Wood Sculpture

Also from Westphalia Press

westphaliapress.org

Wood Sculpture

From Ancient Egypt to the End of the Gothic Period

by Alfred Maskell, F.S.A.

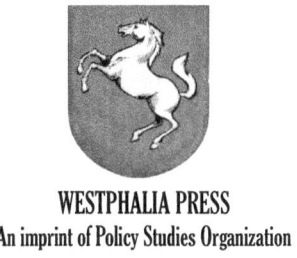

WESTPHALIA PRESS
An imprint of Policy Studies Organization

Westphalia Press
An imprint of Policy Studies Organization
1527 New Hampshire Ave., NW
Washington, D.C. 20036
info@ipsonet.org

ISBN-13: 978-1-63391-692-0
ISBN-10: 1-63391-692-8

Cover design by Jeffrey Barnes:
jbarnesbook.design

Daniel Gutierrez-Sandoval, Executive Director
PSO and Westphalia Press

Updated material and comments on this edition
can be found at the Westphalia Press website:
www.westphaliapress.org

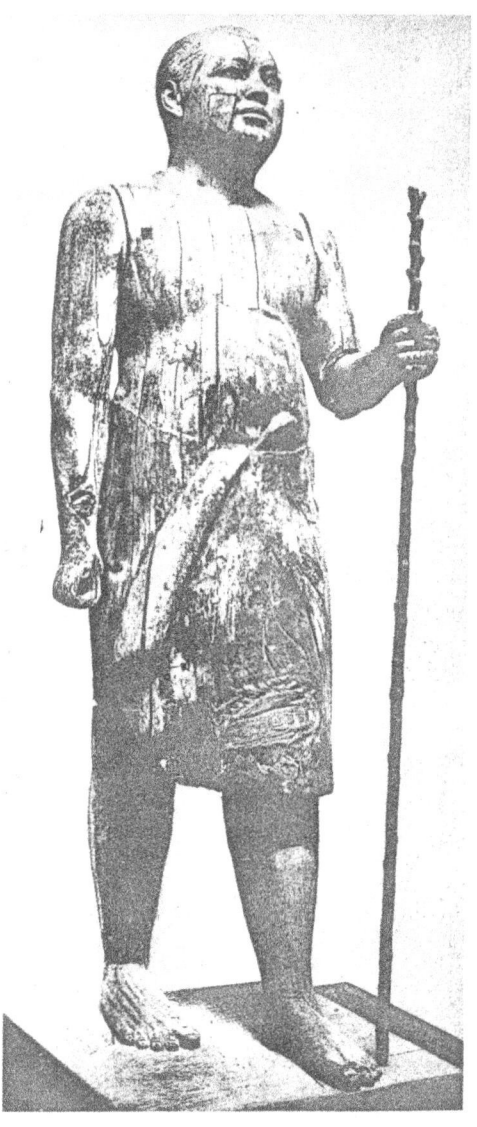

STATUE KNOWN AS THE SHEIK EL BELED. ANCIENT EGYPTIAN
GIZEH MUSEUM, CAIRO

First Published in 1911

WOOD
SCULPTURE

BY

ALFRED MASKELL, F.S.A.

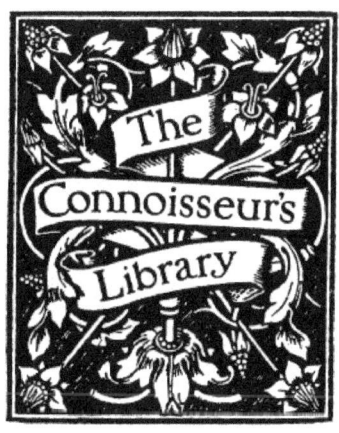

METHUEN AND CO. LTD.

36 ESSEX STREET

LONDON

PREFACE

HARDLY any other division of the arts covers so wide a field as that which is open before us in the study of the use of wood in its decorative applications of every kind. The history of all the arts in all countries from the earliest Egyptian times; the schools of painting, of engraving, and of sculpture in other materials; the goldsmiths', metal-workers', and even the potters' crafts; church lore and liturgiology; the varieties of furniture of every description, ecclesiastical and domestic; the science and art of coins and medals; symbolism, natural history, botany, even heraldry—these things and more, perhaps, confront us from time to time, and present points of contact which cannot be ignored. In endeavouring, therefore, to treat so comprehensive a subject, in a single volume, I cannot but be aware that I lay myself open to the criticism of specialists in all the many divisions with which I may have the hardihood to connect it, and I can scarcely expect to avoid the numerous pitfalls.

After about the twelfth century the quantity of available material is so great that it seemed to me that the only plan would be to restrict the general scope in the main to figure sculpture and to certain decorative work in relief, and to consider what examples could be selected which would best illustrate the evolution of the art and the influences exerted by one country on another. It may be asked why such and such a figure or other work has been included, or why such another one has been passed over. The only answer is that a choice had to be made. It was necessary, also, to draw a line somewhere, and I have done this—generally speaking—at the end of the Gothic period. Whole geographical divisions—Russia, China, Japan, and the East have, perforce also, been left untouched.

The history of domestic furniture already possesses an extensive literature, and our present interest in it is limited to the subjects of the decoration. In the case of such divisions as chancel screens, choir stalls, misericords, bench-ends, and the like, it has not seemed to me necessary to treat them in detail. The student who desires complete information and full lists will consult the special publications to which references will be found in the Bibliography. There are, in addition, numerous articles in the transactions of local archæological societies.

For a work of so comprehensive a character I must admit my many disabilities and restrictions. I cannot pretend to universal knowledge of existing examples of wood sculpture, in all countries and of all ages, which may have claims for notice. In my selections I have given the preference, as a rule, to those which have come under my own notice in our home museums and in many museums and collections on the Continent. I have availed myself largely of numerous notes made at various times during several years, as well as of other assistance whenever I have found anything already collected which appeared to me to be useful. I am free, indeed, to admit that erudition, or even originality, are the least of the qualities—even if I possessed them—for which I should desire credit. My aim is to be readable, and to set forth the subject in the simplest and most intelligible manner. This book is not addressed to those already fully acquainted with the matter, but to the inquiring English reader to whom some of it, at least, may be entirely new. The Bibliography, in fact, shows how few books exist,

PREFACE

in English, in which any information at all—and still less, illustrations—are to be found on many details which are here discussed.

My indebtedness is great to such writers as Bode, in the case of German art, Fabriczy, Fogolari, and D'Achiardi for Italy, Molinier for France, Destrée for the Netherlands, and Habich for the German medallion carvers. Were it not for limitations of space, I should no doubt have availed myself still more largely of the learning and research of these writers.

A word must be said in excuse of imperfections in the quality of some of the illustrations which may not be thought, in every case, entirely satisfactory. The photographing of the objects themselves, in museums, has often been attended with considerable difficulty, from their position in obscure corners, and from the practice of placing under glass. Others have had to be copied from poor photographs in books, or obtained from abroad, and, in the case of some important pieces, it has not been found possible to procure any photographs at all. In some instances, also, there has been the unsurmountable difficulty of adequately rendering the colouring of the sculpture.

But in the matter of the illustrations, generally, my warmest thanks are due to several friends for their very kind and disinterested assistance. Amongst them I must especially mention Mr. George C. Druce, Mr. Francis Bond, Mr. F. L. S. Houghton, M.A., Dom Bede Camm, the Rev. J. W. Banke, Mr. E. W. Smith, Mr. A. G. Thompson, Mrs. George Wilson, Mr. Frederick Evans, Mr. F. H. Crossley, Mr. Aymer Vallance, and Mr. Herbert Read, of the Woodcarving Works, Exeter, who has so ably restored many of the Devonshire chancel screens. To all these I am indebted for valuable aid by the loan of collections of photographs of English carved work, such as screens, misericords, and bench-ends, and, where I have been able to avail myself of it, by leave to reproduce from them. In addition, my publishers desire recognition of permission from the respective publishers or owners to make use of their copyright photographs for plates :—Messrs. Alinari, Florence; Amsler and Ruthardt, Berlin; F. Bromhead, Clifton, Bristol ; Carl Ebner, Stuttgart ; M. Frankenstein, Vienna; A. Giraudon, Paris; Neue Photographische Gesellschaft, Steglitz-Berlin ; Neurdein Frères, Paris; G. Schwartz, Berlin ; Karl Teufel, Munich ; W. Zink, Gotha.

A. M.

April 1911.

CONTENTS

WOOD SCULPTURE

LIST OF PLATES

LIST OF PLATES

WOOD SCULPTURE

BIBLIOGRAPHY

ADDISON (JULIA DE W.): *Arts and Crafts in the Middle Ages.* 1909.

ADELINE (J.): *Stalles de la Cathédrale de Rouen.* 1838.

ADELMANN. *Ueber Riemenschneider.* 1899.

ALBRECHT (R.): *Meisterwerke deutscher Bildschnitzerkunst.* 1896.

ALDIS (E.): *Carvings and Sculptures of Worcester Cathedral.* 1873.

ALLEN (J. ROMILLY): *Early Christian Symbolism in Great Britain and Ireland.* 1887.

ARETIN (FREIHERR VON): *Alterthümer . . . bayrisch. Hauses.* 1853.

ARMAND (A.): *Médailleurs Italiens.* 1883.

AUDSLEY (W. J. and G.): *Polychromatic Decoration as applied to Buildings.* 1882.

AUDSLEY (W. J. and G.): *Handbook of Christian Symbolism.* 1865.

AUSM' WEERTH (E.): *Kunstdenkmäler des christ. Alterthums in den Rheinländen.* 1857-60.

AYMARD: *Album photographique d'archéol. relig.* 1857.

BALCARRES (LORD): *The Evolution of Italian Sculpture.* 1909.

BAUDELAIRE (C. P.): *Curiosités esthétiques.* 1885.

[BAVARIA]: *Die Kunstdenkmäler des Königreichs Bayern.* 1892.

BAYET (C.): *Précis d'histoire de l'art.* 1905.

WOOD SCULPTURE

BECKER (L.): *Leben und Werke des Bildhauers Tilmann Riemenschneider.* 1849.

BECKETT (E.): *Altertavler i Danmark.* 1895.

BERGAU (R.): *Veit Stoss.* 1878.

BERGMANN (J.): *Medaillen berühmter Männer.* 1844.

BERTHIER (J. J.): *La porte de Sainte Sabine.* 1892.

BETHGE (H.): *Decoratir. Holzbau.* 1879-80.

BEZOLD (G. VON): *Anzeiger des Germanischen Nat. Museums.* 1908.

BLOXAM (M. H.): *Principles of Gothic Ecclesiastical Architecture.* 1882.

BODE (W.): *Geschichte der deutschen Plastik.* 1885.
,,   ,,   *Die italienische Plastik.* 1894.
,,   ,,   *Florentine Sculptors of the Renaissance* [Transl.] 1908.
,,   ,,   *Denkmäler der Renaissance Skultur Toscanas.* 1892.

BOND (F.): *Gothic Architecture in England.* 1905.
,,   ,,   *Screens and Galleries.* 1908.
,,   ,,   *Misericords.* 1910.
,,   ,,   *Fonts and Font Covers.* 1909.

BOND (F. B.) and CAMM (Rev. B): *Roodscreens and Roodlofts.* 1908.

BONNAFFÉ (E.): *Le meuble en France au xvieme siècle.* 1887.

BOSARTE (L.): *Disertacion . . . monumentos antiguos . . . ciudad de Barcelona.* 1786.

BOSSCHÈRE (J. DE): *La Sculpture anversoise.* 1909.

BRACH (A.): *Nicola und Giov. Pisano und die Plastik des xiv Jahrh.* 1904.

BRANDON (R.) and (J. A.): *Analysis of Gothic Architecture.* 1903.

[BURLINGTON F. A. CLUB]: *Pictures of the School of Siena.* 1904.
,,   ,,   *Art of Anc. Egypt.* 1895.
,,   ,,   *Early German Art.* 1907.

BIBLIOGRAPHY

BURY (T. T.): *Remains of Ecclesiastical Woodwork.* 1847.

CAHIER (C.): *Caractéristiques des Saints dans l'art populaire.* 1867.

CAHIER and MARTIN: *Mélanges d'archéologie* and *Nouveaux Mélanges.* 1847-1874.

CAHN (J.): *Numismatic Chronicle.* 1904.

CAIN (G.): *La collection Dutuit.* 1904.

CAMM (DOM B.): *Some Devon Screens.* (Pamphlet.) 1906.

CAMPBELL (J. F.): *Popular Tales of the West Highlands.* 1860.

CANETO (ABBÉ): *Monographie de St. Marie d'Auch.* 1861.

CAPART (J.): *L'art égyptien.* 1909.

CAROTTI (Dr. G.): *History of Art* (transld. by Mrs. A. Strong). In progress.

CARTER (JOHN): *Specimens of Ancient Sculpture and Painting.* 1780.

CEAN-BERMUDEZ (J. A.): *Diccionario de los mas ilustres profesores de las bellas artes en España.* 1800.

CHAMPEAUX (A. DE): *Le meuble.* 1885.

,,   ,,   *Dict. des fondeurs, ciseleurs, modeleurs.* 1886.

CHAMPFLEURY (M.): *Hist. de la caricature au moyen âge.* 1871.

CHENNEVIÈRES (P.): *Archives de l'art français* (I. 423).

CHILD (F. J.) *English and Scottish Popular Ballads.* 1882.

CHURCH (A. H., and others): *Some Minor Arts.* 1894.

CICOGNARA (L.): *Storia della Scultura.* 1823.

CLARK (O. W.): *The Misereres in Gloster Cathedral.* 1905.

CLAUDE DE VERT: *Explication simple . . cérémonies de l'Église.* 1720.

CLOQUET (L.): *L'art monumental de la Grèce.*

COCKELBERGS (H.): *Précis historique de la dévotion à N. D. de Laeken.*

COLLING (J. K.): *Examples of English Mediæval Foliage.* 1874.

    ,,   ,,   *Details of Gothic Architecture.* 1851-6.

COMMISSION [PARLIAMENTARY]: *Report on the Cause of Decay in Wood-carving.* 1864.

CONWAY (W. M.): *Early Tuscan Art.* 1902.

CORNELIUS (C.): *Jacopo della Quercia.* 1896.

COURAJOD (L.). *Catal. raisonné mus. de sculpt. comparé du Trocadero.* 1892.

COX (J. C.) and HARVEY (A.): *English Church Furniture.* 1907.

COX (J. C.) and HOPE (ST. J.): *The Chronicles. . . . All SS. Derby.* 1881.

CRALLAN (F. A.): *Details of Gothic Woodcarving.* (Drawings: short text). 1897.

CROUCH (J.): *Puritanism and Art.* 1910.

CROWE (J. A.) and CAVALCASELLE (G. B.): *A New History of Painting in Italy.* 1908.

CRULL (J.): *Antiquities of St. Peter's: or the Abbey Church of Westminster.* 1741.

CZERNY (A.): *Kunst und Kunstwerke in St. Florian.* 1886.

D'ACHIARDI (P.): *Alcune opere di scultura in legno dei secoli xiv e xv.* (In L'ARTE, vii. 1904.)

DARCEL (A.): *The Basilewsky Collection.* 1874.

DARESSY (M. G., and others): *Catal. gén. du musée du Caire.* 1901-1910.

DART (J.): *Hist. and Antiqs. of Cathedral Church of Canterbury.* 1726.

DAUN (B.): *Veit Stoss und seine Schule.* 1903.

    ,,   ,,   *Adam Krafft.* 1903.

    ,,   ,,   *P. Vischer und A. Krafft.* 1903.

BIBLIOGRAPHY

DAVILLIER (BARON): *Les arts décoratifs en Espagne.*
1879.

DEARMER (P.): *Fifty Pictures of Gothic Altars.* 1910.

DEHIO (G.): *Handbuch der deutschen Kunstdenkmäler.* 1905.

DEHIO (G.) and BEZOLD (G. v.): *Die Denkmäler der deutschen Bildhauerkunst.* 1905.

DELABORDE C^{TE}: *Les ducs de Bourgogne au xvème siècle.*
1849-51.

DESHAINES (MGR.): *L'art dans les Flandres.*
    ,,   ,,   *L'art chrétien en Flandres.*

DESTREÉS (J.): *Tapisserie et sculpture Bruxellois.*
1906.

  ,,   ,,   *Etude sur la sculpture Brabançonne au moyen âge.* (See *Annales de la Soc. d'Archéologie de Bruxelles.* 1895.)

DETZEL (H.): *Christliche Ikonographie.* 1894.
  ,,   ,,   *Etude sur la Sculpture brabançonne.* 1894.

DEVILLE (A.): *Comptes de dépenses . . . château de Gaillon.* 1850.

DIDRON: *Etude sur les Vierges ouvrantes.* 1870.

DIEULAFOY (M.): *La Statuaire polychrome en Espagne.*
1908.

[DIJON]: *Catalogue du musée.* 1883.

DITCHFIELD (P. H.) and CLINCH (G.): *Memorials of Old Kent.* 1907.

DOEHRING (O.) and VOSS (G.): *Meisterwerke der Kunst aus Sachsen und Thüringen.* 1905.

DOLLMAN (F. T.): *Examples of Ancient Pulpits in England.* 1849.

DOMANIG (C.): *Porträtmedaillen.*
  ,,   ,,   *Die deutsche Medaille.* 1907.

DOPPELMAYR (J. G.): *Hist. Nachricht v.d. Nürnberg Künstler.* 1730.

DOUAIS (C.): *Les stalles . . . de Sainte-Marie d'Auch.*

DUCANGE (C. D.): *Glossarium.* 1840-50.

WOOD SCULPTURE

Dunlop (J. C.): *History of Fiction.* 1816.
Durand (G.): *Monographie de l'église cath. d'Amiens.* 1903.
   ,,   ,,   *Symbolism of Churches and Church Ornaments.*
[Durham]: *Ancient Rites and Monuments of the Cathedral Church of Durham.* 1672. [Surtees Society.]
[Dursch Collection]: *now in Lorenz-Kapelle, Rottweil.*
Du Sommerard (E.): *Les arts au moyen âge.* 1838-46.
   ,,   ,,   *Les arts somptuaires.* 1838-46.
   ,,   ,,   *Musée des Thermes et . . . de Cluny.* 1852.

Enlart (C.): *Manuel d'archéol. française.* 1802.
Erculei (R.): *Intaglio e tarsia in legno.* 1885.
Erman: *Deutsche Medailleure.* 1884.
Essenwein: *Katalog der in Germ. museum . . . Originalskulpturen.* 1890.
Evans (E. P.): *Animal Symbolism in Ecclesiastical Architecture.* 1896.
Even (E. van.): *Louvain Monuments.*

Fabriczy (C. v.): *F. Brunelleschi.* 1892.
Fairholt (F. W.): *Miscellanea graphica.* 1857.
Falke (J. v.): *Geschichte des deutschen Kunstgewerbes.* 1888.
Ferrari (G.): *Il legno nell' arte Italiana.* 1910.
Finochietti: *Della scultura e della tarsia in legno.* 1873.
Fisenne (L. v.): *Kunstdenkmäler des Mittelalters.* 1880.
Flechzig (E.): *Sächsische Bildnerei und Malerei.* 1909.
Fogolari (G.): *Sculture in legno del sec xii.* (In L'Arte, 1903.)
Ford: *Handbook for Travellers in Spain.* 1846.

xx

BIBLIOGRAPHY

FORRER (L.): *Biographical Dictionary of Medallists.* 1904.

FRULLINI: *Holz Sculpturen.* 1884.

GAILHABAUD: *L'architecture du vᵉᵐᵉ au xviiᵉᵐᵉ siècle.* 1857.

GASQUET (ABBOT): *The Greater Abbeys of England.* 1908.

,,   ,,   *Parish Life.* 1909.

GAUTIER (T.): *Voyage en Espagne.* 1845.

GIBNEY (J. S.): *Subjects taken from Lincoln Cathedral.* 1870.

GIRAUDET: *Les artistes tourangeaux.*

GOLDSCHMIDT (A.): *Studien zur Geschichte sächsischen Sculptur.* 1902.

GONSE (L.): *Les chefs-d'œuvre des musées de la France.* 1904.

,,   ,,   *La sculpture franç. depuis le 14ᵉᵐᵉ siècle.* 1895.

GRAESSE (J. G.): *Guide de l'amateur.* 1871.

GRANGE (A. DE LA) and CLOQUET (L.): *Etudes sur l'art à Tournai.*

GUÉNÉBAULT (L. J.): *Dict. iconographique.* 1845.

HAACK (F.): *Friedrich Herlin, sein Leben und Werke.* 1900.

,,   ,,   *Hans Schuchlein.* 1900.

HABICH (G.): *Studien zur deutschen Renaissance-medaille.* 1906.

HAENDEKER (B.): *Studien für Geschichte der spanischen Plastik.* 1900.

HAMILTON (A.): *The Art Workmanship of the Maori Race.* 1896.

HARROD (H.): *Gleanings among the Castles and Convents of Norfolk.* 1857.

HARVEY (E. G.): *Mullyon, its History and Antiquities.* 1875.

WOOD SCULPTURE

Hastings (G.): *Siena, its Architecture and Art.* 1901.
Heffner-Alteneck (J. v.): *Costumes . . . œuvres d'art du moyen âge.* 1840-54.
Heiss (A.): *Les médailleurs de la renaissance.* 1881-92.
Helbig (J.): *Hist. de la sculpt. et des arts plastiques à Liége.*
Hems (H.): *Rood and other Screens in Devonshire.* 1896.
Hewett (J. W.): *Early Woodcarving in Exeter Cathedral.* 1849.
Hiersemann: *Deutsche und niederländische Holzbildwerke.*
Hirth (G.): *Der Formenschatz.* And in progress. 1877.
Hyacinthe (R. P.): *Hist. de la célèbre statue de N.D. du chant d'oiseaux.*

Jack (G.): *Woodcarving.* 1903.
Jackson: *Woodcarving.* 1902.
Jessopp (Rev. A.): *Studies by a recluse.* 1893.
Jones (O.): *The Grammar of Ornament.* 1856.
Josephi (W.): *Die Werke plastischer Kunst.* 1910.
Jouin (M. H.): *Esthétique du sculpteur.* 1888.
Jourdain and Duval: *La cathédrale d'Amiens.* 1867.
Jupp (E. B.): *The Company of Carpenters.* 1887.

Kellen (D. van der): *Le moyen âge et la renaiss. dans les Pays-Bas.* 1864.
King: *Study Book of Mediæval Architecture.* 1858.
Kleinclausz (A.): *Claus Sluter et la sculpture bourguignonne.* 1905.
Knackfuss: *Monographien.* (See *Dürer, Vischer, Krafft, Stoss,* etc., in this collection.)
Kopera (F.): *Wit Stwosz.* 1908.
Kraus (F. H.): *Geschichte der kirchlichen Kunst.* 1897.

xxii

BIBLIOGRAPHY

LABARTE (P.): *Histoire de l'art industriel.* 1847.

LAFOND (P.): *La Sculpture espagnole.* 1909.

LAMBERT (J. M.): *Two Thousand Years of Gild Life.* 1891.

LANGE (K.): *Peter Flötner.* 1907.

LANGLOIS (E. H.): *L'incendie de la Cath.de Rouen.* 1823.
,,　　　　,,　　*Stalles de la Cath. de Rouen.* 1838.

LEISCHING (J.): *Figurale Holzplastik.* 1908.

LENORMANT (C.): *Trésor de Numismatique et de Glyptique.* 1834-46.

LEPSZY (L.): *Krakau.* 1907.

LEROY: *Materiales y documentos del arte español.*

[LEROY, MARTIN]: *Catalogue of Collection.* 1906.

LESSING (O.): *Holzschnitzereien . . . in Kunstgewerbe Museum, Berlin.* 1882.

LETHABY (W. R.): *Westminster Abbey.* 1906.

LETTS: *Manchester Misereres.* 1886.

LETTU (G. G.): *Guide dans l'église de Sᵗᵉ Marie d'Auch.* N.D.

LEVERSAGE (P.): *History of Bristol Cathedral.* 1854.

LÜBKE (W.): *Geschichte der Plastik.* 1884.

LUCOT (M. LE CHANOINE): *La Vierge de Boulancourt.*

MACQUOID (P.): *History of English Furniture.* 1906.

MADER (F.): *Loy Hering.* 1905.

MAETERLINCK (L.): *Le genre satirique.* 1907.
,,　　　　,,　　*Roger van der Weyden et les imagiers de Tournai.* 1901.

MALE (E.): *L'art religieux du xiiiᵉᵐᵉ siècle en France.* 1902.

MARCHAL (E.): *La sculpture et les chefs-d'œuvres de l'orfévrerie belge.* 1895.

METMAN and BRIÈRE: *Le Bois.* [Photos. only.]

MEYER (A. G.): *Donatello.* 1904.

MICHEL (E.), (ed. by): *Histoire de l'art.* 1905. (In progress.)

MICHIELS (J. A.): *L'Art flamand dans l'est et le midi de la France.* 1877.

MILLER (F.): *Woodcarving.* 1885.

MINNS (REV. G. W.): *Notes on Roodscreens.* 1867.

MOKE (H. D.): *Les splendeurs de l'Art en Belgique.* 1839.

MOLINIER (E.): *Histoire de l'Art.* 1896.

MONGET: *La Chartreuse de Dijon.* 1898.

MONTANET (MGR. B.): *Traité d'iconographie chrétienne.* 1890.

MOORE (T. S.): *Albert Dürer.* 1905.

MOREAU (A.): *Meubles et objets d'art.* 1871.

MUELLER and HEIDELOFF: *Die Kunst des Mittelalters in Schwaben.* 1841.

MUNTZ (E.): *Les Arts à la cour des Papes.* 1878-82.
  ,,   ,, *Les précurseurs de la renaissance.* 1882.
  ,,   ,, *La Renaissance . . . Italie.* 1885.
  ,,   ,, *Histoire de l'Art pendant la renaissance.* 1889-95.

MÜNZENBERGER (E.): *Zur Kenntniss der mittelalterlichen Altäre Deutschlands.* 1885-1890.

MURR (CH. G. V.): *Beschreibung . . . Merkwürdigkeiten in Nürnberg.* 1778.

NAGLER: *Kunstler Lexikon.* 1835-52.

NEUDÖRFFER (J.): *Schreib und Rechenmeisters zu Nürnberg.* Ed. 1875.

NICHOLS (J.): *Illustrations of Manners and Expenses from Churchwardens' Accounts.* 1797.

NIEDERMAYER (A.): *Kunstgeschichte . . . Stadt Würzburg.* 1868.

NIFFLE-ANCIAUX (E.): *Les repos de Jésus et les berçeaux reliquaires.* 1896.

NOAKE (J.): *The Monastery and Cathedral of Worcester.* 1866.

BIBLIOGRAPHY

NOAKE (J.): *Notes and Queries for Worcestershire.* 1856.

[NÜRNBERG]: *Catalogue der originalen Sculpturen.* 1892.

ODELBERG (H.): *Les retables de Strengnas.* [In *Ann. de l'Acad. d'Archéol. de Belgique, t. iii.*)

OTTE (D. H.): *Handbuch der kirchlichen Kunstarchäologie.* 1885.

PACHECO (F.): *Arte de la pintura.* 1649.

[PANNWITZ COLLECTION]: *Die Sammlung von Pannwitz.* 1905.

[PARIS]: *Trocadero. Exposition retrospective de l'art français.* 1878.

PARKER (J. H.): *Glossary of Terms ... Gothic Architecture.* Ed. 1896.

PAULI (R.): *Drei volkwirthschaftliche Denkschriften.* 1878.

PERKINS (C. C.): *Italian Sculptors.* 1868.

„   „   *Tuscan Sculptors.* 1864.

PERROT (G.) and CHIPIEZ (C.): *Histoire de l'Art dans l'antiquité.* 1882. 1890.

PETRIE (W. M. F.): *History of Egypt.* 1896.

PFLEIDERER (R.): *Das Münster zu Ulm.* 1905.

PFNOR (R.): *Ornementation usuelle de toutes les époques.* 1867.

PHILIPPI (A.): *Die Kunst ... in Deutschland und den Niederländen.*

PHIPSON (MISS E.): *Choirstalls and their Carvings.* 1896.

PIOT (E.), (Ed. by): *Monuments et Mémoires.* (In progress.)

PIT (M. A.): *La Sculpture hollandaise.* 1903.

POLLEN (J. H.): *Ancient and Modern Furniture and Woodwork.* 1875.

WOOD SCULPTURE

PRIOR (E. S.) : *History of Gothic Art in England.* 1900.
„   „   *Cathedral Builders in England.* 1905.
PÜCKLER LIMPURG Cᵀᴱ : *Die Nürnberger Bildnerkunst.*
PUGIN (A. W.) : *Chancel Screens and Roodlofts.* 1851.
„   „   *True Principles of Pointed or Christian Architecture.* 1841.
„   „   *Contrasts.* 1841.

QUATREMÈRE DE QUINCY (A. C.) : *Dict. Hist. de l'Architecture.*
QUICHERAT (J.) : *Mélanges d'Archéologie.* 1886.
QUINTERO (P.) : *Sillas de coro.* 1890.

RAHN (J.) : *Geschichte der bildenden Kunst in der Schweiz.* 1890.
RAMÉE (D.) : *Meubles religieux du moyen âge et de la renaissance.* 1864.
READ (C. H.) : *The Waddesdon Bequest.* 1902.
RÉAU (L.) : *Peter Vischer.* 1909.
REBER (F. v.) and BAYERSDORFER (A.) : *Klassischer Skulpturenschatz.* 1900.
REDFARN (W. B.) : *Ancient Wood and Ironwork in Cambridge.* 1886.
RÉE (Dr. P. D.) : *Nuremberg and its art* [transl. by G. H. Palmer.] 1905.
REIL (J.) : *Die frühchristliche Darstellungen der Kreuzigung.* 1904.
REIMERS : *Peter Flötner.* 1890.
RENAN (E.) : *Etat des beaux-arts en France au xivᵉᵐᵉ siècle.*
REYMOND (M.) : *La Sculpture Florentine.* 1898.
RICCI (C.) : *La Mostra Senese.* 1904.
RIDSLOB (E.) : *Das Kirchenportal.* 1909.
RIEHL (B.) : *Geschichte der Stein- und Holzplastik in Oberbayern.* 1898.
RIGGENBACH : *Die Chorgestühle des Mittelalters.*
ROBINSON (F. S.) : *English Furniture.* 1905.

BIBLIOGRAPHY

ROCHEMONTEIX (M. DE): *Les églises romanes de la Haute Auvergne.* 1902.

ROE (F.): *Ancient Coffers and Cupboards.*
„ „ *Old Oak Furniture.* 1905.

ROGER MILÈS (F.): *Comment discerner les styles.* 1896.

ROMBOUT (P.) and LERINS (T. VAN): *Les Liggeren et autres archives historiques de la gilde anversoise de Saint-Luc.* 1872.

RONDOT (N.): *L'Art du bois à Lyon.* 1899.

ROOSVAL (J.): *Schnitzaltäre in schwedischen Kirchen.* 1903.

ROWE (E.): *Art of Practical Wood-carving.* 1907.
„ „ *French Wood-carvings from Museums.* 1896.

RUSKIN (J.): *The Bible of Amiens.* 1880.

SACKEN (E. V.): *Album . . . kunstwerke . . . Ambraser Sammlung.* 1884.
„ „ *Der Flügelaltar zu Sanct Wolfgang.* 1858.

SANCET (L.): *Stalles de la Cathédrale d'Auch.* 1860.

SAUERLANDT (M.): *Deutsche Plastik des Mittelalters.* 1909.

SAUSAY (A.): *Musée de la Renaissance.* 1864.

SAUVAGEOT (C. and L.): *Stalles du xiiième siècle à N. D. de la Roche.* 1863.

SAVAGE (CANON): *Woodwork of Halifax Church.* 1910.

SCARDEONIUS (B.): *De Antiquitate urbis Patavii.* 1560.

SCHAUSS (E. V.): *Die Schatzkammer des bayr. Königshauses in München.* 1908.

SCHEUBER (J.): *Die mittelalterlichen Chorstühle in der Schweiz.* 1910.

SCHLÖSSER (J. V.): *Album Ausgewählter Gegenstände.* 1901.

WOOD SCULPTURE

SCHÖNEMARK (D. G.): *Der Kruzifixus.* 1908.
SCHOTTMÜLLER (F.): *Donatello.* 1904.
SCHUBRINGS (P.): *Die Plastik Sienas in Quattrocento.* 1907.
SCHUETTE (M.): *Der Schwäbische Schnitzaltar.* 1907.
SCOTT (L.): *Filippo di Ser Brunellesco.* 1901.
SENTETZ (P.): *Notice historique . . . Sainte Marie d'Auch.*
SEPULCHRAL MONUMENTS:—
    Baker (G): *History and Antiquities of Northampton.* 1822-30.
    Blomefield: *History of Norfolk.* 1805-10.
    Blore: *Monumental Remains.* 1826.
    Collinson (J.): *History of Somerset.* 1791.
    Cox (T.): *Magna Britannia.* 1720.
    Dallaway (J.): *History of Western Division of Sussex.* 1819-30.
    Eyton (R. W.): *Antiquities of Shropshire.* 1853-60.
    Fryer (A. C.): *Wooden Monumental Effigies.* 1910.
    Glover (S.): *History of County of Derby.* 1829.
    Gough (R.): *Sepulchral Monuments.* 1799.
    Grose (F.): *Antiquarian Repertory.* 1807-9.
    ,,   ,,   *Antiquities of England and Wales.* 1773-87.
    Hartshorne (A.). (See *Victorian County Histories: Northamptonshire.*)
    Hartshorne (C.): *Sepulchral Remains in Northamptonshire.* 1840.
    ,,   ,,   *Funeral Monuments.* 1840.
    Hartshorne (R.): *Effigies of Northamptonshire.* 1867.
    Hutchinson (W.): *History and Antiquities of Durham.* 1794.
    Lipscombe (G.): *History and Antiquities of Buckingham.* 1847.
    Lysons (S.): *Magna Britannia.* 1808-1825.
xxviii

BIBLIOGRAPHY

Manning and Braye: *History and Antiquities of Surrey.* 1804.

Morant (P.): *History and Antiquities of Essex.* 1768.

Stothard (C. A.): *Monumental Effigies.* 1817-32.

Strutt: *History and Antiquities of Essex.* 1845.

Thoroton (R.): *Antiquities of Nottinghamshire.* 1677-1797.

Weaver: *Funeral Monuments.* 1840.

Whitaker (T. D.): *Loidis and Elmete.* 1816.

SERRANO (FATIGATI E.): *Retablos Españoles Ogivales.* 1902.

[SIENA]: *Exhibition of Ancient Art.* 1904.

SINGLETON (MISS E.): *Furniture of our Forefathers.* 1901.

,,   ,,   *French and English Furniture.* 1904.

,,   ,,   *Dutch and Flemish Furniture.* 1907.

SIXT (FR.): *Chronik der Stadt Gerolzhofen.*   ·

SPIERS (R. PHENÉ): *The Styles of Ornament.* 1910.

[SPITZER COLLECTION]: *Catalogue.* 1890-92.

SPRINGER: *Handbuch der Kunstgeschichte.* 1907.

STABB (J.): *Some Old Devon Churches.* 1909.

STABB (J.): *Devon Church Antiquities.* 1909.

STADLER (F.): *Hans Multscher und seine Werkstatt.* 1907.

STÆDTNER (DR. F.): *Deutsche Kunst in Lichtbildern.* 1908.

STEGMANN (DR. H.): *Meisterwerke der Kunst.* 1905.

STIAVELLI: *Pescia nella vita privata.* 1903.

STRAETEN (T. VAN DER): *Jaerboek van S. Lucas gilde.* 1854.

STREIT (T.): *Tylmann Riemenschneider, Leben und Kunstwerke.* 1888.

WOOD SCULPTURE

SUPINO (J. D.): *Arte Pisana.* 1904.

TALBERT (B. J.): *Examples of Ancient and Modern Furniture.*
TALBOT (J. TAYLOR): *Collection at New York.* 1906.
THAUSING (M.): *Albert Dürer.* 1878.
THEOPHILUS. *Essais sur divers Arts.* (French translation of the mediæval work by Cte de l'Escalopier). 1843.
TOENNIES (E.): *Leben und Werke. . . . T. Riemenschneider.* 1900.
TYMMS (S.): *Architectural and Historical Account . . . Church of St. Mary, Bury St. Edmunds.* 1854.

VALLON (E.): *Les monstres dans l'Art.* 1910.
VASARI (G.): *Vite dei . . . pittori, scultori e architetti.* 1550. [And transl. Foster, J. 1888.]
VENTURI (A.): *Storia dell' arte italiana.* 1903.
      ,,   ,, *La Madonna.* 1900.
VINYCOMB (J.): *Fictitious and Symbolical Creatures in Art.* 1906.
VIOLLET-LE-DUC (E.): *Dictionnaire de l'Architecture.* 1868.
VIOLLET-LE-DUC (E.): *Dictionnaire du mobilier.* 1875.
VITRY (P.): *Michel Colombe et la Sculp. franç. de son temps.* 1901.
VITRY (P.) and BRIÈRE (G.): *Documents de la Sculpture française.* 1906.
VOISIN (C. J.): *Descript. Hist. des monums. gothiques des Pays-Bas.*

WAAGEN (G. F.): *Notice sur Hubert et J. Van Eyck.* 1830.
xxx

BIBLIOGRAPHY

WALCOTT (REV. M.): *Sacred Archæology.* 1868.

WANDERER (F.): *Adam Krafft and his School.* 1868.

WEBER (A.): *Leben und Werken des Bildhauers Tilmann Riemenschneider.* 1888.

WIEGAND (O.): *Adolf Dauer.* 1903.

WEISSBECKER (DR.): *Rothenburg ob der Tauber.*

WICHMANNS: *Brabantia Mariana.*

[WILARS DE HONECOURT]: *Album.* (Facsimile by R. Willis.) 1859.

WILDRIDGE (T. T.): *Misereres in Beverley Minster.* 1879.

   ,,   ,,   *Notes on Roodscreens.*

WILLEMIN (N. Z.): *Monuments français inédits.* 1839.

WILLIAMS (L.): *The Arts and Crafts of Older Spain.* 1906.

WILLIAMS (R. F.): *Historical Sketch of the Art of Sculpture in Wood.* 1835.

WILLIS (R.): *Facsimile of the Sketchbook of Wilars de Honecourt.* 1859.

WILLIS and CLARK: *Architectural History of the University of Cambridge.* 1886.

WIMMER (E.): *Mittelalterliche Holzschnitzerei aus der Kirche zu Bechtolstein.* 1873.

WINTER (F.) and DELHIO (G.): *Kunstgeschichte in Bildern.* 1899.

WITKOUSKI (DR. C. J.): *L'Art profane à l'église.* 1908.

WRIGHT (J.): *Some Notable Altars.* 1908.

WRIGHT (T.): *The Archæological Album.* 1845.

   ,,   ,,   *Essays on Archæological Subjects.* 1861.

   ,,   ,,   *History of Caricature in Literature and Art.* 1864.

   ,,   ,,   *Popular Treatises on Science in the Middle Ages.* 1841.

WOOD SCULPTURE

WRIGHT (J.) and HALLIWELL: *Reliquiæ Antiquæ.*
1841.

[WÜRTEMBERG]: *Die Kunst und Alterthums . . .
Würtemberg.* 1899.

YSENDYCK (J. J. VAN): *Documents classés de l'Art
dans les Pays-Bas.*

WOOD SCULPTURE

CHAPTER I

INTRODUCTORY—PREHISTORIC ART—WOOD SCULPTURE IN ANCIENT EGYPT

WE may not, perhaps, be able to claim for wood sculpture that in any examples that have come down to us, throughout the ages or in any land, the general level of excellence has reached as high as that of sculpture in marble or in stone. We may not be able to produce *chefs-d'œuvre* equal to the most famous of those in bronze or in the precious metals. We may have to be content to class it among the minor arts—whatever that indefinite term ought strictly to mean. Yet if we should take but one department, that of figure sculpture, whether we consider it as statuary, as smaller works in the round or as bas-reliefs, it may be fearlessly asserted that undeniable masterpieces have been produced which will bear comparison, at least, with anything in the whole range of the kindred arts. And, as we shall see, it may be claimed that, at any rate in Renaissance times, the creations of the goldsmiths' or the bronze-workers' masterpieces were often first of all conceived and executed in the highest perfection of detail by the chisel of the wood sculptor. Having served their purpose it is unfortunately true that, owing possibly to their fragile or perishable nature, it is but in rare instances that these productions have come down to us. We need not, of course, stay to consider what is obvious, that is the analogy which may be drawn between these models and those in clay or wax of the marble sculptor or bronze founder.

If we have to hew out of wood a figure of monumental proportions, the method by which we accomplish it, the canons of art which we follow, resemble those where the material is marble or stone. For work of lesser dimensions it may be compared with ivory carving. Illustrations will be given of carvings on so minute a scale that they are justly called microscopic, and yet are no trivial *tours de force*. Wood is not like clay or wax, a plastic, or rather, a flexible material. It is for chiselling, not moulding. It has its own special qualities. There are many varieties, and it abounds in the forests throughout the world. It is less fragile, tougher, and more amenable than stone. It has more elasticity than marble, possessing a fibrous nature in various degrees. Certain kinds differ in the closeness of their grain, some being compact, while others are loose and open. Besides differences in colour, wood possesses also many beautiful varieties in its veins and knots, but these are qualities with which we shall not be concerned. Except for tarsia work, and in certain kinds of furniture, they are inconsistent with the aims of the sculptor proper. The colour is of importance, and covers a considerable range from that approaching the ivory white in the elm, through the different shades of box which plays so important a part in our subject, to the deep jetlike black of ebony. Besides the colour, age brings to wood a mellowness and diversity of tone which may be likened to the *patina* of bronze and other metals. And in addition to these qualities it may be dyed or otherwise coloured. As a material the disadvantages are its perishable nature, and the liability to warp or twist, which no amount of seasoning, in some varieties, can counteract.

2

MATERIAL AND PROCEDURE

Considered as a medium for sculpture, wood has a message of its own, which, for those who can truly understand it, must be delivered in a certain way by which it is distinguished from the technique employed when other materials are used. It is especially suited to the expression of the grotesque, and, as its own nature would obviously suggest, to the illustration of plant-form, foliage, and vegetation in their most free-growing character. Yet it must not imitate nature, but inspire the ideas suggested by natural growth, its form, development, and ever-pushing vitality. To do this does not necessarily imply naturalism. The range is immense in the scope afforded between the suggestive conventionality of the art of mediæval times and the mechanical imitation which distinguishes the work of the much-bepraised English decorator of the seventeenth century. The methods of the statuary and figure sculptor in wood differ from those of the marble sculptor in that he goes straight at his work, and employs no pointer. His æsthetic aims and his technique differ. He is impelled towards realism and, almost as a matter of course, towards the addition of colour. The danger in his path is a too faithful dependence on and following of the methods employed in great sculpture in stone, marble, or bronze, or even in forgings and castings in iron. He is apt, at times, to forget the limitations and special qualities of his material.

The first carving in wood was the parent of all sculpture in succeeding ages, and he who first cut it for decorative purposes was the first sculptor. It would have suggested itself to the prehistoric artist as a handy material long before the bone remnant of a feast. For modelling, possibly earth in the shape of some tenacious clay would have preceded it. Then would have come the whittling of a stick or block obtained from the nearest wood. Very soon the savage, with the natural love of man for ornament and display, would have carved the handle of his war-club with lines and curves and patterns, serving at the same time to give it a better grip.

The South Sea islander to the present day decorates his fighting canoe with a deeply incised spiral ornament, which seems to have descended with little variation from the most distant times. The earliest art was an imitation of nature, an attempt to transmit to others, in some tangible form, an impression, appealing to his imagination, of what the artist saw. From that time onwards no one will deny the interest that even uncultured efforts will excite, and the charm from the very naiveness of the expression, provided that these efforts are sincere.

Allusions to wood sculpture and to images of wood in the Holy Scriptures might, of course, be quoted to a considerable extent. In Genesis we read how Rachel stole her father's images and carried them away. In Isaiah the carpenter's and sculptor's crafts are frequently mentioned : for example, how graven images were made, how the carpenter 'marketh out with a compass' and 'maketh it after the figure of a man, according to the beauty of a man: that it may remain in the house' (xliv. 13); how he heweth down cedars and the cypress and the oak, which he uses for various purposes, 'and the residue thereof he maketh a god, even his graven image' (xliv. 17). And it will not be necessary to do more than refer to such passages in ancient history, as where we learn from Pausanias about Dædalus who carved statues, fourteen centuries or so earlier, which still existed in the writer's time; and of the mixed wood and ivory statues in the temple of Athene Atlantis, the statue of Bacchus in ebony, gilt except the face, which was painted ; the Jupiter in wild pearwood, the Æsculapius in willow, a head of

4

Dionysius of olive, and many more, in cypress and other woods, painted, gilded, or inlaid with gold.

Such information as this is, to our regret, almost all upon which we can rely regarding wood sculpture in ancient Greece and the Roman empire: actual existing examples are rare indeed. But of a still more ancient civilization—that of Egypt—we are more fortunate in the remains of statuary and small sculpture in wood which are not surpassed in interest by any other sculptured records whatever. The age of some of them, amounting to thousands of years before our era, is conjectural only. The museum at Cairo, as is fitting, possesses the finest and the greater number: amongst them the famous figure of the Sheik el Beled. The Louvre is rich, in quality at least, but the examples in our British Museum, however interesting in archæological interest, are sadly deficient in beauty and attraction. That we look to Egypt as the cradle of our race, and seek in her monuments for traces of the earliest efforts made by man in the expression of art, is, of course, undeniable. Amongst these earliest efforts —that is of an art which appears to have already attained an extraordinary degree of development and perfection, for the earliest we possess have that character—are the figures and statues in wood, from which two or three will be selected for illustration. More than this cannot be done here, for no pretension is made to an examination of ancient Egyptian art generally, with which these figures are so intimately connected that we should soon be led far beyond our limits and beyond the capacity of the present writer.

At a period of the world's history so remote as to be almost fabulous, but may be counted as at least sixty centuries, if we may judge from the earliest examples of sculpture which have come down to us, Egypt was in possession of a fully developed system of art. This system, whether based on hieratic traditions or on a natural aptitude for the observation of nature, has in its way never since been surpassed. However this may be, we are not in possession of sufficient information to justify any certainty of opinion concerning what canons, if any, were followed by the sculptors of these great portrait figures, whose use and destination will presently be alluded to. To that use, added to the dryness of the climate and to the rifling or systematic examination of the numerous tombs, we owe the preservation of these works of art in a material which, under ordinary conditions, perishes in a comparatively short time. Looking at these wonderful figures, of which we shall examine a few of the most striking, remembering that they are amongst the earliest specimens of art of which we have any knowledge, and that any approach to their actual date cannot be ascertained nearer than within a lapse of time measured by hundreds or even thousands of years, one is struck with admiration and astonishment at the height of their art, the perfection of their execution. We know, without being able to account for the fact, that the farther we go back in the history of the arts of ancient Egypt—notably in the case of sculpture—the more advanced appears to be the standard to which they had attained. From this it would appear that the age of perfection preceded the system of hieratic dogmatism which, in the course of time, became established and ruled by rigid laws. In these wooden figures, as in thousands of other examples of all kinds, in stone and bronze, statues and statuettes, figurines and bas-reliefs, the individualism of the artist is most pronounced. There is evidence of an absolute liberty of expression, of a rendering from nature drawn by the personal observation of each individual artist. They are portraits of men and women as they lived, in the surroundings amongst which their existence had been

6

passed. Whatever the material used, whether it be wood or limestone, granite or bronze, the analogies are so great that it would be difficult to consider them apart, though the wood is naturally most nearly approached to the figures in soft stone. All are of the same type, with the same fidelity to nature, the same lifelike expressions, the same evidence of the use of a living model, the same attention to anatomical detail and method of expressing it. For this method is not a scientifically applied one, the result of established canons of art which later ages produced. There is no undue emphasis, no attempt at producing an artificial effect, no idea of *art* in fact. Yet in its impression-istic manner it suffices. Its naturalism is convincing, expressed by an almost sketchy *résumé* of the principal lines and masses of the subject. It may be that those whose acquaintance with the entire history of the rise and progress of Egyptian art in all its branches is profound, may find an easy solution of the problem which seems to be involved in the consideration of these wooden figures alone. Many questions suggest themselves. What is the date assigned to the figure of the Sheik el Beled? The fourth dynasty? At how many thousands of years before our era is this period to be placed? At any rate at some remote period of man's existence on earth, at a period of which we have no general history, still less a know-ledge of the progress — we see here with astonish-ment a system, a mannerism, instinctively adopted. That is to say, that four thousand years at least before our era we find in Egyptian sculpture an established system of art at such a state of perfection that it continues unchanged during these forty centuries. By what successive stages, slow or quick, by what teaching of principles or canons, by what laborious evolution of technique it was accomplished, that is what we are entirely ignorant about. We are able to study in our museums—at any rate in the great museum at Cairo — innumerable examples, ranging from shreds and tatters to those possibly oldest figures of all, the limestone Hetep and Nefert, as fresh and perfect as if carved last week. But of the evolution of the creative genius—nothing! Yet we are told by Egyptologists that more than nine thousand years ago there flourished in the valley of the Nile a school of free sculpture with a genius surpassing our own. It is a great gap—three thousand years!

The impression produced by these figures will be different on the minds of some from that which is conveyed to others. For my own part I am unable to reconcile the seeming evidence on the one hand of untaught natural genius, on the other of the apparently trained comprehension of principles. In Egypt the practice of statuary is coeval with the earliest efforts in decorative architecture. It would appear that man had no sooner emerged from his primeval condition as a pure savage than he exercised his imitative faculties in an intelligent manner, and set about constructing ideal types of beauty and of manly vigour, reproducing the likenesses of everything that was in the heavens above and in the earth below. Evidently the primitive races would begin to model, and to model well, before any principles of architecture had been evolved, and they would have chosen wood, for its solidity, before clay. With the earliest glimmering of religious sentiment, and the first requirements for the construction of the idols necessary in worship and ceremonial, there would have been a tendency to the establishment of hieratic laws, and of a kind of pictorial language for which no very high degree of perfection in expression would have been necessary. Certain types would have been formed, and perpetuated by transmission from age to age, before the idea occurred of endeavouring to make a direct imitation of those which nature provided in every form

8

of life around. It was not always ignorance, or inability to do better, which produced the archaic groups and figures which we associate in a general way with the monuments of ancient Egypt. It was deliberate choice guided if not dictated by hieratic prescription. And so we find in statues and bas-reliefs certain conventions in conjunction with considerable skill in rendering the human form and the suggestion of movement. The body is fronting, the head in profile: the whole weight is thrown on the soles of the feet: one foot is generally advanced, the right in the case of men, the left of women and children, and so on. As time went on two currents were formed and proceeded on two different principles. The one rigidly adhered to the precepts and dogmas imposed by hieratism; the other, which finally triumphed, was in the direction of emancipation from these trammels and restrictions. But, in accordance with the laws of evolution which Nature causes to be repeated over and over again, in art as in more important matters, the triumph, or arrival at perfection, is followed by decadence. The early loyal efforts at faithfully reproducing nature little by little induce suggestions of what she teaches. We learn to appreciate the ideal, and little by little the highest perfection of its expression is arrived at, only to fall again, little by little, without pausing for a moment until, as an anticlimax, imitative realism is the miserable result. It is not without reason that a question of too great importance to be followed in a single chapter has been hinted at. It is not only in this early history of peoples that we have to remark this phenomenon, this unchangeable law. In one form or other we shall encounter it repeated over and over again as we pass under review the arts of many nations from the times when we are in possession of evidence of their beginnings under conventional forms held captive by the restraints of priestly domination, until emancipation from these restrictions leads to the free study of nature herself. We shall be confronted everywhere by evidences of the forces of the hieratism of convention opposed by the struggle to represent beauty as it is in nature, unrestrained by the trammels of tradition. And no sooner is the height of beauty in the ideal reached than it is followed by decline and degradation and the change to a completely new system, which in its turn follows the same path. Early sculptural art in Egypt seems to have possessed a considerable amount of originality and understanding of nature, bound though it was by hieratic laws, even if less rigidly than they were imposed later on. In our own history the subjection to theocratic doctrines and the imposition of traditions by priests held peremptory sway during a long succession of centuries. The emancipation began only when Gothic art was nearing its apogee, and reached absolute freedom with the triumph of the Renaissance.

Ancient Egyptian statues and statuettes, when not representing deities, are—in whatever material—without exception, portraits of individuals executed with the utmost exactness and fidelity to the prevailing characteristics and habits of life of the person whose memory it was desired to preserve. We are not called upon to follow here, in any detailed way, the manners and customs of the people. It is sufficient to remember that all these statues found in the tombs are, as it were, the 'doubles' of the deceased personage whose embalmed body lies in the decorated cartonnage case and massive sarcophagus. Briefly stated, the idea was that the spirit, separated at death from the body, required a material support of some kind for the continuance of its existence or at least some kind of local habitation. The body itself was preserved by embalming; otherwise the soul would die a second and definite death. And as the mummy itself might disappear, it was represented by one or more statues—exact representations of the dead—by which life was perpetuated. We may gather, indeed, that these reproductions had to be, as far as possible, absolute facsimiles of the form of the deceased, with no concessions in the elimination of imperfect features, no attempt at the ideal, no flattery in exaggeration of beauty and expression : in short, a real body in stone or wood as the case might be, with more than photographic detail. Thus could a second himself, clothed as he was clothed, in his most accustomed attitude, wearing the insignia of his rank, or bearing the usual instruments of his occupation, take his place in the tomb as the familiar resting-place of the soul. Are they then works of art? It is a question perhaps not difficult to answer. But we may be sure that they must have been posed during life and the result of long observation. And it is because there is evidence in them of appreciation and of capability of seizing salient points and of omitting the unimportant in a masterly manner —whether intuitive or acquired by training we know not—because of this impressionism, that we should place them on so high a level. For we must not assume that the copying was so very exact and mechanical. On the contrary, the artist knew how to emphasize by exaggeration. He knew, for example, the importance of the eye, as the key to character, as the messenger of thought from the brain. We are struck at once in such statues as that of the sheik, or especially of the scribe, in that of the princess Nefert, and in all those which are really portraits, with the vitality of the head, the reality of the expression. In those in wood with which we are now particularly occupied, the size and power of the eye was heightened by means of an artificial one, an inlay of coloured marble, or some vitreous substance. The Egyptians, it is true, were in the habit of increasing the apparent size in life by the use of *kohl*, and the exaggeration is to be found in all their portraiture, in the admirable funeral masks and the like, and even in the colossal granite statues which represent, if they are not strictly, portraits of the rulers. What is not to be forgotten is that it is held that our wood and other statues are older still by centuries than any of the colossi. Still, in dating them, we cannot be guided solely by our artistic perception. We are at the mercy of the Egyptologist and must accept his ruling. Otherwise we might ask for evidence of tendencies to idealization, and conclude that Egypt must have long been at the height of her civilization before her art had arrived at such a conception. And when we come to reckon with such figures as the sheik or the scribe we feel that the sculptor must have been perfectly well aware of the impossibility of translating into wood or stone that which has other qualities : that his method implied convention, that he could only succeed in conveying an impression, that all he could give was petrified life and arrested motion. The statue in wood known as the Sheik el Beled was discovered by Mariette in one of the tombs of the necropolis of Memphis. It may be taken as a type of the Egyptian of the period, but so little has this changed in the course of sixty centuries or more, that we are told that no sooner was it seen by the native workmen engaged in making the excavation, than they cried out, 'It is the sheik of the village!' And so, whoever he may have been in life, and whatever his occupation, that is now, and always will be, his designation.

A short description only will be required to supplement the illustration here given (*Frontispiece*). He stands solidly planted on both feet, holding with raised left hand his long staff or walking-stick, head cropped close (perhaps for the addition of a wig), fat, jolly face, rather low forehead ; short, thick nose ; intelligent, obedient eyes ; quiet, contented smile, as if resigned to his position as a minor local official ; broad shoulders ; prominent, fleshy breast ; hips, arms, and legs too solidly constructed, and furnished with an indication of tremendous muscular development ; long, flat feet, admirable suggestion of movement in the easy and natural pose as if stopping for the moment—that is the man known sometimes also as Ra-em-Ke, the name of the owner or inhabitant of the tomb. It is the art of the nude, and art of an advanced kind, whether of natural genius or by training. Either hypothesis is tenable.

The question of the colouring of sculpture will form later on an important section of our subject. The practice was certainly prevalent in the earliest art of Egypt, and may be briefly referred to here with regard to such figures as the one just described. It was, indeed, usual to colour men figures red or a deep reddish brown, the women yellow, more or less deep according to their lower or higher social position, representing, as it were, delicacy of complexion. Generally speaking, it may be said that in the painting of sculpture the Egyptians either had no knowledge of, or did not care for, the use of tone. It may be that they disdained an attempt at absolute imitation, and were satisfied with a conventional treatment without break or shadow. The seated scribe of the Louvre is coloured a uniform red of equal value. His eyes, as we find also in wood figures, are formed of an opaque white quartz, in which is set the pupil of clear rock crystal, and this is again surrounded by eyebrows and eyelashes of engraved bronze. For wood, the work was covered with fine linen closely adhering by means of some colloid to every portion of the surface, and upon this was a layer of thin plaster upon which colour was applied on the same principle as in the case of stone. The system is, in fact, identical with that of the Middle Ages, and, as we shall see, described by the monk Theophilus and Cennino Cennini thousands of years later. We cannot here examine at length a number of examples, even of those in one museum alone. It must suffice to confine our attention to a few which are typical. A fragment of a figure, as far as somewhat below the waist—probably of a slave—is also in the Cairo Museum. The head, with the hair or a wig carefully curled, is no less powerfully executed than that of the sheik. It is ascribed to the fifth dynasty. Eton College possesses a fragment of a figure representing an old slave, with completely bald head, of the time of the first Theban empire. Finally, in the museum of the Louvre is a beautiful statuette of the priestess Toui. It is of a dark polished wood, of a fine grain : of acacia, sycamore, or of the Egyptian locust-wood perhaps, for all these were used, together with ebony, sometimes plain, sometimes coloured and gilt. Of charming proportions, clothed in a thin transparent robe, she wears a magnificent thickly tressed ceremonial wig, such as we find so commonly in much earlier times. For we have arrived now at the eighteenth dynasty, two thousand years later than the scribe, and still there is no difference in style or in technique.

It is not only, however, great sculpture and figures in the round which call for attention amongst these ancient wood sculptures. There are also numberless bas-reliefs which cannot be particularized. We are compelled by limits of space to confine ourselves in the main to generalities. But there is also some quite small work which is often so fine in character that it is impossible to pass it over. These are the carved spoons for perfumes and the little toilet ornaments and utensils which are to be found in many museums. The handles of the spoons are carved with human figures and with a variety of motives of the most fascinating description. We find, for instance, in the Louvre, the graceful nude figure of a young girl swimming, and holding a waterfowl; another, walking in a lotus-grove, and gathering a bud. The Liverpool Museum possesses a delightful figurine which appears to be an article of toilet use, to contain perhaps *kohl* or some ointment. It is of a type which is not uncommon also in alabaster or terra-cotta : a man, bending under the weight of a huge vase which he carries on his back, one arm upraised behind him to support it, the other hanging down or resting on his thigh : precisely, in fact, as we see a *hammal* at his task, in the streets of Cairo to-day, climbing slowly and laboriously the steep ascent to the citadel. It seems to be a portrait from life of some slave, and M. Jean Capart, who describes it (*Revue archéol.*, 4ème série x. 372), points out that the form of the handles of the vase, confined to the eighteenth dynasty, allows us to be precise as to date. Other examples of wood sculpture of all kinds present themselves in profusion. Amongst them a brief reference must be made to the remarkable bas-reliefs on six panels of wood, found by Mariette in a tomb of the third dynasty and now in the Cairo Museum. They are portraits of the deceased, one *Hosi*, and admitting the conventional method of representation, the head in profile, the body, and even the eye, as if standing full face, the intuitive knowledge of art and the great cleverness of execution are surprising, at such a remote epoch. We are not now, however, endeavouring to follow the history of sculpture in Egypt even in this one branch of the art. Should we do so we should find the two currents already alluded to, the ideal and the real, strongly illustrated. We should discover in the outline pictures on the monuments of what a power of suggestion these early artists were capable. As an example, there is the painter colouring a statue, from Thebes (see *Champollion, plate* 180). It is the art of leaving out, and we must admit that the latest achievements of the French caricaturist Sem, or our own Nicholson, have their prototypes in these almost prehistoric times. We all see things of this kind with different eyes, and may or may not entirely agree with the observations made by Mr. Flinders Petrie in his *History of Egypt*.

But they are very much to the point. He says: 'The sculptor's work and the painter's show the same sentiment—a rivalry of nature. They did not make a work of art to please the taste as such, but they rivalled nature as closely as possible : the form, the expression, the colouring, the glittering transparent eye, the grave smile, all are copied as if to make an artificial man. The painter mixed his half-tints and his delicate shades and dappled over the animals or figured the feathers of the birds in a manner never attempted in the later ages. The embalmer built up the semblance of the man in resins and cloth over his shrunken corpse to make him as nearly as possible what he was when alive. In each direction man, then, set himself to supplement, to imitate, to rival, or to exceed the works of nature. Art, as the gratification of an artificial taste and standard, was scarcely in existence, but the simplicity, the vastness, the perfection and the beauty of the earliest works, place them on a different level to all works of art and man's device in later ages. They are unique in their splendid power, which no self-conscious civilization has ever rivalled, or can hope to rival, and in their enduring greatness they may last till all the feebler works of man have perished.'

We are led, then, if only by the consideration of the few examples of the art of wood sculpture which limitations of space permit us to pass in review, to questions of very great interest. But with regard to these questions no certain answer is forthcoming. Hypotheses and theories are not wanting, it is true, but we can come to no definite conclusion. It would appear that at a time so remote as the period of the fourth dynasty—shall we say four thousand years before Christ?—the civilization of Egypt had arrived at its highest point, and that perhaps another four thousand years had passed during which the progress of this civilization and the evolution of the arts had been going on. It would appear, also, that the earliest works of art of which we have any knowledge are, as Mariette has said, fine in themselves and no less fine if compared with the work of dynasties which are supposed to represent the most flourishing ages of Egypt. The most striking feature of this earliest art is its intense realism: the understanding of and fidelity to nature even when conventionally expressed. It would appear, further, that, at the beginnings of the fourth dynasty, art was dependent on and strongly influenced by religion, its ceremonies and hieratism. As in the west, thousands of years later, all art was religious art, at least in an extended sense. We cannot, however, be certain that we are in possession, now, of the finest art of all. There may yet be in store for us, to be revealed by further discoveries, still greater surprises. So far as we can judge at the present time the earlier the art, the greater are the evidences of refinement, whether from instinct, from a long process of training or imported by some conquering race, we know not. And, further, that somewhere about the time when documents become abundant, there was a period of decadence forming a temporary break.

The remains of ancient Greek or Roman art in wood which have come down to us are so few that hardly more than a bare reference can be made to them. No doubt the earliest attempts in the awakening civilizations of these peoples were, as elsewhere, rude resemblances to the human figure. The beginnings of art of this kind have always followed a like tendency: something more in the nature of a representative symbol than an effort to reproduce an actual likeness. Beauty, for the pleasure it might give, was not thought of. So far as our knowledge goes, the extreme archaicism of the early Hellenic religious sculptures was intentional. The national museum at Naples possesses a wooden image of Diana which sums up the retention of this deliberately intended feeling. It has been called the ' Diana of the archaic smile.' And, amongst other rare examples, is a seated statuette, in wood, of a goddess with a child on her lap, which was found about 1872 in a tomb at Troussepoïl, in Vendée. The group, nearly three feet in height, in attitude and expression and draperies, bears a remarkable resemblance to the Madonna statuettes of the Romanesque period, and perhaps explains the legends of miraculous images found from time to time (see *Mélanges archéologiques*, 1885). In this connexion a passing reference may be made to the groups of Isis and Horus, of which an interesting example in ivory —so like wood that it is not easy to say whether it is so or not—is in the Egyptian gallery of the British Museum.

CHAPTER II

WOOD SCULPTURE IN THE EARLY MIDDLE AGES AND LATER

THE perishable nature of wood has already been noticed. If we may add to this its small intrinsic value, the want of consideration from which decorative work of any kind must suffer as fashions change, and the recurring vandalism which seems to be a law of nature, it is not surprising that our information concerning the art of sculpture in wood, even of our own early era, should be so scanty. In the turbulent times of which we know so little, excepting that men's chief occupations were strife and tumult—in the Dark Ages as we call them—the goods of the Church were the only ones respected, and even these suffered. Some ivories have come down to us perhaps because they could be turned neither into money nor fuel. But wood—it was burnt or left to kick about in garrets as fashions changed, to become worm-eaten, rotten, and powdered! Even in the most recent times, many of us can remember how the to-day so highly prized Chippendale furniture could be bought for a song, and was considered fit only for the nursery or the attic. Such a thing as an example of Norman furniture could not be found in England, and anything earlier than the thirteenth century is of extreme rarity. We do not even know the name of a single English furniture-maker or carver of Elizabeth's time. In England, in France, in the Netherlands, revolutionary and reformation troubles caused destructions of the most sweeping kind. The churches were the only museums of those times, and they themselves were the first to suffer from the insensate fury of iconoclasts.

Thus it is that we can hardly pretend to begin any history at all before, at earliest, the eleventh century. There are, it is true, preserved in various collections, certain archaic rarities with traces of decoration, such as the coffin of St. Cuthbert at York, the reading-desk of St. Radegonde,[1] in the convent of Sainte-Croix at Poitiers, some gates and doorways in France and Italy, or the Romanesque sculptures of the Christiania Museum. The last named are the twelfth-century doorways of churches, of which there are reproductions in the gallery of casts at Kensington, and there are also some arm-chairs and other furniture with a decoration of a similar character.

The reading-desk of Saint Radegonde—if we are really justified in assigning to it such an early date as the sixth century in which she lived—is, of course, a precious monument, on account of its unique position as an example of wood-carving of the time. With regard to the character of the decoration, this is merely an application of themes and sculptural methods derived from the sarcophagi of the fifth and sixth centuries in Italy and southern Gaul, and may have been executed three or four centuries later (see *Mél. d'archéol*, iii. 78). The vine-wood doors of the church of Santa Sabina in Rome have already been referred to in my ' Ivories ' of this series (p. 252). They are usually ascribed to the sixth century, but the whole subject involves so much that is debatable and connected with early Christian

[1] St. Radegonde, wife of the French King Clotaire. She founded the abbey, or nunnery, of Poitiers, which she called the Holy Cross, on account of a relic of the true Cross which she caused to be preserved there. The Normans in England had a great devotion to her, and there were several churches and convents under her dedication; notably the one at Cambridge, which, at the reformation, became the present Jesus College.

PLATE I

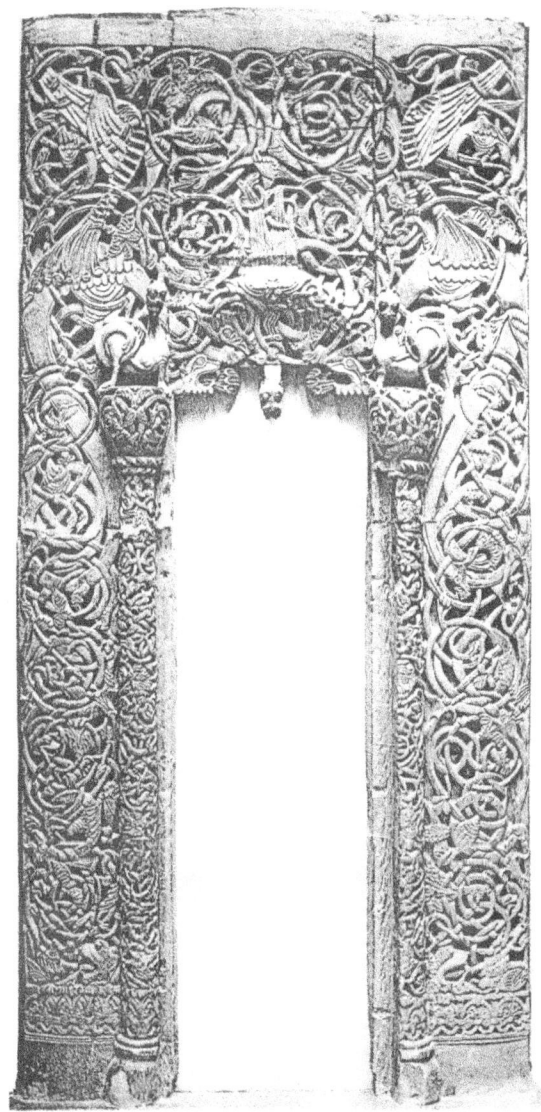

CHURCH DOORWAY. SCANDINAVIAN. TWELFTH CENTURY
CHRISTIANIA MUSEUM, NORWAY
PAGE 21

art generally that I shall content myself with their bare mention. It is extremely doubtful that they should be given so early a date, notwithstanding their close analogy with the sarcophagus style. The reader may be referred, for an erudite notice concerning them, to the paper by M. Kondakov in the *Revue Archéologique*, N.S., xxxiii. 360. It is right to observe that such an authority as Molinier had no doubt that they are Roman work of the early sixth century, and by no means due to sculptors working under Greek influences of a later date.

The Scandinavian doors (Plate I.) allow us to form a very good idea of the kind of decoration in sculptured wood of early mediæval times. We find in them the usual interlaced foliage work, with which fantastic figures are intermingled, dear to the northern races : a style which persisted so long that though we may have grounds for an attribution to the twelfth century they may well be later. A close examination of the subjects drawn from old Norse mythology—perhaps from the Nibelungen—would be most attractive. Amongst them we seem to have, for example, Siegfried blowing the furnace, forging his arms, fighting the dragon, and so on. The execution is admirable, and has the further interest that the style is inspired or borrowed from English or Celtic sources of the eleventh or twelfth century. We must remember also that Scandinavia was not evangelized until the eleventh century, no long time before the date assigned to these church doors. However this may be, they illustrate the usual type of sculpture in wood of the Carlovingian empire in the Romanesque period. There is nothing original or peculiar to Scandinavia. The system is borrowed from the prevailing fondness elsewhere for convoluted foliage ornament twisted and knotted in elegant curved lines symmetrically arranged and intermingled with mythological figures and grotesques :

21

conventional, yet in a certain way realistic. We need not here pursue its more remote oriental origin. With regard to design and technique, a similar fashion is to be found on other early doors, for example those of the eleventh century of the cathedral at Puy. We have here again, in the scenes of the life of our Lord, the same system of deeply cut subjects in a style resembling champlevé enamels, the surfaces quite flat without any relief whatever, and the added colour, of which there are traces, would make the resemblance still closer. Other examples of the kind might be given, and if we were to follow the subject still more closely we should find that this kind of dug-out decoration in wood—in chests for example—continued until quite late times. We shall take note, later on, of the coffer in the Cluny Museum of late thirteenth or early fourteenth century work, but it will be an evidence of an almost sudden awakening and of the beginning of times when an entirely different character of ornament will afford examples in profusion. In France the earliest known piece of furniture is the armoire of the church of Obazine (Corrèze). It may possibly be referred to the twelfth century, but it is almost entirely unornamented. Our principal concern will be with the madonna and crucifix figures. Of these some noble specimens yield in no way, in merit and interest, to those in other materials of pre-Gothic times. The condition of Europe, and indeed of what constituted the civilized world at the time now occupying our attention, offered but little opportunity for the cultivation of the arts. It had hardly recovered from the terrible anarchy produced by the invasion of barbarian hordes in the eighth century which had covered it with ruins. Men's attention was wholly absorbed by wars between nations and disputes amongst powerful chieftains. They had no time to trouble about the comforts and luxuries of life. Those whose minds turned to religious subjects were resigned to the idea that the time for providing for future generations was past, and that the year 1000 was an ominous date, destined to see the end of all things. It is, perhaps, more than a remarkable coincidence that this period of anxiety should be succeeded by one of greater tranquillity, and that the arts of peace should, as it were, immediately enter upon an era of activity. The very year 1000 gave the signal for an enthusiasm in church-building. But although in our own country the Norman invasion, later on, brought with it the genius and feeling for art of another race, we were still far behind in that of architecture and sculpture : in all the arts, indeed, except those which were practised in the seclusion of the monasteries, or in metallurgy, for which we had the advantage of possessing rich stores of the necessary materials. The twelfth century continued the advance, and the coming of pointed architecture, which was everywhere adopted, spurred on the cultivation of all the arts, wood sculpture no less than the others. If, then, we are forced to begin our history at comparatively so late a date as the eleventh century, it coincides with a time when every industry was beginning to awaken from the lethargy under which it had so long stagnated. In the working and ornamentation of wood the imagination of the artist was no longer limited to always the same interlaced patterns mingled with fabulous animals, the human figure characterized with always the same stiffness, unnatural attitudes, and monotonous gravity of expression. As the twelfth century progresses, painters and sculptors gradually begin to abandon the hieratic methods under which they had hitherto worked. It is almost an *art nouveau*. Where, in the older system, there was neither undiluted realism nor idealism, but only the restrictions of a traditional convention, there begins to be an approach to an understanding of nature. Draperies are no longer confined to a uniform system of long, straight, and narrow folds, but the sacred personages begin to wear an approximation at least to the costume of the period which the artist had daily before his eyes—this, of course, except in the case of the most sacred of all. We are nearing the time of an absolute revolution in architecture, when the Abbot Suger builds his church of Saint Denis, when Chartres and Reims uprear their famous façades, and when England is in no ways behind other countries in enthusiasm and accomplishment. And when we remember that the great edifices had each and all to be filled with sculpture in wood as well as in stone, and that the controller of the whole was the master builder—or architect as we should call him now—it will be seen that these general references are not without importance in relation to our particular subject. The more so because the functions of the master builder were not limited to those of the modern architect. He could and did carve a statue or the capital of a pillar as well as plan and measure and decide upon curves and angles, and whatever may have been the freedom permitted to individual sculptors, their part was entirely subordinate to his conception of the whole work. The importance of this consideration cannot be too much insisted upon.

We are, however, still confronted with a paucity of examples in wood sculpture until the end of the thirteenth century. But before we enter into the succeeding one, when there will be much less reason to complain, there are a certain number of statuettes, especially of the Virgin and Child and of crucifix figures, which are highly instructive. Throughout the fourteenth century wood-carving follows the same lines as the stone sculpture of the cathedrals. The various departments of art are not specialized, the trained workman is not confined to any particular branch. Many are at once architects, painters, sculptors, image-

24

makers, huchers, or, as we should say, cabinet-makers. And this condition of affairs continues to at least mid-sixteenth century. Architecture and the architectural completeness governed everything. Under the master builder, retables, stalls, figures, and even such minor accessories as thuribles and other sanctuary requisites, were simply motives for decoration in accordance with the general plan. All decorative work bore an architectural aspect. Even in furniture, chairs, tables and benches, bedsteads and chests, were panelled with window tracery, adorned with little buttresses and pinnacles, and, between the panels, with carved niches and canopies : surmounted also, in the case of ceremonial seats, or even of rich domestic furniture, with an elaborately-carved dais. There was an overmastering tendency to lavish ornament everywhere, not only simply decorative ornament, but also pictorial and didactic. There was a propensity in the choirs of cathedrals, and even of parish churches, to an over-rich display, which took the place of the refined simplicity which had characterized the previous age. We shall see this at its culmination at the close of the fifteenth century, when the aim seemed to be to employ all the resources of the wood-carver's skill in the production of a veritable encyclopædia of the arts and sciences, and of religion, together with an epitome of the domestic life, manners, and customs of the time. This meant, indeed, the whole science of theology, for theology embraced all knowledge, and the method of imparting it to the illiterate people was by means of these great illustrated books which every one could read. The language was the language of symbolism, and the imagery was drawn from every conceivable source, both sacred and profane; from the romances of chivalry or the mystical bestiaries of the thirteenth century. The transformation effected by the end of the fourteenth century was complete, but we shall not attempt to trace it to all its sources and in every land. Italy had not yet begun to exercise the special influence which, a century later, was to become so powerful and far-reaching in the creation of an entirely new system. It is to Flanders that our attention will be drawn over and over again in succeeding chapters. It is true that the courts of Philip vi., of John ii., or of Charles v. were centres of all the arts, but the chief impulse was given by such masters as Claus Sluter, or André Beauneveu, and by such work as the *puits de Moïse* at Dijon. The artistic relations between the Netherlands and the Courts of Philip the Bold and of Philip the Good, and the fusion later on with the house of Austria, have an important relation with our subject. Indeed, during the three centuries or so with which we shall be more particularly interested, we shall meet the Fleming at every turn. We shall not be able to neglect him even in his painting. The influence of painting upon sculpture may be indirect, and it cannot be said that a school of the one creates a school of the other, yet it may act very powerfully upon it, as will presently be insisted upon. We shall find, then, the Fleming almost cosmopolitan in his character. By nature homely, and a lover of his own chimney-corner, he is industrious, and as a bread-winner has no hesitation in expatriating himself, and even in attaching himself to another nationality. And so we find him now Burgundian, now a Frenchman, now German, now so far a Spaniard that we have to deduce his origin by his Flemish name disguised in Spanish form. In our own country we owe to him the Angel choir of Lincoln, one amongst many evidences of the employment by us of Flemish artists during at least five centuries of the greatest activity in the arts in England. The productions of the wood-carver's skill of Brussels or of Antwerp enjoyed a world-wide reputation, and were exported to every other country. Had it not been for the destructions at the Reformation our churches would probably even now abound in triptychs and retables and roods from these celebrated workshops. One of the difficulties in our study of the evolution of the art of wood-carving will be to recognize that as centuries progress changes are rarely sudden. One style supplants another almost imperceptibly. Innovations would not be accepted at once, and time would have been required before the newer system triumphed. Nor would changes have occurred simultaneously in every district : even in the same town the old fashion would have kept its admirers. Therefore it is that style is not always evidence of date. It would not be easy to make a just comparison between the refinement of the thirteenth century, the progress accomplished in the fourteenth, and the new spirit of the Renaissance in the fifteenth. There was in fact, in the fourteenth century, a pause which was marked, a halt in preparation for the spring forward which was to follow. During that interval there was an indulgence in a kind of extravagance. The art was less refined, less spiritually inspired, with more dexterity, perhaps, than perfection in execution. A new era had opened in the gradual emancipation from religious domination. Craftsmen were formed into corporations, and the hieratic rule of the monastery lost its autocratic power. So long as the arts proceeded along lines rigidly marked out by dogma and tradition, the free study of nature was kept in check. But the increase of luxury made its wants felt in another direction. The laity now began to have a say in the matter. And so there came about a freer system which required a different organization of labour. Huchers and joiners separated from the ordinary working carpenter, and those with natural aptitudes for that line began to study ornament for its own sake. The demands on their talent were no longer exclusively confined to the requirements of the altar, although even for the decoration of the sumptuous furniture of the rich man's house they knew no other theme than that inspired by religion. The great artists of this period of awakening were pioneers, the results of whose efforts on emancipation soon became manifest in every land. An understanding of art thus catered for seems to have been innate, in those days, in the meanest of people. What the public was capable of appreciating found an ever ready supply. Art was vulgarized in the best sense of the term. It became a necessity to the inhabitants of the smallest hamlet. If it was to be found at its highest amongst those who worked in the great capitals, or for princely mansions, the village carpenter, in his untrained way, possessed an unconscious perception of its canons, and he was successful in applying them because he could both design and execute. Yet still, and for two centuries longer, the great abbeys were the source from which everything proceeded. They were the inspirers and the directing force. As the Rule of the great Benedictine order had provided, so it was still. Every monk was not obliged to be an artist, but every monastery was a hive of artistic industry, a workshop of trained architects, illuminators, calligraphists, sculptors and carvers in stone and wood, founders and chasers, and enamellers, in iron and bronze and in the precious metals. They were the instructors and they set the tune, even if their pupils were less dependent upon them than formerly. Our thoughts in this direction naturally turn to our special subject, and it is difficult to avoid a certain amount of generalization which may not in every case be strictly accurate. We find in wood sculpture, as in the minor arts as a rule, little evidence of originality of conception. The artist's themes were found for him, and their arrangement followed the traditionary methods. They had the work of the masters of sculpture in stone to inspire

28

them, and their task was to transpose into the key of wood that which had originally been phrased to suit the needs and qualities of another medium of expression. Nor can it be said that they were always successful, and this, indeed, because their art was not specialized. In the fifteenth century we arrive at a more intelligent effort to understand the human form, and to follow its study: a study which monastic sentiment had so long barred and proscribed. The great effect which resulted was in the treatment of draperies. To this subject we shall have more than once again to turn our attention. Early Christian and early mediæval art disliked and entirely neglected the body as a form of beauty. The head alone received attention, the use of drapery was to conceal the human figure. It fell in long straight folds and hid even the feet. In Italy, up to the end of the twelfth century, the sculptural arts had fallen into complete decadence, and even in the early days of the thirteenth she was still in arrear of other nations. But a movement was preparing which was not to be without its effect upon the particular subject with which we are concerned. We shall consider presently, even if it must be in a somewhat restricted manner, sculpture in wood of the great schools of the trecento and quattrocento of Pisa, of Florence, and of Siena, and we shall be able to include amongst those who practised the craft the names of the greatest masters of sculpture of those glorious times. Again, we shall find that there was no exclusiveness, and that a close connexion existed between the painter and sculptor and worker in the precious metals.

The early history of sculpture in France is vague, and we have little to show in wood. The Gaulish provinces, after the Roman conquest, suffered, as elsewhere in Europe, from the invasions and oppressions of the conquerors, and little chance was left for the peaceful arts. Their refuge was in, or in the neighbourhood of, the great monasteries, and there, no doubt, were established the only schools for the practice of wood and ivory carving. Later on we shall find examples in profusion to show that the wood sculptors of France were as distinguished as those in other branches. Paris became the centre, and, at least up to the fifteenth century, was the instructor in the arts of the whole of Europe. But, as in the case of ivories, we have little precise information and no names. Or if, as is probable, we may take it that the ivory carvers worked also in wood, it is to them that we must go to include a Jean le Scelleur, who in 1315 was employed for Philip the Long, a Jean le Brailleur, the ivory carver of Charles v., a Jehan de Couilly, or a Jean de Marville at the Court of Burgundy. But that court will supply us with some names of notable carvers of Flemish origin of very great importance. Other royal inventories show also the esteem in which the woodcarver's art was held; for instance, in that of Charles v. there is mention of 'tableaux istoriez, crucefilz, ymages de bois, un de quatre pièces que Girard d'Orléans fist,' and in the inventory of Philippe le Bon wood figures are entered under 'ymages d'or et d'argent.'

In Germany we shall be mostly concerned with the wood-carving of quite late mediæval times, at a period of transition when the tide of the Renaissance was flowing fast and rapidly changing the condition of things which had so long continued. We shall find two distinct regions, that of the north where vast forests of oak prevailed, and that of the south where softer and more resinous woods were also used. It is to the work of the southern masters, to the schools of Würtemberg, of Würzburg, of Rothenburg or Nürnberg, and of Suabia generally, bordering on Italy and Switzerland, that attention will be chiefly directed.

In Spain, wood-carving, always in a flourishing condition in the early Middle Ages, continued to be

none the less so in later Gothic times and throughout the period of the Renaissance. If, at the end of
the fifteenth century and beginning of the sixteenth,
the prevailing fashion as exemplified in the choir
stalls of that period is frankly French, and if the
designers and carvers of so many magnificent choirs
and retables have French, and, especially, Flemish
names, they worked in conjunction with Spanish
artists. But the art they display is a borrowed and not
a national one, and so it must be considered. Yet it is
Spanish.

In England we are met by even a greater penury of
existing examples than elsewhere, and although in
Gothic times the fabrics of our great cathedrals, abbeys,
and parish churches attest that we possessed a national
art in no way inferior to other countries—in some
styles taking the lead—yet the destructions of the
reformers and Puritans have left us in wood sculpture
almost nothing. Practically, we can show only the
choirs and choir stalls, chancel screens and bench ends,
and the splendid roof-work, so peculiarly English.
Happily, these still exist in not inconsiderable numbers.

Without the aid of wood few arts would be possible,
and in itself its peculiar qualities make it applicable to
every form of sculptural decoration. The sole fault
with which we can reproach it is the liability to decay.
No material is more amenable to the chisel or graver.
The varieties are very numerous, and its own natural
colours and capability of high polish demand, of
necessity, nothing additional. It is no part of the plan
of this book to enter generally into the natural history
of the various kinds of wood, but a few brief
remarks concerning those which have been generally
used in decorative sculpture will not be out of place.
Oak, of course, has ever been the most popular,
especially amongst ourselves in mediæval times. In
the German schools, also, of the end of the fifteenth

31

century—at Calcar, Xanten, and other great centres of the northern division, oak was almost exclusively used. In France the northern schools remained faithful to it long after some softer woods were employed in more southern regions. Indeed, one may say, generally, that oak is an infallible sign of northern workmanship, walnut of the provinces south of Burgundy. But there is no rule without exceptions, and in later times, in the schools of Philibert de l'Orme, Pierre Lescot, Jean Goujon, Germain Pilon or Ducerceau, in the île de France, and in the provinces bordering on the Loire, walnut was exclusively used. So also with regard to the Lyonese schools in Burgundy, Auvergne, and Dauphiné, oak furniture is to be found. But walnut was certainly the fashionable wood of the Renaissance, of the times of Louis XII. and Francis I. Nearly all the great Burgundian pieces of this period are in walnut. Again, in Italy, the same wood with its beautiful grain and rich colour and hard close texture, besides possessing a variety peculiar to the country, and in great profusion, was the favourite for her magnificent choir stalls. Figtree was occasionally used in Italy, and corkwood, for its lightness. There are, for instance, a life-sized statue of the flagellation in the church of S. Giovanni al Monte, Bologna, and a St. Sebastian in the Salting collection at South Kensington of the first-named wood, and crucifix figures to which reference is made later on, in corkwood. Walnut, indeed, has always been a favourite, especially in southern countries. The Spanish wood-carver was naturally partial to it, for it has always been common in his country, and oak on the contrary scarce and necessary to be imported. The early Spanish carvers, even long after the Moors had been driven out, used the wood of the cedar, cypress, pine, and other resinous varieties ; the pine of Cuença being particularly esteemed.

32

VARIETIES USED

The immense pine forests of Germany will, of course, prepare us to find this wood largely employed, and we shall come across some remarkable panels in the museum at Kensington of the south Bavarian school of the fifteenth century. From the nature of the grain and arrangement of the fibres it was best adapted for flat or not very high relief; for coffers and panels rather than statues and statuettes. We may recall also the Scandinavian doors previously described.

Boxwood has peculiar qualities which distinguish it from almost every other wood. Unfortunately it is not to be obtained in pieces of any but comparatively small dimensions. Notwithstanding this, the examples of figure work, in boxwood, to which we shall come presently, are masterpieces which stand in a distinct category, and from this point of view are not to be surpassed amongst the whole range of sculpture which forms our subject. Some, indeed, will hold their own in comparison with the statuettes of bronze and other figure work of the periods to which they belong.

Beech, elm, yew, and chestnut—if not so commonly selected—might all be illustrated by examples. Mahogany was not known in mediæval times, nor did the sculptor appear to have any leaning towards the woods with ornamental grains such as maple or satinwood. For marquetry these, of course, would appeal, but the prevailing fashion of adding colour to all sculpture in whatever material, to which attention will be drawn in a succeeding chapter, would have been one reason, amongst others, for neglect. Sycamore and acacia, tamarisk, cedar, rosewood, and, for inlay, sandalwood were favourite woods of the sculptor in ancient Egypt, and, in the days of the highest civilization of Greece and Rome, we learn from such writers as Pausanias the lavish use of ebony, cypress, cedar, oak, sycamore, yew, willow, ash, beech, maple, hornbeam, plane, mulberry, lemon, palm, holly, poplar, walnut, and

33

pear. But, indeed, every existing wood has doubtless served the purpose more or less at one time than another. Lime is a soft wood, pliable to the tool, not given to splintering, and taking a stain well, that we shall meet very frequently indeed in the work of the Franconian sculptors of the fifteenth and sixteenth centuries: in the figure work of Veit Stoss and Riemenschneider and their contemporaries. In England we find it very commonly used for the imitative festoons of garlands, fruit, and bird-life of Grinling Gibbons and his school. The white description which they selected is, however, peculiarly subject to the attacks of insects, and the gum or glaze with which the finished work was covered preventing their escape, the result was that in numerous cases the whole interior was eaten away, leaving mere shells or skeletons. Pearwood also was a favourite with the sixteenth-century statuette carvers. It is light, close grained, moderately hard, and not given to warp or split. Harrison, in his description of English woods and marshes in Holinshed's *Chronicles*, written in 1577, speaks of houses formerly built of sallow, willow, plum, hardbeam, and elm, in which men were content to dwell, and that 'oak was in manner dedicated wholly unto churches, religious houses, princes' palaces, noblemen's lodgings, and navigation : but now all these are rejected, and nothing but oak any whit regarded.' *Bois d'islande* is frequently mentioned in old French and Flemish contracts. According to the statutes of the corporation of *charpentiers huchiers* of Paris in 1382, this and walnut, ebony, pear, elm, maple, guelder, and some others not easy to identify, were much used. Regulations are very precise, showing the esteem in which the craft was held, and how fine work was only to be practised by masters. Care was taken that the wood should be of the finest quality, thoroughly seasoned, without knots or shakes, and that green

34

ebony should not be used instead of black, nor pear, nor other wood, instead. Yet of this hard lasting ebony I do not know that a single mediæval example could be found. The statutes of corporations are all of the same character, lengthy and minute in detail, and the same evidence of care in selection of material and quality of the work will be found in such contracts as that for a rood-loft for a remote Cornish parish which elsewhere is here quoted.

The question of the preservation of wood-carvings from decay is an important and interesting one. The maladies to which the different kinds are liable vary, of course, according to the several species : so also do the attacks of the enemies to which they are subject. Chestnut was disliked and condemned by Wren, who considered that it became rotten sooner than oak. Yet the famous roof of Westminster Hall is made of it. The question is one of technical interest. It will suffice to mention that in 1855 a Royal Commission was appointed to consider it. The evidence and report may be consulted with profit.

It must be admitted, of course, that we have few remains of wood sculpture to be compared with the figures of Chartres, of Reims, or of Amiens, but it may be remembered also that until full sixteenth century, when the classical turn in taste was becoming overmastering, this art exercised more general interest than any other. It was the medium above all others of appealing to the popular imagination and, after all, popular taste in those days represented the nation to a greater extent, in point of numbers and concentration of classes, than it does now. Learning and an appreciation of the refinement which characterized the imagery of the thirteenth century would have been confined to the few. This ultra-refinement was, no doubt, for the court and the higher clergy. But the mass of the people had provided for them a system of education which, whether it approached near to or fell far short of the greater sculpture in stone, undoubtedly was the means of keeping up a high standard of taste amongst them. What still remains for our admiration is evidence, when we consider the facilities it offers for decay and destruction, that at one time the abundance must have been almost incredible. With the disappearance of the multitude of images in this material coincided—account for it as we may—the decline in general taste. From the other side of the mountains came the invasion of classical ideas which demanded marble as the great medium of plastic expression. Great, no doubt, was this art, unsurpassed in its appeal to the intellect, but it was caviare to the general. Wood and even stone were abandoned : wood was good enough for the cabinet-maker, and to him it was relegated. With it died also the age of colour in sculpture.

Besides the question of durability, the paucity of early examples of wood sculpture may be accounted for by causes from which all sculpture had suffered in common with the other arts, owing to the unsettled state of the western world. There had been everywhere almost a total want of originality, a copying from antique bas-reliefs by men who in artistic intelligence were hardly above the level of the artisan. It was not until the close of the eleventh century that a real awakening of the sculptural arts begins to be apparent. Then came the crusades and the intercourse with the east. Workmen of all kinds accompanied the armies and brought home with them the oriental systems of ornament, which they adapted to their already existing methods and national feeling. Syria was able to furnish friezes, bas-reliefs, the capitals of columns and other architectural details, and figure work, but for pure statuary there was no indebtedness. It will not be wholly without value to remind ourselves of the capture of Antioch and Jerusalem, and of the virtual occupation of the Holy Land in the first crusade, of the second crusade preached by St. Bernard, of the third under our own King Richard, of the fourth, and of the fifth which will bring us to the fall of Constantinople in the third year of the thirteenth century. During all this time the influence of the monastic establishments on the arts was gradually diminishing and guilds were organizing. They were the true revivalists who restored the art of sculpture to the position it had lost : a restoration which, though apparently a sudden one about the beginning of the twelfth century, had no doubt been prepared for by long years of persistent training. The Cluniac order, already established more than a century, was the most active centre, and exercised a powerful influence on the arts of the whole region of the west. It was the most learned, if not indeed the only, order of the time really learned in the arts. Its houses covered France and Spain, and at a later period Italy, Germany, and England, while at the same time its relations with the east were constant. We should expect then to find in those examples of wood sculpture that can be adduced, the influence of Byzantine hieratism, and the conventional systems of draperies. It is not easy to resume in a few words these influences, nor should an undue weight be given to those resulting from the operations of the crusades. Other causes had, since a long period, caused an immense influx of Greek monks into Europe, who had brought with them manuscripts and other works of Byzantine art, and the commercial relations with Italy—with Venice especially —had helped to spread these things in Germany, France, and England. The southern schools of France — Limoges, Toulouse, Poitiers, Provence — and the Rhine provinces were at the close of the eleventh century absolutely Byzantine. We must suppose that, in the wood-carving of those days, there were also those long-limbed emaciated figures, pearl-bordered long clinging robes and pointed shoes that we find in our ivories. It is to the monks of Citeaux and of Cluny that we owe the beginnings of an observation of nature, some attempts at least at dramatic movement, some attention in their figures to the life which they saw around them. It is indeed against these very methods that St. Bernard fulminated his famous diatribe. The statuary sculptor, turning to nature, had begun to draw from it under idealized forms what he saw with his eyes. It is the age of idealism which will lead, slowly but surely, as suggested in the introductory chapter, to realism. The monastic artists of the twelfth century prepared the way by the partial emancipation at least from Byzantine formulæ. They must have contributed the earliest impulse, for they alone were the instructors and employers of labour. The beginning of the thirteenth century was the beginning of a new order of things. The control of art initiative has to pass out from the cloister into the world. Lay corporations and lay workers supersede the monk in the direction of works, though still almost the only art is that which is devoted to the service of religion. The courts of kings and nobles are too much occupied with warlike pursuits to make much demand for the luxuries of domestic establishments. But a spirit of communism is abroad. Guilds are established—trade unions in fact —which bind themselves to obey codes of regulations which they themselves have drawn up, instead of submitting to the orders of enclosed corporations, ignorant of the life outside and of the demands which it is beginning to make. Independent schools are formed, entirely emancipated from the monastic yoke. It must, however, be admitted that it is not easy to be absolutely precise regarding the relations between these independent workers and the great abbeys. The general direction of architectural and sculptural work for the use of the Church must still have been in the hands of the latter, and the changes were gradual. But a more settled condition of social life had begun to prevail. In the troublous dark ages, between the seventh and eleventh centuries, the producers in every craft took refuge under the shadow of the monasteries, where they followed their apprenticeships and worked afterwards in submission to what was the ruling power. Continual wars and local strifes hindered any kind of artistic activity among the mass of the people. With the new era new ideas took the place of the former rigidity of rules, and the freedom was everywhere welcomed, even by the secular clergy. Yet, though the lay element had come in, sculptor monks still moved about from province to province, from country to country, and we cannot be precise regarding the question how far this or that work is peculiar to the locality in which it appears to have been introduced. For direction, the science must still have come from the learned, the travelled ones of the monastery. Geometry, drawing, the principles of Greek art, the science of symbolism and the rest—all these it was their province to transmit to the lay apprentice, who might then be left to his individual inspiration. The lay artists, following, no doubt, the principles in which they had been educated, enjoyed a greater amount of intellectual liberty, and used their intelligence to discard whatever hide-bound regulations they considered to be no longer up to date. They wanted a freer choice of subject and of methods of expressing it. One must imagine also that the workmen moved about more freely from place to place, forming themselves into bands under a master crafts-man whenever they heard that some great work—as for example the building of Canterbury—was in progress.

CHAPTER III

THE THIRTEENTH, FOURTEENTH, AND FIFTEENTH
CENTURIES—GUILDS AND CORPORATIONS

AT the close of the twelfth and in the opening
years of the thirteenth century there was a
wave of enthusiasm, an immense activity in
church-building everywhere. Abundant liberality provided for the erection of imposing cathedrals in the cities,
of magnificent parish churches even in the most remote
districts and amongst sparse populations. The spirit
which was the real moving one in all this—in our own
country especially—has always been a difficult one to
account for. With every allowance made for the piety
of the age, there can be no doubt that it was largely due
to the development of civic life, the prosperity of trade
generally, the crusades and intercourse with the east,
and to a new-born understanding of, and enthusiasm
for, the industrial arts, which procured a call for their
employment, and a response to demands consequent on
increasing luxury and ideas of comfort. It was a
national movement. But the Church in those days was
the only centre of life and movement, and afforded the
chief medium of expression for the artistic tendencies
which had become so developed. If, then, there were
piety and a desire to beautify the house of God, there
was also an appeal to the judgment and admiration of
men, which in this regard had hitherto, in conformity
with monastic rules, been rigidly suppressed. As Dr.
Jessopp writes : 'The immense treasures in the churches
40

were the joy and boast of every man, woman, and child in England, who, day by day, and week by week, assembled to worship in the old houses of God which they and their fathers had built, and whose every vestment and chalice and candlestick, and banner and organ, and bells and pictures, and image and altar and shrine, they looked upon as their own and part of their birthright.' (*Studies by a Recluse in Cloister, Town, and Country*.)

The artist sculptor, no longer tied to the copying over and over again according to a formula supplied to him, looked for the motives of his ornamentation in the human, animal, and vegetable life around him. The vine was not the only symbol, and if symbolism were required it was open to any one to apply it from all the flora of nature, and so, as we shall see, in capital and corbel, in roof and screen, in sculptured stone, or carved wood, he would use the clinging ivy, leafwork and fruit of oak, the trailing eglantine, the fern and all the common plants and fruits familiar to his locality. Happily for his art, the traditions derived originally from the cloister taught him to avoid mere imitation. The guilds, however independent in the working of their regulations, were still under the control of the Church.

A guild or corporation was a kind of large family comprising all those who aspired to the craft it practised. It had its various grades of apprentice, craftsman, and master, the last an office of honour often accorded to some great lord. It possessed, usually, its own chantry chapel in the cathedral church, its hall, its processional banners, benevolent fund, collars, jewels and other insignia, and enjoyed numerous civic privileges. To this day, as is well known, the shadow remains in our city companies and in various guilds in other countries. The purpose of their existence was a practical one, always, however, in submission to or under the influences of religion. A notable circumstance is that in every country these associations were placed under the patronage of St. Luke. The origin of the invocation is uncertain. It is known, of course, that in hagiology St. Luke is considered to have been an accomplished painter and sculptor. Some, however, hold that, by a fortuitous circumstance not unparalleled in the rise of legendary stories, the founder of the system was a Florentine painter of holy life, and of the same name, in the twelfth century. The image makers — *tailleurs d'images, imagiers, beeldersnyders* or *beeldemakers*, amongst other appellations in France and in the Netherlands — were the sculptors of the Middle Ages with no distinctions as to material, whether stone, or wood, or ivory. The system of their guilds probably differed but little in the various countries, and at the beginning, at least, they worked freely and independently. Paris was the first—about the end of the fourteenth century—to combine in one corporation the guilds of the imagers with those of the painters and illuminators, and to bring them under a stringent code of statutes. The *huchers* or *huchiers* (Flem. *screenwerkers*) were a lower class of workmen, makers of chests and furniture of all sorts, and the architectural part of choir-work as distinguished from the imagery. All, whether carvers of images or other decorative work, coffer-makers, huchers or table or bench makers, were under the master carpenters, and the strictest regulations were enforced regarding the quality of wood to be used. In Flanders the profession of wood sculpture was one of the most ancient in the guild of Saint Luke, and by the end of the fifteenth century formed a distinct corporation, undertaking such important works as were everywhere in evidence; choir and stall work as at Rouen or Amiens, or the great retables for which the wood-carvers of the Netherlands were everywhere famous. The principle upon which

42

the guilds were founded was that of a community under the direction of a master mason or a master carpenter as the case might be, the whole subordinated to the general plan which, while prescribing the position and dimensions of, for example, a capital or a frieze or the arrangement of stall work, left the artist sculptor free scope, in his own particular department, for individual expression. Not otherwise can we understand the creation of the elaborate choir work of Amiens, or of Ulm and so many others. The idea must be grasped generally, as it would be impossible to consider it here in its details. The most important thing to remember is the subordination to the general conception of the edifice both in form and colour, and that every portion, from painted window to the *jouées* of the stalls, played its part in the production of the harmony. Subject to this there was a general absence of specialization and particular distinction among the arts. Most men were practised in several. The system implied local government, popular interest and readiness to help in any capacity. As Ruskin says in his *Seven Lamps of Architecture*, the master workman must have been the person who carved the bas-reliefs in the porches, and to him all others must have been subordinate. The number of sculptors was so great that it would no more have been thought necessary to state regarding the builder that he could carve a statue than that he could measure an angle or strike a curve. At a sale of autographs at Sotheby's in the present year was one of Ruskin, to a friend, in which he declares that 'neither Gilbert Scott nor anybody else can build Gothic or Italian,' and this, because architects are not now also sculptors. 'All real work in these styles,' he continues, 'depends primarily on mastery of figure sculpture.' However arbitrarily conveyed, the dictum is one which cannot be too strongly insisted upon. The French sculptor Rodin, in a conversation reported by Frederic Lawton in his *Life and Work* of the artist, expressed the same idea. He said: 'the aim of the Gothic artist was to fashion something that should have its full meaning and produce its full effect only in the place where it was to stand. They carved for the architecture, not for themselves.' We are aware what importance is to-day attached to the position of the conductor of an orchestra, and how greatly it differs from the time-beater of fifty years ago, how he holds supreme control of the whole, and how, as it were, through this control, he plays every instrument which composes it. This, it would seem, was the office of the mediæval master builder.

The earliest regulations concerning carvings in wood are very precise. The wood was submitted to the most rigid selection by officials appointed for the purpose, in order that the quality, seasoning, and freedom from knots and shakes should be guaranteed. There are no end of regulations concerning careful and correct morticing and so on. Nothing in a figure was to be joined, except in the case of a crucifix, for which three pieces were allowed. Finally the marks of the corporation and of the sculptor were impressed.

When the fourteenth century opened, while Gothic art was still in its full splendour, the new tendencies towards a return to nature as distinguished from the conventions imposed by scholastic philosophy may be said to have more than asserted themselves. There was everywhere, in sculpture as in painting, a desire to profit by the personal observation of nature, and to deduce from this what we call realism. Under the altered circumstances which have been briefly indicated in the preceding pages it is not surprising that the condition of the artist sculptor and the artist painter should have been immeasurably raised. The first was no longer a mere craftsman, a chipper of stone or wood working to order with ideas supplied to him—by rule of thumb, indeed, as the Greek carver of icons works to this day. Instead, he found himself in a position of relative independence. He became, in fact, a personage of considerable importance in the social scale. Great princes and nobles sought him out and attached him to their courts, not merely as their servant, but as a confidential friend. So it is that at the courts of the dukes of Burgundy, at the end of the fourteenth and beginning of the fifteenth century, we find Claus Sluter and his companions part of the princely households: Sluter himself *valet de chambre* to Philip the Bold, in those days equivalent to a title of nobility.

We have little information concerning the condition of wood sculpture in France in the twelfth century. Examples, as elsewhere, are wanting. It is probable that, in common with monumental sculpture in stone, it preserved the ancient traditions, and was exercised principally in the southern provinces, and in such centres as Toulouse. To this region we are indebted, no doubt, for numbers of the archaic crucifix and Madonna figures, which will be noted later in their place. In Poitou, la Saintonge, Normandy, the Ile de France, Picardy, or Auvergne, the ornament was still confined for the most part to the friezes and capitals of pillars derived from Byzantine models. But in Burgundy—at Vezelay or Autun for example—the Cluniac order had reached an immense development and influence. Where the principal Cluniac monasteries were situated, statuary, though still modelled upon the conventional hieratism, had made considerable progress. It is necessary to say modelled on, for it was more adaptation with entirely French differences of features and drapery than unintelligent copying. In the Ile de France and Normandy statuary was non-existent. Poitou and Toulouse were in complete decadence. There was, of course, the mid-twelfth western doorway of Chartres with its statuary. But in most regions the type was rigid, individuality of the personages represented wholly lacking. The thirteenth century dawned, and the great change was effected by the organization of the laity outside the enclosures where art had so long been in the hands of dreamers poring over their books. French furniture, earlier than the thirteenth century, is confined to the very few existing, practically unornamented, pieces of the type of the Obazine armoire. But this, with its extreme simplicity, is a model of solid elegance, and the long iron hinges are, as decoration, charming and sufficient in themselves. What images we have in wood of the first years of the fourteenth century certainly begin to show a more realistic character. Instead of the conventional, smiling, simpering type, they appear to be more approaching real life, at any rate to have been suggested by a living model. The ivory 'bend' continues, but this is merely fashion. As the century progresses the tendency to exuberance and overloading in response to the demand for display, both ecclesiastical and civil, is marked. However this may be, no department of artistic industry in France showed more splendid results than are found in the examples of wood sculpture generally which still adorn so many of the cathedrals throughout the country. In the earlier days we find some difficulty in distinguishing a type or method which we can call national, nor was the art of wood sculpture so diligently practised as by the Fleming, or in Germany where the material was more abundant. The Flemish wood-carvers seem to have long preserved the lead throughout the fourteenth century, and in the fifteenth one is always tempted to ascribe to Flanders the most striking examples of figure work. The general character was the same, and the overlapping of frontiers, added to the practice of bands of workmen being engaged far from their own homes —not to mention the ubiquitous Fleming—renders the task of distinction still more difficult. It is certain, however, that towards the middle of the fifteenth century there was one district where sculpture of all kinds, including wood-carving, was practised with remarkable activity. This was in Touraine, and examples from that school are the more interesting on account of its connexion with the courts of the dukes of Burgundy, and because from it we may gather some precise idea of the quality of French art in wood of that period. Some then, of which the French origin is certain, may be selected. The first belong to the region of Tours, about the middle of the fifteenth century, and apart from their individual charm their interest is heightened from the fact that Michel Colombe and his compatriot, Jean Fouquet, established their workshops in that district. These are three panels of oak acquired by the Louvre about fifteen years ago : part of a set, for a few others are known in private collections. On each, in low relief, is an angel holding a shield on which is represented one of the instruments of the Passion : the nails, the winding-sheet, the purse of Judas, and the rods. All are characterized by a similar type of face and figure, by the outstretched wings, the same model of smiling face and arrangement of the hair, the long straight folds of the alb-like garments, and a peculiarly marked bending of the knees. At one time, in the church of Ronzières, in Touraine, they were formerly coloured, and traces of this remain under the later and badly added daubing. Nothing could be more French, nothing more simply elegant and natural. Instead of the arbitrary exaggeration of the angular folds which distinguish the Flemish draperies of the period, the lines of the tunics fall gracefully and naturally ; the details of the wings and of the hair are indicated with precision, yet without undue prominence, and one cannot help remarking with what art the sculptor has expressed the value of an accessory such as the scourge. And yet one asks oneself are these the work of an established workshop, almost a commercial product, or rather, as one feels, due to some simple inhabitant of the district, naturally endowed, and so more touching in their spontaneous feeling? In the Victoria and Albert Museum are some larger panels of walnut, with angels bearing shields, of the Savoyard school of the early sixteenth century, which are worth comparing with those just described (Plate II.). The general type was a favourite one everywhere. In England, on bench ends and other places many will be found.

Whatever may have been the relations of French art with other nationalities in the more northern provinces, here, in Touraine, it is of the country undiluted. At the same time at this period changes were imminent. The Italian invasion was rapidly approaching. In the concluding years of the century the court of Charles VIII. was making its progress through the province, and bringing in its train Italian masters for the decoration of the royal castles of Amboise, of Blois, or of Chambord. It is small wonder, therefore, if the simple native art-workers were tempted to learn from and assimilate the new style. They were no less clever than their teachers, and here, and through the assimilation, arose the French Renaissance. For, in accordance with the genius of the national character, they took the idea only and worked it out for themselves in their own way.

In the same connexion of ideas a brief reference may be made to some examples of French Burgundian statuary work in wood and stone of the fourteenth and fifteenth centuries in the region of Autun. An important collection of these figures is to be found in the Musée Rollin at Autun. These have by no means the high value and artistic merit of the Tourangelle examples, local and personal though some of them may be. Several, indeed, such as the St. Andrew, in wood,

PLATE II

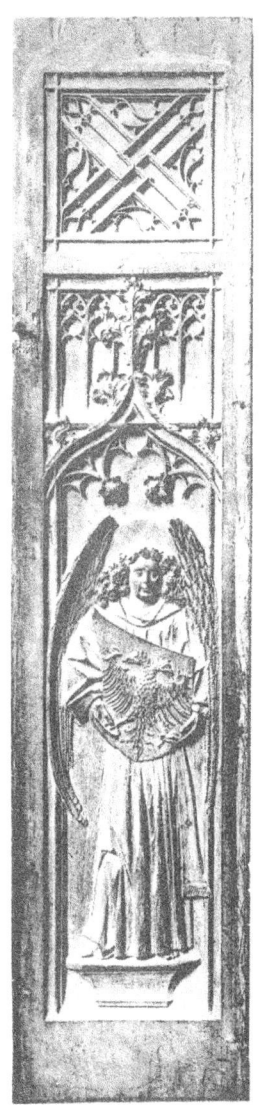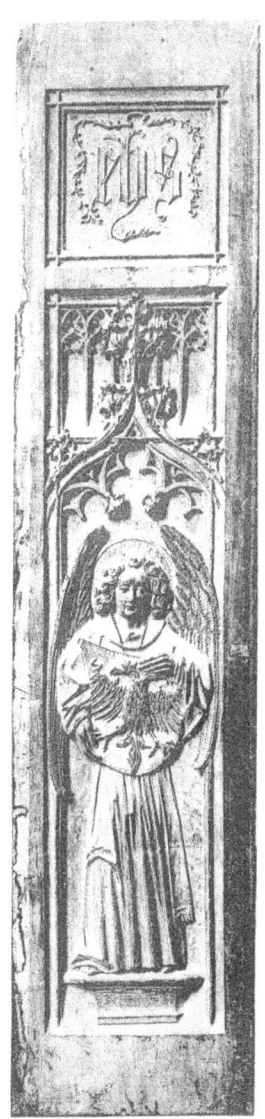

PANELS WITH ANGELS. SOUTHERN FRENCH (SAVOYARD)
SIXTEENTH CENTURY
VICTORIA AND ALBERT MUSEUM
PAGE 48

make us pause before we can persuade ourselves that they belong to the region, and are not importations from very much farther north. But there are others— for the most part coloured—which are of interest as examples of local characteristics and of various influences steadily imposing themselves in these districts at a period of transition, while yet Gothic methods and feeling held the field. A remarkable portrait statuette of a man in the hunting costume of the time of Louis XIII. is important from its absolute naturalism, for although it is said to represent St. Hubert, or even St. George, there appears to be not the smallest trace of any saintly character or attribute. The reader must be referred to the article and illustrations in the *Gazette des Beaux Arts* for November 1909.

The end of the fourteenth century might present some difficulties if we should attempt to draw deductions from the political conditions of France, especially in the northern provinces. Under our own King Edward III. the English were still, roughly speaking, in possession of Picardy, and of most of the south-western part of the country from north of Poitiers to Spain, and bounded on the east by Auvergne, Touraine, and Languedoc. The southern provinces were lost at his death, but England still retained Aquitaine and Guienne. In the beginning of the fifteenth century Paris itself becomes an English town. But the strongest influence of all, particularly affecting our subject, was caused by the political circumstances which joined together the French and Flemish possessions of the dukes of Burgundy. Nor is it, perhaps, altogether a factor to be neglected that it was these dukes, especially the first of them, Philip the Bold, who—vassals though they were supposed to be of the kings of France—aided the English in the conquest of the country. They were our allies at Crécy and at Poitiers. But it was the marriage of Philip with Marguerite de Valois, heiress of Flanders, that brought about the decisive influence on the arts. The dukes of Burgundy, in their unrestrained passion for display and magnificence, were able to gratify it through the vast wealth which the possession of the richest industrial towns of Flanders afforded them. The two courts combined formed a centre of splendour and extravagance. The sovereigns surrounded themselves with luxuries, and gathered together an army of workers, painters, sculptors, goldsmiths, and retainers of all kinds who flocked to them, from the French provinces still held by England, to assist in the adornment of their numberless palaces and castles. Two streams of art met at Dijon, the French capital of the duchy. It was a time when Flanders had become the principal centre of art in Europe, when Van Eyck, Rogier Van der Weyden, and their schools were the teachers and directors, not only in painting proper but, to a very great extent, in all the arts, and in an especial manner in that of wood-carving. From Brussels, Antwerp, Tournay, Bruges, Ypres, Ghent, or Liége, craftsmen came in swarms, or followed the court as they moved between the two great capitals.

It was at Dijon that Philip built the *Chartreuse* of Champmol, and for its church were made in 1391 two great retables, notable landmarks in the history of wood sculpture. These were the work of the Flemish artists Jacques de Baerze and Melchior Broederlam. There, too, are the magnificent *sedilia* for priest, deacon, and subdeacon, made by Hennequin of Liége. These are but a few examples of the wood-carvers' skill at the Chartreuse, where the art itself had established a school of no inferior importance amongst the other schools of sculpture. Of the sculptors, if precise information is lacking concerning the parts played by each in divers works, we know the names at least of the leaders—Jean de Marville and his nephew and successor, Nicolas or Claus Sluter, the architect of the famous tomb of the founder,

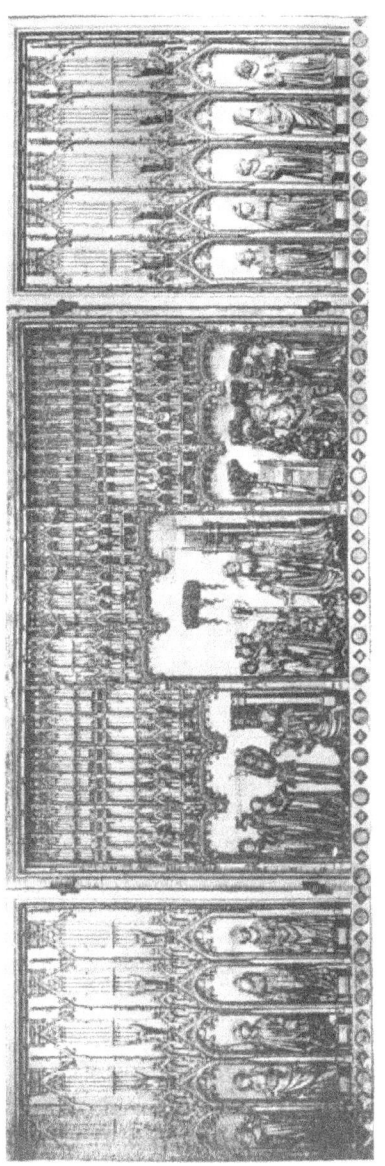

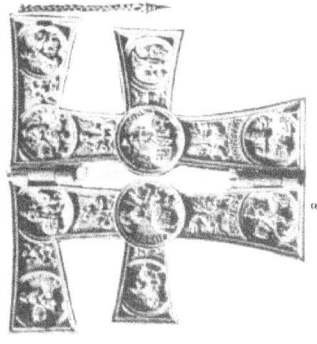

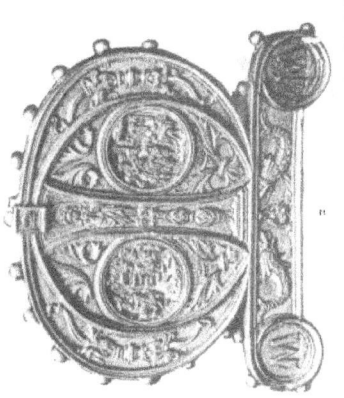

1. RETABLE. FLEMISH BURGUNDIAN. FOURTEENTH CENTURY. DIJON MUSEUM
2. CARVED LETTERS. FRANCO-FLEMISH. SIXTEENTH CENTURY. LOUVRE MUSEUM

PAGES 51, 199

and of the hardly less famous ' Puits de Moïse.' Each of the retables consists of three panels of figures in full relief, with foliage and flower work in dead gold on backgrounds of colour. The central subjects are from the gospel narrative—the decollation of St. John the Baptist, the Visit of the Magi, the Crucifixion and Entombment—legends of SS. Antony, Catherine, and Barbara, and others drawn from the Golden Legend. Over all is the most remarkable architectural design of sculptured arcades of any that we possess in wood, so refined and delicate is it in detail and in general effect. The whole, except the flesh tints and some of the draperies, is fully gilded. The question of the extent of the influence of the Fleming on French art is a complicated one. These great retables, amongst other sculpture at Dijon, we know are due to Flemish artists, and the masters, such as Sluter, in the service of the duke, seem to have set their faces against employing any but their countrymen. Yet the art, whatever its origin, was fostered in France, and if the stranger came in it is probable that, as elsewhere, he assimilated much of the spirit and preferences which he already found in the country. Nor was France, at the time, unused to dramatic treatment of sacred scenes in the manner of the retables. The churches of Dijon, of Autun, or of Vezelay, of Albi, of Toulouse, and indeed throughout the east and south of France, can testify to this. But we are inclined to marvel all the more at such exceptionally fine and original work as that of Sluter and his school when we remember that when these master-pieces were achieved Donatello was yet to be born, and Michael Angelo to be unheard of for more than a century later. This Flemish art is, therefore, an important link in the chain of the arts between the traditional methods of Niccola of Pisa and the evolution accomplished by the great names of the Renaissance on the other side of the Alps.

WOOD SCULPTURE

Wood-carving as applied to the decoration of domestic furniture of a luxurious kind at the end of the fourteenth and throughout the fifteenth century differed hardly at all from that which characterized the choir and other woodwork for the service of the church. Immense thronelike seats were covered with sculptured panels, carved with window tracery, and with subjects in various degrees of relief, taken from Scripture or from lives of the saints. From the summits of their monumentally high backs projected broad canopies supported by traceried vaultings, with saintly images and other figures in full relief, in every way comparable with the choir and screen work of religious edifices. In addition to the panels with religious subjects we find others with the linen pattern in many varieties, or with intricate arrangements of floral leaf-work, pendentives, arcades, corbels, pinnacles, colonnettes, figures of angels and cherubs, and a general decoration borrowed from architectural systems and enriched with every imaginable caprice. Nothing but innumerable illustrations could give an idea of the infinite variety. Bedsteads of the fifteenth century are of extreme rarity either in France, the Netherlands, or in England. But we can gather from miniatures, or from the carvings of such stall-work as at Amiens, that these, together with the great armoires, the dressers and credence tables, were of a like architectural character and profusion of ornament. Bedsteads of this period are more common in Germany. In general the form was either that which we now call half-tester, the head, foot, and canopy elaborately carved, or a kind of boxed-in enclosure or alcove. A typical example is illustrated by Mr. Baillie Grohman in the description of his castle at Matzen in the Austrian Tyrol (*see* ' *The Land in the Mountains* ').

Throughout the Gothic period in France it would be useless to attempt to distinguish styles in the various provinces. Practically there was but one, and to ascribe this or that example to a particular district is very often purely hypothetical. Nor, without devoting more space to one country than would be justifiable, is it possible in a book of this kind even to allude to numbers of examples of monumental wood sculpture which possess from so many points of view an interest apart from the beauty which distinguishes them. This is the case, for example, with such illustrations of pure Gothic, and the mixture of Gothic and the classic of the Renaissance, as we find, together with a perfection of execution, in the flamboyant central doors of Rouen, or the great doors of the cathedral of Aix. Of the latter the attention of the reader may be called to the excellent reproduction in the gallery of casts in the museum at Kensington.

The characteristics of Flemish art of the periods with which we are most particularly concerned are not easy to define. Strong in its influence upon others, it is itself the result of numerous foreign impressions. From its geographical and political position the country has been, turn and turn about, now half French or Spanish, now under the strong influence of her German neighbour: affected by the dynastic alliances with England under Charles the Bold of Burgundy, or, again, with those of Austria and Spain. In general, the art of a people reflects the character and inclinations of the race. The Fleming, so sincerely attached to his home, was essentially a traveller in search of business, with the natural consequence that the artist who travelled, whether to sell his wares or to learn the methods of other countries, was the means of a reciprocal interchange of ideas, and brought back with him those which he assimilated. It is necessary also to classify the artistic output. This included the purely commercial productions under the authority of the guilds, and, on the other hand, those of the artist freely working in a foreign country or for a foreign master. In every land we find him at work. To France, and to Paris especially, the master imagers of the schools of Brabant came in great numbers, many, no doubt, to stay. There is voluminous documentary evidence to show that they were employed in the ornamentation of churches throughout the whole country. It must suffice simply to mention Rouen, and the stalls and the great crucifix carved by Mosselmen for the cathedral. The exportation of retables to France was constant during two centuries, and many are still in evidence. In Sweden, also, some of the finest examples of the fifteenth century exist to this day. In Italy, Flemish artists and their retables were received with enthusiasm even in the days of the greatest of the quattrocento sculptors. In the succeeding century the names of numbers settled in the country could be gathered. The artistic relations with Spain will be considered later on. Finally, as regards our own country, the relative positions naturally encouraged commercial relations and brought about those of art. We imported largely, no doubt, altarpieces and screenwork. It is hardly necessary to quote the case of Westminster. In old records, references to the employment of Flemish workmen are frequent, and of payments such as to Hawkin de Liége, and the 200 marks 'which the Lord the King commanded to be paid to him for making the tomb of Philippa, Queen of England.' In 1441 there is mention of a dispute between Wm. Cerebiss, a Scotch merchant, and a monk of Melrose Abbey, acting on behalf of Corneille d'Aeltre, a master carpenter of Bruges, who was to supply certain stalls for the abbey after the fashion of the stalls of the church of Dunis in Flanders. It is necessary to bear in mind the geographical position of the Netherlands, and we must not forget the overlapping of frontiers—of Holland, France, and Germany—

so that it is not always easy to distinguish between Dutch and Walloon, French and German. Still, on the one hand, the Walloon is French in language and genius, refined and inclined to the ideal; on the other he is German, more simple, more patient, more practical, rough in manner, and with a preference for matter of fact, that is to say, towards realism. On this side, too, he is, at times, decidedly coarse. There are among the misericords of the fifteenth century certain examples which the *esprit gaulois*, even of that free age, would disavow. It is useful to remember that the Walloon provinces of the French tongue were in the thirteenth century those of Artois and Hainault—including Valenciennes—Cambrai, Arras, Liége, Namur, Brabant, Lille, Tournai, and Lorraine.

It is not proposed to discuss here at any length a very difficult and perhaps thorny subject. This is the tendency to realism, and its rise and evolution, which is so characteristic of the art of the Netherlands. It will be found strongly marked in the retables and single figures with which we shall principally deal, and without seeking to decide on the origin or the reciprocal influences which may have accompanied its growth, it may at once be taken that the close of the fourteenth century shows it at its height. Till quite the end of the twelfth century, Flemish sculpture had continued to adhere closely to the old traditions, and remained sunk in a dull subservience to, and unintelligent copying of, conventional types. In the thirteenth, Flanders followed almost as servilely the culture of the French provinces, and so far adopted the language and ideas that the distinction between the sculptures of the two countries is, as in the case also of ivories, sometimes difficult to establish. In that century, in France, the ideal in sculpture was at the height of its refined grace and charm, and still in complete subjection to the mystical element and the most rigid rules of ecclesiastical discipline.

French fashions and ideas of all kinds invaded the Low Countries with resistless force, and the triumph in sculpture was complete. Of realism, such as the next century developed, and the fifteenth carried to its utmost limits, there is no trace. It is not to be inferred, however, that the Flemish sculptor was content to copy from French models, but that the sentiment once introduced and understood was eagerly assimilated and followed, sometimes with national differences, but as often without. Arrived then at its height at the period when the apparition of the brothers Van Eyck, and of their school, startled the world of art, it is hardly surprising that the part played by Flanders in the introduction of the new feeling should be somewhat exaggerated, even to the point of giving to Flemish artists the credit of an absolutely new invention. We must by no means conclude that the process of evolution was anything more than slow and gradual, or more hurried in Flanders than in France. The word once given to go, it was as if those who practised the arts had to submit to a long apprentice-ship in an entirely new system, and to abandon a great deal that they had learned under an antiquated and now discredited system. The emancipation from the old fetters was a long and tedious process. But liberty was in the air, the cause was a popular one. People learned by themselves what they had hitherto accepted in a mechanical manner. They began to understand how to make use of nature as a model, and how to give life and movement to their figures, a dramatic element to the composition. Mighty again was the revolution involved in the understanding and true use of perspective. It is not with France only that com-parisons are to be made in considering the beginnings of realism in the early days of the Renaissance. In the fourteenth century Italy, equally with Flanders, disputed for the lead in the development of the arts.

56

Equally to them both is due the signal for a movement which went direct to nature for inspiration. The chief propagator in Germany, Spain, England, and Northern Europe, was the untiring Fleming.

Nowhere is there such a complication of detail, such elaboration of ornament, such a masterly use of polychromatic decoration, such a change in style from the sobriety which in the midst of its richness characterized the altarpieces of Dijon, as in the great retables of the fifteenth and sixteenth centuries. Striking in their perspective arrangement, they are more pictorial than pure sculpture. A well-known French critic, M. Bonnaffé, has said of this Flemish figure work that the proportions are somewhat squat, that they lack the German realism, French elegance, and Italian great manner (*grande allure*). The assertion is too sweeping : numerous instances would show almost the exact contrary, although as a general impression, with the exception of the comparison with Germany, it has reason enough in it. The figures are shorter and blunter than in similar French work, the modelling harder, and the draperies treated with an exaggeration of sharp angular folds which is especially distinctive of the realistic art of the late fourteenth and fifteenth centuries. Carried into Germany, the system, even with the best Franconian masters, became a perfect craze, in which all reason seems to have been thrown to the winds. There will be ample occasion presently to note examples. As the fifteenth century advances the taste for realism is still more marked in the details of flesh modelling and in the expressions of human passions almost violently displayed. The sobriety of the old conventional form of garments, founded on classical traditions, is discarded. Virgins and martyrs, the Saint Catherines, Magdalens, and Margarets are presented to us in the holiest of scenes as ladies of fashion in the richest costumes : patriarchs and apostles are in the dress of the period. In the Netherlands, perhaps more than anywhere else, it was the age of wood-carving, the churches filled from floor to roof with sculptured altarpieces, screens, and choir fittings, episcopal thrones, tabernacles, and font covers, carrying high into the air their elaborately-carved pinnacles. An equal demand on the wood sculptor's art came also from the palaces of the wealthy, and, above all, so far as the happily preserved existing monuments can testify, from the Hôtels de Ville and other corporation buildings of the great cities. Some names of the designers and sculptors of these great works we know. At Bruges, Jean de Valenciennes did most of the sculpture of the Town Hall, and carved in 1386 the richly-vaulted ceiling of the great *Salle des Échevins*. One example — the most widely-known perhaps — of the monumental decoration so frequently found in the municipal buildings, must suffice for all. It is the great chimney-piece of the *Palais de Justice* at Bruges. An excellent reproduction has for many years been included in the collection of casts in the Victoria and Albert Museum. It brings us, of course, to the very end of the period to which it has been necessary to restrict this book : indeed, in this regard, it somewhat oversteps our limits. Finished in 1532 by Guyot de Beaugrant and Lancelot Blondeel, it is only with the statues, busts, and other ornament in carved oak, by Herman Glosencamp, that we are particularly concerned, but it would be impossible to dissociate from them the rest of the work. A most admirable feature is the harmonious mixture of the black marble statues bordered with alabaster and the great oak figures. Spanish taste is apparent throughout, especially in the proportions of the figures, though the union of the two countries was not till some twenty years later. Still we know that de Beaugrant was in relations with Spain, and that he died there in 1551. The character

58

of ornament applied to luxurious furniture differed not at all in Gothic times from that already noticed in French work. Magnificent examples are to be found in museums, ranging throughout the three centuries which we are now considering in their general aspect. It is fortunate that we are still able to examine so many important specimens, and in this way to supplement the deficiency of examples of ecclesiastical work resulting from iconoclastic devastations. The history of these incidents, indeed, singularly resembles our own. The internal troubles of religious wars from about 1566 to 1584 commenced the disasters. It is marvellous that anything in the churches, then, as it were, the museums of every country, survived the outrageous treatment to which they were subjected. M. Dehaisnes in his *Art Chrétien en Flandre* tells us, quoting from contemporary documents, how the sectaries and their adherents 'jettent par terre et brisent touttes les images, autels, épitaphes, organes, sepultures, ornements, calices, sacrements et toute chose servant au service de Dieu.' (Letter of Margaret of Parma to Philippe II.) Churches were whitewashed to adapt them to Calvinistic methods, amongst them Notre Dame of Antwerp, then one of the richest temples of Christendom. But worse almost was to come later, as in our own bad days of the seventeenth and of the first half of the nineteenth century, so close to our own time. On the establishment of the government of Albert and Isabella, the restoration of Catholic worship brought with it an immense impulse to revive its ancient splendour. It is the time of St. Charles Borromeo. He sends Jesuits to direct the new style of decoration adopted, and in accordance with the Roman ecclesiastical style, which took kindly to the rococo and theatrical in churches, the Jesuit system in sculpture triumphs. Whatever may have been the value to art in general, great as it was, of Italy's part

in the Renaissance, we can only deplore the influence of
St. Charles Borromeo on church ornament: an influence which pursues us to this day, in Jesuit taste in
the decoration of altars and in statuary. The cult of
the tawdry is almost elevated into a dogma. Instead
of the instructive retable in carved wood or stone, of
which Flemish art provided so many noble examples,
this was replaced by the colonnaded high altar with
interrupted pediment. Rubens is substituted for the
glorious Primitives, and everywhere, in sanctuary and
nave, on the altars, in pulpit, and in the newly introduced confessional boxes, appears the debased classic.
Balusters instead of panels, twists and scrolls, vases
and pyramids, obtrusive glories amongst impossible
clouds, cherubs and angels of theatrical type, and
Madonnas in copes and monstrous crowns, take the
place of the pathetic figures of Gothic times. Everything seems to shout at us and to glory in its vulgarity.

CHAPTER IV

RETABLES IN FLANDERS AND GERMANY

THE genius of the masters of wood-carving is nowhere more admirably displayed than in the retables or altarpieces which, in Flemish art especially, have now to be considered. It is not to be wondered at that they should have brought forth the highest efforts and the most loving care, for, on the one hand, they were destined to complete and decorate the most holy part of a church, on the other, the sculptor was called in to supply in many cases a fitting framework for the masterpieces of a Van Eyck, a Memling, or a Van der Weyden. Not always, of course, was the carved work merely a framing for the painted pictures. Often, indeed, the entire retable is of wood, a picture with its perspective planes in some measure correctly disposed. In size and variety of arrangement also there were many differences. In the chapter on boxwoods we shall come across some extraordinary *tours de force* of tiny altarpieces, if we may so term them, microscopically carved. They are not, perhaps, strictly retables so much as objects for private devotion. Still we must place them in the same category. The altar and its surroundings in primitive times was characterized by an extreme simplicity and absence of ornament. It is sufficient to remember that the bishop sat behind it, in the apse, to show that not even a curtain intervened, much less so solid an erection as a reredos. Even when the priest took his place in front, and until quite late mediæval times, there was nothing on the altar but the chalice, the book, and, while they were still used, the diptychs. The enclosure of the choir with its arrangement of stalls seems to have been approximately coeval with the appearance of great fixed altarpieces. The earliest examples which we possess of both date from the thirteenth century. At the same time, it is to be noticed that they appear to be already of a settled type —a type which for the choir stalls has scarcely varied down to the present day — so that for some time previous something in the nature of an altarpiece may have formed a groundwork for decoration. Metal work was the forerunner. In Italy we have the *Pala d'oro* of St. Mark's of the twelfth century, and goldsmith's and enamel work was probably general elsewhere, to give way to stone or wood, more or less according to locality. In the fourteenth century we arrive at an age when everything that ingenuity could suggest tended to exaggerate novel ideas in architectural arrangements and the accessories of church furniture. Men's ideas were centred in the church. It was the mainspring whence proceeded all their interests and even their recreations. In the smallest village the adornment of the church occupied every mind, and possessing a higher appreciation of the beautiful and a more general diffusion of good taste than nowadays, people were ever on the look-out for a suggestion of novel ideas culminating at times in extravagances for the mere pleasure of doing things in some startlingly original manner. The earliest fixed construction corresponding with the later triptychs or polyptychs is the retable carved in soft limestone formerly in the church of the Carrière Saint-Denis at Paris: a picture in stone forming a kind of screen at the back of and resting on the altar. It was nowhere the custom to make the altar a fixture against the east wall. There was a space between, and the early retable served to support and conceal a large reliquary over the ambulatory. A tabernacle on the altar itself has, at most, the authority of the last three centuries. Two lights or even one sufficed, nor was it the custom to place flower-vases, candlesticks, reliquaries, or other ornaments upon the holy table. Even the book and its cushion were brought and taken away by the acolyte as they are, or should be, now. As, then, innovations succeeded each other, the retable became an adjunct upon which the utmost skill of architect and sculptor was lavished. It attained the proportions of a towering edifice, with pinnacles covered with every description of architectural device, with niches and statuary, pendentives, canopies, and tracery of all kinds, soaring up to the roof of the building.

The German retables are distinguished by their fanciful construction and the lengths to which the system was carried, and in Spain the development was still greater. Our present interest is with the smaller variety, of wood, either decorative or pictorial work in themselves, or forming in addition a framing for paintings. A Flemish retable of this description consists usually of a triptych formed by a central portion with a movable wing on either side, hinged so as to fold in on the centre when required. Sometimes the wings themselves are subdivided. Every portion is lavishly carved with scenes and figures in relief. The central panels naturally present the principal scene, often with innumerable figures in full relief and in a landscape perspective, crowned and surrounded by every description of architectural ornament. Thus we have, in astonishing abundance, arabesques of foliage, fruit and flowers, statuettes, pendentives, pilasters, groinings, corbels, *culs-de-lampe*, crestings, canopies, niches, lace work ; in short, speaking of the framework only, every conceivable detail and architectural device on a small scale which monumental sculpture in stone presented on a larger one.

There are characteristic differences between the

Flemish and German systems. That is to say, taking them as a whole, for the geographical positions of the two countries and their artistic relations naturally prepare us to find similarities of general style. In the one, so far as it is distinctly German, we have, for example, the upper part of the work ornamented with a range of floral crestings; the Flemish is plain. Canopies without supporting columns are more usual with the latter, and we do not find here such commonplace features as the veil of open-worked thorny twigs and branches, the too realistic vegetation, and such fantastic caprices as the tops of the pinnacles curled round like the volute of a crosier. There is, in the German work, too much which would be more appropriate in wrought-iron. These features, however, need not be insisted upon, because our limitations confine us more particularly to the figure sculpture, and general observations without numerous illustrations would be liable to be misunderstood. As a rule, the Flemish retables of the fifteenth century are evidences of the perfection of skill attained by the wood-carver in the declining years of Gothic feeling, and of conscientious work, with as much sobriety as the prevailing taste for exuberance of detail permitted. When, however, we are inclined to criticize them, as we find them now, under glass in a museum, or in a church with altered surroundings, we must not forget the positions which they were created to occupy. This was not under the garish light of a modern gallery, but in the soft obscurity, perhaps, of a guild or convent chapel, discreetly lighted by windows of painted glass proportioned to its size, or by the dim oil lamps and tapers of its altar and shrines. So many retables contain paintings of the great masters, above all by the French and Flemish primitives of the same date as the sculptures, that it is reasonable to suppose that the painter had more than a little to say with regard to their general character, if indeed he was not responsible in many cases for the design, and at times, for the execution also. It is impossible to examine them, and the work later on of the Franconian, Suabian, and Bavarian schools, not to speak of those more immediately connected with Flanders, without seeing the indebtedness to, and absolute copying from, the masters of painting, whether directly or through the medium of the engravers. The Creglingen altarpiece and innumerable others have their models in, for example, the paintings on the wings of the well-known altarpiece, the 'Adoration of the Lamb.' These things are but the attempt at a translation into another medium of the masterpieces of a Van Eyck, of a Rogier de la Pasture, or of the Cologne artists, by whom even Van Eyck was inspired. The influence of these men invaded everything, and we find their formulæ everywhere the example to be followed. What else are such details as the long wavy curls in separate strands of Riemenschneider's Magdalen, of the Madonna of Brussels workmanship in the Bossy collection of the Louvre, or that charming fragment of a Virgin and Child statuette in the Cluny Museum, also of the Brussels schools, which with others we shall notice in a succeeding chapter? Or again, the drapery, broken up into an infinite complication of angular folds, upon which the German wood-carvers brought to bear their own developments in treatment? The question of the participation of Roger Van der Weyden, and of other great painters as sculptors, is not one that can be discussed here. It is still unsettled. M. Maeterlinck, in the *Gazette des Beaux Arts* for 1901, has devoted a long study to it, and seems to bring at least *prima facie* evidence that Roger, before his apprenticeship as a painter, had worked the chisel of the imager. Nothing is more likely and more in accordance with the spirit of the times. Yet we know little of his history and early life beyond the fact that he was born at Tournai about the year 1400. Tournai had long been celebrated for important schools of sculpture, and had exported far and wide its productions and artists—in earlier times, for instance, its black fonts to England—and at the end of the fourteenth century it held the foremost position in the art which Brussels and Antwerp wrested from it in the following century. From the little more of which there appears to be some documentary evidence, we may gather that Roger's master, Robert Campin, was a sculptor as well as painter. M. Maeterlinck concludes that it is certain that Van der Weyden often painted statues and retables, and, if the great carved retable of Ambierle, which has been attributed to him, is not by his hand, there would appear to be evidence not only from style, but documentary, that he is responsible at least for the painting of the sculpture, and for that of a number of other famous retables. Amongst these, for example, may be placed that of the Comte de Nahuys, and one which is perhaps the finest of all Flemish examples, the retable of Claude de Villa in the museum at Brussels. (See E. Jeannez, *Le retable d'Ambierle en Roumais*, in *Gaz. archéol.*, 1886.) It is interesting to note that Waagen, many years ago, was already persuaded of the influence which the Tournaisian schools exercised not only on sculpture but even on the great Flemish painters. In the present state of the question, it is remarkable that this far-seeing critic should have expressed his opinion that 'in the same way that the most famous painters of the Roman and Tuscan schools studied the great gates of Ghiberti of the Baptistery at Florence, so also the brothers Van Eyck and Roger van der Weyden of Bruges were inspired by the sculptors of Tournai.' (*Messager des Sciences et des Arts*, vol. ii.)

In Gothic times the practice was universal of painting and gilding sculpture of all kinds in stone, wood, ivory, and even metal. There seems to have been an absolute dislike for monochrome, which appeared to be incomplete without the aid of the painter to give it the finishing touches. Frequently, no doubt, painter and sculptor were the same individual. As the subject will be treated at greater length in a succeeding chapter, it need only be said here, that although such a striking work as the great Flemish altarpiece at South Kensington is now uncoloured, and perhaps may never have been intended to be otherwise, yet other marvellously fine pieces of the same character, such as the retable of Oplinter in the museum at Brussels, were fully coloured and gilded. There can be little doubt that the painter and sculptor worked together. It was from her Flemish neighbours that Germany received the first impulse towards realism, and when we come to consider presently some of the most striking examples amongst the mass of German altarpieces of the fifteenth and early sixteenth centuries, the evidence of their indebtedness to Flemish art will be manifest. In the treatment of the subjects, and especially in the mannerism of the drapery, the inspiration is from the great masters of painting rather than through the medium of the carved retables. Generally speaking, and especially in the work of the more southern provinces, the German retables give an impression of an arrangement among decorative surroundings of a number of detached figures or statuettes : almost doll-like, and in the worst cases suggesting a puppet show. In the case of the Flemish, and in the north German work, influenced by the proximity of her neighbour, we have a more pictorial, more lifelike representation of the scenes and characters ; the perspective is studied, the picture is complete, instead of being formed by isolated figures. The Flemish treatment is more refined, more suggestive of the active collaboration of the painter with the sculptor. The German, even in such a typical example as Michael Pacher's altarpiece at St. Wolfgang, expends himself in a profusion of details, for ever adding independent elements, and elaborating the ornament till not an unoccupied space remains. Taken singly, individual figures in the retable just mentioned are admirable. Their grouping is almost fortuitous, as of an assemblage which might have been collected from various quarters. Yet Pacher was painter as well as sculptor.

It must be admitted, also, that in the case of some altarpieces, both Flemish as well as German, the toy-stage-like effect is not wholly absent. The composition is divided into a number of compartments or separate stages, peopled with little figures playing their parts in some sacred drama. It is the representation, on a small scale, of a mystery-play, and, indeed, from these entertainments, so popular in the Middle Ages, the idea may have proceeded. It is still continued in the 'Cribs' which it is customary to erect in so many Catholic churches at Christmas time. Even in the best examples of the retables the scenic illusion is unavoidably present. The stage itself is sloped, so that the figures which occupy the hinder planes may be plainly visible, and there is frequently no difference in their respective proportions wherever they may be placed. There is an attempt at producing within a constricted area the effect of greater space for the action of the piece than is really the case. The groups and details of the landscape stand out with startling stereoscopic-like sharpness. The dramatic movement is so striking, and the resemblance to a piece in action so great, that one almost expects to find wings or side scenes from which other characters in the drama will presently emerge and play their parts upon the stage. At the same time one must not forget the evident relationship between these carvings and the storied panels of the diptychs and triptychs, caskets and mirror-cases which, with less advanced ideas of perspective, delighted our mediæval forefathers.

In about the second half of the fourteenth century wood-carving was in a highly flourishing condition in the province of Brabant, notably in the towns of Brussels and Antwerp. Reference has already been made to the organization of the guilds which were universal at this period, and nowhere ruled with greater strictness than in the Low Countries. At Brussels and at Malines the wood-carvers seem to have belonged to the guild of the *Quatuor Coronati*, the stone sculptors and other allied crafts forming a separate corporation under the invocation of St. Claude and his four fellow-martyrs. Before wood-carvings could be placed on the market they had to satisfy a jury that they were made of properly seasoned oak or walnut and of the proper thickness. This examination satisfactorily passed, a mark was impressed on the piece, which seems, as a rule, to have borne some relation to the arms of the town. According to M. Destrée, who is our principal authority, the mark of an open hand or a castle belonged to Antwerp, and especially to the guild of huchiers charged with the marking of retables. The mark for Brussels, for polychromed work, was BRVESEL in Gothic characters enclosed in a rectangle. Another corporation mark of Brussels is a mallet ; and a shell, a fleur-de-lis, a compass and a kind of comb with four teeth, would seem to be those of the sculptors. But the whole subject of marks is somewhat involved and awaits further investigation, and careful examination of examples in various museums. Unfortunately these indications are not, in general, easy to discover, hidden away, as they often are, in the most out-of-the-way corners. They are none the less important, for even if we are unable in many cases to name the actual carver of a retable or other piece of sculpture, we may at least be certain of the school to which he belonged. Every craft was necessarily connected with a guild, and thus the work issued from a particular source, and stamped with its mark, was bound to have a family resemblance. No doubt there was more personality in the details of work in mediæval times, in which more than one artist had a share, than there is in our own day. Still, there were probably commercial workshops, or, as we should say, carving works. Except for their independence, our modern system would not show much difference. For example, a considerable quantity of screen and other wood-carving, not excepting figure sculpture, for the use of churches, has now for some years been executed at Exeter, and there are at least two principal firms. The productions of each house are not so difficult to distinguish. On the other hand we hear, for instance, that this or that screen, or pulpit, or bench end, or figure, has been carried out by Messrs. so-and-so. But of the identity or celebrity of the actual designer or carver we know nothing.

The mallet corporation mark of Brussels is found, amongst other examples, on a St. Michael, and on a Madonna group in the Louvre, and on Jan Borreman's retable of St. George in the museum of industrial arts at Brussels. We shall come across Borreman—or Borman—again in a succeeding chapter. He and his son Pascal or Passier were among the greatest and most prolific Brabant sculptors of the end of the fifteenth century. The great retable with the story of the Maccabees in the Brussels Museum is by the elder man, and is marked with the mallet and compass. His retables are especially free from the faults which were just now indicated. The figures are not suggestive of puppets, the planes are correctly disposed, the perspective excellent: the architectural features, in which the influence of the Renaissance is apparent, are free from the fantastic exuberance of ornament frequently found elsewhere. The compass

PLATE IV

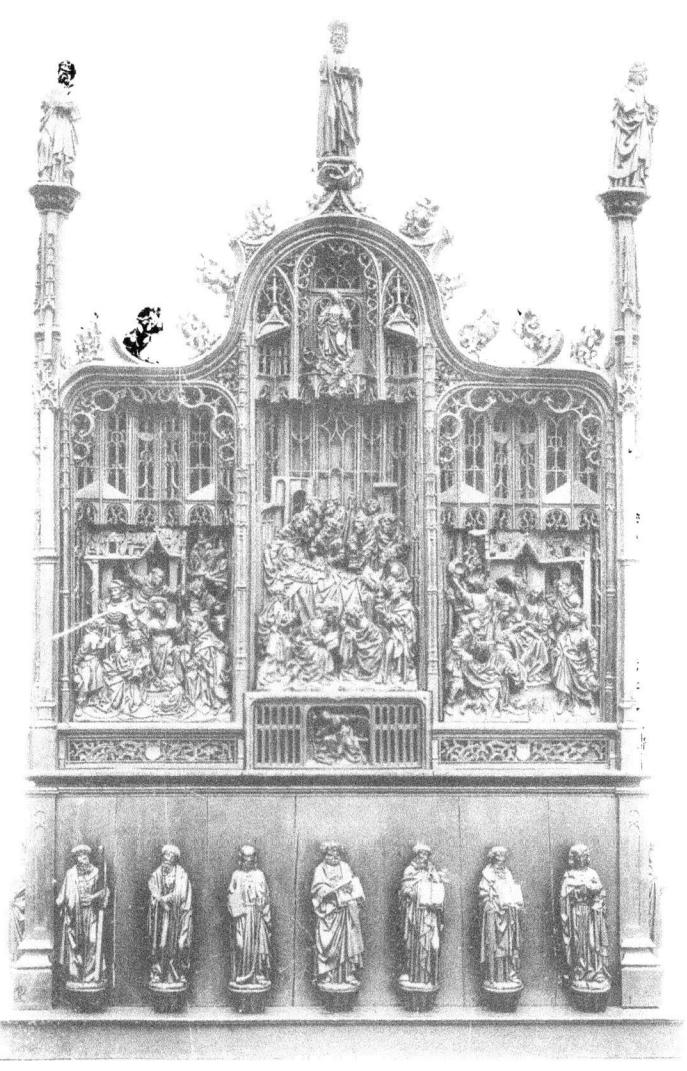

ALTARPIECE. FLEMISH. FIFTEENTH CENTURY
VICTORIA AND ALBERT MUSEUM
PAGE 71

seems, for example on the retable of Claude de Villa, to be a mark of the *screenwerkers* generally, who worked in concert with the image makers. To them was allotted the part of carrying out the general architectural forms. Then came the turn of the composer of the picture, the sculptor of the figures, and the painter and gilder. An interesting document exists among the archives of Louvain, in which Jan Borreman agrees to execute by his own hand all the figures of a certain piece of sculpture to be made by the *screenwerker* Petercels.

Our national museum at Kensington acquired so long ago as 1855 an extremely fine specimen of an altarpiece of the latter part of the fifteenth century. It is of considerable dimensions, uncoloured—in its present condition at least—and, of course, of oak. The illustration here given will obviate the necessity of more than a brief description (Plate IV.). The general formation, with a central panel and two wings is much the same as in many others of the style and period, but plainer and not so rich in ornament. The figures of the apostles, now placed upon it, may or may not have been originally connected with it. The principal subject represents the death of the Virgin : on the wings are the Nativity and the Visit of the Magi. We may remark that the character of the drapery is excessively *tourmenté* in the multiplicity and the arrangement of the folds. The piece is said to have come from the cathedral of St. Bavon at Ghent. It would be interesting if we could verify this origin. The fine retable, formerly in the church at Anderghem, and now in the Brussels Museum, is a good example of the coloured and profusely gilded Flemish flamboyant style of mid-fifteenth century. Within a moderate compass the groups of figures form a living composition, each in its way superior to more realistic work, as, for example, in the choir at Ulm. Naturally, Belgium and the museums of the chief city of the modern state are rich in specimens.

71

WOOD SCULPTURE

In the Museé du Cinquantenaire are some superb examples, which alone are sufficient to illustrate the subject at its best. These are the retables of Haekendover, of the Cte. de Nahuys, and above all that known as the retable of Claude de Villa. The first-named is an instructive example of the preservation of types, for though, without doubt, work of the end of the fifteenth century—perhaps by Maître Devis or Jan van Connixloo—the costumes and architectural style are of a century earlier, carrying us back to the formulæ of Jacques de Baerze at Dijon. The retable of Claude de Villa (Plate v.) is a triptych, with each compartment crowned by an architectural decoration of ogival arches, the points of which at one time may have carried statuettes of which the *culs-de-lampe* now only remain. The rest of the tabernacle work is a mass of delicate tracery, lacelike in complication, yet of extreme lightness. In the centre is the principal subject, the Crucifixion. Allowing for some differences, and for more or less detail, this is the type of the pictorial compositions which are general in this class of altarpiece, and may be thus described: In a landscape a mountain of figures—men, women, soldiers on horse and on foot, the crowd of sightseers, officials and legendary figures that we associate always with the sacred scene—leads up to the extremely tall and narrow-limbed cross. On either side of this, on similar crosses, are bound the thieves, contorted in agony. With the exception of the most holy personages, all the figures are in the costume of the period, that is, of the last quarter of the fifteenth century, the date of the work itself being about 1460 to 1470. The patrician ladies of the crowd, and even some of those whose names the scriptural narrative and legends attach to the sacred event, are in the richest robes of brocade and tissue of the latest and most extravagant fashion: *décolletées* and decked with chains and jewels. Amongst

72

PLATE V

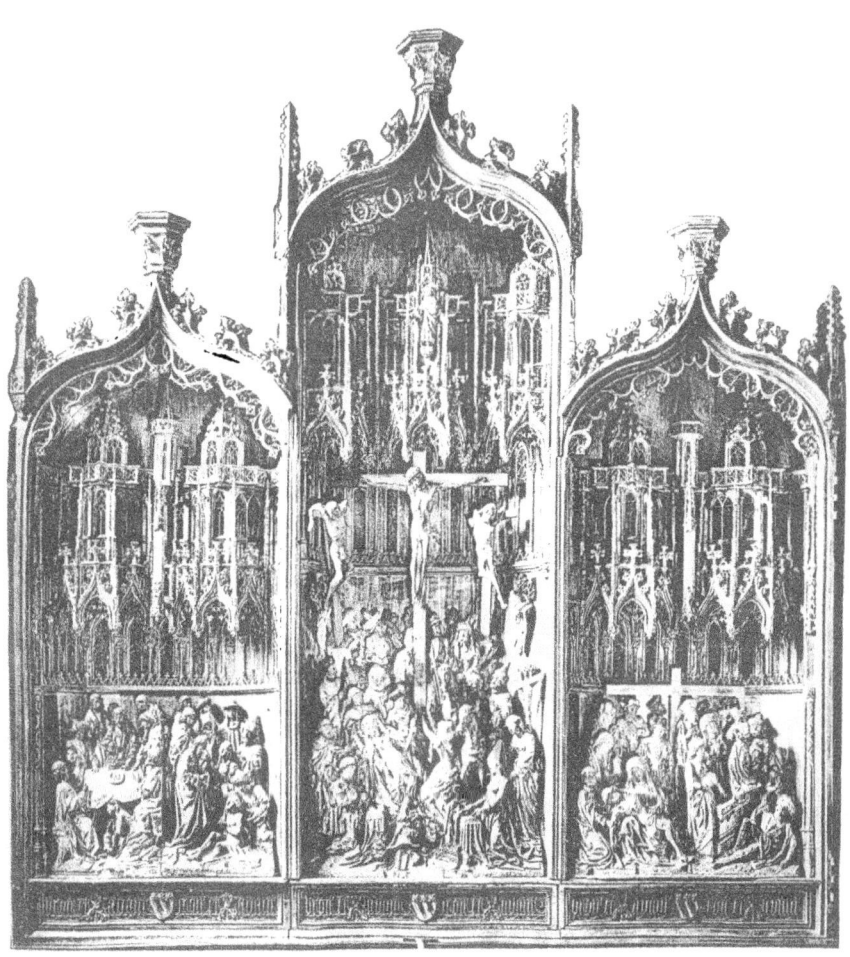

RETABLE OF CLAUDE DE VILLA. FLEMISH. FIFTEENTH CENTURY
BRUSSELS MUSEUM
PAGE 72

them are the noble donor and his wife. They kneel each at a draped prie-dieu, on which are their books of devotion, he in full plate-armour, with by his side his helmet with the mantling, surmounted by the family crest—a horse's head—on the usual fillet: she in a simple dress of the period and wearing the *hennin*, the steeple-shaped headdress of ladies of quality. In the wings, of which two remain, are, beneath similar rich tabernacle work, other scenes in the Passion—the Last Supper with the Magdalen washing the feet, the raising of Lazarus, the Deposition and the Resurrection. In the last scene the type of the angel at the tomb seems to carry us back to models and the feeling of two centuries earlier.

There can, of course, be no question of further insisting, in relation to compositions of this kind, on the connexion with the great Flemish schools of painting, with which they are contemporary. Every one may determine for himself to which well-known masterpiece this or that work is mostly related, and how much it has directly borrowed from it or from others. It is thought that the retable of Claude de Villa possessed at one time additional wings, painted, perhaps, by Van der Weyden. What was his part in the sculptured composition? Did he, perhaps, furnish the design? However it may be, nothing can detract from the skill of the sculptor who, himself perhaps also the draughtsman, translated his design with all its sentiment and colour into sculptural forms. The history of the important piece just described is known. It was made to the order of a noble Piedmontese family, the head of which, Claude de Villa, had perhaps official relations with Brussels. We have, in this circumstance, an interesting example of the high reputation which Flemish work enjoyed in Italy at such an important period of Italian art when so many great names were preparing to dazzle the world. Most touching is the treatment of the scenes of the Passion that we find in this and so many other similar works of the period. It is unnecessary to refer to them in detail, or from this point of view to make comparisons with the paintings. Often, as here, the pious founder is to be seen with his wife, kneeling with clasped, uplifted hands, he in warlike attire, she with long, trailing robe and the *hennin* headdress with its flapping wings and long veil falling from the point : forming, as it were, part of the composition, and yet addressing themselves in prayer to the central figure. Here, as more commonly, perhaps, a favourite treatment of the subject in Flemish art than elsewhere, the blessed Virgin is supported fainting in the arms of St. John and the holy women. As we look to-day at the method of picturing these sacred scenes there seems to be nothing incongruous in a Magdalen at the foot of the cross attired in a rich *décolletée* costume of the Middle Ages, of other women in *hennin* or turban-like headdresses, in the dresses of the chief priests and officials, the arms and accoutrements of the soldiers and their sturdy Flemish horses. It is the poetry and piety of the last days of Gothic times combined, before the completed Renaissance of the sixteenth century made the cultivation of religious art more exclusively the property of the rich, and we may be grateful that we owe to the art of wood-carving an expression of sentiment which in talent of execution reached a height in its way comparable with that of the masters of painting.

CHAPTER V

WOOD SCULPTURE IN GERMANY IN THE FIFTEENTH AND EARLY SIXTEENTH CENTURIES

THE flourishing period of German art in wood-carving extends from about the middle of the fifteenth, to the middle of the sixteenth, centuries. If, during this period, it cannot be said that Germany took the lead, at any rate it was conspicuously in the fore-front, and the output of figure work for the adornment of altarpieces and shrines, for choirs and choir-stalls, was nothing less than prodigious. But the extent of the empire was great, and we have to consider the reciprocal influences exercised on its various constituent parts, its commercial position on the main route between the Alps and the north, between Venice and the Flemish and Dutch capitals; on the other hand, internal conditions of government, the absence of centralization, the exist-ence of several Free towns, and the restricted means of communication between the provinces, making, for example, Saxony and Thuringia dependent on Franco-nian schools of art—all these things combining to produce a complication so diverse that it is impossible to treat the subject comprehensively as a whole within reasonable limits. Nor can we forget also that the period with which we shall be most concerned is pre-cisely the one when there was almost a general upheaval in everything connected with the arts, resulting partly from the advancing religious changes, but above all from the strides which the principles of the Renaissance

75

were making.   It is true that Germany remained steadfastly faithful to Gothic ideas until close on the end of
the fifteenth century, and resisted the Italian invasion
longer than other countries.   All art continued to be
exclusively religious.   Even when the enthusiasm for
antique styles had established itself in the German
Renaissance, still, more than with other peoples, Gothic
methods of treatment, in the ornament derived from
natural forms, predominated.   The ideas of the transitional period found in Germany a favourable soil for
their development.   Gothic here, modern framing there,
with old models revived and adapted, we find greater
independence in the design and construction of separate
ornaments, less subordination to the general architectural motive, more freedom and an increased intelligence
of the individual artist resulting from the extensive
travels in other countries which were the rule in his
wander-years, before he set up for himself with the
grade of master.   Remains of earlier art in wood are,
as elsewhere, scarce.   There are a few—for example the
doors of St. Maria im Kapitol at Cologne—but we shall
not stay to consider these.   There are also a certain
number of twelfth-century Madonna figures and colossal
crucifixes which may find brief mention in the section
devoted to early figure work of this kind.   And certainly,
if in wood we can advance absolutely nothing to form a
link between this archaic figure work and the newly
awakened realism which characterizes the prolific period
of the decline of Gothic ideas, it must not be forgotten
that in the thirteenth century the great cathedrals of
Bamberg, of Naumberg, and of Strassburg, were adorned
with statuary which vied with, even if it were derived
from, that of Chartres or of Reims.   The earliest impulse
towards naturalism in German wood-carving was undoubtedly from the Netherlands.   Reaching first the
neighbouring provinces, the new system spread rapidly
throughout the empire, and in those more distant from

its source would seem to have been adopted with more freedom than in the north-west, where we find very numerous importations of the most imposing of Flemish retables and the like. Indeed, these are more numerously represented in North Germany and in Sweden at the present day than in their country of origin. We shall be particularly occupied with the retables and the single figures made to adorn them, of that part of the empire in the district of the Upper Rhine comprising the Franconian and Suabian schools. There will be found, of course, a general character which, while strongly allied to that of Flanders from which it sprung, possesses its own distinctive, absolutely German type. The faces of the women are rounder and more of a simple peasant order, those of the men bony, haggard, and ascetic in the case of the older ones; the hands have peculiarly long and knotted fingers; the hair of the men is of a uniformly adopted fashion of masses of thick curls, so uniform as to become monotonous. The draperies, especially towards the end of the period in question, carry to the utmost extravagance the complications and angularities of folds, breaking up into innumerable crooked tucks and pleats, which, far from being suggestive of reality, present, on the contrary, an appearance unlike anything which ordinary stuffs could assume. The inclination towards naturalism becomes more and more pronounced until it develops into attempts at reproducing realities in the human form, regardless of beauty for its own sake, which are almost revolting. It is the cult of the ugly, which, from time to time in all arts and in all periods, seems to exercise such a strange fascination. It will be necessary to confine our attention almost entirely to the most important of the two great districts or groups, which may be distinguished roughly as North German, with the Lower Rhenish provinces around the centre of the wood-carving industry at Calcar, and the South

German, with which are associated the Franconian and Suabian schools and their far-spreading spheres of influence. In the South German area, in contradistinction to the sway still held elsewhere by painting over the plastic arts, it will be found that sculpture took the lead and imposed its influence, whether for good or bad, upon the art of the painter.

It would not be possible, in a work of a general character, to examine minutely the differences which may exist in the character of German wood sculpture throughout the various divisions of the empire. To do so would involve a study of German art not only in sculpture generally, but also in painting; a consideration of the various influences at work during the period of less than a century, with which we shall principally deal, and these also with relation to their evolution in previous times. As already remarked, the quantity of wood-carving still existing in the shape of retables and single figures, in addition to decorative panel and architectural work for the adornment and accessories of choirs, is prodigious. Museums and every village church possess examples of altarpieces and statuary. But although so numerous, these adornments of the altar, as we find them in the churches, are by no means universally of a high artistic character or of more than local interest. As, then, we are not engaged in a general study of the art of the empire, or even proposing to attempt a comprehensive account of its sculpture in wood, our attention will be confined to a certain number of examples, for the most part selected from the second of the two great districts or groups before mentioned. In general it will be sufficiently accurate to assume that during the period in question— that is, roughly speaking, from the first half of the fifteenth to the second half of the sixteenth centuries— the character of the retable art and of its accompanying figures has a generic similarity throughout the empire.

GERMANY

A marked characteristic is the indebtedness to the art of the Netherlands, to the great masters of painting of the Flemish, Dutch, and Suabian schools, and to the direct or indirect influence of the contemporary German engravers and etchers. This influence may indeed from time to time be called, rather, collaboration. In certain cases—for example in that of Veit Stoss—the artist will be considered by some to have been more distinguished as an etcher than as a sculptor. That the wood-carver was very often a painter also, is of importance from another point of view: that is to say, with regard to the actual colouring of the sculpture.

If we should look around such a fairly representative collection as is to be found in the department devoted to wood in the Bavarian National Museum at Munich, the general similarity just alluded to can hardly be disputed. It is not always easy, even for an expert, to distinguish the productions of the Franconian, Suabian, Westphalian, High German, Low German, Rhenish, Bavarian, or Tyrolese schools : and experts themselves will differ considerably in their ascriptions. It is not, of course, intended to assert that we should have any difficulties with regard, say, to distinguishing characteristics of a Lübeck school of the fifteenth century or others which we associate with Rhineland work, but it will be unnecessary to concern ourselves with minute territorial distinctions. Nor does it follow that because we find such and such an example in such and such a neighbourhood that the latter is necessarily the place of origin. Artists themselves moved about a good deal. Amongst the finest, if not the finest, work of Veit Stoss is the altarpiece at Cracow several hundred miles from the town of his adoption and the school with which he is identified. Further than this, our information concerning the sculptors themselves and anything positive to guide us in the ascription to them of any definite piece is, as elsewhere almost up to the sixteenth century, scanty and vague indeed.

We shall devote considerable attention to several important pieces attributed to Tillmann Riemenschneider, to Veit Stoss, and to Conrad Meit. Yet whatever value (and this no doubt is very great) may be attached to the judgment of some leading critics in assigning certain works to these names, it is, after all, very often a matter of pure conjecture, and we have no positive evidence in support. There is, as yet, no finality in the assumption that Riemenschneider is the master of the Creglingen altarpiece, of the Anna selbdritt group and the Adam and Eve busts at Kensington, that Veit Stoss executed the statue of St. Roch in the Ognissanti at Florence, or Meit the busts in the British Museum. Over and over again we meet with work which may be by Stoss, but which we have no real authority for characterizing otherwise than of the Nürnberg school. For example, the fine figures of our Lord and the Apostles of the Deokarus altar, or the Madonna in a flame-glory of the Sebalduskirche: or, of greater importance from its connexion with the Madonna of Nürnberg, the Pietà of the Jakobskirche. We do not know for certain whether Dürer or Wohlgemut or Peter Vischer worked in wood. The mystery surrounding the famous Madonna of Nürnberg is greater still. Though some confidently see in it the style of Stoss, others are equally struck by resemblances to that of Vischer or Krafft. The fact remains that it stands by itself, as it were, the single masterpiece of a genius of whom we know neither the name nor any other work with which to compare it. Again, the kinds of wood used furnish us with no safe guide. Limewood was very general in Franconia as in Bavaria and elsewhere, and if on the other hand oak was almost exclusively used in some districts, we find it also throughout the empire. Thus it is that although there may be a remarkable similarity of style—with regard to several of the best examples which may be selected for illustration—there is considerable difficulty in finding not only the master to whom they are due, but even the school. Although the art of figure sculpture in wood was more popular in Germany, and more widely practised than anywhere else, it hardly succeeded in attaining an elevation comparable with that of Flanders or of Italy. Exceptions which will presently be noticed are remarkable indeed, the more so because they are distinctly original and national, and find their like in the wood-carving art of no other country. However reasonable, then, it may be to form certain groups, the positive identification with a particular artist is often impossible. To take but one only of several cases which might be quoted—the 'Vergänglichkeit' ascribed to Riemenschneider. This might be given to almost any one of the greatest names from Brussels to Munich, and certainly is more impressed with Renaissance than with Gothic feeling.

Among the general characteristics of German figure work of the late Gothic period, varying in importance as time progressed, are the somewhat stunted proportions of the men, their large heads, bony and elongated faces, and strained expressions, the long strongly marked hands and long thin fingers, the stereotyped fashion of wiglike curly hair, the placid, sweet-smiling and decidedly round-faced type of the women, and the evident striving after a realism which, under the still existing restraints imposed by Gothic tradition, was not to be attained until a change in these ideas brought with it a free study of the nude. Added to these, a passion for treating the draperies of figures with an exaggeration of angular folds which becomes irritating. This exaggeration of a style of which they were by no means the inventors is well expressed by the French

term *tourmenté*, and in German sometimes *Schnitzstil*.
Wood was the national glory, everywhere employed for
countless single figures and panels in low and high
relief, as a rule richly painted and thickly gilded. In
the altarpieces, following the example of the Netherlands, but applying it in a different way, there is a
striving after pictorial effect by placing the figures in
different planes. The workers were no mean artists.
Well instructed in their apprentice days, the practice
was general of passing several wander-years, as the
German term has it, of travel, before attaining a standing as a master. The two great divisions from which
it is proposed now to draw examples for illustration are
those of Franconia and Suabia. Briefly summarizing,
we may define sufficiently for our purpose, Franconia
as one of ten circles into which the empire was divided,
bounded by Thuringia and Hesse Cassel on the north,
by the upper Rhenish provinces on the west, by Bohemia
on the east, and by Suabia on the south. Suabia
extended to France on the west and to Switzerland on
the south. We shall include therefore the schools
which we may term Franconian, Suabian, Bavarian,
and Tyrolese, and the towns of Nürnberg, Würzburg,
Augsburg, Munich, Rothenburg and the Tauber district, and Ulm. Incidentally, for special reasons, we
shall travel to the extreme north, to Lübeck and
Schleswig and Danzig of the Baltic provinces, to
Cracow in Poland, to Zwickau in Saxony and elsewhere. Artist life of lower Franconia became almost
concentrated in Nürnberg, more strikingly so in the
case of wood-carving than in any other department.
In the popular idea no other art is more identified with
that city. We shall not, therefore, expect to find much
independence in the immediate neighbourhood. At
the same time Würzburg, some sixty miles to the
north-west, had, since Bamberg lost the pre-eminence
in sculpture which distinguished it even so late as the

middle of the fourteenth century, acquired a distinction which places it, so far as wood is concerned, in prominent rivalry. Its independence of the Nürnberg schools, and its condition of individual development, was in great measure due to its connexion with the neighbouring Suabian art which in the middle of the fifteenth century was, especially in painting, substantially in advance of that of Nürnberg. The name of Riemenschneider has conferred on Würzburg a celebrity of a similar kind to that which, in the case of Nürnberg, is connected in popular esteem with Veit Stoss. Another important centre is to be found in Rothenburg in the valley of the Tauber in Bavarian Franconia. These lower Frankish schools show in a remarkable degree the characteristic calm and stolid severity which are striking features of much of the German retable work. The same feeling is expressed by the single figures. An emotional dramatic motive, with exceptions which will be noted, as a whole is absent. In the best examples what one finds is a series of well-conceived and delicately handled single figures and groups. In a large number of cases, however, they are the work of self-taught or untrained men who were more or less able craftsmen. When there was question, therefore, of such an important work as the altarpiece or shrine for the relic of the Precious Blood in the chapel for that purpose in the Parish Church of St. James at Rothenburg, it is not surprising that the authorities should have gone elsewhere. Their choice of an artist for the central group was Riemenschneider, of whom we shall presently hear a great deal more.

The Suabian provinces had been distinguished in sculpture from early times. From early in the fourteenth century we meet with great work at Ulm, at Stuttgart, at Esslingen, at Augsburg, in Bavaria and throughout South Germany. The Suabian temperament in art, which we recognize also in our wood-carving, is simpler, more homely in character than the almost truculent excitability and striving after, if not attaining, dramatic expression which seems to characterize that of Franconia. But it would appear that the latter school soon wrested from the Suabian its pride of place in sculpture, giving the tone to almost the whole of the empire.

The great altarpiece in the Victoria and Albert Museum, fully painted and thickly gilt, which will be briefly described later on, offers a sufficiently characteristic example of the style which prevailed in South German districts at the end of the fifteenth and beginning of the sixteenth century. Of different degrees of merit, these sculptures abound in the village churches, not often of so high a character as the example which the museum was fortunate enough to acquire so long ago as 1859, but as a rule of very great interest from the sincerity and quaintness of the treatment, the homely character frequently expressed in the peasant type of the figures, the insight into details of costumes, and of the manners of the period, and the obviously devotional feeling with which, at so late a time, when the Renaissance and reforming ideas were making a strong impression, pervade them. Still, for the proper appreciation of such altarpieces as that at Kensington, one must imagine them divested of colour, for despite its gorgeousness and the rich and thickly laid-on gilding, it would then be seen that the sculptor was by far the greater artist of the two: allowing that they were perhaps identical personally. That Augsburg should not figure so prominently as Nürnberg or Würzburg in sculptured woodwork of a religious character is due no doubt to the terrible destructions consequent on the Reformation. What little is to be found in museums we can only assign by conjecture to this city. Two important pieces, however, will be mentioned presently. The Bavarian and Austrian provinces have much in common with the Suabian, and the work of the Tyrol is, as one would expect, nearly related to that of upper Bavaria. We shall find its best expression in the altarpieces and figure work of Michael Pacher, and in the figures of the Virgin and Apostles at Blutenberg. While we have to recognize the influence which, from its geographical position, Italy could not have failed to exert, the art at the same time is unmistakably German. The village churches and chapels of the old castles of Bavaria and the Bavarian Tyrol have long furnished almost a gold mine in the way of old carving in profusion, from statue work to furniture, to the museums of Vienna, Munich, and other places. The whole district in fact, from Hohenschwangau and Innsbruck on the north, Meran and Salzburg and Lindau in the centre, to Botzen on the south, has been ransacked for the treasures which abounded. Cartloads of altarpieces, shrines, panellings, elaborately carved bedsteads and furniture of all kinds, now adorn many museums and private collections. Tyrolese Gothic has a character of its own. As an example may be cited the bedstead belonging to Mr. Baillie-Grohman, to which allusion has already been made. It has more originality, individual taste, and inventive skill, is less dependent on a conventional imitation of architectural forms; is simpler, more solid, less given to fretwork, geometrical forms, and fantastically twisted pinnacles and other dragged-in ornament than we find in northern work or even in that of Franconia and Suabia. Oak and other of the harder woods were not common, and therefore not often used. Instead, we find pinewood frequently, larch, lime, and chestnut. There is an absence of too exact finish and measurement and an admirably free treatment of plant-form growth, ever varying in luxuriantly convoluted and twisted forms, but not a realistic copy of nature. At times one is reminded of the character of the emblazonments of German heraldic mantling.

In Saxony the best wood-work is strongly suggestive of the influence of Nürnberg, but the local style is, in general, distinctly lifeless, impersonal, commercial work, with an absence of any beauty in the type of the faces. The figures are lanky and badly proportioned, and even in the draperies one finds nothing more than an unintelligent copying from the woodcuts and copper prints of the time. On the other hand, we are confronted in the Pietà of the Marienkirche at Zwickau with a masterpiece which, allowing for exaggerations due to the prevailing taste of the time, may claim a place among the best which the Franconian artists can show. The Thuringian school, in evident touch with those of Nürnberg and Würzburg, is distinguished by the name of Valentine Lendenstreich. Amongst his other work is an altar in the chapel of the castle of Schwarzburg, Rudolstadt, dated 1503. In common with many wood sculptors of his time Lendenstreich had no hesitation in copying or freely adapting from Schongauer and other engravers, and even directly from the school of Riemenschneider. About an hour from Rudolstadt, in Thuringia, is Neusitz, where in the late fifteenth century there was evidently a considerable industry in the carving and painting of altarpieces. In the parish church is a retable with the characteristic doll-like figures under canopies, painted and gilt: perhaps by Lendenstreich. But throughout Thuringia the work of the second half of the fifteenth century lacks artistic distinction. It is not that it is undeserving of any notice, but, strongly influenced by the school of Würzburg, much of the better class is very likely the imported work of Franconian masters, and cannot call for separate notice merely on account of its position.

In the northern districts bordering on Belgium

86

and Holland, there is a wealth of Flemish altar-work, exiled, no doubt, during the wars of religion in the Netherlands.   Flemish artists, also, would have emigrated, and the opportunity would have been taken of acquiring their services.   Their altarpieces were, indeed, scattered elsewhere, besides, and examples are still to be found in France and Spain, and especially in Sweden.   Nearly all are of the pictorial character, and, although some fine specimens may still be seen in museums in Belgium, it is to the North German churches and to Sweden that we must go for a very large number: to Lübeck, Calcar, and Xanten, and to the museum of Stockholm for retables formerly in Swedish churches.   Calcar itself was at one time the centre of a great school of wood sculpture, but this was in almost complete subjection to the art of the Netherlands.   It is now a small town of little im-portance.   The style, then, is in general Flemish. Elaborate scenes are included in the central division, or in panels on the wings, with multitudes of figures in perspective; such, at least, as this was under-stood at the time.   We find very commonly the story of St. George and the dragon and the rescue of the princess: one part of the legend in the foreground, another on a higher plane amongst a landscape of a hilly country, with towns and castles and winding roads.   These altarpieces are not always of the same date throughout.   Some panels are evidently much earlier than others, and we find, also, Gothic figures and scenes placed amongst quite late Renaissance and rococo surroundings.   The variety and wealth of detail in these compositions is astonishing.   It would be difficult to find a parallel elsewhere to the height of dramatic treatment of the scenes in the life of our Lord, and the legends of the saints.   The high altar at Calcar is an astounding piece of elaborate pictorial carving.   More subdued but quite as effective is the retable of the Brief-Kapelle in the Marienkirche of Lübeck (Plate VI.), the work, in all likelihood, of Jan Borman of Brussels about the year 1518. Probably a considerable number of these altarpieces are the work of Westphalian artists.

The wood sculpture of Cologne of the fifteenth century must be briefly passed over, although there is much to attract attention. Yet, even in such figures as those of St. George, which are so common, where the saint is in full armour, bearing a sword with a wavy edge (an extremely good example is in the Rothschild bequest in the British Museum), there is an affectation in style more appropriate to a mignon of the courts : mincing, rather than of the intrepid soldier. In German wood sculpture of the fifteenth and sixteenth centuries it is impossible to help remarking a very considerable absence of originality both in subject and treatment. It is true that the same holds good in respect to other departments of art, but with these we are not at present concerned.

For a complete understanding of the sources from which the sculptor drew his inspiration, a study is necessary of the work of the wood engravers and etchers ; of Dürer, Burgkmair, Beham, Schongauer, Virgil Solis, and many other contemporary masters of ornament. Even the greatest of those with whom we shall presently be concerned—amongst others, Riemenschneider, Wohlgemut, Stoss, Haguenauer, or Daucher —were not only indebted to these sources for ideas, but whole panels of their most admired altarpieces are direct copies from them. How far also they were directly influenced by the Flemish and German masters of painting, by the Van Eycks, the Memlings, and Van der Weydens, and, in particular, by the Cologne school of the fourteenth century, is a subject to which it is necessary to draw attention, though it cannot be followed here in detail. It must suffice to say that

PLATE VI

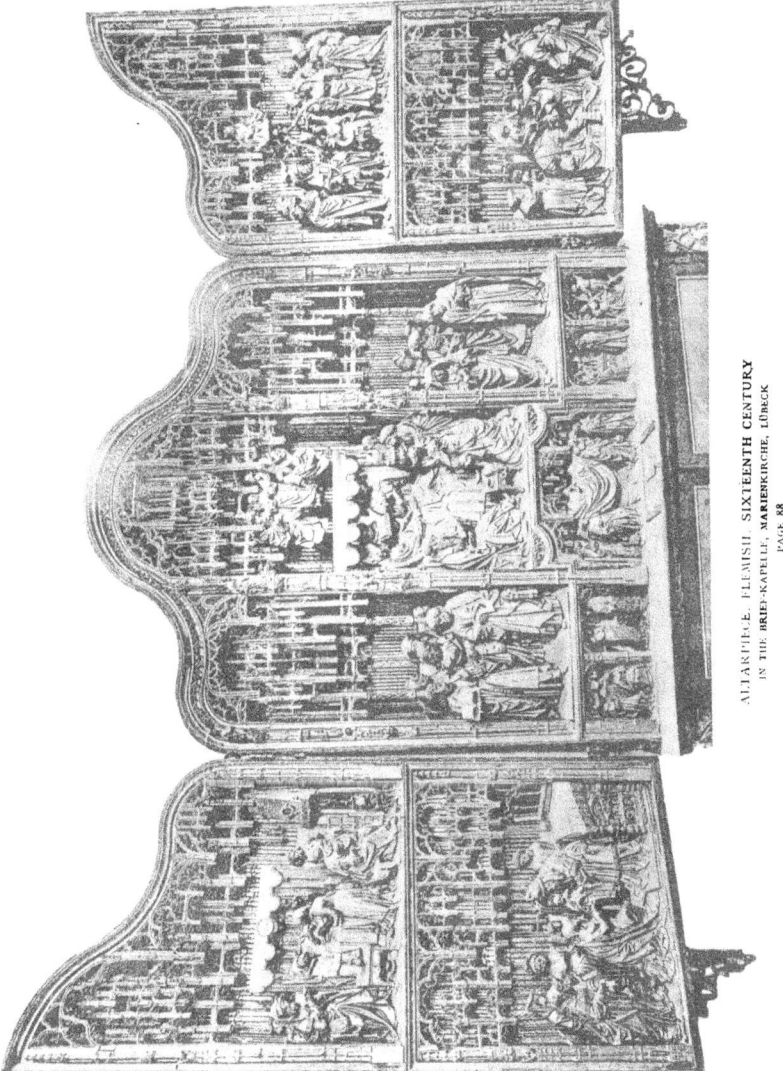

ALTARPIECE. FLEMISH. SIXTEENTH CENTURY
IN THE **BRIEF-KAPELLE, MARIENKIRCHE,** LÜBECK
PAGE **88**

it is connected not only with every remarkable example to which reference will presently be made, but also with innumerable other altarpieces and single figures of the fifteenth century in the churches and museums throughout the country. Whether directly derived from paintings or from the work of engravers, the practice is often not merely a case of inspiration, but of actual copying, in the composition of the subject. The arrangement of the folds and the disposition of the draperies, the fashion of a mantle, a veil, or a head-dress, the type and costume of such a figure as the angel of an Annunciation group, the expression, and, especially in the women, the very model herself, the flowing hair in long straight slightly curling strands—all this and more is, it may be said, but the system of the time, and the interchange of ideas amongst all the arts was general. Still, it would be remarkable, per-haps, if a Riemenschneider should have been unmoved not only by the Flemish primitives, his contemporaries, but also by those earlier Suabian schools, the glory of his own country. Beautiful and inspiring indeed is a Stefan Lochner, to whom Dürer himself in his journal of travels to the Low Countries contributes his meed of enthusiasm. From such a one—amongst so many more whom we know only by the titles of their works —from these followers of the earlier Dutch and Flemish mystics, came the strengthening of the impulse which, without entirely abandoning the ideal, was to add to it a homely personal realism. It would be a matter of difficulty, no doubt, to apportion the relative indebted-ness to this or that source, for with Stefan Lochner ends the distinct character of the Cologne school. After him, German, Dutch, and Flemish are merged in one, or at least the differences are not great. The Germans go for instruction to the studios of Bruges and Louvain, and the greatest of Flemish painters are called upon to contribute their masterpieces to the churches of the empire. When, however, we find such frequent relationships in subject and treatment between the sculptured altarpieces and the work of the wood-engravers and etchers, we are led to inquire how far there was collaboration between their authors. We know that in many cases such great men as Dürer were on intimate terms with the sculptors, their contemporaries: he himself a pupil in Wohlgemut's studio, as Riemenschneider was also. Was, then, Riemenschneider, for instance, in later years, free to copy or adapt for his altarpiece, now in the Bavarian Museum, Dürer's 'Decollation of St. John the Baptist,' or did he do so at the engraver's instigation? For this is a direct copy of Dürer's woodcut of 1511. There is no Dürer cypher or so-called monogram, it is true, but we seem to be face to face with a similar problem to that involved in the question of so many honestone and wood reliefs and medallions on which it is found: a question still awaiting a final answer. Did Albert Dürer himself use the chisel of the sculptor? From his training, from the artistic methods of the time, the absence of specialization, and the fact that we know that so many others were at once painters, engravers, etchers, goldsmiths, bronze-casters, and sculptors in stone, limestone, wood, or ivory, it is only natural to suppose that he did. From time to time the saleroom still professes to furnish examples. As lately as October 1906 a small boxwood statuette of an old man, from the Keele Hall collection, was ascribed to Dürer and sold at Christie's for 430 guineas.

The question is of more importance when we come to consider the boxwoods and medallions of the early part of the sixteenth century. But when we find so prominent a wood sculptor as Veit Stoss almost as prolific in etched work as in sculpture, and, to cite but one example—the central panel of his altarpiece in the Academy at Cracow which is a reproduction of one of his own etchings—it would be interesting to determine what, in general, were the relationships between the two crafts. That Dürer and his art exercised a considerable influence on the arts of the German and Italian Renaissance during the last quarter of the fifteenth century, still more up to the time of his death in 1528, and even afterwards, is, of course, unquestioned. The studio or workshop of Wohlgemut is of considerable importance in the history of our subject, and here Dürer was apprenticed in 1486 as to the best master of painting of the day. Then he travels extensively for his *wanderjähre*—to Italy, as far as Venice, to Colmar, Augsburg, Innsbruck, the Tyrol, Trent, Basel, Strassburg—before establishing himself in his native city, Nürnberg, at that time the centre of German art. The first years of the sixteenth century take him again to Italy for a long residence, and there he enjoys the society and friendship of the great Italian painters, engravers, and sculptors: of Raphael, Bellini, Mantegna, and Marc Antonio. More years pass before his visit to the Netherlands in 1520 brings about a decided influence in his change of style. But it is almost the close of his life. Adam Krafft is dead (1509): Veit Stoss and Riemenschneider die within a year of each other (1530-1531), the one at the age of 90, the other over 70. Dürer's influence is, again, markedly strong in the work of the boxwood carvers and medallion-makers. Amongst these he had the greatest admiration for Conrad Meit. It is not only on honestone reliefs and boxwood medallions that the Dürer cypher, the famous 🄰 adopted by him in 1497, so frequently calls for explanation. The imperial gallery at Vienna possesses the admirable carved wood frame for the great picture known as the ' All Saints,' or the Adoration of the Trinity, and it bears this cypher. As

Thausing says, in his *Life of Dürer*, 'There can be no doubt that Dürer superintended the carving, rule and compasses in hand. For who at Nürnberg but himself could have designed anything which so completely breathes the spirit of the antique . . . the spirit of classical forms?' Within the panel of the tympanum appears, in high relief, the Saviour, as Judge of the world, between the Virgin and St. John : at each end are angels in the round, blowing trumpets, and there was another, now missing, at the top. Sculptures in wood, ivory, and honestone, bearing the monogram are numerous. This, decorative in itself, was easily forged, if, indeed, the term may be applied, and that it was not used, in some cases at least, by permission. The British Museum possesses the honestone relief of the birth of John the Baptist, now generally attributed to Georg Schweiger, who would seem to be the author of many others. The Pierpont Morgan collection has the famous honestone Venus Kallipyge, for which it would seem certain that Dürer made the drawings, two of which now remain : one in a MS. volume in the Dresden royal library, the other in the collection of Professor Blasius at Brunswick. But the relief itself may be the work of Hans Daucher. In the Victoria and Albert Museum is a small pearwood panel, acquired in 1858, with the 'Judgment of Paris' in low relief, bearing the monogram in the foreground of the landscape. Bartsch describes the etching by Dürer from which this was copied (*Peintre graveur*, vii. 134), but as without the monogram. A boxwood panel in the Morgan collection is after a woodcut by Hans Burgkmair. In the Vienna Imperial Museum are two round boxes in boxwood with portrait reliefs which are free copies from Dürer's 'Frederic the Wise of Saxony' : within is written in pencil '*fyt Stoss den elder,*' an attribution no doubt of some early critic. A small walnut panel in the Kensington Museum is a

92

copy, with slight differences, from the lower half of a well-known painting of the Rhenish school of the fifteenth century, the 'Paradise' picture in the Frankfurt Museum. Martin Schongauer and Hans Sebald Beham were, amongst other masters of the upper German schools, simply mines from which to extract ideas and turn them into sculpture. From these the adapters took especially the fashion and fall of the draperies and the angular folds in which they delighted. Schongauer was perhaps more drawn upon than any other. Wohlgemut copied many of his engravings, and even the small boxwood statuettes of the Madonna—there is an example in the Kensington Museum—are sometimes, as this one is, practically copied from his work. Riemenschneider's altarpiece in the Marienkirche at Salzwedel is from a Schongauer etching: and the Madonnas in glories of flames, what are they but direct imitations of the little German masters of the fifteenth century? The boxwood medallions to be noticed in a succeeding chapter, even in the case of such artists as Daucher and Haguenauer, are sometimes copied from paintings. For example, the portrait by Haguenauer of Henry VIII. is after Holbein's miniature at Windsor, and the 'Alchemy' and 'Grammar,' in the Louvre, are of Dürer inspiration, tempered by Italian influences. So again, we have the panels with the triumph of Maximilian by Daucher, after Dürer. All this, no doubt, in some cases is legitimate enough, and the transcription is often admirable, and comparable in a certain sense to the masterly work of the line engraver or etcher who translates into tones of black and white the colour of a painting. On the other hand, the literal rendering of a black and white engraving —so far as it can be called literal—by the contours of a sculptural relief approaching the round, or in the round itself, is contrary to the character of the two arts, and leads to abuses of which examples are but too frequent.

93

CHAPTER VI

THE FRANCONIAN, BAVARIAN, AND OTHER GERMAN
ARTISTS AND WORKSHOPS OF THE END OF THE
GOTHIC PERIOD

IT is to be regretted that we are in possession of so
few names of importance which can be attached
to the crowd of sculptured work still remaining
in the churches throughout the country, or now trans-
ferred to many museums and private collections in
Germany and elsewhere. At the same time it must be
repeated that the merit is very unequal. There are
masterpieces, but there is also a vast quantity of poor
work which has little call for notice beyond its curiosity
value and the sentiment which may attach to the
subject, or local interest. Concerning such things
monographs are not wanting. The number of artists,
and of work, of the first class to which it is necessary
to refer in any detail, is therefore restricted: limited,
in fact, to hardly more than half-a-dozen names during
the last century of Gothic art and the transition. Of the
later date, the workers in boxwood and the medallionists
will furnish a separate chapter. What we shall be
concerned with is almost exclusively religious art in
the form of retables and altarpieces, and the statuettes
and groups which in many cases were made for them.
But, when all is said and done, there still remains the
greatest doubt to whom, amongst those named, we can
definitely assign certain of the most important pieces.

94

Signed work is of the extremest rarity, and documentary evidence almost wholly wanting. We are ignorant even of the birthplaces and dates of birth of Veit Stoss or of Riemenschneider.

The pervading similarity of style and technique, outside the exceptional pieces which will be selected, has already been noticed. It must be borne in mind that these men worked also in stone or bronze, and we must be prepared to find that in many cases the methods and actual technique of the sculpture in stone and wood are almost indistinguishable. In addition, painter and sculptor were in Germany, as elsewhere, intimately connected and dependent on each other. Workshops and schools existed which were controlled or directed by such masters as Wohlgemut, and work turned out commercially to order. Imitation and copying from the masters of engraving were rife, and if there were certain mannerisms they were often those which were fashionable, and common alike to the graphic and plastic arts. Nothing would be more satisfactory than, could we but do so, to feel that we could distinguish a Riemenschneider by a mannerism in style or execution which could be called peculiar to him and to no other. We can get near this, it is true, as will be shown later on, but no further. Probably the masters of the boxwood models for medals, or for figures, did not confine themselves to this small sculpture alone, but, at least in their earlier days, would have had a practical acquaintance with, and have worked in the large ateliers whence proceeded the great altarpieces of Creglingen or of Schwabach. Doubtless there were boxwood carvers before Hans Schwarz. But with him we are brought to the beginnings of the Reformation, when the disuse of images, or at least the demand for them, must have greatly diminished. Yet the zeal of the iconoclasts does not appear to have affected Germany in the way it did England or Flanders. To this day some of the finest carved altarpieces with images, or the great crucifixes of the Roods, are to be found in the Protestant churches. But its effects, and the revival of classical ideas in art, turned the attention of artists towards the glorification of individuals rather than to the illustration of devotional ideas. Piety was no longer the sole incentive. Disregard for fame gave place, happily for posterity, to a more general desire to perpetuate a name. Besides the statuary work of the great altarpieces, the architectural surroundings or framings—often with elaborate canopy work and plant-form tracery—cannot be left entirely out of account, though it is not now proposed to deal with it in detail. There is ample material to form a separate subject, and the names of some carvers who seem to have been especially devoted to it are known. For example, the characteristic framing of the altarpiece of the Precious Blood at Rothenburg is ascribed to one Erhart. Foliage and intertwining open work of branches and tendrils, often of a wild and thorny character, were much affected, especially for the curtain-like veil which often hangs from the upper parts of the shrine. There was room for the exercise of any amount of capricious fancy and pleasant play of branch and leaf-work, flowing in every direction, sometimes abruptly broken off, sometimes mingling with and losing itself in purely architectural motives of corbel or *cul-de-lampe* ; disguised in pinnacle form, or a pinnacle itself curled and twisted into the shape of a half unfolded leaf or opening bud. A wilderness of vegetation and absence of symmetry in accordance with nature's own methods, a naturalism as of things really growing, and in all stages of growth from the bud to the full bloom, or already decaying leaf or stem, a perpetual reminder of growth on earth even in its unspoken application to the holier themes with which it was connected—all this may be found carved out of a material than which no other is so appropriate, though it is found also in abundance in stone sculpture, in the ironworker's forgings, or the goldsmith's hammered metal-work. We are bound to connect much fine work with the productions of Wohlgemut's workshop. In an atelier under one master of many pupils—and he a painter who perhaps never carved himself, but left this part of his altarpieces to his pupils and assistants—there would be naturally a great similarity in style. His young men were no doubt allowed to follow pretty freely their own bent, with the advantage of his advice and supervision. Little is known of those who worked in the same studio as Riemenschneider, but the names, at least, of many of his contemporaries may be gathered from the municipal archives of Würzburg. These young artists travelled largely, and learnt to assimilate foreign styles, interchanging ideas also with all parts of Germany, with the Rhine or Baltic provinces, with Thuringia and Saxony, Bavaria and the Tyrol, Bohemia and Poland. Riemenschneider himself is first included in the list in 1483, but as painter associate only, not as sculptor. Of others, who may also have attained an equally high standing, we know only the names. With him were contemporaries : for instance, Lorenz Müll of Landsberg, Michael Bolz of Volkach, Michael Weiss, Ulrich Hagenfurter, Paul Polsterer, Hans Metz, and others, but these are but names. Of their work and manner we know nothing. Amongst them may lie concealed, perhaps, even so sympathetic and great a master as the creator of the Nürnberg Madonna. It would seem to be the fashion, at present, to ascribe to Riemenschneider anything remarkable of the school, especially if it is distinguished by a certain type of face and curling hair. It is unfortunate that it is only for the less distinguished work that we are able to rely on documentary evidence. His reputation, however, need not rest upon what is merely conjecture, as in the case of the St. Anne group and the Adam and Eve busts at Kensington, while we may give him with certainty such fine work as the effigy in stone of the Prince-Bishop Rudolph von Scherenberg in Würzburg cathedral. There is a good reproduction of this monument in the gallery of casts at Kensington.

CHAPTER VII

VEIT STOSS—RIEMENSCHNEIDER—PACHER—
MULTSCHER—BRUGGEMANN

EVERY lover of German old-world cities knows Nürnberg, its narrow streets, and the old-fashioned houses with their half-timbered and slim-turreted fronts, their richly ornamented gables, and angles decorated with carved figures. Everywhere there is evidence of the inborn art of the people of mediæval times, and of the religious feeling of the age. There is little need to name its famous monuments, popular all the world over; the Schöne Brunnen, or the little goose-man. If the name of Adam Krafft is mainly associated with stone sculpture, Peter Vischer and his family with bronze-founding and metal-work, that of Veit Stoss is the one which has been generally connected with the wood-carving art of Nürnberg. Indeed it may be said to have been the only one in popular estimation of German wood-carving until recent years, when those of Riemenschneider, Multscher, Hans Schwarz, Conrad Meit, Hans Wydyz, and a few others, have come to the front with some information concerning them, resulting from the unwearied industry of German writers. It will be sufficient to note that not one of these names appears in the historical introduction to the large official catalogue of wood-work in the South Kensington Museum, published in 1874, which up to the present day continues to be the only one of that collection. Nor do we find them alluded to—to name

99

no other histories of art—even in such a presumably comprehensive compilation as Bayet's *Précis de l'histoire de l'art*. Veit Stoss stands, then, as the official representative in Germany of wood-carving of late Gothic times. For all that he was no Heaven-sent leader. He but followed in the footsteps of others, who as originators were greater than he. Amongst them we know the names of two at least: Hans Multscher, hailing from farther north, and Michael Pacher, a South Bavarian or Tyrolese master. Of the beginnings of the art of wood-carving, or of the sister arts of stone sculpture and metal work, which made Nürnberg famous, we are almost entirely ignorant. Documents and municipal archives give us some names of artists, but for identification of work with which to connect them, hardly anything. As a rule Veit Stoss's earlier altarpieces show that he merely followed a style already fully developed. He used the same models, or rather derived his type of woman figure from the same stereotyped one — small, narrow-busted, and with sloping shoulders—which had come to be the only one recognized: the same draperies, the same mixture of conventional costume and of the fashion of his day. Little is known of the date or place of his birth, or even of his nationality. Although Cracow may have been his birthplace, and his origin Polish, Nürnberg may claim him as a true son of hers, and his family had definitely settled there. In the archives of that town a document is preserved—the contract for the execution of his great work, the altarpiece of the Marienaltar of the cathedral—in which he is called 'Magister Almanus de Norimberga.' The son probably of a coppersmith, Michael Stoss, he was born certainly as early as 1447; for it would seem that he himself had a son born in 1464. Without going further into questions that are more proper for a biography, we may take it that Veit Stoss left Nürnberg to settle in Cracow in 1477. He had served his apprenticeship, perhaps, and accomplished and learnt a good deal in the travels of his *Wanderjähre*; no doubt had already visited Cracow, had become a master, and, as the early work of his long life shows, his art was full-blown. After a stay of almost twenty years in Cracow, where he must have executed a considerable quantity of wood-carving, and applied himself also to etching, Stoss returned to Nürnberg, and appears to have worked in the studio and wood-carving shop of Michael Wohlgemut. There, if not solely responsible for the altarpiece of the parish church of Schwabach, his, no doubt, is the carved centre-piece representing our Lord and the Blessed Virgin enthroned between St. John and St. Martin of Tours. It is interesting to notice that in all Wohlgemut's altarpieces the central place of honour is of carved wood, the wings painted. Thausing, in his *Life of Albert Dürer*, makes some cogent remarks with reference to the carved work which applies, in a general way, to the Franconian wood sculpture of the period. He characterizes the figures as 'slender and graceful, the faces, though uniform and round, childlike, with an innocent look characteristic of the old Cologne school: *antiquated, stationary art*, in glaring contrast to Wohlgemut's paintings of the side-wings.' The general arrangement, painting, and gilding of these central figures was probably superintended by the painter. It is impossible for us to know, now, how to apportion the credit for the carved work which at this period (1508) issued from Wohlgemut's establishment, as we must call it, for it had become little more than a factory. The painter concerned himself with the panels of the altarpieces alone: the carving was left to Stoss and his assistants and pupils. We shall presently return to the subject of the altarpiece of Schwabach and its connexion with the one at St. Wolfgang by Michael Pacher, an earlier work which

Stoss must have known and more or less copied from.

Veit Stoss's first business at Cracow on settling there in 1477 was to undertake the carving of the great altarpiece of the Marienkirche in that town, a work which required twelve years for its completion. Considered by many as the finest of the German retables, we may take it as representative of the general arrangement of this class of work in the southern division of the empire. One of the largest and most elaborate, at least, it still, although restored and repainted, presents in essentials its original condition. As the church and this altar in particular are dedicated to the Blessed Virgin, it is not surprising that the subjects should be those illustrative of her life. It is the life as we know it in the language of the Rosary, of the Joyful, Sorrowful, and Glorious mysteries. Triptych in arrangement, the high central shrine rests on a predella carved with the gnarled and almost leafless branchwork of the tree of Jesse, bearing figures representative of the genealogy of the Virgin. The principal subject in the central division of the triptych gives us her death, or at least—for it is an unusual method of representing even the earlier stage of the Dormition—the last phase in her life on earth. She is in the act of gently sinking to the ground, kneeling, and supported by one of the apostles, surrounded by the others and some holy women. Above, still in the central division, is the Assumption, beneath pinnacled canopy work, and above this again, amongst elaborate architectural details, figures in niches, foliage, borders, and other ornament. The wings are carved in low relief—within, in six divisions with scenes from the life of our Lord, on the outer sides in twelve compartments with similar subjects, mostly of the Passion. On the tomb itself, in the Resurrection scene, is the monogram, or more properly the cipher, ⚏ of the master.

PLATE VII

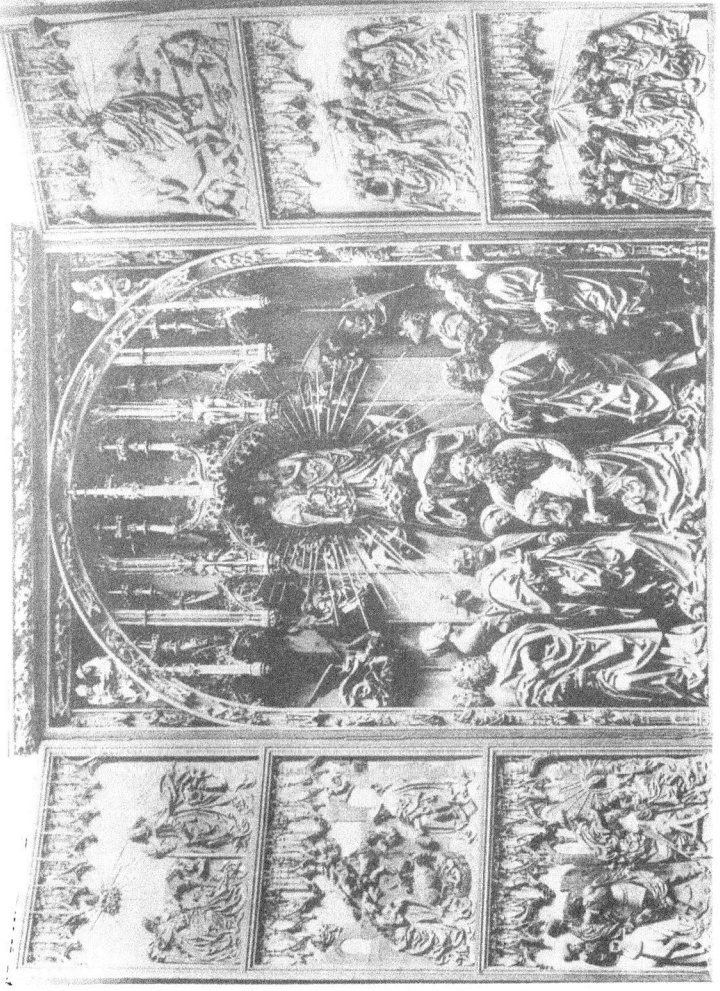

ALTARPIECE BY VEIT STOSS. FIFTEENTH CENTURY

IN THE MARIENKIRCHE, CRACOW

PAGE 162

VEIT STOSS

Technically we have here, in Stoss's earliest great work, an admirable illustration of his style for figures in the round, and in low relief. Those in the central group are somewhat larger than life size. The strongly marked anatomy of the heads of the apostles, the long bony hands and fingers with their swollen veins, the deeply cut and many-folded tumultuous draperies completely concealing the figures, the style of the hair and beards; and, again, the slender, small-busted type, and costumes of the women in the low reliefs of the wings, are all highly characteristic landmarks upon which to base conclusions with regard to other work attributed to Stoss. There is in the apostle group an almost wild oriental type, associated with the artist's own temperament. The heads are those of ascetics, impulsive, filled with enthusiasm, rough uncultured men for the most part. The women, tender and lovable, with a distinction between the mother of Christ herself and the other women who, in the costumes of the period, are merely burghers' wives or daughters. Taken as single figures there is life and movement in the expression and attitudes of those in the central tableau. Yet, as a composition, it has the faults of the German system of assembling, as it were, a number of puppets, rather than, as in Flemish retables, a more pictorial perspective method. It suggests an impression of a stage grouping without the scenery. There is a disregard of any logical arrangement, except a general decorative effect. The draperies are subordinated to this, and have little relation to the position and movements of the figures they cover. But no one will dispute the poetical treatment of the whole. For, if the eye may wander from group to group, from panel to panel, every detail is full of suggestiveness. What ideas, indeed, are not evolved, from that central kneeling figure, what suggestions relating to the ending of that earthly life, which we are left to fill up for ourselves!

WOOD SCULPTURE

Many altarpieces, single figures, and panels are with
more or less certainty attributed to Veit Stoss. Madonna
statuettes are numerous, the Holy Child, as a rule quite
unclothed and lying, according to the fashion generally
prevailing, somewhat across in the arms of His mother.
The face of the Virgin is almost always from the same
model, or it would be more correct to say, of the same
accepted type : very long, loose, wavy hair, unfortunately
often crowned with a monstrous crown, as was so much
the fashion not only in sculpture, but in graphic representations generally. It would be impossible to give
here a list of works attributed to Stoss. Their variety
also is very great, ranging from those of high quality,
as the Cracow retable, to others after his return to
Nürnberg, of very indifferent merit. For an appreciation of his style at his best, the altarpiece of the parish
church of Bamberg, representing the adoration of the
Magi, would form a very fair example. This is a
quite late work if executed, as it is said, about 1533,
when the sculptor would have been at least eighty years
of age. Of his low reliefs we may class amongst his
very best work the panels in limewood of the Ten Com-
mandments, now in the Bavarian National Museum.
The influence of the Italian Renaissance, wherever he
may have derived it, is strong in these, and from the
costumes of the women and hats of the men we must
again date them very late in his life : not earlier than
1520.

With no intention of entering into its artistic
merits—indeed with a difficulty of repressing the expression of a feeling of wonderment that a reputation
should be founded on work of such a character—it
would be impossible to pass without notice the famous
Englische Gruss — the Angelical Salutation — in the
form of a Rosary wreath, with more than life-sized
central figures, hanging from the vault of the choir of
the Lorenzkirche at Nürnberg. These hanging pieces,

PLATE VIII

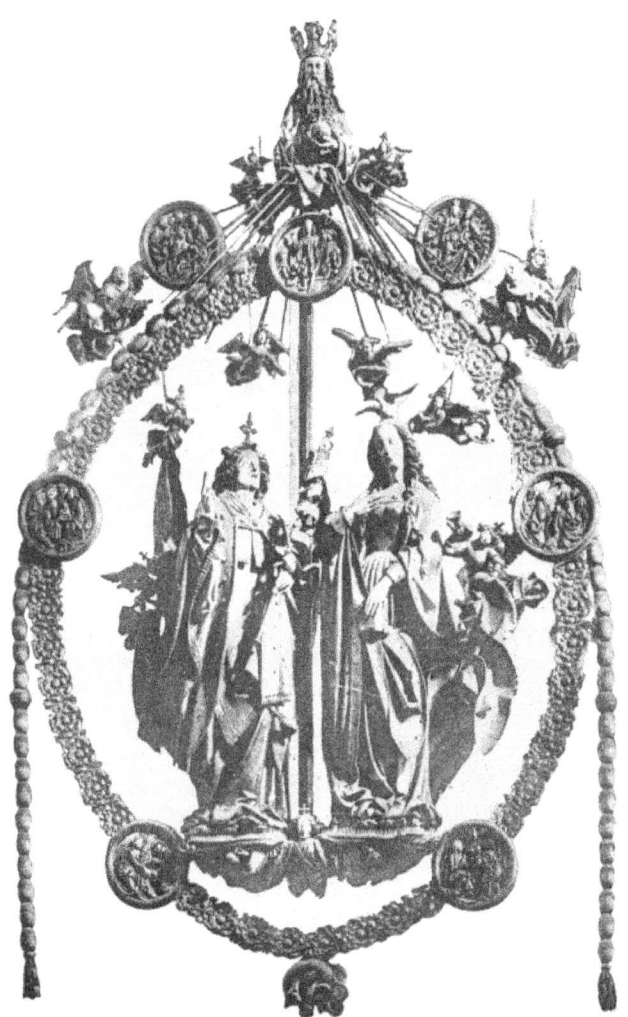

HANGING WREATH. THE ANGELICAL SALUTATION. BY VEIT STOSS.
SIXTEENTH CENTURY
CHURCH OF ST. LAWRENCE, NÜRNBERG
PAGE 105

and other *Rosenkränze*, seemingly attempts to copy, in wood, paintings such as those of the Cologne school of the early fifteenth century, enjoyed great popularity. The arrangement is almost childish in this work by Veit Stoss of 1517, as in others of its kind, including the one by Riemenschneider in the church of Volkach. Apart from this and its general vulgarity, neither the drawing, composition, nor execution entitle it to consideration as a work of art. The pose of the two principal figures is affected, the expression of the faces unattractive, the hands and position of the limbs those of an artist's lay-figure. There is neither style nor consistency in the treatment of the draperies; the bust of the Almighty at the top is almost revolting in its toy-like suggestion, the rosary paternoster medallions are gingerbread-like, the floating angels of the Christmas-tree type. These and other details are, in conjunction with an absence of any redeeming feature, unaccountable, except from the point of view of playing down to the level of popular demands. A somewhat similar work—at least on similar lines—is the Rosenkrantz tablet in the Nürnberg Museum. Veit Stoss was a great maker of crucifixes. The best, perhaps, are those of the high altar of the Lorenzkirche, of the Spitals-kirche, and of the church of the Ognissanti in Florence.

Whatever may be the undoubted high merit of such examples as the retables of Cracow and of Bamberg, on the other hand, if we are to accept some work attributed to him, Veit Stoss descends to the extreme commonplace, not to say vulgarities, and to a pandering to the taste in devotional representations which nothing but the chauvinism of his countrymen could demand to be admired. One looks with astonishment at the puerile taste and composition, and the inferior execution of such pieces as the group of the Coronation of the Virgin in the Nürnberg Museum and at many of his

Madonnas, for example, the Maria of the Stosshaus or
the smirking and truly wooden Heilsbronn Madonna
now in the Nürnberg Museum.   It is indeed puzzling
to compare such things with the charming etched work
of the master : with the Madonna of the apple (Bartsch
No. 3), the St. Geneviève holding a lighted candle, or
the Pietà (Bartsch 2), all of which have a close relationship with his style and feeling as a sculptor.   Veit
Stoss certainly lived to a great age, probably at least to
ninety-five.   In private life he seems to have been of a
troublesome, quarrelsome character : so much so that
in a town council decree he is called an *irrig und
geschreyig Mann*, and for some grave offence was condemned to be branded on both cheeks.   In his last
years he became quite blind, and died between the
years 1530-1540.   Of the many figures ascribed to Veit
Stoss, we may reserve for the section dealing with the
work of unknown German sculptors the Eve of the
Louvre, the St. Roch of the Church of the Annunziata
at Florence, and the crucifix of the Ognissanti at
Florence.   There will be naturally some comparisons
between his style and that of Riemenschneider.   There
is, for example, a St. John holding a chalice, in the
Berlin Museum, which, ascribed to him, might with
more reason be given to the school of the latter.   It
would not be easy to do full justice to his reputation
from every point of view without very numerous illustrations.   Our National Art Museum at Kensington
contains no example of the work of Veit Stoss, nor
even, for authenticated ones, does the museum of the
Louvre.

Amongst all the German wood-carvers of the
end of the Gothic period there is no more interesting
figure than that of the Würzburg master, Tillmann
Riemenschneider.   The interest which attaches to him
is all the greater on account of the problems which are
connected with the attribution to him of certain of the

finest pieces of German wood-carving. These questions involve at least three of the most important examples of the late mediæval work. They affect our own museum at Kensington, in which are to be found the charming busts of Adam and Eve, which for a long time were labelled as the work of Albert Dürer, and the group of SS. Anne and Joachim: the Imperial Museum of Vienna, which possesses the painted group of three figures known as ' Fleeting Life' (*Vergänglichkeit*): the Louvre and the recently acquired so-called Venus: and besides these—perhaps the most important with regard to suggestion of style—the altarpiece of the Lady altar of Creglingen, a little village in the valley of the Tauber, in South Germany. Now, it is almost solely on the strength of these masterpieces that we are able to concede so high a position as a wood-carver to Riemenschneider. It is true that we have other work undoubtedly by his hand which places him on a level as a stone or marble sculptor with Vischer or Krafft, his contemporaries, and that there are a considerable number of altarpieces, such as those of Rothenburg, Dettwang, or Münnerstadt, of statuettes and other groups, sufficient to establish a high reputation. Nevertheless, the main interest lies with the greater works just mentioned, whose authorship remains at the least doubtful. It would be impossible, within our present limits, to present the whole case, and it must be admitted that the consensus of opinion is, so far, in favour of Riemenschneider. Generally speaking, however, there is nothing compelling acceptance, and it would be wiser to leave them in the category of those other works in painting, engraving, and sculpture which we are accustomed to designate as by the Master of such and such a subject: as in the case also of the Nürnberg Madonna, to which we shall presently devote considerable attention.

The Würzburg school stands, with that of Nürnberg, in a singularly independent position, if we may judge from the strong influence which it exercised far and wide. It is unfortunate that our positive information concerning the works which emanated from it should be so scanty, because a considerable number of names, at least, can be gathered from the archives of the city. Amongst them is Riemenschneider, but it is by no means safe to attach his name to everything, even of the best, which bears the impress of the school. Certainly none is more widely quoted as representing lower Franconian sculptural art. Thilo, Teyl, Dile— Riemenschneider, or Rymschneider, or Master Dill, with other variations, as we find him named in documents and archives of Würzburg, appears to have belonged to a family of Saxon origin which had established itself at Würzburg. The date of his birth is unknown, but as he was said to be a little over seventy years of age in 1531 when he died, and as he was inscribed as an associate of the Guild of St. Luke in 1483, we may take it that he was born about 1460. From other evidence it is probable that his birthplace was Osterode, in the Hartz district, that mountainous chain in North Germany that we associate with the famous Brocken. Of his civic life as a burgher of his adopted town information is abundant, but as we are not now particularly concerned with biographical details, we need not stop to consider this at length. It will suffice to mention his marriage and early widowerhood, and that he occupied high positions in the city council and became Burgomaster. A three-quarter length profile portrait of Master Dill, probably the work of his son Jorg, dated 1519, is in the possession of the Archæological Society of Würzburg, a medallion in the parish church of Creglingen, and a bust in the Pietà of the church at Maidbronn. In accordance with the custom of his time he began, on the conclusion of his apprenticeship, his *Wanderjähre*, and probably

108

travelled principally through Franconia, Suabia, and in Poland, no doubt devoting considerable time to the art centre of Nürnberg. But we have no certain information where, or under what master, he may have studied, and can only conjecture the influences which went to form his style. He must have been familiar with Wohlgemut's studio, possibly even a fellow-pupil with Dürer, whose designs he afterwards followed in more than one of his altarpieces, and, whatever personal qualities were afterwards developed, his early training was strongly influenced at Nürnberg. But this would hardly have been through Adam Krafft, whose first dated work is in 1490, when Riemenschneider had been already some time a master. Veit Stoss, though somewhat an older man, he would have known also; but however much similarity in treatment we may find between the two, these are due to the following by both of the same traditions rather than to personal relations and community of feeling. The temperaments, indeed, of the two men and their methods of expression were widely different. By nature, Stoss was rough and undisciplined, as was his character in general; wanting in refinement, indifferent to a research of beauty, his work giving no evidence of a nobility of feeling, descending to the commonplace and even to vulgarity: his madonnas often coarse and of pure peasant type. Riemenschneider shows in his work an amiable disposition, almost womanly refinement, sincerity of purpose, and a tender sympathy with the sentiment he endeavours to illustrate. His saintly women are chosen from an idealized type of young, fresh, and innocent German womanhood, with an open candid expression from which a certain smiling coquettishness in no way detracts. We must not, however, forget the sources which influenced him in this respect. He was fond of clothing his holy women in the costume of the time, whether of the gorgeously apparelled lady of fashion or with the plain wimple and stuffed head-dress, or of the serving maid as in his St. Martha. If we are to accept the attribution to him of the disputed Eve or the Magdalen, he was not, in his later years at least, averse to the nude, but his inclination towards naturalism would never have allowed him to become coarse and offensive as it pleased others of his contemporary wood sculptors to be. In common with the practice of the Lower Franconian and Suabian schools generally, his work, even for altarpieces, was limited, except for low reliefs, to single figures and small groups arranged in rows, without attempting dramatic effect as a whole. This may be said without excepting even such compositions as the Creglingen or Rothenburg retables. We do not expect from him strong stagelike treatment. A group such as the Anne and Joachim fragment at Kensington has plenty of story to tell in a quiet way, and the greatness of his talent is fully exemplified in the twelve seated apostle figures in the Bavarian National Museum. These are figures, fragments no doubt of an altarpiece, than which no others could be better chosen as typical of Riemenschneider, in character, in design, and in handling. They are, of course, intimately connected with the ascription of the Creglingen retable.

The German schools of the little masters of engraving were, in the early days at least of Riemenschneider's apprenticeship, still in their infancy. To Schongauer in particular must be traced something of the type of the women's faces which is almost constant in his altarpieces and in his single figures, from the Eve, in stone, of Würzburg, to the Magdalen of Münnerstadt. We have no documentary evidence of his *Wanderjähre*, but if he did not actually travel in Italy or Flanders he must have been well acquainted with the work of the great masters of his time. Prague was not far off, and the early Bohemian school of painting would have been familiar to him. He must have seen many great Flemish retables even in his own country, but as a rule he did not attempt to imitate their pictorial style, reserving for the wings, and in lower relief, his skill as a narrator of stories. As an artist Riemenschneider was faithful to the last to Gothic traditions. Excluding such a disputed piece as the Vienna Allegory, there is hardly a trace of Italian influence and the Renaissance. Throughout all his work it would be difficult to find anything resembling the undisciplined independence of Veit Stoss. It is dignified, calm, logical, restrained. He never overdoes—as was so common a fault of his time—the expression of the painful, harrowing sides of the sacred scenes. In general, his figures, so far as the draperies permit us to characterize them, are slim in proportions, the shoulders narrow and sloping, the heads of the men large, and rendered larger by the wiglike profusion of curling hair: those of the women, on the contrary, small. The cheek-bones are exaggerated in prominence, the hands long and rather thin, the veins strongly marked, the fingers also long and delicately formed, but the hands small almost to distortion in his later work. The women's figures have the same straight falling shoulders, long oval faces, somewhat almond eyes, small breasts, very commonly the little finger bent over the next one, the feet rarely showing. The heads of the evangelists in the Berlin Museum are decidedly too large. Often, especially in the late work, the contour of the face runs from the prominent cheek-bone in a sharp narrow angle to the chin. And for the younger type we have as in the St. Totnan, St. Kilian's deacon, that constantly recurring sweet-smiling, rather sly, pretty boy or blarneying youth.

What cannot fail to strike the student of figure work of the Riemenschneider school is the hardly ever varying type of face either for the men or the women. We might say that they were all from one model, but that it is not likely that the living model was used at all. His men have all the same strong family resemblance, as of one stock, from the grandfather down to the youngest grandchild. Not only so, but the women belong to the same family also. There is a wearisome, ever-recurring repetition of the same conventionally curling locks, flowing in wiglike fashion over the shoulders, but for this we must blame the exigencies of the prevailing taste. For the Madonnas, though the type of face is so constant in form and expression, there would seem to be two varieties, but mostly a dark round face with broad forehead, sometimes bareheaded, sometimes with a veil simply draped on one side. The sentiment expressed is one of youthful grace and humility. The Holy Child is also always of the same type: curly-headed, lying across on the right or left arm of His mother indifferently, the upper leg bent upwards. But all this is not original, or confined to Riemenschneider, but merely the prevailing style of the time. On the other hand there is a treatment of the mouth in his holy women which is decidedly characteristic. The eyes, somewhat diverging, have a languishing expression. The neck, thick and sturdy in the men in conformity with the German fashion in art of the time, is thin and graceful in his women figures, and in the younger men. One might go so far as to say that the same model is to be found in the Magdalen of Münnerstadt and the St. John the Evangelist of the Berlin Museum. Generally, the influence of Wohlgemut in the Madonna figures is strong. The older women follow the customary types. If the name of Riemenschneider is to be attached to the St. Anne group in the museum at Kensington, it will be in evidence of masterly execution, of a technical use of his chisel with which no comparison can be made in any other German work of the kind. The study of the draperies is important. There is, of course, first, the conventional type proper to the figures of the apostles as we find it in those in the Munich Museum and in the Creglingen altarpiece. Generally, they would seem to be of a thin, somewhat stiffened, linen material, the long pleats crinkled up, as it were, and breaking off at acute angles : forming in this way a decorative arrangement of lines which seemed to hit the taste of the time, but led to extremes of exaggeration which, according to our ideas, are unmeaning and irritating, besides being monotonous. They form a series of plane surfaces set up at various angles : a succession of numberless small spiny folds. The idea is conveyed of a suddenly arrested movement converted into a frozen rigidity. The Zwickau Pietà, which is elsewhere noticed (pp. 86, 138), is an example of an admirable work in which this system is carried to excess. The whole question concerning it is, however, one in which the styles of the wood and copper-plate engravers of the time, and that of the Flemish, Cologne, and other schools of painting, have to be taken into account.

Riemenschneider was probably not strong in the anatomy of the undraped figure. The time had not arrived—for him at any rate—of emancipation from ecclesiastical traditions and restrictions. Even if we allow him the authorship of the Eve of the Louvre, his position would not be a high one, and the stone Eve of Würzburg cathedral has no claims for consideration from this point of view. On the other hand, the head, at any rate, of the masterly stone sepulchral effigy of Bishop Rudolf von Scherenberg in the cathedral of Würzburg is apparently evidence of consummate knowledge and truthfulness. But may not this be due to some extent to the practice of making *post-mortem* casts which was becoming usual in late mediæval times ? Riemenschneider's sculpture in stone hardly comes within the scope of this book. As a matter of fact, though it cannot be altogether left out of account by the student or admirer of his work in wood, the relationship is slight, and points of contact would not be easy to determine. For my own part I can attach little value to the endeavour to establish a theory, as one critic at least has done, connecting Riemenschneider with the Master of the Nürnberg Madonna through some analogies of costume with his sepulchral effigy of the Countess Dorothea von Wertheim at Grünsfeld. It was to stone sculpture that he seems first to have applied himself, and one of the earliest pieces from his hand—the tombstone of Prince-Bishop Rudolf, of which there is a cast in the Kensington Museum—would of itself suffice to assure his reputation. I am free to admit that I have derived no assistance concerning the questions which have arisen of the authorship of some important works attributed to Riemenschneider from comparison with the style or technique of his work in stone.

We may now turn to the retable of the *Herrgottskapelle* at Creglingen, an example which, rightly or wrongly, has been accepted as typical of the *style* of Riemenschneider (of this there should be no doubt), and, on the other hand, is amongst those pieces about which reasonable scepticism may be permitted as to his authorship. The date of the work is probably from about 1495 to 1499, and an ascription therefore to Riemenschneider must in the first place put out of the question the date 1487 carved on it, for Riemenschneider was then an apprentice at Würzburg, having gone there in 1483. In any case it is interesting to note that the most important work of both Stoss and Riemenschneider was executed at a very youthful age. The central group represents the Assumption of the Virgin, the figures a little less than life size. The apostles, some kneeling, are gathered in

PLATE IX

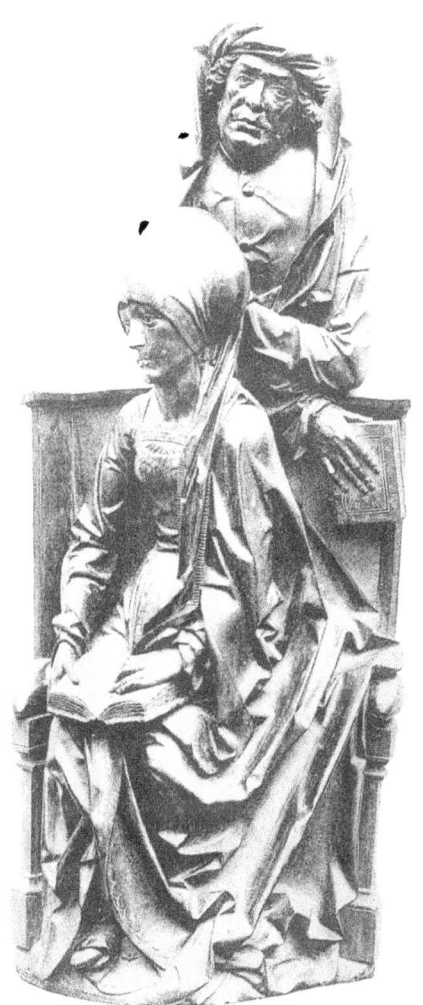

GROUP. ST. ANNE AND ST. JOACHIM, SUABIAN SCHOOL.
EARLY SIXTEENTH CENTURY
VICTORIA AND ALBERT MUSEUM
PAGE 116

two groups below, watching the ascent borne up and attended by angels. On the wings, in rather high relief, are scenes in the life of our Lord, and on a panel is an extremely characteristic group of two angels floating in the air upholding the miraculous Veronica handkerchief. The wing panels with the angelical salutation have neither original character nor are they good in execution. In the Annunciation scene, on the left wing of the triptych, the following of a master of painting such as the *Maître des Moulins* in the same subject is apparent in the composition generally, and even in such details as the disposition of the draperies and the flow of the train of the Virgin, the form and position of the bed, the book, the reading-desk and other accessories. But the two groups of the apostles are admirable in the expression of the figures taken separately, and in the treatment of the draperies. The retable, which measures, over all, about 21 feet in height by 10 in width, with the wings open, is not painted nor was it intended to be, and although we have many examples of the sculptor's painted and gilded retables and figures, we have no knowledge what may have been his part in this decoration.

As the altarpiece of Creglingen was to be left un-coloured, the carving had to be worked up to the highest perfection of finish. In some other cases bad workmanship is, to some extent, concealed. One finds too, not unfrequently, these carved works cleaned of the original polychrome, and redaubed with modern painting. Indeed we should be grateful that we may now admire in the pure surface of the wood such admirable appropriateness to the material and per-fection of execution as in a group which the museum at Kensington possesses. This is a fragment from a *Sippenaltar* with the figures of the parents of the Blessed Virgin.

A very few descriptive remarks are needed to

accompany the illustration here given (Plate IX.).
It is a portion, no doubt one half, of an arrangement
very popular in Germany known as a Sippenaltar,
or Anna selbdritt group. Elsewhere the term Holy
Family is, it is well known, usually applied to the
Virgin and Child, St. John Baptist, and St. Joseph.
The Anna selbdritt groups are very frequently found,
the main idea being St. Anne teaching her daughter to
read. But there is generally the strange inconsistency
of the Blessed Virgin grown up and holding the Holy
Child, even if herself standing or sitting on the lap of
her mother. We shall find this, for instance, later on,
in the case of a group in the Kensington Museum there
called English work (Plate XXXVIII.). In an example
in the Erfurt cathedral by Riemenschneider, or of his
school, Anna holds the Holy Child on one arm, and on
the other a doll-like crowned figure of His mother with
an open book on her lap. In another, in the Bavarian
National Museum, the elder woman is seated, the Holy
Child stands on her knee, and the Virgin, grown up,
is seated on her other knee, learning to read from the
usual open book. Often again the holy women are
seated side by side, the Child playing between them.
A divided piece, of which, however, the two halves are
still existing, is in the Bavarian National Museum
(No. 1247). This, also, is of the Franconian school,
and here we have St. Anne and St. Joachim, St.
Joseph, Salome, and Alpheus, but the Infant is absent,
and it is not a reading lesson. The Kensington group
(Plate IX.), if by Riemenschneider, may be quite late in
date: the costume and stuffed headdress pointing to
some time between 1495 and 1520. It was at one time
attributed to Georg Syrlin of Ulm, and indeed it is not
easy to dissociate the Suabian and Würzburg schools. A
piece composed in an identically similar manner is said
to be in the possession of Prince Ottingen-Wallenstein.
As an example of this particular side of German wood-

116

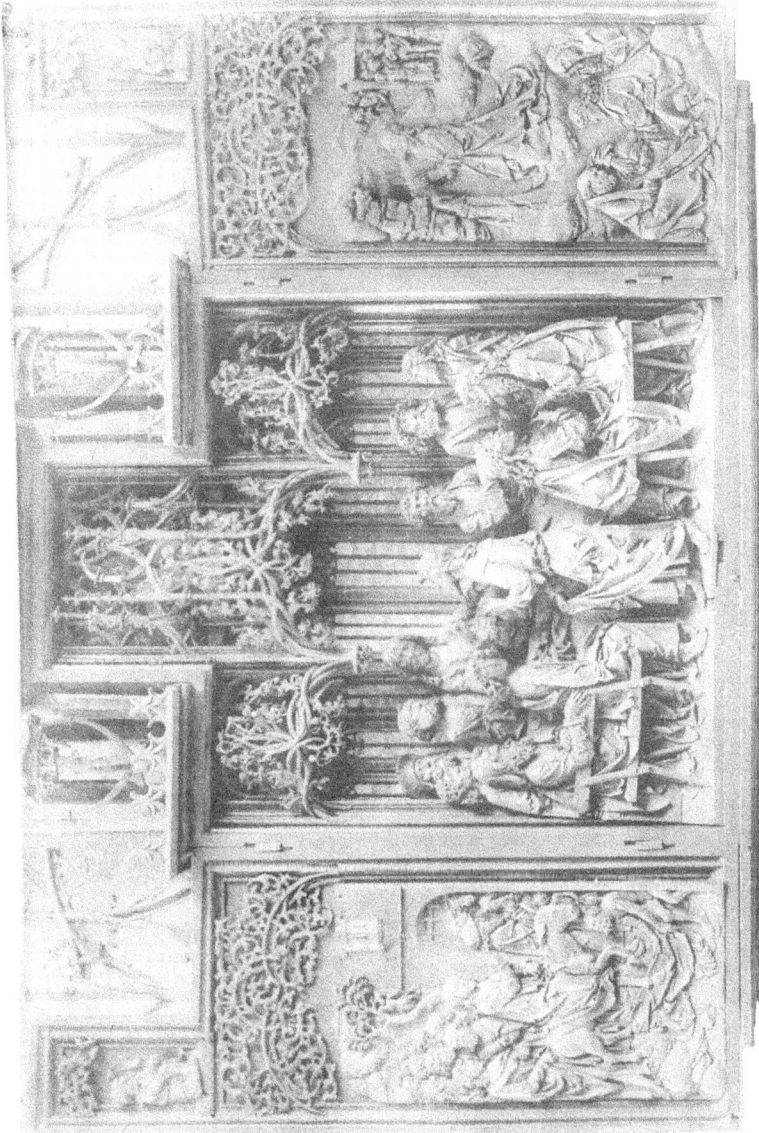

RETABLE OF THE ALTAR OF THE PRECIOUS BLOOD, BY RIEMENSCHNEIDER. FIFTEENTH CENTURY

JAKOBSKIRCHE, ROTHENBURG

PAGE 117

carving of the late Gothic period, the Kensington group, by whomever executed, is unsurpassed, and must be ranked among the masterpieces of the art. The figures are human beings, portraits, it may be said perhaps, from life models. The drapery no longer conceals the admirably posed figure and arms of the seated woman, and though we may regret the still somewhat *tormented* folds falling in veil-like form from the headdress, yet even these are masterpieces in that particular style. And above all to be remarked are the clean sharp-cut handling and precision of the chisel, the understanding and right use of the material, absolutely to be distinguished in this case from the technique of stone sculpture, and the wonderful treatment of the hands of St. Anne, to which, in wood, for their art, I can only compare those of the Nürnberg Madonna.

Comparisons have been made between this figure and the stone monument of the Countess Dorothea von Wertheim by Riemenschneider. There are analogies, it is true, in the form of headdress and in the drapery folds, but nothing could be less convincing by way of proof of the identity of the sculptor than the general feeling. The designer of the one, great as he might be according to older traditions, is still wedded to convention, with no sign that he has yet taken advantage of the new realism. The other has worked straight from nature. The question is, are they or can they be the same man?

A work more definitely characteristic of Riemenschneider's style, and in some ways a finer piece than the Creglingen retable, is the one known as the altar of the Precious Blood in the church of St. James at Rothenburg, in the Tauber valley (Plate x.). We need take the central group of figures alone—they are those of Our Lord and the Apostles at the Last Supper—and compare them, for example, with the twelve apostles of the Munich Museum. They are a little less than life size, very fine indeed in composition and in technical execution, and far outweigh in importance the low reliefs on the wings and the long spiny pinnacle work and other ornament characteristic of late German Gothic. Although of a different character from the scenic grouping of Flemish retables, the arrangement has a certain dramatic force, the naturalistic figures seemingly engaged in an animated conversation with Our Lord and with each other. There is an earnest solemnity in the figures of these men, all with that family likeness already remarked upon, the somewhat too large heads, the flowing curly hair, and all, except four, bearded. There is but one of a different type : a rounder, fuller, shaven face. The middle figure, standing in the foreground, and carrying a purse, of course is Judas. The exposed parts of the figures—the hands and feet—are of the best style, the draperies of soft thin stuffs, of the prevailing type and not exaggerated. In its intense naturalism this fine altarpiece may indeed be called truly representative of German work of the kind, of southern German or Suabian origin. From documentary evidence it may be confidently assigned to Riemenschneider, and we can be well content to accept it as an example of the best work of this class of his school. At the same time, in several other cases, there is no obligation to go further.

Still without positive authentication, and yet of even more value in the endeavour to lay down a type in which we may reasonably recognize the style of Riemenschneider not only as the wood was left by the chisel, but also with the full addition of colour and gilding, is a charming shrine with predella, in the Munich Museum (No. 1330), (Plate xi.). In the centre are three nearly life-sized statuettes, the Blessed Virgin, St. John the Baptist, and St. Sebastian. It is, of course, of no particular consequence that we

PLATE XI

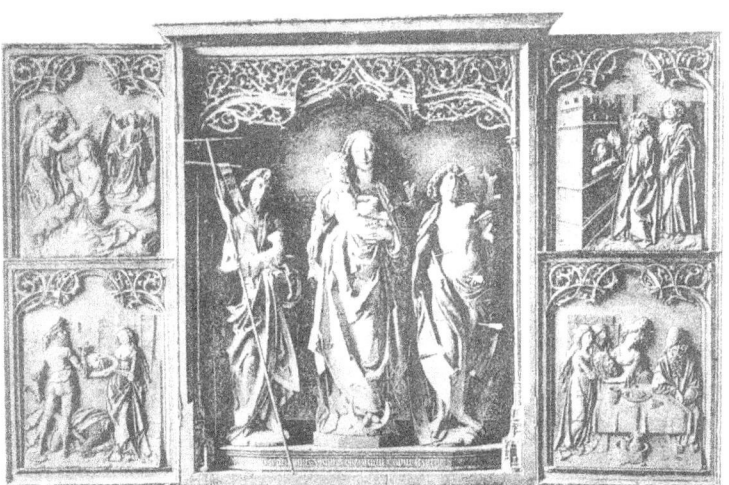

ALTARPIECE. GERMAN. FIFTEENTH CENTURY
MUNICH MUSEUM

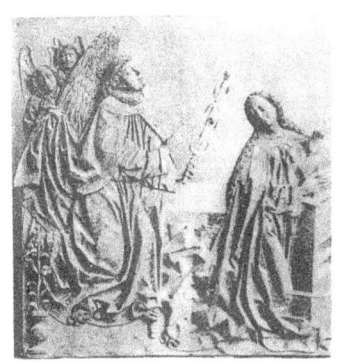 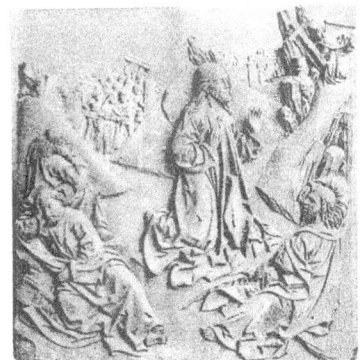

PANELS. ASCRIBED TO VEIT STOSS
MUNICH MUSEUM
PAGE 118

find them so grouped, and we may consider them as single figures. The wings have, in low relief, the subjects taken from Schongauer's and Dürer's engravings to which allusion has already been made: the baptism of Christ after Schongauer (Bartsch 8), the decollation after Dürer (Bartsch 126). In passing we may note the decapitated body of St. John Baptist clothed, as it were, in a curly *maillot* of hair, as we shall find presently the Magdalen in the Münnerstadt altarpiece. The Madonna statuette is of the style which we should wish to characterize as typical of Riemenschneider. Simple and unaffected, sweet in expression, smiling, with the grace and charm in their German way almost of an early French fourteenth-century Madonna group, both Mother and Child are of a refinement without mannerisms, that would be difficult to match in anything of the kind which has come down to us. All three figures would well bear more detailed description. They represent the religious art of Germany in the hands of a master born and nurtured in Gothic traditions at a period when many influences were at work, portending changes of an absolutely revolutionary character, and are in themselves standing evidences of the effect of these changes at the close of his career when the old order was so soon to be utterly and entirely displaced by the new. The date of the work can hardly be later than 1515.

We must pass by the third very fine altarpiece ascribed to Riemenschneider—that of the Holy Cross at Detwang, remarking only the crucifix as an example of his work of that kind, and come to the one of the parish church of Münnerstadt in the same neighbourhood. We have here a work which can be authenticated from the archives of the town, and one of Riemenschneider's earliest productions when he could hardly have been more than thirty—perhaps only twenty-five—years old. It is, in fact, the earliest of which there exists documentary evidence of date, and it is not altogether unimportant to note—in relation to the principal figure—that the freestone Eve of Würzburg cathedral is nearly contemporary. The altar is dedicated to St Mary Magdalen, and we seem to have in it the mixed histories of the Magdalen of the gospels, of Mary the sister of Lazarus, and the legend of the Penitent of the desert. Portions of this altarpiece were dispersed about a hundred years ago, and we shall only concern ourselves with the central figure now in the Munich Museum (Plate XII.). This is the Magdalen of Münnerstadt—a figure standing almost on tiptoe, with hands clasped, the face of the type which is, or should be, associated with Riemenschneider's Madonnas and women figures—for example, with the Assumption of Creglingen—long ringlets streaming over the shoulders, the body almost entirely clothed with a tight-fitting *maillot*, as it were, of silky curls, leaving only the bosoms, feet, and hands exposed. The idea is curious. It can hardly be asserted that at any period of his career there is evidence of intelligent study of Italian art or models on the part of the German sculptor. Yet this figure suggests, in pose and in the treatment of the limbs, the following of Italian influence : for instance, Donatello's John the Baptist in the Church of the Frari at Venice, or is to be compared with such a type as Benedetto da Majano's Magdalen. This last the Italian master presents as an aged emaciated figure, clothed in long flowing hair, with a suffering expression : the attitude and clasped hands, however, are similar. But the German Magdalen is plump, smiling, graceful, made up, as it were, in travesty. If devotional, the feeling is expressed in a different way, though one is not much surprised that in a later age those responsible for the Münnerstadt altarpiece considered the figure to be inappropriate, and caused it to be removed.

PLATE XII

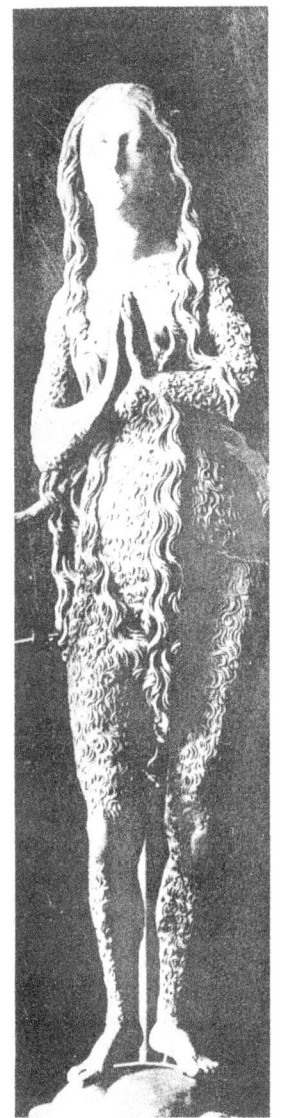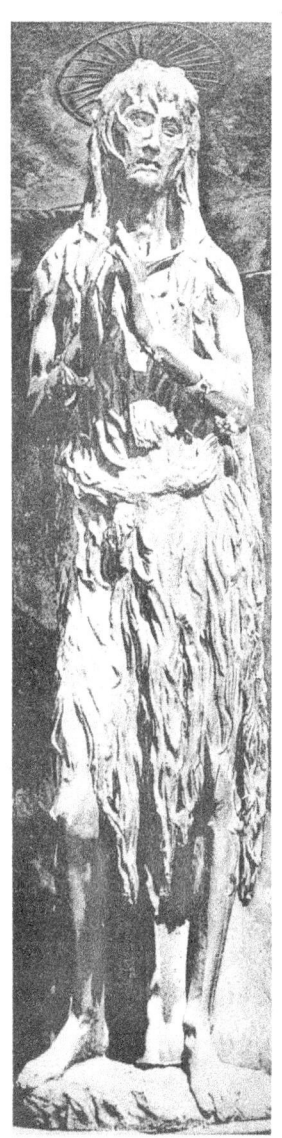

1. THE MAGDALEN OF MÜNNERSTADT, BY RIEMENSCHNEIDER
MUNICH MUSEUM
2. PENITENT MAGDALEN, BY DONATELLO
BAPTISTERY OF CATHEDRAL, FLORENCE
PAGES 120 - 256

RIEMENSCHNEIDER

The tombstone of Tillmann Riemenschneider was discovered in 1822 in the course of some reparations to the churchyard near the cathedral of Würzburg. The master is represented in his official costume as a member of the City Council. The inscription runs: 'Anno D^{ñi} MCCCCCXXXj am abent Kiliani starb der ersam und Kunstreich Tilmann Rimenschneider Bildhauer burger zu wurczburg dem got gnedig sey Amen.' Beneath is a shield on which is the sculptor's mark or cipher ✗

The so-called busts of Adam and Eve in the Victoria and Albert Museum seem to have been obtained about fifty years ago, and were then, and for many years after, said to be the work of Albert Dürer. Mr. Hungerford Pollen's official catalogue, published in 1874, which, however much out of date, still remains the only catalogue, or even list of the woodwork of the museum, says that these busts were 'probably executed from some sketch or drawing of Dürer, not by that artist himself, whose works of sculpture are exceedingly scarce.' It is hardly too much to say that forty years ago very little attention had been paid to German wood-carving, and such names as Riemenschneider and Meit were unknown, in England at least. Whether these small busts represent our first parents, and whether they are completed works in their present form, or fragments of full-length figures, will not affect our judgment that they are masterly in idea and execution to the highest degree. Both are represented in the first bloom of youth, Adam with an intense earnestness of expression, the eyes large and wide set, the contour of the face diminishing from the cheek-bones in a somewhat acute angle to the chin, the mouth and lips of the utmost delicacy of modelling, the chin dimpled, the ears partly showing under the thickly curling masses of hair which almost conceal the forehead.

There is a thoughtful, melancholy, almost worried expression. Clearly, here, there is Italian influence, and evidence of more than superficial knowledge and training. Yet there was reason in the early con-nexion (to call it no more) with Dürer: even Van Eyck, in these two figures, would not be so very far a cry. Eve, again, is a mere girl, hardly developed, sweet smiling, full of intelligence, her hair divided over the forehead and gathered in a great twist round the head, the eyes and mouth those of a twin sister to Adam. In the modelling and general treatment of eyes, eyebrows, and lips, there is, notwithstanding, a curious divergence which cannot be passed over in the argument.

These two most important works are now labelled as by Riemenschneider, and it must be allowed that at the present time this ascription has received almost universal acceptance. But for those who have carefully studied not only what we have documen-tary evidence to justify us in giving to him, but also the disputed works such as the Eve of the Louvre, the Creglingen altarpiece, or the Anna and Joachim group, surely the grounds for this judgment must be far to seek. Should we not find, on the contrary, much which would seem conclusively to show that though we may, almost in desperation, look around for some master with which to connect them and fail to find him, the name of Riemenschneider is not the one which, without any hesitation, springs to the lips? What work, indeed, that we know to be by him is to be selected to be placed beside these busts for comparison? The very material—pearwood—from which they are carved is one which, at the least, would have been unusual with him, and contrary to his general style. His work is nearly always in oak or limewood, and one would think that we should look rather for the artist amongst the class of his contemporaries who were

PLATE XIII

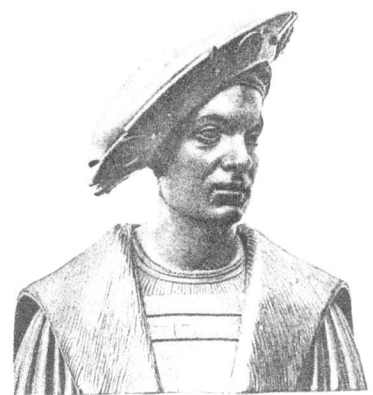 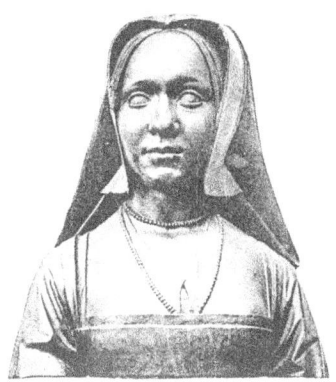

1. PORTRAIT BUSTS. BOXWOOD. SIXTEENTH CENTURY
BRITISH MUSEUM

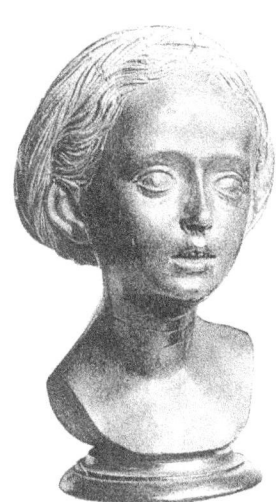 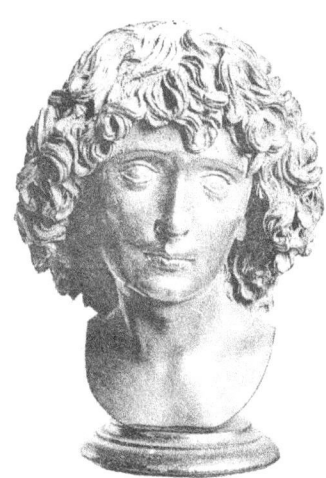

2. BUSTS. PEARWOOD. GERMAN. SIXTEENTH CENTURY
VICTORIA AND ALBERT MUSEUM
PAGES 122, 156

PLATE XIV

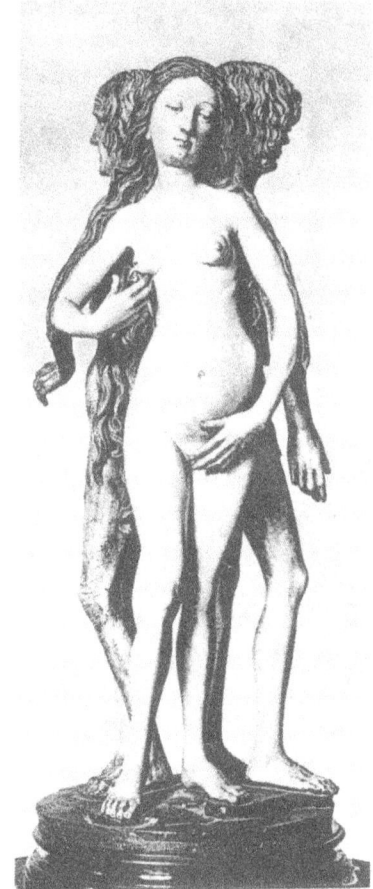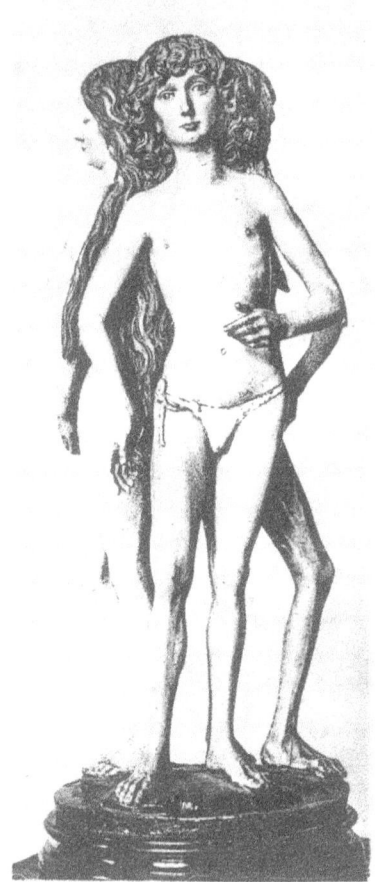

GROUP. "*DIE VERGÄNGLICHKEIT.*" ("FLEETING LIFE") OR "*JUGEND, SCHÖNHEIT, UND HÄSSLICHKEIT*"
(" YOUTH, BEAUTY AND UGLINESS ")
POLYCHROMED. SIXTEENTH CENTURY, SCULPTOR UNKNOWN. AMBRAS COLLECTION, IMPERIAL MUSEUM, VIENNA
PAGE 124

connected with the goldsmiths—the Meits or Ludwig Krugs. It is difficult indeed to appear to differ when so much unanimity seems to prevail. So lately even as 1906 these busts were lent to the exhibition of the Burlington Fine Arts Club and were there ascribed to Riemenschneider. Yet, we may still be permitted to hold a contrary opinion, and in a case of this importance to express it. For my own part, while I feel that I have no alternative name to offer, even as a suggestion, I am totally unable to see the same feeling, the same style or handling, much less so great a talent, in the sculptor of the Magdalen, of the Creglingen altarpiece, of the Munich apostles—even of the Anna and Joachim group—as in these busts. They belong to a different age: to a movement, at least, with which there is no evidence to show that Riemenschneider was connected, or even sympathetic.

At one time it seemed to be the fashion to attribute any kind of fine figure work to Riemen-schneider. Even so long ago as 1857, before the days of illustration by photography, when Ausm' Weerth published his fine work *Denkmäler des christlichen Altherthums in den Rheinlanden*, the wonderful group of coloured figures known as the 'Vergänglichkeit' in the Imperial Museum, Vienna, was ascribed to him, and we may take it here under his name. It is an allegory or personification of 'Fleeting Life'—perhaps, rather, a 'Memento Mori'—designed to impress upon us the vanities of human existence. Dances of death, whether single figures or in groups, were favourite subjects in late Gothic times: for example, amongst other celebrated series, the painting by Hans Baldung (1476-1545), in which is represented a young girl nude, an old woman, and Death. In the 'Vergänglichkeit' (Plate XIV.) we have three nude figures standing back to back: a youth, a girl in her full beauty, and a decrepit old woman, marked with all the infirmities of age, even to realistic and repulsive details of flies crawling over her yellow shrunken skin, and other horrors. It is a masterpiece by an artist with consummate knowledge of the treatment of the nude : of such training and practice in the antique as we have no reason to believe fell to the lot of Riemenschneider. His school had been rather that of Gothic traditions, dying out, no doubt, towards the end of his life, but, still, more tenaciously adhered to in Germany than anywhere else. The unknown carver is more likely a Renaissance master of a considerably later date. We have in it realism at its highest, yet not such absolute following of nature, as with less consummate art is pushed to extremes by Wydyz, Daucher, and others, in their small figures and panels for caskets in boxwood, pearwood, and honestone, which are frequent in mid-sixteenth century work. The Vergänglichkeit group is fully coloured, and is still in the original leather case in which it was enclosed when acquired from the Augustinian collegiate church of St. Florian in Upper Austria, having an opening through which each figure of the group, turning on a pivot, could be exposed in turn. The ascription to Riemenschneider would seem to have arisen in one of those haphazard ventures or guesses, started one scarcely knows how, or by whom, which by repetition in course of time acquires authority. If it rests on anything at all, it might be on some fancied resemblance to the Eve of Würzburg, but this is of quite another type of art. It is suggestive also to notice that Tönnies, in his monograph on Riemenschneider, thinks both this group and the Adam and Eve busts to be by the same hand. Equally contentious as to origin, and similarly ascribed to Riemenschneider, on account of a certain resemblance to the type of some of his Madonnas, or of his Magdalen, is the Eve of the Louvre. There is, of course, a striking analogy in form and expression of the face, in the

PLATE XV

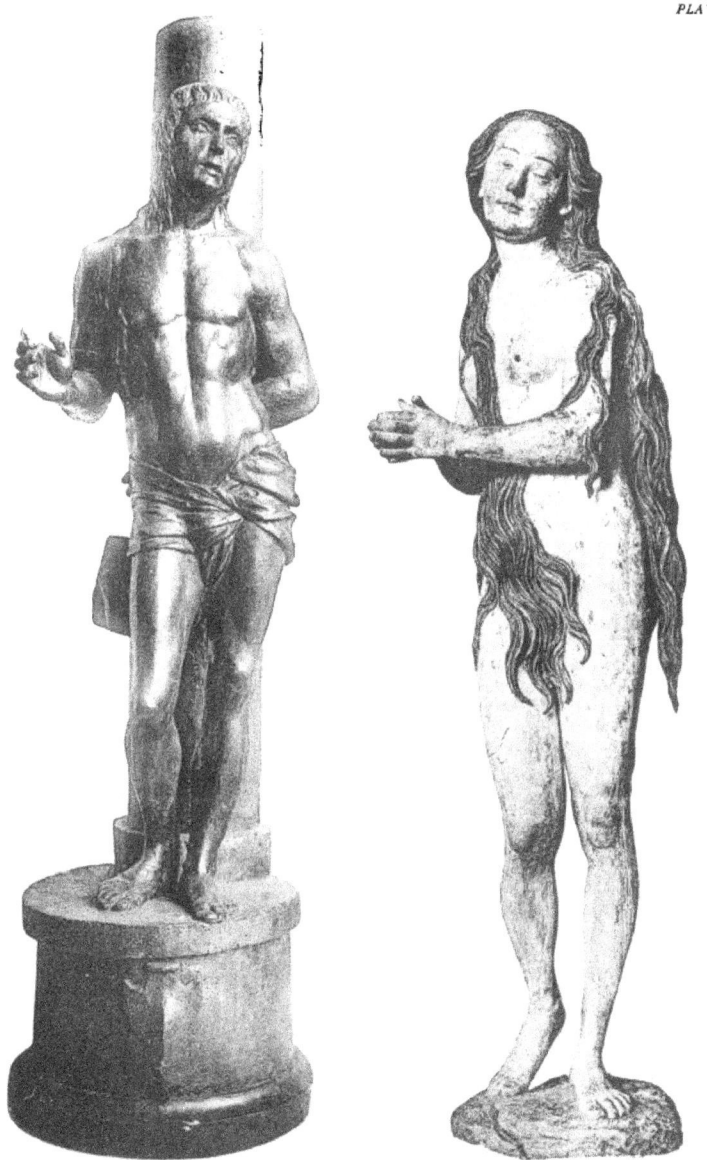

1. ST. SEBASTIAN. ATTRIBUTED TO CRISTOFORO FOPPA
VICTORIA AND ALBERT MUSEUM
2. EVE. POLYCHROMED FIGURE. ATTRIBUTED TO RIEMENSCHNEIDER
LOUVRE MUSEUM
PAGES 135 - 258

PLATE XVI

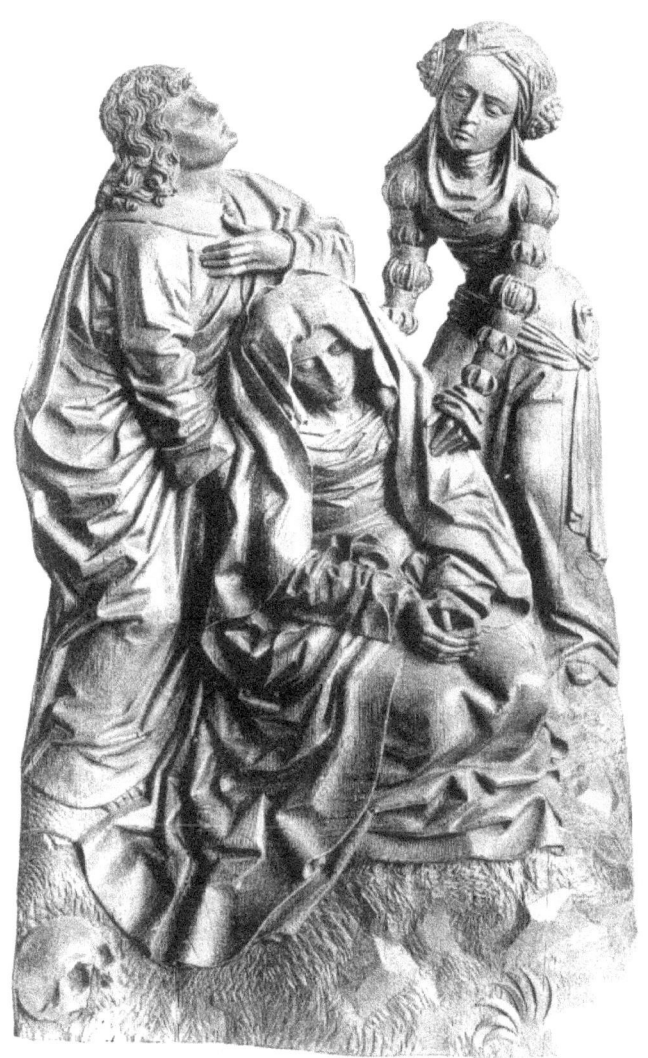

treatment of the long flowing hair in long wavy separate strands, and to a certain extent the anatomy. Yet, while it is by no means unreasonable to accept the ascription to Riemenschneider, we may remember that the type or model was a favourite one with others of his school. Besides, as a work of art, the Eve in wood is greatly superior to his Eve in stone. Entirely German, of the school, and with some of the mannerisms of that school, of the Magdalen, it is much nearer in refinement and elegance to the level of the Vergänglichkeit group. Equally with the latter it is coloured, and it is right to say that the reproduction here given is, on this account, faulty. By Daun, this Eve has been given with certainty to Veit Stoss. He finds the style of Stoss in the prominent chin, the short neck, the thick upper lip, the nose, the eyebrows ; and analogies to other carvings, and in etchings, by the Nürnberg artist. It is not easy to follow him here. On the contrary Veit Stoss would seem to be the farthest removed of any sculptor of the time that could be selected.

There are two groups in the Salting collection of the Victoria and Albert Museum ascribed to Riemen-schneider, one of which is here reproduced (Plate xvi.).

For many characteristics of the Franconian schools of the latter part of the fifteenth century, we may refer back to an earlier wood-carver of the Bavarian or Austrian Tyrol, Michael Pacher of Bruneck. Exactly how far and how much of the development of the art of the Nürnberg and Suabian masters may be traced to his influence would be difficult to lay down with precision. He is the master and leader, rather, of the art of the more southern districts of Upper Bavaria and of the Tyrol. It is necessary to pass quickly over all these German altarpieces, although every village church, almost, possesses them, together with single figures which, if not in every case of the highest art, have considerable attraction from their quaintness and originality. The National Museum at Munich has, of course, an admirable collection of the finest examples. Little is known of the history of Michael Pacher. Born at Bruneck in the Pusterthal, about 1430-1440, he flourished probably about the middle of the fifteenth century, and died at Salzburg in 1498. Both painter and sculptor, he is most generally recognized as a master in the former art. Living near Italy it was natural that he should be influenced by the Italian, and especially the Venetian schools of painting, and this influence may be, to a certain extent, traceable in his carved wood. Still, in this, it is not very marked, and he remains distinctly German. Amongst other famous altar-pieces by Michael Pacher, the most remarkable is the one made for the church at St. Wolfgang in 1477. Indeed, it is in many ways unsurpassed by any others in the empire. Pacher, as already mentioned, was in the first place a great painter, and in this piece his talents in both directions are admirably conjoined. He loved rich colouring, rich garments, crowns and jewelled ornaments, and we have all these in profusion. The subject is the Coronation of the Virgin, or perhaps rather her reception in the heavenly kingdom. Mary kneels, with crown on head, before the Almighty, Himself crowned, robed, and throned as an earthly potentate, the right hand raised in blessing, the left resting on an orb. The Blessed Virgin herself wears a golden mantle with a long train in voluminous folds, treated with the mannerism which is characteristic of the time. Her head, already crowned with a gorgeous crown, is modestly bent and inclined to one side. The large single figures on the right and left are St. Wolfgang, patron of the town, and St. Benedict, who is represented as a mitred abbot bearing a crosier, and holding in one hand the poisoned chalice. The mitre, of course, is by artistic licence. Around, in a magnifi-

126

PLATE XVII

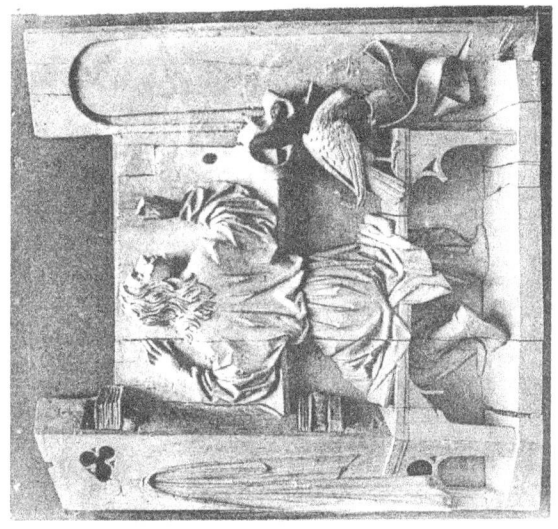

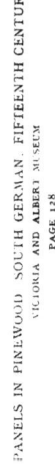

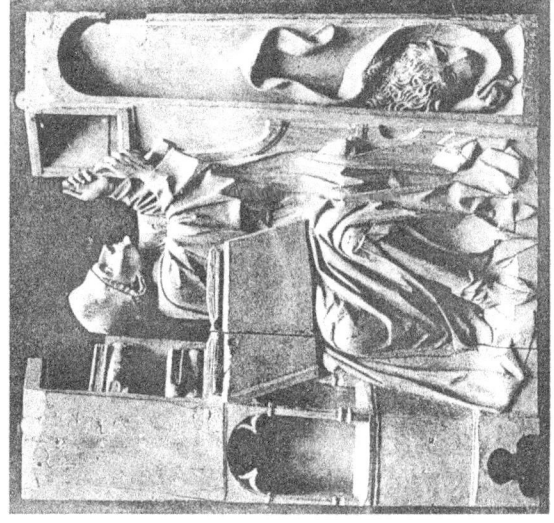

PANELS IN PINEWOOD SOUTH GERMAN FIFTEENTH CENTURY
VICTORIA AND **ALBERT** MUSEUM
PAGE 128

cent setting of pinnacled architectural work, with rich pendentives, are numerous figures of angels, floating here and there in the air, singing and playing on musical instruments, and joyously acclaiming the solemn spectacle which represents the last of the glorious mysteries of the Rosary. It is, however, hardly a perspective composition, but rather the usual grouping of single figures. Yet this is done with dramatic effect, far more masterly in arrangement than are so many of the later Franconian altarpieces.

For Pacher's art as a painter, and for other details of his sculptured work, I cannot do better than refer the reader to the admirable series of articles by M. Auguste Marguillier in the *Gazette des Beaux Arts* (3ᵉᵐᵉ pér. tom xi. 1894). Until recent years almost unknown, he is entitled to a high place amongst the masters of the old German schools. To establish this claim it should almost suffice to name the panel with the 'Circumcision' of the altarpiece of St. Wolfgang. Others, of lesser merit, in the same work, were formerly attributed to Wohlgemut, but now to the master's brother, Friedrich, and other assistants. In the Pinacothek of Munich, at Innsbruck, and at Augsburg, more, again, may be studied. For sculpture, the archives of the town of Gries record the contract made with Pacher in 1471 to carve a retable for the church, which was 'to be useful, precious and complete,' representing the Coronation of the B.V.M. and other subjects, with numerous figures and busts of saints. This one is in similar style, though not so elaborate, to that at St. Wolfgang. The latter also is of very large dimensions, measuring about 36 feet in height by 21 in width when the wings are opened. It is a noble work of a master in painting, in architecture, and in sculpture.

The altarpiece at Schwabach by Veit Stoss, or at least executed under his direction in Wohlgemut's workshop, has already been noticed. Dissociating in each case the question of painting, this work bears so remarkable a resemblance to that at St. Wolfgang, especially as regards the central subject, which is an almost absolute copy, that the merit of the Nürnberg work must be considerably discounted. Even as a copy it lacks Pacher's refinement and evidence of training in the best schools of painting.

In the Victoria and Albert Museum are four panels of pinewood, which, according to the labels of forty or fifty years ago, are of Pacher's school. The most, perhaps, that can be said, is that they are representative of those southern mountainous districts of the Bavarian and Austrian Tyrol where the art of wood-carving has ever found, as it finds to-day at Ober-Ammergau, a congenial home. They are quaintly pictorial, these four evangelists, and in somewhat high relief, each seated at his work, in his study as it were, in his own homely surroundings, even though these details be contemporary with those familiar to the artist. Here they sit on their benches, their backs turned partly to the spectator, their books on little shelves in alcoves above them, engaged in one way or another, all with every air of naturalness, which is most charming. St. John sits almost upright, the face in profile, his arms raised and elbows leaning on the desk, as he mends his pen, the legs in easy attitudes seen beneath the bench. But I see nothing to lead us to attach to these panels the name of Michael Pacher, or his influence.

Hans Multscher of the Upper Suabian school is a still earlier master of wood-carving, and again a painter of great merit. There is a considerable collection of his wood sculpture in the Lorenzkapelle at Rottweil, whither it was brought from the Capuchin church at Wurmlingen in 1851. Unfortunately we are in the same condition of ignorance concerning his life as confronts us in the case of so many other

128

PLATE XVIII

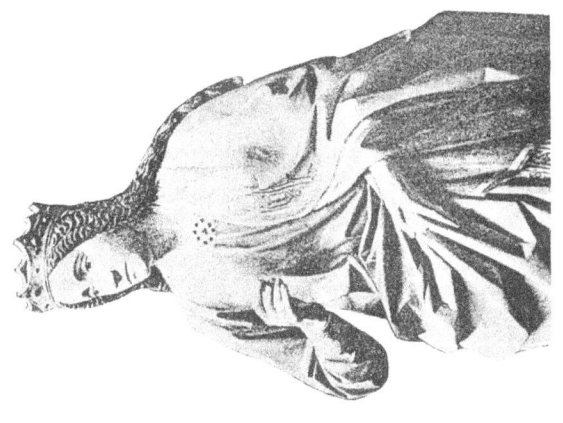
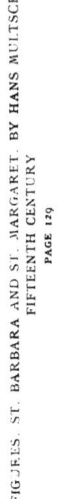
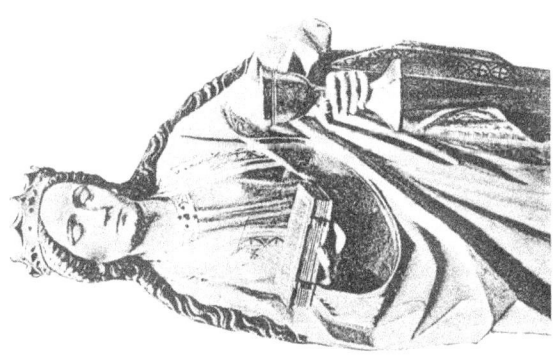

FIG. JE.E5. ST. BARBARA AND ST. MARGARET. BY HANS MULTSCHER.
FIFTEENTH CENTURY

PAGE 129

HANS MULTSCHER

German wood sculptors of the period. From scanty information we may glean that, besides his reputation as a painter, he was famous also for his work in wood and stone. The great altarpiece of the Frauenkirche at Sterzing in the Tyrol is by him, and the curious group in wood of our Lord riding on the ass, at one time in St. Ulrich's Convent at Augsburg, is connected with his name. The latter subject is one very frequently found in German fourteenth-century wood-sculpture. Two illustrations of Multscher's figure work are here given; the Saint Barbara and Saint Margaret of the church at Sterzing (Plate XVIII.). We have no positive evidence, it is true, that Multscher was a painter of pictures. Of his work there is nothing authentic except in sculpture. In 1433 he made an altar for the cathedral of Ulm, of which, however, but little now remains. His figures are in general of a different character from the stern, austere type of the later Gothic period. The women are of more mature age, yet shapely, attractive, and unaffected. Multscher was certainly a master of his craft, and as we have comparatively so little of the Suabian schools of wood sculpture of the early fifteenth century, the collection at Rottweil is particularly valuable. But it must suffice to call strong attention to it, without considering it in detail.

So also with other remarkable examples by unknown late Gothic sculptors of the Upper Bavarian schools. In particular, the very fine statues of Our Lord, the Blessed Virgin, and of the Twelve Apostles in the Klosterkirche of Blutenburg. One of these, that of the Madonna, is perhaps as fine as anything in wood of the period, which could be brought forward. It has technically considerable analogy with, and artistically may stand as high as the Madonna of the Nürnberg Museum.

The last-named famous figure is perhaps better

known, and has exacted more admiration, at least of a popular kind, than any other example of mediæval wood-carving. We can give it no name but that of the Nürnberg Madonna; we are absolutely in the dark with regard to its origin. But it must be said also that not only has speculation been baffled concerning the unknown sculptor whose creation it is, but there exist also some differences of opinion as to the measure of art which may be claimed for it. Nor can we be certain even with regard to the subject: whether, indeed, it is a figure of the Madonna at all; and if we may take it so to be, whether it is the Virgin of one of the joyful mysteries, of the glorious, or of the sorrowful ones. For according as it may impress us, we may have here the Virgin of the Annunciation, or of the Assumption, or—in the calmness and happy joy of resignation—of the sorrowing mother at the foot of the cross. Few, indeed, will hesitate to accept it as one of the two figures, the other being St. John, which were so invariable and universal accompaniments to the rood figures in every country. But so different may be the effects produced on different minds, that while some see in the expression of the face a happy, joyful expectation, the statue has long been known in Germany as the *Schmerzensmutter*—the Mater Dolorosa. Are, then, the eyes ecstatically joyful, with the tenderness of love fulfilled, or are they almost overflowing with suppressed tears, betraying an unspoken lament, which asks for no consolation? Is it the Magnificat, or the theme of the Stabat Mater, that is expressed by those clasped, uplifted hands which, in their exquisite modelling, are in themselves masterpieces, and evidences of a craftsman to whom not one of those with whom we have dealt, and no unknown sculptor of existing woodwork of the period can compare? Bode in his early work on German sculpture, published in 1885, was of opinion that, although the place of origin of

130

PLATE XIX

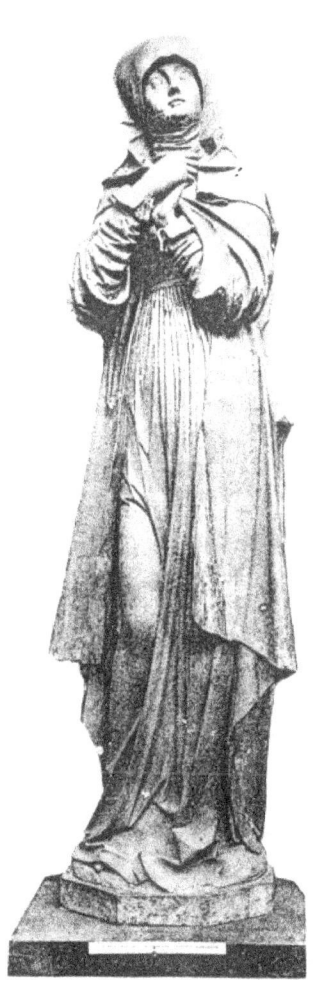 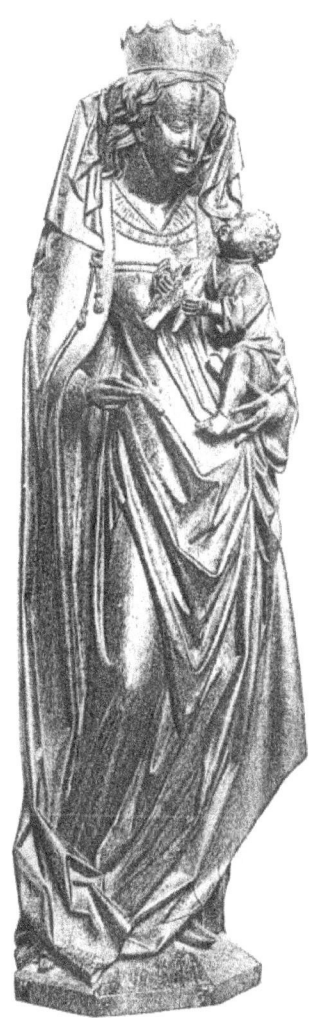

1. THE MADONNA OF NÜRNBERG. SIXTEENTH CENTURY. SCULPTOR UNKNOWN
GERMAN MUSEUM, NÜRNBERG
2. MADONNA. RHENISH. FIFTEENTH CENTURY
LOUVRE MUSEUM
PAGE 130

this figure was said to be Gnadenberg in the Palatinate, the impress of the Nürnberg school of the sixteenth century is too strong to be doubtful. We may be content with this. At the same time the question may not be altogether unworthy of consideration, Is it even German? Admirers of every Nürnberg sculptor of note have striven to claim, for the particular object of their study, the credit of this work. Adam Krafft the stone sculptor, Peter Vischer the bronze founder, the master of the Blutenburg Madonna, the master of the Pietà of the Jakobskirche in Nürnberg, Veit Stoss, of course, and perhaps even Riemenschneider, have each in turn found their advocates. We cannot now stay to consider all these claims and the arguments upon which they are founded. Not infrequently, after the manner of German minute research, an analogy will be found, and driven to a conclusion, in a resemblance to some isolated detail of drapery or attitude: for example, in the figure of the lady in the sixth of Veit Stoss's Commandment plaques. And if, on the one hand, the enthusiasm of eminent critics has been aroused, on the other we meet now and then with terms of disparagement which do not err on the side of moderation. Daun (and M. Louis Réau follows him) quarrels with the proportions of the figure and with certain mannerisms. Daun holds that the figure is too lank, the head and face much too small, that according to the canons of art the normal figure is $7\frac{1}{2}$ heads long, and this Madonna almost 9; the shoulders are too small, the undeveloped bosom too high, the hip-joint too high, and so on. We need not go too deeply into these points, but as to proportions generally: in the first place, the intended position of the figure has to be taken into consideration. If it is one of a rood group, it would probably have been placed at a considerable height. Vasari distinctly lays down that when statues are to be in a high position, and there is not much space below to allow one to go far enough off to view them at a distance, they must be made one head, or two, taller. And even without these conditions innumerable instances in statuary and painting could be cited, in which the proportions are equally exaggerated. The canons of art in this regard are not rigid and invariable. As Flaubert says, 'the conception of any work of art carries within it its own rule.' (*Chaque œuvre a sa poétique en soi, qu'il faut trouver.*) And Dürer, that while the artist must in no ways abate what is essential to truth, neither must he lay what is intolerable upon nature. But here there is surely nothing intolerable, but an added grace and charm, and in another place in the great German master's discourses on proportion we learn that departures from rule are variations such as the artist specially intends, so long as one deviates without having the air of monstrosities or negligence. Almost all the older writers have discoursed on the proportions of the human figure. Vitruvius's proportion was eight heads as the extreme limit for a normal adult. But many artists make the figure nine heads high, thus: for throat and neck, $\frac{1}{2}$; chin to top of forehead, 1; torso, 3; pit of throat to shoulder, 1; arm to wrist, 3; instep to sole, $\frac{1}{2}$. Far greater exaggerations are frequent in painting. To take but one haphazard, a reproduction of which lies before me as I write, a St. Ursula group by Antonio Vivarini in the seminary of St. Angelo at Brescia. Here the Ursula is no less than eleven heads high, and the attendant virgins are almost as disproportionate. And again, in later times, it would be superfluous to point to the example of Michael Angelo. All this is of course among the commonplaces of art, and though perhaps but superficially stated here, may be of interest to those to whom it is not familiar in relation to the present example. It was through no ignorance, nor, on the other hand,

PLATE XX

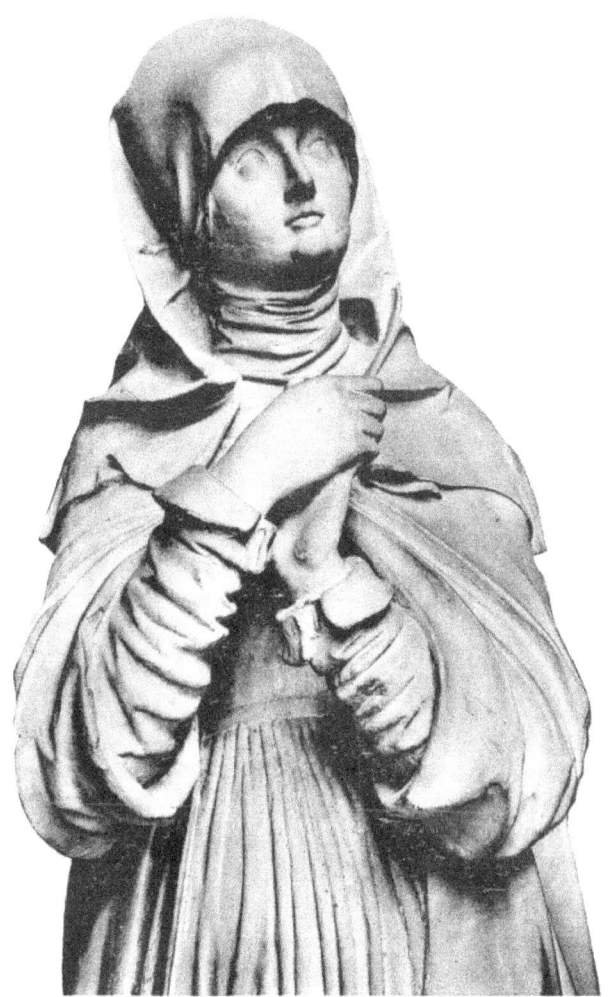

THE MADONNA OF NÜRNBERG FIFTEENTH CENTURY
NÜRNBERG MUSEUM
FROM THE CAST IN THE VICTORIA AND ALBERT MUSEUM
PAGE 132

from an abuse of licence, that the artist chose to present to us as he did this admirable figure. He wished to produce on our minds a certain emotional effect, and he instinctively, if at the same time with intention, followed what his imagination dictated to him. Reconstruct the Nürnberg Madonna according to the most restricted canons. Would it then have continued to extort admiration as it has done? To find fault with it on these grounds is the cheapest of criticisms. A second objection, upon which Daun is somewhat contemptuously strong, is the protuberance of the figure, accentuated, as it is, by the position in which it stands. But this is due to a common fashion of the time, beloved by artists: comparable to the exaggerated twist which, whether or not derived from the curve of an ivory tusk, was so much affected in sculpture and in painting in the thirteenth and fourteenth centuries. One might as well condemn the Van Eyck in our National Gallery—the so-called Arnolfini and his wife. And again, what if the figure does not declare plainly its meaning, or bear the same message to all? And even if we accept that we are to connect it with a *Schmerzensmutter*—a rood figure—an acquaintance with German art of the period would show that the expression of the mother's grief was not always painfully exhibited. We need only go for an illustration of this to the great master who, we may well imagine, inspired the author of this figure. We may take, for instance, Dürer's series of the *Sieben Schmerzen* in the Dresden gallery. The Nürnberg Madonna will need but little defence for the readers for whom these remarks are written. For my own part, I am free to confess that I cannot easily rid myself of early impressions produced when I first saw it, removed from Nürnberg to the exhibition of German art at Munich in 1876. A word more may be added with regard to the character of the drapery. This is certainly a departure, and a welcome one, from the prevailing style of the period. It is a harking back to older and better traditions. We feel ourselves rather in the atmosphere of the Italian trecento, from which this sane system, as we shall find it in French art in wood of the fifteenth century, such as the statue of N.D. des Ardents in the Cluny Museum was derived ; in many more, also, in wood, which may be remembered in the exhibition of French primitives at Paris in 1904, and we shall find it where we might be inclined to find also if not the same sculptor, at least one whose art was similar if not greater, in the Blutenburg Madonna figure already mentioned.

There is one more group whose connexion with the Nürnberg Madonna would appear to be unmistakable. This is the Pietà of the Jakobskirche in Nürnberg, which is supposed to be the work of Veit Stoss. Without accepting this, we must not omit to notice the judgment of Doctor Bode in his history of German sculpture (1885 edition), when he says that the relationship between the Madonna and the Pietà is so great that they must be the work of one and the same master. The head of the Virgin is in both almost the same: the large, fine, expressive eyes, the full lips, the arrangement of the veil are repeated, and no question can remain that the statue is a Madonna and no other saint. But the known authenticated work of Veit Stoss ought surely to place beyond doubt the idea that it was in any way likely that he could either have conceived or executed either of these two works. I cannot admit the possibility. It remains to be noted that both the group and the statuette have been for many years painted a dull olive green. Whether originally polychromed or not, or what was the character of the colouring, we have now no means of knowing. It is to be hoped that the attempt will never be made to add anything of the

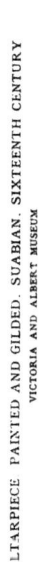

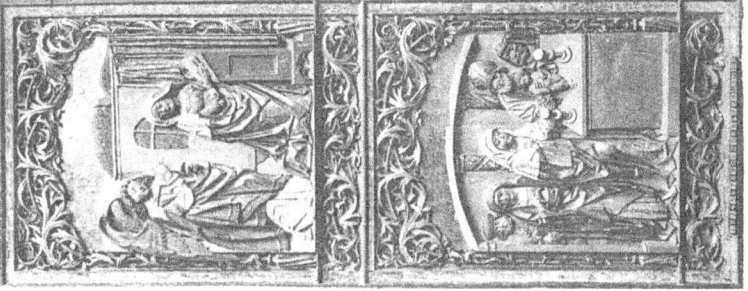

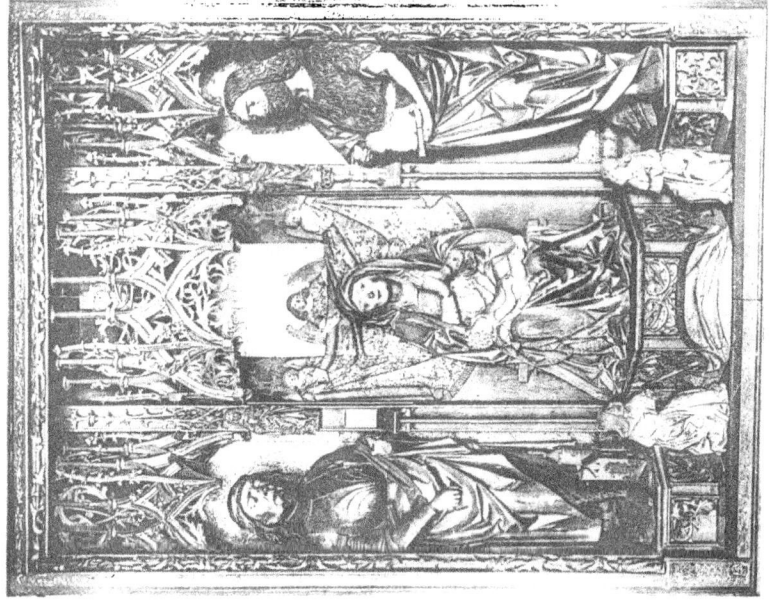

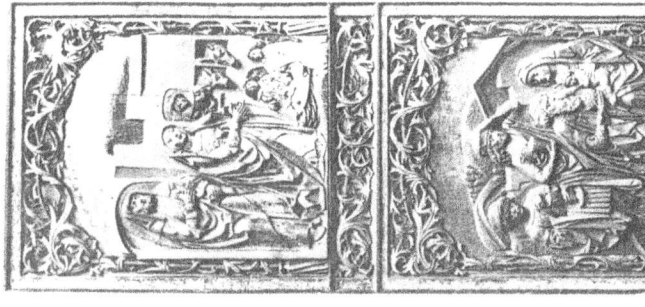

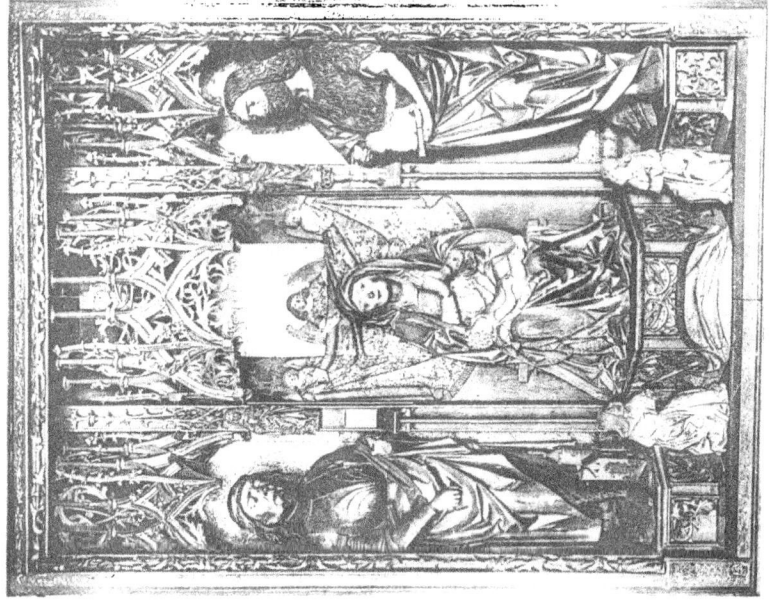

PLATE XXI

ALTARPIECE PAINTED AND GILDED. SUABIAN. SIXTEENTH CENTURY

VICTORIA AND ALBERT MUSEUM

PAGE 136

kind. Reproductions of all sizes of the Madonna abound, in various materials, for the most part libellous; but even when from moulds taken direct from the figure itself they are not entirely successful, neither is any photograph. The earliest history we have of the figure, which is probably of limewood, is that it was about the year 1829 in the Kaiserkapelle of Nürnberg, whence it was removed in 1876 to the Town Hall. It is supposed that it came originally from the church of the Dominican order dispersed in 1807, and was restored—if one may use the term—and painted with a uniform coating of green in 1825.

The number of altarpieces, groups, and single figures in wood throughout Germany is enormous. The quality no doubt is mixed, and many possess little merit. There are, however, not a few—and we should naturally expect to find this to be the case at such a period of artistic activity—that demand especial notice. We cannot, of course, in a book which is not confined to German art in wood, follow them all. A few brief remarks must suffice for some others. Among the altarpieces, those to be found in the more northerly divisions, strongly influenced by the art of the Netherlands, and themselves transmitting this influence to the rest of the empire, have been perforce omitted in favour of the more original and national art of the southern provinces. Calcar and Xanten were centres of industry in this kind of work, and if we were concerned with lists of distinguished names we should include the altarpieces of Loedewick, Bogaert, and many others. At Lübeck, wood-carving is richly represented by innumerable magnificent examples of sculpture in wood. Amongst them, and again at Güstrow and at Danzig, we find the fine work of the Flemish master Jan Borman of Brussels, the wings of his altarpieces painted by his compatriot Barend van Orley. The Flemish and Dutch influences here and in the Calcar neighbourhood are strong, both of sculptors and painters. Still further north, on the shores of the Baltic, we have what is considered by some to be one of the finest pieces of woodwork of the kind in Germany. This is the great altarpiece in carved oak by Hans Brüggemann made in 1521 for the Klosterkirche at Bordesholm, and now in the cathedral at Schleswig. As separate compositions, the central group of the Crucifixion and the fourteen or fifteen lesser panels, crowded with figures in full relief, are astonishing in their animated arrangement and dramatic force. The pity is that they are framed in a setting of niggling and commonplace cut-work tracery and distorted architectural motives which one can hardly conceive to be from the same hand. Probably they were not, and with the single figures—our Lord in Majesty, Adam and Eve, a Madonna, an angel with a pillar and another with a cross—are of even later date. At least, they foreshadow the rococo which later on invaded the land and are hardly worth serious consideration. We shall not stay to consider how far Brüggemann was indebted to Flemish teaching for his art. Certainly the central group of this altarpiece, with its many groups in a kind of stereoscopic perspective, of which there is a cast in white plaster in the Kensington Museum, follows its best traditions, and is admirable in arrangement and in execution. In Suabia altarpieces of another character abound. As we are forced to summarize, it will be best to take for this type and to illustrate the great painted and gilded triptychs acquired by the South Kensington Museum so long ago as 1859 (Plates XXI. and XXII.). Of the early part of the sixteenth century, the first consists of a central panel and two wings. The principal subject is the Virgin with the Infant seated under a canopy of late German Gothic style. On one side of her is a figure

PLATE XXII

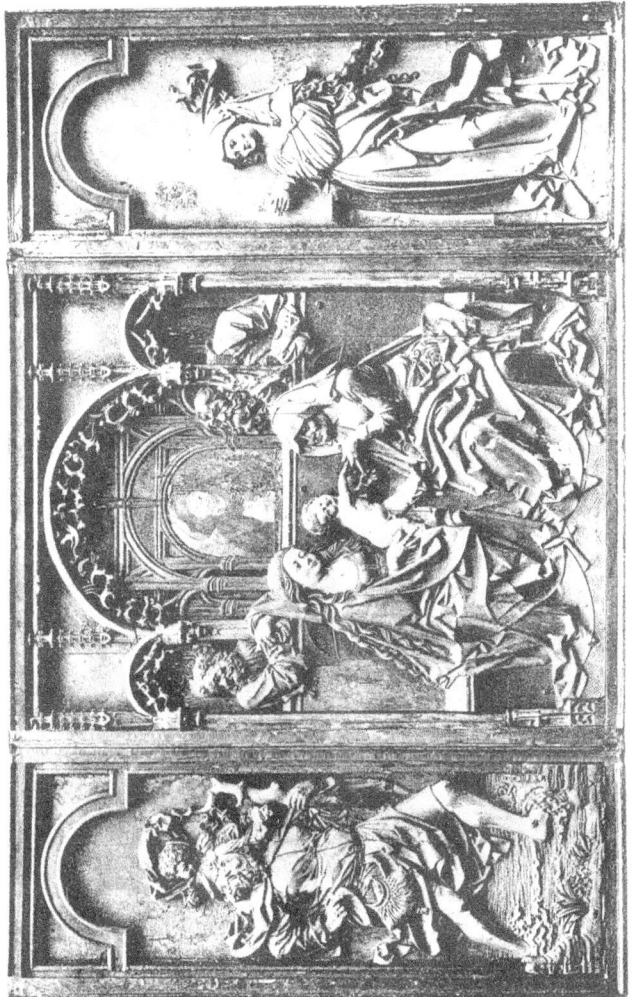

ALTARPIECE. SUABIAN. FIFTEENTH CENTURY

VICTORIA AND ALBERT MUSEUM

PAGE 137

of St. John, on the other, another, perhaps a local saint, and on the wings, in low relief, four subjects in the life of Our Lord and His mother. In the second example (Plate XXII.), we have in the central compartment a Holy Family group with SS. Anne, Joseph, and Joachim : on one wing is St. Christopher, on the other St. Mary Magdalen. The whole is in very high relief, very thickly coated with gesso, painted and heavily gilded and burnished. In another the central part represents, with almost life-sized figures, scenes from the life of Saint Margaret, all elaborately coloured and very thickly gilded. Generally speaking, nothing could be more representative of the religious taste and feeling of the time : the homeliness and peasant type of the figures and accessories, the simple innocence and absence of any idea of a great art fitted for the requirements of princes and nobles, at the same time giving the best and richest to the church, the quaint treatment, the details of the martyrdom, the valuable information to be gained concerning the costumes and manners and customs of the time—all this, and more, is of infinite charm and attraction in such pieces for those who will take the trouble to examine them.

Of Suabian origin, of mid-fifteenth century, by masters under Flemish influence, and followers of Van der Weyden and the Flemish schools of painting, are such altarpieces as those ascribed to Friedrich Herlin in the Jakobskirche at Rothenburg, at Dunkersbuhl and Bopfingen, to Hans Schülein or Schüchlin (1469) at Tiefenbronn, and many magnificent ones in the cathedral of Ulm and in the neighbouring provinces. Space, however, cannot now be spared to consider these and such other typical ones, in the arrangement of the statuary figures and busts placed amongst the somewhat eccentrically treated late Gothic architectural work, as we find, for example, in the great altarpiece of the Kilianskirche at Heilbronn, in the Tauberland. Of a more northerly school, if indeed we are justified in ascribing the production to Saxony, it would be difficult to pass without mention the fine Pietà group in the Marienkirche of Zwickau. In any case, there is more than a little suggestion of its connexion with the Würzburg and Franconian schools, as must be said also of the High-altar piece in the same church, of an earlier date, and from Wohlgemut's workshop. The Pietà is, of course, a fragment of a crucifixion group, the Mother weeping over the body of the dead Christ, just taken down from the cross. The Italian inspiration, from Mantegna perhaps, can hardly be doubtful, altered for German feeling and the taste of the time. We need not be asked to admire the exaggerated treatment of the drapery, in which the German artist saw a decorative beauty of arrangement. As in so many other examples, the predilection for this style shows clearly that this was its object rather than any idea of truth to nature. Even in the drapery of the loincloth of a crucifix figure, the sculptor, the painter, or the engraver was not to be restrained from an indulgence in widespreading or floating twists and curls which could have had no other origin and tended to abuse.

Of single figures it remains to notice an illustration of the favourite practice of representing holy personages in the rich costumes and amongst the surroundings of the period. Examples abound. Two fine groups are those of SS. Gereon and Catherine of Siena, and SS. Sosimus and Barbara, in the Nürnberg Museum. Both retain their original colouring, and are of Franconian origin, probably from Augsburg. The first-named pair are here illustrated (Plate XXIII.), and we may note how the costume of the lady has the sweep in the folds, suggestive of the school, and the elegance and decorative value of the large and full sleeves gathered

PLATE XXIII

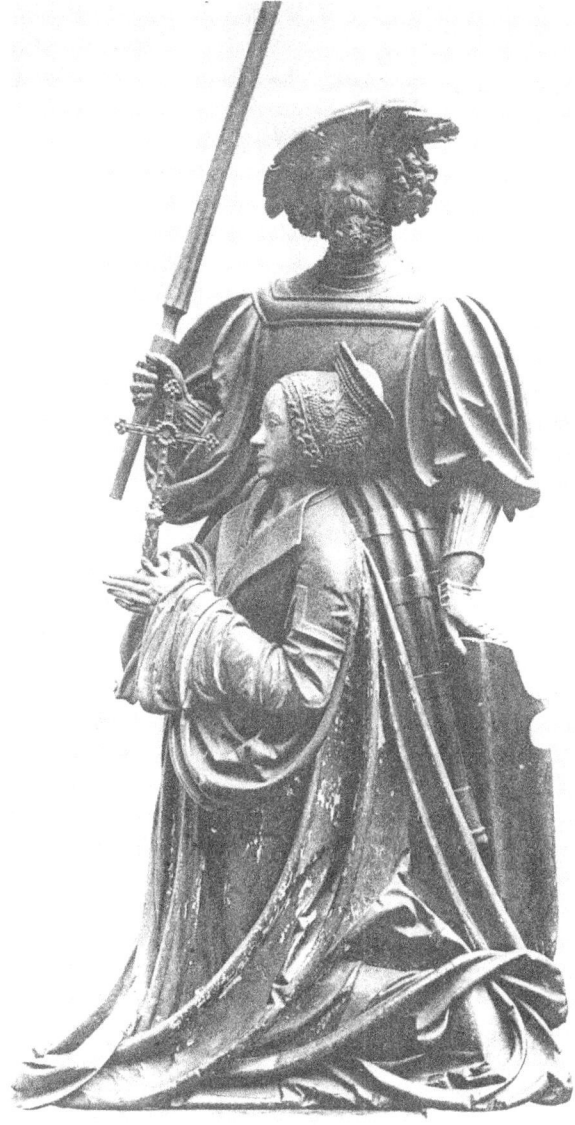

POLYCHROMED GROUP. SS. GEREON AND CATHERINE. AUGSBURG WORK.
SIXTEENTH CENTURY
NÜRNBERG MUSEUM
PAGE 138

PLATE XXIV

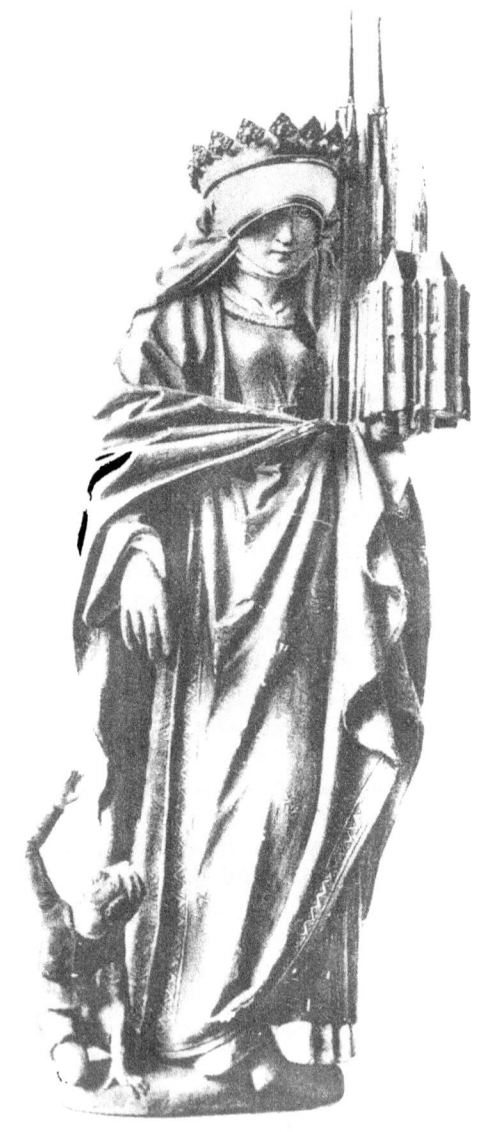

POLYCHROMED GROUP. ST. ELIZABETH
IN THE ELIZABETHKIRCHE, MARBURG
PAGE 139

together over the wrists. The expression 'the lady' is intentionally used, for there is no obvious suggestion in either figure of the saint supposed to be represented. No doubt the heads are portraits of some noble personages who held these saints in special devotion, and admirable, from this point of view, is the head of the lady. Again we have absolutely no clue to identify one who must have been a very clever artist. Not one of the names we have been able to select to illustrate late fifteenth-century wood-carving could in any way be suggested. Yet, even in these figures, Gothic feeling still lingers, though the sixteenth century is far advanced. To my mind, the group is full of suggestion with regard to the changes in progress. A few words must be said for a beautiful statuette of Saint Elizabeth in the Elizabethkirche at Marburg. It is a noble figure that many will be inclined to place on an even higher level than the better known and more popular Nürnberg Madonna. The style, the carefully executed details, and the handling of the drapery, are indicative of a later date than the latter. The head is bent and covered with a veil which almost conceals the eyes. She carries in one hand a model of the cathedral, and a diminutive urchin crouches beside her. The figure is fully coloured. The costume, and the quaint hood and wimple, suggest late fourteenth century, but the small-bosomed figure, the beautifully modelled hand, and the general style of the folds of the drapery, place it not earlier than the second half of the fifteenth. However we may look at it, it is a charming example of the realistic art of Germany towards the close of the Gothic period.

CHAPTER VIII

SCULPTURE IN BOXWOOD—FRANCESCO DA SANT'
AGATA—CONRAD MEIT—HANS WYDYZ

WE have been engaged, for the most part, in the preceding chapters with wood sculpture on a comparatively large scale : with figures which, in many cases, have claims to be considered on a par with great sculpture rather than with that to which the vague term of minor art is frequently applied. This is notably the case with regard to Italian and French work of the early and later Renaissance, and to some examples by German masters of the close of the Gothic period. But in the whole range of our subject there is perhaps no division which offers so much attraction, and is of so great general interest, as that which relates to the small figure work, usually executed in boxwood, and to the still smaller and amazing *tours de force* which, in default of a better term, we must class as microscopic sculpture. Examples of the latter kind, though not very numerous, are to be found in almost every great museum or collection, and without exception it may be said, are of the highest class, apparently proceeding from one workshop of the beginning of the sixteenth century. *Tours de force* though they may be, they are not to be confounded with clever turnery work, which, however wonderful in its way, and evidence of patience and dexterity, can make no pretensions for consideration as art. Skilful work of the latter kind has been known in all ages. We are familiar, for instance, with such things as the enclosing of numbers of tiny spoons or other reproductions on the most minute scale, in a nut or cherry stone: with writing the Lord's Prayer in the compass of a silver penny, and so on: and with the delightful little Japanese netsukes in ivory and wood. The microscopic wood-carving, which will presently be considered, is of another character. It may be compared with the beautiful ivory book-cover of the thirteenth century in the British Museum, which contains, within a space of six by four inches, thirty compartments carved—with what may truly be characterized as fine art—with as many subjects in the history of the Passion of our Lord. It has been illustrated and described in my *Ivories* (p. 159) of this series. We will, however, take first the figures in boxwood, pearwood, and soft woods, which in comparison with those just mentioned are proportionately as much larger as the life-sized statues are to these themselves. Amongst them the busts of the so-called Adam and Eve in the museum at Kensington have, for other reasons, found an earlier place. These boxwood figures—as in the case of the wood medallions to which we shall also presently come—are, speaking generally, more to be connected with the *atelier* of the goldsmith, or bronzist, than with that of the wood sculptor, whose line was the production of large figures for altarpieces and the like. It can hardly be doubted, in fact, that their genesis was often due to the requirements of the metalworker, or founder, as models or patterns: not, of course, wholly excluding them as treasured objects for the cabinet of the collector. Our examples will be, for the most part, German work of the sixteenth century, but in more than one we shall be forcibly impressed with the Italian spirit, transmitted through the influence of such masters as Dürer, Schäufelein, Vischer, or Fletner, and, generally, through the continual contact with Italy of German artists in their wander-years and afterwards. It will be unnecessary, also, to refer again to the continual copying from the engraved works of these and of other masters of ornament. Italy itself will furnish us with our finest example: but it would seem probable that such figures were produced only in a few places in Venetian districts, if we may judge from the scarcity of existing specimens. Boxwoods were probably more worked in Augsburg than elsewhere in Germany, and, as the great centre for goldsmith's work, this is no more than we should expect. But Nürnberg was hardly less prolific. At Basel, almost on the frontiers of Switzerland, we shall meet with Hans Wydyz, and it would not be easy to be precise with regard to the locality of the work of Conrad Meit. Other French and Flemish work in boxwood of the highest possible excellence exists in such museums as those of the Louvre and of Kensington; but admirable as may be the specimens which we should select, these are of a character and of a date later than that at which we are now, with some exceptions, obliged to stop, and must remain for some future opportunity. Speaking generally, it may be said that small sculpture in wood hardly appealed to the genius of Italian art. They preferred to deal with larger effects, although, no doubt, in northern Italy, in Lombardy or in the districts of Verona and Vicenza, there was a considerable industry for church purposes. But this consisted of panels with pictorial subjects in relief, or figures and statuettes for devotional use, turned out in quantities in trade workshops, copied or adapted from paintings and sculpture. Still, although we are carried beyond the limits of date and style, to which as a general rule we are restricted, it would be impossible to avoid dealing in this chapter on box-woods with the figure of Hercules which the Wallace collection is fortunate enough to possess. It is a *chef d'œuvre* of the most pure Renaissance art, one, too, of which recent research and the identification with a contemporary record enables us to name, with certainty, the sculptor. Yet beyond the bare name, we are still almost completely in the dark regarding the life-history and achievements of one who must have been in the first rank among the artists of his time. Not only so, but the story of the acquisition of the piece itself is almost equally mysterious. Its *état civil* and the roll of its former possessors would be of considerable value could they be discovered. Lost sight of for three hundred years at least, though doubtless cherished in many collections, M. Bonnaffé was the first to identify it with a figure of Hercules described by Bernardino Scardeone in his work *De Antiquitate Urbis Pataviae*, published 1560. It will suffice to translate the following extract from the Latin text, p. 374 : ' Every one is astonished at the boxwood Hercules of the Paduan goldsmith Francesco da Sant' Agata, which may be seen at the house of the well-known antiquary Mark Antony Massimo of Padua : of such exceeding beauty of form and approach to human truth that certainly neither Polycletus in bronze nor Phidias in ivory could have rendered it in a more expressive manner. The high price testifies also to its extreme merit, since hardly six ounces of box-wood are estimated at, it is said, a hundred gold crowns. This Francesco, as may be imagined from the work in question, was a very great sculptor : it is surprising that he should have left nothing more in wood than this remarkable Hercules, the admiration of every one, and esteemed at so high a price. He sculptured this piece, as I have heard, in his leisure moments, in the year 1520.' We have, then, no more precise knowledge of Francesco da Sant' Agata than that he must have been a very famous sculptor and goldsmith of the early cinquecento. In 1520 the Paduan school of

marble sculptors and bronzists was everywhere celebrated, and no doubt the sculptor of our Hercules was
in the company of such craftsmen as Vellano, Donatello's pupil, and Vellano's still more famous pupil,
Riccio, maker of the famous paschal candlestick of San
Antonio at Padua, of Minio, of Giovanni Mosca, the
medallist, and many others, goldsmiths as well as
sculptors.

The Hercules of the Wallace Collection (Plate xxv.)
is a figure about ten and a half inches high, standing
erect, and in a defiant attitude, brandishing a huge club,
which is swung round to the back of the head in the
manner in which a modern golfer uses his weapon.
The perfect proportions of the figure, the absolute
knowledge of anatomy, and its treatment in accordance
with the highest classical traditions, the life and expression of movement do not require to be insisted
upon. In addition, there is the perfection of finish in
execution, knowledge of the material, and even the
charm of the beautiful piece of boxwood, as perfect
to-day in colour and in exquisite polish, or patina, as
when it left the sculptor's hands, four hundred years
ago. By general admission, this figure, which from
its comparatively small dimensions may attract but
little general attention, is to be counted amongst the
chefs-d'œuvre of the Italian Renaissance at that epoch
when Cellini, whose name was afterwards to be so
famous, could only have been beginning his career, and
must have known and studied it. It is a finer figure
than the well-known bronze Hercules of the Ashmo-
lean Museum, which it resembles in pose: the youthful
head is more graceful and attractive than that of the
quite elderly man of the latter piece.

We have little cause to doubt that the signature OPVS
FRANCISCI AVRIFICIS · P · connects the Wallace Hercules
with the Paduan Francesco, and that he was a goldsmith.
It seems to have been discovered in some unknown way

PLATE XXV

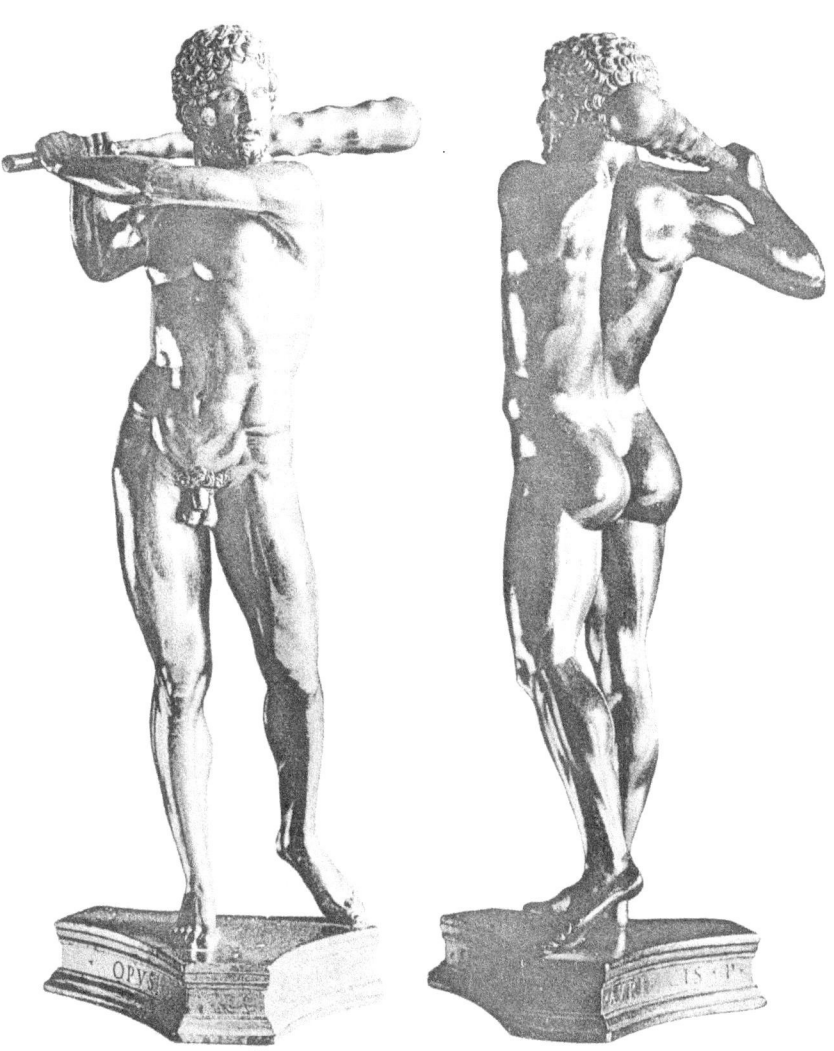

STATUETTE. BOXWOOD. BY FRANCESCO DA SANT' AGATA. SIXTEENTH CENTURY
WALLACE COLLECTION
PAGE 144

by M. Debruge Dumesnil in the first half of the last century. At his sale it was sold to the elder Carrand for 300 francs. By Carrand's son it was sold to Comte Nieuwerkerke, and came with the latter's collection into the possession of Sir Richard Wallace. It is not a little interesting to note that this work of art, valued in its own day at £200, was in the nineteenth century esteemed at £12 only, at any rate acquired for that amount. And how could Carrand *père*, whose magnificent collection of *chefs-d'œuvre* was bequeathed by his natural son to the Bargello at Florence, have parted with it? The habits of both father and son were eccentric. The elder Carrand had an admirable taste and the luck to collect when objects of art of the Renaissance and *moyen âge* were more easily to be acquired than later on. He himself, though he exchanged, never sold, and would hardly have parted with this figure. The son, without being learned in any way, had the *flair* of the dealer, and with it the instincts. It would be instructive to know at what price Count Nieuwerkerke acquired from him the Hercules. There can be little doubt that boxwood figures will become more and more sought after, and from their extreme rarity—that is, when of the highest class—will, as they fully deserve to do, attain prices in the market not inferior to the ivories of the thirteenth century. There is in the Berlin Museum a youthful nude figure in boxwood, with uplifted arms, which Dr. Bode also attributes to Francesco da Sant' Agata, and also a St. Sebastian : both, no doubt, Italian of about the same date as the Hercules, and masterly in style and execution.

Boxwood, at the end of the fifteenth and beginning of the sixteenth century, was becoming a favourite material, and displacing ivory in Flanders and in Germany: and not only by the *imagiers*, but naturally, at such goldsmiths' centres as at Augsburg, for use as patterns. But, of course, fine patterns would be esteemed as cabinet-pieces, and about this time also the practice of making portrait medallions was coming in, and followed by the best masters of small sculpture in wood and in lithographic or honestone. Before its dispersal in 1890, the Spitzer collection was especially rich in this class of work. We cannot now follow the fortunes of that which was dispersed in various museums and in the great private collections of Pierpont Morgan and others. Amongst it, and now in the Louvre, is a charming example of the fashion to which allusion has already more than once been made here, of representing holy personages in the gorgeous costumes of the time. None, of course, would suggest themselves more readily than the Magdalen in the days of her impenitence. We have her here in an elegant *décolleté* costume, of the richest character, looking up-wards with hands raised in an attitude of prayer, and holding a rosary. It is early sixteenth-century work. From the same collection the Louvre has also a fine Venus, which the eminent former keeper, Molinier, thought to be by Hans Schwarz—a boxwood sculptor with whom we shall presently meet as the earliest and best of the medallion carvers—and a fine bas-relief, with the favourite subject of a Young Girl and Death. The latter, which bears his monogram, is no doubt rightly attributed to him. The Venus is an example of a prevailing and rapidly increasing taste of the time amongst German sculptors of small work of all kinds, which there will be frequent occasion to note. The Renaissance, and the passion for naturalism had changed the ideals and the con-ditions of artist life. There was a rage for this kind of sculpture in Germany, and all were not masters who followed it. Doubtless this Venus has its merits and shows a not unpractised hand, but even if that hand is of Hans Schwarz himself it is governed by the German

146

predilections of the time. She is not beautiful, this woman of the people with a knotted handkerchief on the head, hands of exaggerated length, and limbs which by no means can be associated with classic grace. It is a naked Gretchen, and, this conceded, we may be prepared to accord not a little admiration to the talent of the artist in his reproduction from his model, and his technical skill. In the boxwood figures, plaquettes, and bas-reliefs of this time, we meet but rarely the devotional subjects which up to about fifty years before were almost the only themes. They preferred to work from Italian bronzes, to adapt from a Venus of Giovanni da Bologna perhaps, or to copy from innumerable wood-cuts or etchings. There are few German statuettes in boxwood of saints : what there are, exhibit more pleasure in rich contemporary dresses than devotional ideas. Religious fervour was dying out, as it became more paying to work for the luxurious requirements of princes than for the love of the church. There is almost a contemptuous making use of holy figures and legends for their purely decorative value or to satisfy some æsthetic feeling which the growth of the Renaissance encouraged. The boxwood semi-classical St. Sebastian in the Louvre, for example, is purely pagan : or again, in that of the Berlin Museum one has to make diligent search for the marks of the arrows before accepting that title instead of perhaps an Adonis or a Narcissus. Both Dr. Bode and Fabriczy have published the beautiful pearwood relief, in the Berlin Museum, of the head of St. John Baptist on a charger upheld by *putti*. The size for one piece of wood—16 in. × 13½ in.—is remarkable. The group bears the signature FRANCISCVS · JVLI · VERONEN, possibly, but by neither of the first-mentioned authorities thought probably, identical with Francesco da Sant' Agata. Dr. Bode comments upon the 'great want of proportion in the figures, a certain lack of freedom in the carriage of the

147

two angels, a stereotyped manner of arranging the hair, and obviously slight knowledge of the human form' (*Burlington Magazine*, May 1904). That is as may be, but at least the head itself is masterly and painter-like in conception and expression. It would be easy to continue the selection of boxwood figures and groups from various collections which, if not all of the highest distinction, present points of interest, but without multiplying our illustrations beyond our limits, mere lists would become tedious. Amongst such pieces, of somewhat late date, the figure of a Canon kneeling in prayer, at one time in the Odiot collection and now at Kensington, deserves attention. This small box-wood figure, inscribed ' Broeder Cornelis van der Tyt A° S 1562,' is evidently a portrait, and of remarkably careful execution in such details as the texture of the surplice, of the knitted gloves, and of the robes. We are still confronted with the same difficulties with regard to authorship as has been the case with so much carved woodwork of German, Flemish, and French origin. But although it is only quite lately that particular attention has been directed to these most charming works, recent research has begun to afford at least some means of classification.

The great influence of the Netherlands on the arts of other countries, and the high reputation of its sculptors during the thirteenth, fourteenth, and fifteenth centuries, have already several times occupied our attention. It is, indeed, hardly surprising that this should have happened when we consider the artistic genius of its people, and in addition the dynastic conditions and the changes in government which brought them into close contact with so many different countries. In 1369 Philip the Bold, son of the King of France, united the Courts of Burgundy and Flanders by his marriage with Margaret, heiress of Count Louis ii. Under the princes of the house of Burgundy, John the Fearless,

Philip the Good, and Charles the Bold, who married Margaret of York, sister to Edward IV., the luxury of their Courts was unsurpassed, calling for the employment of the best artists from the countries with which they were connected. In 1477 Flanders, through the marriage of Mary, daughter of Charles the Bold and Margaret of York, with Maximilian, falls under the dominion of Austria, and Burgundy returns to France. For the moment we need not concern ourselves with the subjection of the Netherlands to Spain about, again, another hundred years later (1555).

At the death of Philippe le Beau in 1506 the government of the Low Countries was confided by the Emperor Maximilian to Margaret of Austria, widow of Philibert of Savoy, whom he named Regent or governess. This princess was even more strongly inclined to luxurious display and the encouragement of the arts than her predecessors. Her early years had been passed at the Court of Savoy, where the Italian Renaissance had already begun to assert itself, and she was therefore naturally influenced by the Italian artists who had there established themselves in considerable numbers. Yet during her short married life the attractions of the Flemish style had not been lost upon her even if they had not been entirely those of her predilection. At the death of her husband she conceived the project of erecting a magnificent tomb both to his beloved memory and as a place where she herself should rest. For this purpose she sought for artists amongst the greatest of the time who should be capable of uniting the principles of Gothic art, as she knew it, in its French and Flemish forms, with those of the Italian Renaissance which had already become strong in its all-conquering course. In the same way she chose for the superb monument which she caused to be erected in the church of St. Nicolas of Tolentino at Brou (Bourg-en-Bresse), Lucas van

Berghem as architect, and with him John of Brussels and Conrad Meit. With the two former we are not particularly concerned, but the art of Conrad Meit, and its relationship with our boxwood carvings, is a matter sufficient to necessitate some slight references at least to the monument generally and to the Regent Margaret herself. The tomb is one of the most beautiful sepulchral monuments in existence. It is a mass of rich Gothic work with numbers of figures in marble and alabaster. Beneath the most richly carved canopy work are the recumbent effigies of Philibert and his wife, the latter twice repeated—in death and in life—and of his mother, Margaret of Savoy. Completed in 1526, the Regent herself died and was buried at Brou in 1530. Conrad Meit—'Conrad Maistre, notre tailleur d'ymages,' as he is styled in documents in the archives of Lille—seems to have entered the service of Margaret of Austria about the year 1514. There is documentary evidence also that he made for her in 1518 two figures of Hercules, one of wood and one of bronze, a box-wood Christ as the Gardener, and two portraits of herself. Our information, generally, concerning Meit, is still but scanty. We do not even know with certainty what portions of the monument at Brou, erected on French soil, are due to him. But if a sculptor in Flemish employ, he was nevertheless a true German. A figure in alabaster of Judith, presently to be noticed, is signed by him CONRAT · MEIT · VON · WORMS. As, unfortunately, we have evidences only of style to guide us for purposes of comparison between the sculptured figures at Brou and those in alabaster and boxwood with which we are particularly concerned, it will be sufficient to confine ourselves to the beautiful effigy on the lower part of the monument, representing the Regent lying in death, and one from among the numerous *putti*, or cherubs, in alabaster. Doubtless, besides the architect Lucas van Berghem, Meit had many assistants, and probably he himself was not the sculptor of all the beautiful Renaissance *putti* on this Gothic tomb. It would carry us too far and must be left to the reader to follow for himself the comparisons in detail which are of interest with regard to some boxwood figures presently to be noticed. He will find ample material and excellent illustrations—which our limits prevent us from giving here—both of the tomb and the figures in the article by Wilhelm Vöge in the Year-Book of the Prussian Art Collections, Tom. xxix. There is one figure at least, the one most important for our purpose, which may be accepted as the work of Meit. It is the *putto* with the gauntlet. Whether Meit had ever been in Italy is not known, but un-questionably his art was strongly influenced therefrom, and we cannot forget also his friendship with Dürer, who became intimate with him when he visited the Low Countries in 1520. Dürer speaks of him as 'mysterious,' and as known in Italy as Corrado Fiammingo—prince of Flemish sculptors. And, again, as 'that excellent carver, whose equal I have never met.' A German of the Palatinate by birth, his figures of Judith, and those of Adam and Eve which we shall presently connect with him, are unmistakably German also. Yet, even if by him, we do not know the date of their execution, and when we consider his experience at the Court of Margaret of Austria, his probable long sojourn at Brou, and in all probability his journeys to Italy, it is difficult not to be inclined to consider him as belonging to Flanders.

The learned curator of the Berlin Museum has also addressed himself particularly to the small sculpture work of Meit in an article in the *Annual* before men-tioned (Tom. xxii.). If I am not mistaken he still ascribes to him not only the boxwood statuettes of Adam and Eve in the Gotha Museum, and the similar ones in the Austrian Imperial collection, but even the portrait busts in the British Museum (which the authorities there have not ventured to describe further than as of a man and woman), the bust in the Berlin Museum which is almost identical with the first of these, and the one in the Bavarian National Museum so nearly alike to the other. In considering the series of Adam and Eve full-length figures—and I venture to say that the busts attributed to Riemen-schneider in the Victoria and Albert Museum are in the same category—we have to take as our starting-point an admirable alabaster statuette in the museum at Munich representing Judith with the head of Holofernes. In all the numerous German figures of this kind and period—either statuettes or small bas-reliefs—we cannot fail to notice the tendency towards, and fondness for, an exaggerated naturalism. It was not a striving after the representation of beauty for its own sake; there was no attempt at a realization of Greek ideals, but inspired, no doubt, by some mistaken idea of the Renaissance, there was an almost brutal determination to go straight to nature, omitting nothing, modifying nothing. In the alabaster statuette the Judith of the scriptural narrative is absolutely naked, with an uncompromising realism that finds a parallel nowhere but in Germany. The youthful figure is strictly the artist's model as he found her, far indeed removed from any attempt at idealism. The too long body is set on thick short legs, with very sloping shoulders, flabby and squat; the anatomy is some-what lost in the plump flesh-covering. It is not the figure of a strong active girl, but rather of one too well nourished and enervated: chosen perhaps from some notion of suggestion of the East and the nearest to that according to the German idea. It must surely be conceded that in this, as in the other figures of similar character, the intention of the artist was the presentation of a vision of beauty as he himself conceived it to be. The fault lay not with him, but in the want of a better model. Vasari, in his *Lives of the Painters*, speaking of Dürer, says that he would have done better work if he had had better nude models : 'for these,' he says, 'must have had ill-formed figures, as indeed the Germans, for the most part have, when undressed, although one sees many in those countries who, when dressed, appear to be very fine figures.' Yet there certainly had not been for a considerable time any particular avoidance of the nude, from life, and Meit's contemporary, Lucas Cranach, in his pictures shows no want of elegance and seductive, if German, models. Granted, however, the too obtrusive naturalism, the work is admirable in technique and in directness of touch : admirable in the rendering of soft satiny skin, and in suggestion—if no more than suggestion—of the muscular anatomy which is too fully furnished. The head itself is masterly, and one could wish to find no fault in the sweetness of expression, and the refinement in the arrangement and treatment of the curly hair. Too sweet is the smile : too seductive to accompany the gruesome horror of the severed head which the girl sustains with one hand. It would seem, then, almost to come to this, that it is the technical handling, the execution of such a work which is borne in upon one, more than its intrinsic charm. It is no first effort or production of a natural untaught genius. Meit must have already known a good deal about Italy. Yet the figure is German.

In the boxwood statuettes of Adam and Eve, of the Gotha Museum, we are confronted, though certainly from another model, with even more realistic fidelity to nature, with the same masterly rendering of soft satiny skin and somewhat flabby flesh in both the male and female figures, the same short bodies and short thick legs : similar handling of the curly heads, similar narrow very sloping shoulders, and small, hardly developed, bust of the Eve. Adam's head is proportionately much too large, and, granting the imperfections of the model, the lumbar muscles and folds of flesh below the waist are very finely expressed in the back of the figure. The technique of the Adam and Eve of the Imperial Museum, Vienna, at one time in the Boehm collection—this boy and girl Adam and Eve—presents striking similarities with that of Meit's *putto* at Brou. Adam, indeed, might be not more than about twelve years old. His almond-shaped eyes have a languid expression, and his mouth is half open as if speaking and gently remonstrating. The hair is differently treated from the Adam of the Gotha Museum: it has more of the character of stone work, and of the alabaster of Brou. We find in the Eve the same bulging forehead as in the Judith, but the bust is more fully developed though still of extremely youthful type. The pair are probably much later than that of Gotha, in which there is no trace of Italian influence.

We may be very well content with these two pairs of figures of our first parents, in which they are in the first blush of newly created youth, and it would be difficult to decide which is the most charming. That is to say, when we have got over the novelty of the first impression of the mannerism and of the naïve and apparently untutored art. Meit must have known Dürer's famous Eve of 1504, and it is difficult to imagine that the influences by which he would have been affected during his long connexion with the court of the Netherlands should not have weaned him from his too German proclivities, and inclined him—as in the later days of his friend Dürer—to Italian refinement. The sculptor of these figures may have been assisted by Dürer's plate, but he evidently worked from a living model. It can hardly be asserted as conclusively proved that they are from the same hand, however strong the analogies may be, but that they are

PLATE XXVI

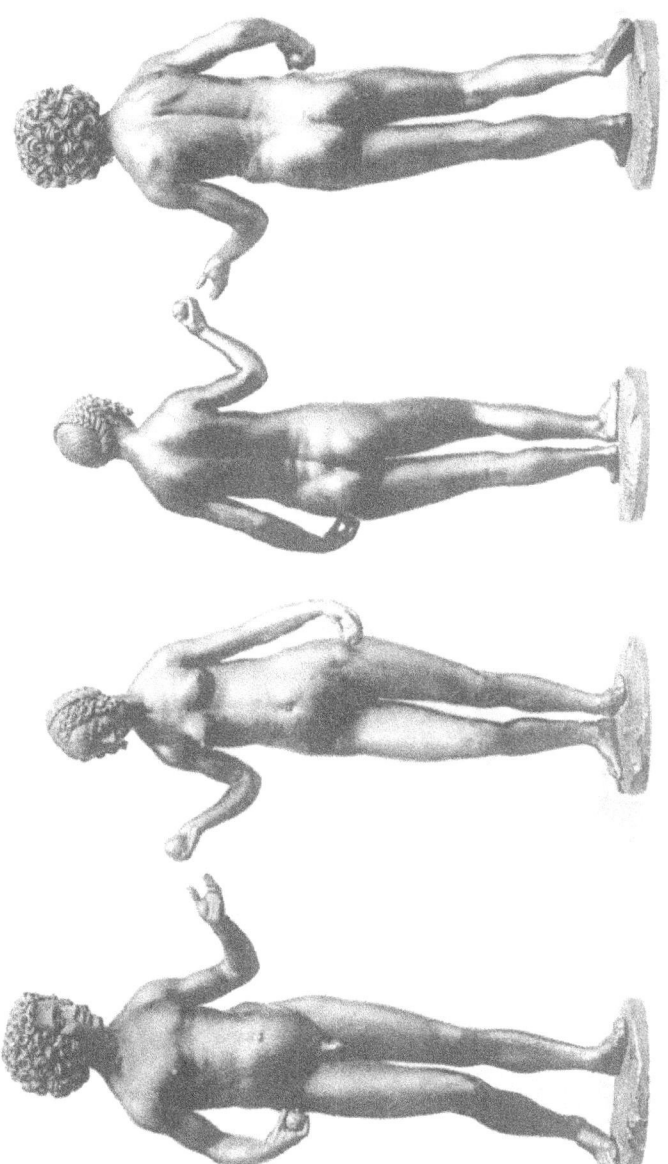

STATUETTES. ADAM AND EVE. BOXWOOD. SIXTEENTH CENTURY
BY CONRAD MEIT. GOTHA MUSEUM
PAGE 154

nearly related, and that Conrad Meit was no stranger to them may be accepted as certain. Of them all I should like to associate with him the Vienna pair and the busts in the British and Berlin museums.

We have not yet done with the interesting figure of the Regent of the Netherlands and with her favourite sculptor. In the collection bequeathed to the nation by Baron Ferdinand de Rothschild, known as the Waddesdon bequest, from which also other treasures have been selected for this book, are two portrait busts. They are, according to the catalogue, of walnut, and represent a young man and a young woman in the costumes of the early sixteenth century. As examples of skilful portrait sculpture, neither too realistic nor over idealized, they would be remarkable in any material, and are, therefore, of still greater interest in that they represent in wood, with the others with which they are connected, the highest excellence of any examples which could be produced. Whatever ultimate conclusions we may come to, there is certainly not a little to be said in favour of the supposition that in the lady we have a portrait of Margaret of Austria herself. There is in the Bavarian National Museum another bust in many respects identical, which Dr. Bode unhesitatingly considers to be of that princess. In the British Museum example Margaret is in widow's weeds, so that if the ascription is correct it would not be difficult to be fairly accurate as to date: that is to say, not earlier than 1504 or later than 1530. And, if we may judge the age of the lady, she would be somewhere about forty. The museum catalogue, however, thinks this to be about twenty to twenty-five. Beautiful, Margaret was not, perhaps, though her sepulchral figures at Brou are full of sweet expression, but with little resemblance, it may be said, to these busts. In the busts there is no flattering, toning-down of the rather puffy features, and though that of the British

Museum is the younger of the two, in both there are the same broad, thick nose, fleshy cheeks and chin, and prominent thick lips. The Renaissance Museum in Berlin possesses, curiously enough, a bust of a young man which is also as nearly identical with the one in the London Museum as in the case of the lady. Very interesting is the man's costume : the fur-bordered robe and the broad hat half covering the elegant net which confines the hair. The latter fashion came in in the first quarter of the sixteenth century, probably not earlier than 1515, and was common throughout the greater part of Northern Europe, and even in Italy, during almost the whole of the century. We shall find it repeated again and again in the medallion portraits next to be considered. In itself, it disposes of the earlier identification of the busts with Charles the Bold and Margaret, sister of our own King Edward IV. The medallion on the hat of the London male figure (that on the Berlin bust is now missing) bears a St. Margaret killing the dragon, and the motto IE · NE · SCAi : very possibly a medallion of a much earlier date than the time of the wearer. The costume of the British Museum lady, with the plain, partly open chemisette, close-fitting body, and well-executed drapery of the loose sleeves, and the simple bead necklace, is much more elegant and attractive than the pleated *guimpe* which conceals the neck and bust in the case of the Munich figure. Judging from the costumes, then, and the apparent age of Margaret, if it is she, the date of these busts would be about 1520-1530. But Philibert died young in 1504. The young man cannot, therefore, be that prince. What, then, is the connexion? And, again—if Dr. Bode is correct in the case of one at least—what is there to explain two such similar figures as those of the lady ; both to be ascribed to Meit, but the one in widow's weeds for a husband who died in 1504, the other more youthful? In addition to this we are to be precluded by the costume from dating, what seem to be companion busts, earlier than 1515, when Margaret, however devoted a wife we know her to have been, would surely have put off her mourning. But yet again, is it the same personage in both the busts of a lady? In the one case it will be noticed that the hair is smooth and straight, in the other wavy. Can we then be certain that in either we have a portrait of Margaret of Austria? Perhaps not, and it may be remarked that while Dr. Bode unhesitatingly identifies with her the Munich bust, he cautiously labels the British Museum one a '*junge Frau*' only. Finally, we have also in the British Museum a boxwood medallion of the Regent, which offers practically no resemblance to the busts in question. A brief allusion must be made to the fine honestone busts in the Dreyfus collection at Paris, which represent a younger man and woman in almost identical costumes with the wooden ones, and are evidently by the same sculptor. That is, by Meit, if it be he in any one of the cases. The material here used would seem still further to complicate the question. A short mention must suffice also for two rather larger busts in wood, said to be of Philip the Bold and the Elector Frederick II. in the Munich Museum: probably Augsburg work of about 1540. They have been attributed to Haguenauer, to whose medallion work we shall come presently.

Every country, in Gothic and early Renaissance times, had its own favourite, or popular, subjects. In Germany and the Netherlands none was more so, in painting and in sculpture, than the story of our first parents. We are familiar with the Adam and Eve of the Ghent altarpiece. There are famous examples by Dürer and the other great etchers and engravers, and figures and busts innumerable. Such are the busts at Kensington, or, again, such bas-reliefs as the small pearwood panel in the same museum with the Dürer cipher or signature, and there are many others in metal or honestone. Even in wood we could not attempt to follow them all. But it is necessary to take one more pair. They introduce us to a comparatively new name, although, unfortunately, it is hardly more than a name, so scanty, as usual, is our information concerning the bearer. In the Basel Museum there is a group of small boxwood figures—about six inches in height —of Adam and Eve, which have much in common with the type with which we have just been occupied. In this case they form part of a pictorial representation of the Fall. The boxwood figures are set on a landscape ground of limewood. Eve smilingly holds out the apple to Adam, and, in the background, is the tree with the serpent. In both we have again the same unrestrained realism in which a by no means perfect model is relentlessly copied, defects and all. Less physically plastic, perhaps, than the type from which Meit worked his Judith, it is the same short and plump Eve dear to the German taste of the time. Her head is charming, the soft waving hair restrained by the fillet encircling it. But the Adam surely is a wretched creature. He is thin, weak, flat-chested, narrow-shouldered, with prominent collar-bones, thin, almost muscleless, limbs with unduly-strained sinews, and the too-large curly head characteristic of this art of the time. Eve smiles seductively as she tenders the apple. Adam is distressed, hesitating, imploring. There is perhaps more art in these figures, after all, than we might be inclined to accord to them from a first comparison with the more attractive pair of the Vienna collection. The presence of the initials—H on one block of limewood, W on the other—has led to the opinion of recent critics that we are to ascribe this group to the sculptor of the Visit of the Magi (also in wood) in the cathedral of Freiburg-im-Breisgau. That is to say, to a certain

PLATE XXVII

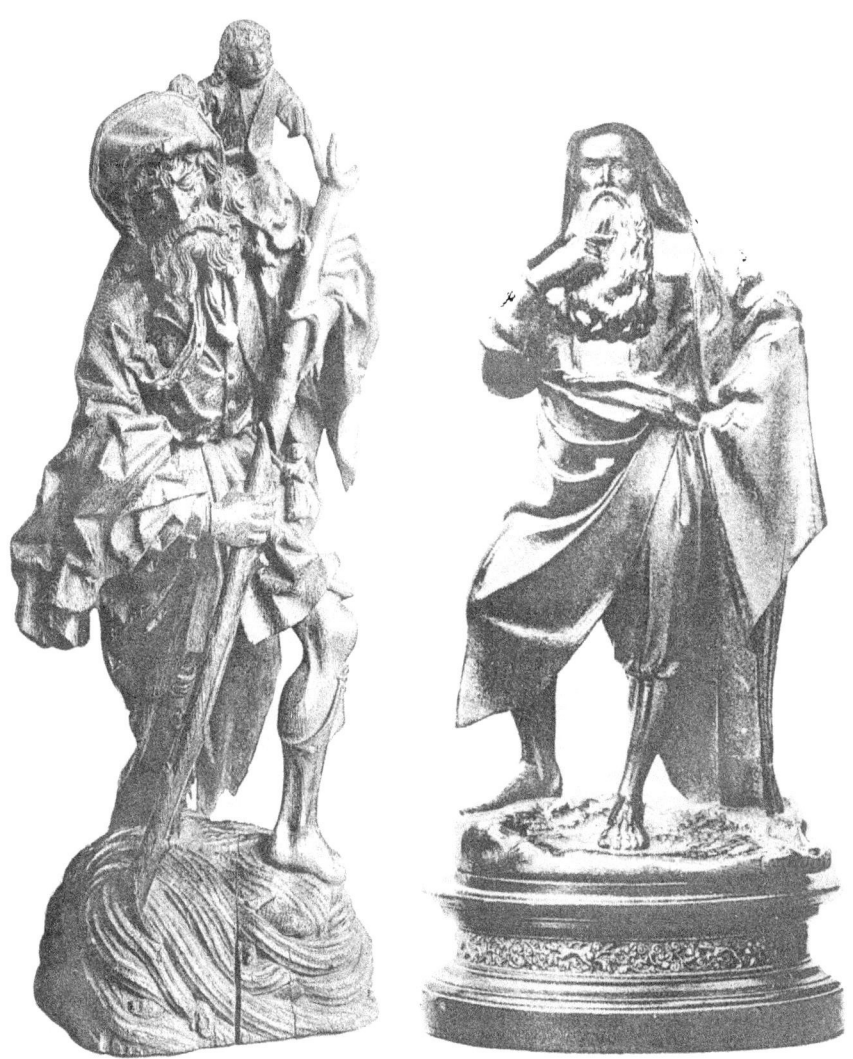

HANS WYDYZ

I. O. Wydyz if the inscription with the date 1505 is to be relied upon. But of this Wydyz we are without any further information, nor can there be any certainty that the signature refers to a sculptor. If, however, we take it to be that of the Master of the Freiburg altarpiece, we may conjecturally also connect him with a Martyrdom of St. Sebastian in the Kaiser Friedrich Museum, Berlin. Some see in this, too, a strong resemblance to the Basel Adam. But it is entirely unsafe to rely upon such weak analogies, for which other circumstances might easily account, and though the figure of the martyr may fairly be connected with the style of the sculptor of the altarpiece, it would not suffice to establish an affinity with the Basel piece. The Adoration of the Magi is surmounted by figures of Our Lord, the Virgin and St. John, and if there should be grounds for ascribing this group and the one below to the same sculptor, then we should be fairly on the way towards giving to him also the Adam and Eve. In the figure of Our Lord blessing and in the crucifix we have, as typical of the sculptor, the three folds of flesh below the ribs (although the body is nearly upright), the contracted waist, the peculiar curve of the hips and the anatomy of the arms. There are points in the group of the Martyrdom of St. Sebastian which may be compared with a fine boxwood figure, which it will be convenient to take here, but with no idea of suggesting that they are by the same sculptor. It is the figure at one time in the Bonnaffé collection, supposed to be a portrait-statuette of Wenczel Jamnitzer the great Nürnberg goldsmith: possibly, even, a self-portrait. It is plainly a masterly piece, representing an elderly long-bearded man, draped in a flowing mantle, more suggestive of the bronzist's or goldsmith's art than of the qualities of wood sculpture for its own sake. The Basel St. Sebastian has a certain resemblance to it in the pose of the left leg, in the general movement, and in the

159

anatomy of the foot. There is, of course, evidence of considerable acquaintance with Italian art, but it is far behind the Jamnitzer figure in originality, in nobility of expression, and in simple elegance of the drapery. The subject of boxwood and pearwood figures generally can hardly be left without a passing reference to the very powerful group, in pearwood, in the Waddesdon bequest, representing Antæus supporting the wounded Hercules. It stands almost a foot in height, and is said to be Flemish of the late sixteenth century. We have here another instance of the uncertainties which still surround us. Whether the origin be of Flanders, of Nürnberg, or even of Augsburg, might surely be conjectured, but in each case no artist's name suggests itself, or country, except Italy, from which we may be sure it did not proceed.

CHAPTER IX

GERMAN MEDALLIONS IN WOOD

IN a comprehensive work of this kind, in which an endeavour is made to give a general idea of a very extensive subject, it becomes advisable from time to time to clear the way. Every division with which we have to deal is of importance, greater or less as the case may be, and in reality demands a monograph. The subject of medallions in wood is also intimately connected with that of the sister arts of cast and struck medals, and here we come into especial contact with Italy and her great bronze sculptors and goldsmiths, and with the plaquettes and panels in lithographic stone which form such a feature of German art of the sixteenth century. These, again, cannot be dissociated from the great names of Dürer, Wohlgemut, and so many other wood engravers and ornamentists. While, therefore, diversions from the principal subject are inevitable, the limits of this publication make it imperative that they should be allusive only. Nor will it be possible to do more than make a choice of three or four from among the most distinguished of the German boxwood medallion sculptors and of their work, and this as examples of wood sculpture only, without reference to those in metal. Medals are coinlike pieces cast or struck in metal, or carved in wood, either as finished memorials, and works of art in themselves, or for pattern pieces to be reproduced by casting in metal. Those with which we are now concerned bear for the most part portraits in relief of distinguished personages of the time, or of less important people, who delighted in having them executed much in the same way as nowadays the aid of the photographer is called in. They were portable likenesses for friendly exchange: expensive, no doubt, but all classes indulged in them according to their means. An artist who was in fashion, such as a Haguenauer for example, would no doubt have counted amongst his patrons every one distinguished in art, in letters, or in other ways, as in our own times the portrait drawings by Richmond abounded. Thus it has resulted that, apart from their merits as works of art, these medallions form a remarkable addition to our knowledge of the personal appearance of many celebrated personages, and of the costumes, especially the headdresses, of the period. Medallic art is due to the Italian Renaissance, and it will be unnecessary to trace the steps through which it may have been introduced thence into Germany, where our earliest example is not before 1520. Vasari attributes it to Vittore Pisanello, who died in 1451, and the names of Sperandio, Pastorini, Boldu, and many others of the last half of the quattrocento, are familiar to those interested in the subject. Generally speaking, the difference in the practice between Italy and Germany is, that in the one case the medallic art was in the hands of the great painters and sculptors, in the other, of the wood-modeller for the goldsmith as a special branch of his profession. Yet in Italy all great artists passed through an apprenticeship, at least, with the goldsmith. Brunelleschi, Donatello, Ghiberti, Ghirlandajo, and many other great names could be mentioned. This, because the goldsmith, as Mr. Perkins has so well put it, was a master *par excellence* in all the arts. He was an architect for the columns, niches, pilasters, pinnacles, and tracery which enriched his productions, a sculptor for statuettes and bas-reliefs, a painter for enamels, an engraver for niello. He had to forge and hammer iron and gold and silver, to cast in bronze, to model in wax, in wood, or in clay. The Germans preferred casting to striking for their coins and medals, but it was not until the sixteenth century that they got the idea from Italy, and so followed it that they became, in this art, portraitists of consummate ability. We need not here inquire into the origin and development of coinage in Germany, and the connexion it may have with our wood medallions. In point of date it has been said that the fine *Schauthaler* of the Emperor Maximilian heads the system. In Italy the earliest medals were all cast by the *cire perdue* process. Caradosso and Francesco Francia were the first, it is thought, to strike medals from engraved dies. If these admirable works have not always the boldness and individuality of those modelled direct, they are specimens of the height of perfection in execution to which the goldsmith's art could rise. Of Francia's work in boxwood the Louvre possesses a beautiful relief: a Pietà. The German is first of all a wood-carver, and, as the early sixteenth-century workshops abounded in sculptors of small figures, panels, and the like, it was natural that they should imagine the production of round, instead of rectangular, portrait reliefs, and make them, first, for their own sakes and not as patterns for casting. It was not, perhaps, much earlier than about 1530 that the latter practice became popular, and that the lithographic or honestone reliefs were used in the same way. And even then it is hard to imagine that so many charming works—for example the Pierpont Morgan Venus in honestone—would not have been esteemed, and first made, as cabinet-pieces. The wood medallion continued in favour until Peter Vischer's influence introduced, from Italy, more generally, the method of casting. It was a distinctly national art in a country where carving in wood had acquired such a hold. Many of these beautiful sculptures are so delicately and minutely executed that they take an independent position even amongst other wood-carving. They are cameos in wood.

The two great cradles of the rapidly-growing goldsmith's industry in Germany, destined shortly after to attain so high a development and such remarkable prosperity, were Nürnberg and Augsburg. These also, and in particular Nürnberg, were the most fruitful districts in the working of small sculpture in box, pear, and other fine-grained woods, and in the calcareous stone used much later on for lithography, which we refer to generally as honestone. The preference of Nürnberg was for stone : Augsburg for wood. At the same time it is not easy—it may be said to be almost impossible —to distinguish, in every case, the productions of these two great centres. Still, as a rule, each of the great masters confined himself to one of these materials. Of the two, the highest art remains with the wood. It requires greater artistic qualities in the right understanding of its varied qualities, a surer hand, and more care in execution. The more pliable soft stone is less varied in its qualities, and almost as amenable as wax to minutiæ, sharpness, and delicacy of detail. For high artistic merit there is really little comparison possible between the fine bold individuality of a relief in wood, when handled in the style of Schwarz, and the cold mechanical character and too fine finish of even the best among the honestone workers. Doubtless both have their charm, and the methods used do not generally differ greatly except in the case of such a master as Hans Schwarz. It is necessary also to bear in mind the double purpose which these productions were often intended to serve. As has been already stated, the goldsmith had the choice of wood, stone, or wax, and, in wood, several kinds besides box and pear.

MEDALLIONS

The sculptor of these miniature portraits was required to be a master in the rendering of human lineaments, and in the character and peculiarities of his subject, no less than in great sculpture and in painting. So far as we know, there was no previous preparation in clay or wax, but he worked direct on the wood. We shall find, even, very evident points of distinction between a wood-carver such as Haguenauer, and such honestone workers as Fletner or Daucher. Again, in making general comparisons—and we cannot here go further than that—it is not only the medallions which have to be considered. But the honestone was as a rule, some busts apart, confined to bas-reliefs, and these sometimes of considerable dimensions. Our main interest for the present lies with the series of portrait medallions in wood. Of the masters, Hans Schwarz is the earliest of whose personality we have any definite information, and he is also the greatest. To him we can assign a fairly large number of examples. Of other important medal masters Friedrich Haguenauer is the most interesting and prolific, and there will be something to say also of Ludwig Krug, Hans Kels, Hans Daucher, Peter Fletner, Hans Culmbach, and Jakob Fugger. In these portrait bas-reliefs it is impossible not to be struck by the general air of realism, and by the conscientious fidelity to the individuality of the subject, not only in the features, but also with regard to the particular characteristics and carriage of the person portrayed. The observation of nature is exact. There is, in the best and boldest specimens, a scrupulous avoidance of flattery, and of retouching away natural defects. The portly burgher, for example, loses none of his corpulence: on the contrary it is emphasized, sometimes even to the extent of exciting our amusement or ridicule, and, without any malice, the puffy cheeks and usual characteristics of the *bon vivant* are nothing extenuated. Facility of execution, a firm, rapid, and decisive touch are evident : sometimes fatally so, even with the best masters. It is true also that there was a tendency towards excessive exactness and sharpness of detail which are not in accord with the highest expression of art.

For fine bold workmanship, and in breadth of touch, Hans Schwarz is distinguished to a degree which places him in a category distinct from that occupied by his later rival Haguenauer. We do not look for mechanical precision in art as evidence of perfection of execution. On the subject of medallic art Quatremère de Quincy, in his *Essays on Art*, has some apposite remarks which are worth quoting. He says, if it may be permitted to summarize them :—' The art of the composition of *médailles* consists in the reduction to their lowest terms of every subject, every action, every figure, so that each may be not merely an insignificant part of the whole, but the whole clearly indicated by that which is only a part. From this arises the necessity of distinguishing in each subject the feeling, which is the chief or central point. In this way a system of studied abbreviation is accomplished, which reduces each composition to its most simple expression, so far as its moral or physical signification is concerned : not only so, but which gives to the persons or figures represented the value of that ideal language of which they are the visible signs.' It is true that he is speaking not so much of portrait medallions as of those with historical compositions, and that his remarks are addressed in particular to the work of the eighteenth century medallist, Duvivier. But the language is no less applicable to our present subject. As great talent is required in the life-like rendering of individual expression in these bas-reliefs as in the art of the portrait painter. The sculptor seizes the point of view best suited to his purpose, and he would seem to be more successful with the profile portraits than with the full-face, or even the three-quarter face. In profiles the form of the head and face, the line of the nose, the contours of the chin, the eyebrow, and the eye itself, are rendered with more lifelike and impressive fidelity. Illusion is produced by the play of light and shade and the different degrees of relief. Almost without exception the known portrait medals of Haguenauer are in profile; where they are full face, for example in his Friedrich van Embrich, his Johann von Aich, or even his Mercator—of whom he made two others, much finer—they are strikingly inferior. It would seem that the back of the head is of the highest importance in the expression of character in bas-reliefs. The full-face must have strongly marked points, as—to quote another amongst the few we have of Haguenauer—that of Jakob von Strassburg, to give equal facility of rendering.

Many boxwood medallions are known, often not inferior in merit to any of Italy in bronze of the same period. Large numbers are in public museums and private collections, and, of course, in such storehouses of German art as the museums of Berlin, Dresden, Gotha, Vienna, or Brunswick. But, unfortunately, in the majority of cases, though we may be able to identify the portraits them-selves from inscriptions or other indications, the sculptors' names are unknown, or, at the best, uncertain. The greater number may be attributed to the Augsburg workshops. Italian medals were much more frequently signed. As regards Germany, it is not only the boxwoods which are unsigned. The anonymity applies also to the greater number of cast or die-sunk medals which are scattered in rich profusion throughout most collections of importance. In point of fact, when we are concerned with any attempt to classify, we are reduced to the method adopted by

Erman of assigning examples to artists using certain monograms, when, even, we have this slight information to go upon. And amongst these anonymous masters are to be found specimens of no less high character and interest than the work with which a Schwarz or a Haguenauer may with more or less certainty be identified. For these and other reasons already given, our attention must now be confined to a few of the most distinguished whose work is known, viz. Hans Schwarz, Hans Kels, Haguenauer, Krug, Dachauer, and, incidentally, Peter Flöttner, or Fletner. Fletner was, no doubt, one of the most distinguished pioneers of the German Renaissance, but his wood-carving is not of the class, for chronological and other reasons, to which the present review of German wood-carving is especially directed. Certain medallions and bas-reliefs are attributed to him, in some cases for no better reason than as, in the same way, anything fine about which there is no authentic information is associated with Dürer or Michael Angelo. Fletner was a versatile genius, and his influence on the art of his time was very great. In a general way he was a decorator : designing chimney-pieces, ceilings and so forth, and doubtless employing many hands. There are in the Louvre a number of reliefs in wood with floral swags, *putti* playing, and the like, derived from the Italian after the manner which, later, became such favourite subjects with Flemish and German sculptors in ivory. Born probably about 1480, working at Augsburg, and for the most part at Nürnberg, he died in 1546. Although we know little of his life, his drawings and architectural designs exist in considerable numbers. They cover a most extensive range, and include designs for goldsmith's work, altars, altarpieces, organ fronts, choir stalls, furniture, panels, plaquettes, and reliefs of all kinds and interior decoration. A large number were exhibited at the Burlington

FLETNER—SCHWARZ—HAGUENAUER

Fine Arts Club Exhibition of early German art in 1905. No doubt he was in business relations with the workshops of the great metal workers such as the Vischers. He belongs essentially to the later Renaissance. Of his existing work there are the choir stalls of the cathedral at Berne, in which his own portrait, winged as a cherub, though a bearded one, appears on a misericord. In the Waddesdon bequest is a fine oval medallion, with the subject of Lot and his daughters, said to be by Fletner: probably a copy of an engraving. The Victoria and Albert Museum possesses a boxwood medallion of Joachim Rehle (Plate XXVIII.), and a large number, in silver and other metals, exists, of which the honestone or wood models can also, in some cases, be identified.

Our two foremost figures in the art of medal-carving in wood are Hans Schwarz and Friedrich Haguenauer. Of both of these little has been known until recently, when the researches of Professor Georg Habich have resulted in some light being thrown upon their work, especially with regard to Haguenauer, through the discovery of a MS. by him, and other documents in the archives of Augsburg. The initiation of the practice of medallions in wood may justly be claimed for Hans Schwarz. Born at Augsburg about 1492, he was apprenticed to a wood-carver of the same family name, Stephen Schwarz, and worked subsequently at Nürnberg. Artist life in that city seems to have been particularly tumultuous, for like his contemporary, Veit Stoss, he had to leave on account of a brawl, and we have no trace of him after 1527, the date of his last known medal. This little we can gather from Neudorffer, the indefatigable chronicler of Nürnberg art, who calls him the best *conterfetter* of his time. And with regard to his family we know also that his father, Ulrich, also an artist, is represented in Holbein's votive picture of 1508. In his medal work, as in his figures and reliefs, Hans Schwarz was consistently Gothic. Intimately connected, no doubt, with Dürer — who seems to have been associate or mentor of every craftsman of his time—the traditions of Gothic art in which he was brought up, were never, so far as we can positively judge, abandoned for any flirtations with the Italian spirit then making its insidious way. The contrary of this may be asserted, and for proof we might go to the few pieces—for example in the Louvre—which, though unsigned, are accepted as by him. Of his first known work—a relief with the Entombment in an architectural framing, at one time in the Felix collection (figured in the catalogue of 1886 No. 938)—Habich says that the influence of Donatello is evident, and that Schwarz soon left his Gothic sympathies behind. But beyond the framing, which is purely Renaissance, it is hard to see what there is of Donatello in the subject itself. What is remarkable in his medals and reliefs is his absolutely personal style: strong, dashing, impressionistic, and in striking contrast with the somewhat laboured precision and minute finish of his contemporary Haguenauer, whose medal work begins, as far as our present information goes, almost in the very year when that of Schwarz leaves off. Schwarz was the Rodin of his time, and, as the precursor of German medal work, his style, owing little to German traditions and sympathies, is still less connected with, or indebted to, Italian modellers and casters. His drawing is bold: a few lines, a few firm strokes; rude, perhaps, and uncompromising. He was no flatterer, and in no way inclined to spare the strongly marked lines of the face. Whether instinctively acquired, or by a course of training, his knowledge of the anatomy of the head must have been great. We see this in his treatment of the formation of the skull beneath the skin, and in the hanging cheeks of the aged. His figures, however, are mostly hatted, and his style is certainly more forcible when they are not.

Unfortunately, the broad-flapped hat of the period was so much in favour both for men and women that not one in twenty of the medals of the time is without it. Of the remainder, most wear the curious close-fitting cap with a flap at the back, which was afterwards affected by the reformed clergy. The number of Schwarz's medal works in Nürnberg is considerable. He was *the* Nürnberg medaller as Haguenauer was afterwards of Augsburg. For the rest, in contra-distinction to Haguenauer his full faces are especially distinguished. Expressed with a few touches, they are lifelike—speaking likenesses, indeed, to use the familiar expression. One cannot help remarking the clever use of rasp and point in the treatment of the drapery ; and the whole arrangement, the placing of the figure in the circle and the value given to the headdress, is more pictorial than the dry neat finish and photographic detail of Haguenauer.

We are again indebted to the researches of Dr. Habich for additions to the very little information hitherto available concerning the next of the most important among the German medal makers. The earliest documentary accounts from which we may gather particulars of the life of Haguenauer are in the archives of the city of Augsburg, in which he first makes an official appearance about the year 1531. He appears to have been the son of a famous Strassburg sculptor, Nikolaus Haguenauer, the maker of a great carved altarpiece, now no longer existing, in the cathedral. As was the case with so many of his contemporary artists who worked in corporations, his talents were versatile, and he was at once painter, sculptor, goldsmith, and stained-glass maker. Early in his career Reformation troubles caused him to leave Strassburg (he was on the Catholic side), between the years 1520-1530, but we have not much certain infor-mation concerning the countries visited by him. They were, indeed, rapidly changing times, which affected in many ways the sentiment and fortunes of artists. The old exclusively religious requirements in the art of Gothic times had, under the influence of the classical Renaissance, turned the demands upon them into other channels, and with the Reformation came a marked decrease in emotional piety. The glorification of holy personages in heavenly spheres was discouraged, and gave place to that of living individuals. Princes, rich merchants, town councillors, goldsmiths, and others who were in the foremost ranks of literature and art, with their wives and families, were no longer only to be commemorated by their monuments after death, but caused a new demand for their portraits in life, which had hitherto been almost unknown. It is at least remarkable that out of the immense number of medals of the first half of the sixteenth century—and not all of them are portraits—a religious subject is rare indeed. There exist, happily, a large number of Haguenauer's cast medals, and not a few fine examples of his medallions, or patterns, in wood in various museums, and our British Museum possesses some rare specimens. The museums at Berlin, Munich, Augsburg, Nürnberg, Karlsruhe, Donaueschingen, Frankfurt, Stuttgart, Cologne, and some others in Germany, are naturally the strongest. Haguenauer's art, as we find it exemplified in these, differs considerably from that of his immediate predecessor, by which he seems to have been in no way influenced. He was, indeed, as independent and, to a certain extent, as original in one direction as Schwarz was in another. The work of Schwarz is direct, bold, decisive, impressionistic, and decorative. As an aid to identification many will find that in his portraits, whether drawings or medal work, there is a peculiar treatment of the eye which is remarkably characteristic: a piercing, penetrating expression, rather directed upwards. Very striking also is the treatment of the hair in his men models : a method which has no analogies in the work of his later rivals, Haguenauer or Kels. Or we may take, again, the modelling of the underlip and the angle of the chin. These and other distinctive features are recognizable at a glance, though without numerous illustrations it would not be easy to describe them in so many words. Indeed, it would be risky, within our limitations of space, to pursue further such questions of detail which, if but superficially stated, are liable to misconstruction. The reader may be advised, if he has not access to originals, to compare in the numerous plates of the articles by Habich to which reference has been made, such examples as the medals of Hans Tummel, of Ursula Imhoff, Anna Pfinzing, Margaret Tetzel, or Friedrich Pelham—to name no more of many which might be cited. Shortly, may we not say that a Pfinzing—and there are several—is recognizable, at a glance, as by Schwarz? For his full-face portraits what a finely modelled, convincing likeness is that of the young man in a broad-leafed slouched hat, embroidered shirt and furred robe of which there is a boxwood in the Munich Museum! Of his wood medallions we have, so far as I know, no authenticated examples in English museums or private collections. At South Kensington there is a fine cast in bronze of Urban Labenwolf dated 1518.

If we may compare shortly the genius of the two men, we shall find that although the work of the one begins, or comes into fashion, in the very year in which we lose sight of the other, Haguenauer was —as has already been stated—no follower of or in any way influenced by the earlier master. He struck out an entirely independent line for himself. He is of the Renaissance, while Schwarz remains Gothic. Exactness, finished precision, and dry, mechanical technique are nowhere strong points with Schwarz. In his work it is the satisfying results of the living image, the powerful use of strong lights and shades, forming a general decorative effect, which strike us. We hardly notice the manual dexterity, nor do we feel called upon to inquire into the methods which were used. In the other case we admire the technical *tours de force*, the academical correctness, the dexterity of the turner added to the talent of a finished draughtsman. Not that Schwarz was devoid of talent for figure-drawing. However he may have acquired it, more than one delightful example exists in the collections of prints and drawings of the Berlin, Bamberg, and Leipzig museums. The art of Haguenauer is less personal, accurate almost to the extent of niggling, descending to particulars of detail, and, as it were, sharply focused. It is generally of a lower relief, and would have appealed more to the sympathies of our own medal workers of the sixties of last century than the broader style which the critical art judgment of the present day would demand. At the same time, it is evident that, from the demands made upon him, Haguenauer was led into the error of over-production. What concerns us principally is, of course, his work in wood, and, amongst the comparatively small number of wood medallions to which we are able to refer, there are some which may place him on an equal level with Schwarz. What a strong portrait, for example, is that of the unknown individual, with close-cropped and partly-shaven head, and in buttoned coat with a hood to it, in the museum at Brunswick! Lesser characteristics by which we may be guided in assigning work to Haguenauer are the style of the lettering, the small ornaments used by him, the position of the subject in the field, and the decoration of the reverse. The inscriptions, it may be said, were often added by gluing letters to the model or impressing them on the mould for casting, sometimes evidently by means of printer's type.

174

Haguenauer's medal work was not exclusively confined to portraits, and his reverses were sometimes classical: for example, the 'Liberalitas' in the Berlin Coin-room, and the 'Girl extracting a Thorn from her Foot.' But this side of his art is not remarkable. Besides medallions, the Kann collection possessed a fine rectangular relief portrait of Bishop Philip v. Freising, than which nothing is more characteristic of his style in wood ; and, indeed, at its very best. It is a half-length, almost facing, the head turned in profile. The bishop wears the Reformers' cap, a kind of rochet, and over this a fur-bordered gown, the folds of which fall almost as in the draperies of the earlier Gothic schools. The clean-shaven, strongly-marked face, with the loose hanging folds of cheek and chin, has nothing of flattery about it. We do not know whether, in his later years, he followed their creed, but about 1543, when at Cologne and Bonn, Haguenauer made a number of portrait medals of prominent reformers. Amongst them, in the Berlin Coin-room, is the boxwood pattern for the medal of Melanchthon, then about the age of forty-six. It is on a plain field, without any rim, rather hard in treatment, but the face full of character, and of the type of the Caspar Hedio in the Brunswick Museum. The British Museum possesses a cast of this, and also, amongst others, of Mercator, Lauchberger, and Thomas v. Rheineck, and in the Waddesdon bequest are a bust of Hans Hanschel dated 1544, and another of Goedart van den Wier dated 1542, both attributed to Haguenauer. Without a sufficient number of illustrations it would be uninteresting to follow the series in detail, and a comprehensive list of works, according to artists, is not within the plan of this book. Two more original wood models, however, may be noticed. In the Munich Museum are the two large medallions of Sebastian Ligsalcz and his wife Ursula. Ursula wears what seems to be a looped man's hat of the period, and beneath it her straightly-combed hair falls in a long plait down her back. The man's headdress is more like a woman's cap, but it is really the netted fashion of the period, as an under headdress, and to be found on other portraits. The lady is neither beautiful nor youthful for the age of twenty-eight given to her by the inscription on the edge. The medal has the additional interest of an inscription in ink, stating that I (Haguenauer) at the age of 44 ' dis in holz abguntervetten und schneiden,' so that, if an autograph, we may deduce that Haguenauer was born in 1473. All Haguenauer's medallions are not in boxwood. They are sometimes, for example, of walnut or pearwood : and the very large one in the Munich collection of Cristof von Nellen is of maple. This is a very fine portrait of a great noble of the time, distinguished by his huge bulk and powerful physique, about whom there are many interesting anecdotes. He is represented as extremely portly. The Victoria and Albert Museum is not strong in wood medallions. The best is a small one of Ulrich Ehinger, dated 1533, which might well be by Haguenauer. It would be impossible, within our limits, to follow in detail other wood sculptors who produced medal work. Amongst the best known is Hans Kels of Kaufbeuren, who worked in Augsburg. By him there is in the Morgan collection, on loan at South Kensington, the original model of a medallion of Barbara Reihing of Kaufbeuren. She wears a close-fitting dress, with a chain over it, and her hair in a net. A bronze cast of this is in the collection of Mr. Max Rosenheim. Hans Daucher, or Daher, to whom some of the wood medallions may be attributed, was one of Augsburg's most distinguished sculptors. But his reliefs in honestone are his chief distinction. This was an Augsburg speciality, not being known in Nürnberg before 1508. With regard to these, and to the

176

sculptor generally, it must suffice to refer to the two reliefs in the Morgan collection at South Kensington, relating to the Triumph of Charles v. (1522), and to mention that Mr. Peartree (*Burlington Magazine*, 1905) proposes to name Daucher as the author of the famous Venus panel in the same collection, which bears Dürer's cipher. Mr. Peartree doesn't mention them, but he may have had in his mind also Daucher's honestone reliefs in the Bavarian National Museum, in which the nude women, holding shields with the arms of the Dukes of Brunswick, are certainly in no small degree reminiscent, both in design and execution, of the Morgan plaque. Daucher is credited with having made the stalls formerly in the Fugger chapel in the church of St. Anne at Nürnberg, and a fine group of the ' Deposition ' in another Fugger chapel at Augsburg. On the other hand there is, according to Mr. Peartree, direct evidence that he worked also for the Fuggers a ' Resurrection ' in Schloss Wellenburg. But this seems to be a pitifully poor piece of rococo character which would hardly redound to his credit. To such other medallionists, distinguished also in other departments of wood-carving, as Ludwig Krug, Hans Culmbach, Hans Reinhardt, Valentin Maler, or Jakob Fugger, it is possible to devote only a passing attention. Ludwig Krug of Nürnberg, of whose short life little is known, and whose medal work must also be classed, for the most part, as uncertain in attribution, worked probably between the years 1522-1532. He was a goldsmith, and Neudorffer praises his diesinking. Two examples of his silver medals are in the Victoria and Albert Museum. Of Hans Kels there is a group in boxwood in the Nürnberg Museum, with country people dancing, but it is rather trivial, and suggestive of the advancing rococo style. On the other hand, the rich and elaborately carved draughtboard and draughtmen by him in the Ambras collection, Vienna, is a very fine example of woodwork, generally, of this class. It is of many woods combined: oak, box, lignum vitae, satinwood, and pear. The board itself is a most elaborate work, with portrait medallions and borders of foliage and fruit, birds, and animals, and scenes of the chase. Some of the smaller medallions, with figures and scenes, have almost the character of the microscopic work to which the next chapter will be devoted. The draughtsmen are carved with a great variety of scriptural scenes and with classical and other profane subjects. The whole work is minutely described and figured in photogravure in the Vienna *Jahrbuch der kunsthistorischen Sammlungen*, iii. 53 (1885). Hans Dollinger was another contemporary Augsburg wood-carver to whom, however, few medallions in wood can be assigned. His reputation lies chiefly in his stone reliefs. The Rothschild bequest has eight interesting examples of boxwood medallions, amongst them one of John of Leyden, leader of the Anabaptists, and another of Maria, wife of Maximilian ii., by Antonio Abondi of Milan, who worked for that emperor and for Rudolph ii. In the same collection also is a fine panel in pearwood, measuring $6\frac{3}{4} \times 5\frac{3}{8}$ inches, with a three-quarter length figure of a young man in doublet, flat cap, and extravagantly slashed and beribboned doublet and hose.

The question of Albert Dürer's influence on the wood-carving of his time, and the use made by sculptors of his designs, has already received attention. In connexion with medal work it is again opened, and we have to consider not only whether this great artist himself carved in wood, but also whether some important medals and other reliefs, with or without his well-known signature, are the actual work of his hand. It is a momentous subject, upon which critics have greatly exercised themselves. It is more than likely, indeed we may be certain, that in accordance with the general practice of art in his day, Dürer would have been exercised in the use of the chisel. He worked as a goldsmith in his father's workshop, and, well versed in the art in all its branches, left it to become a painter. But nothing can be deduced from his diary and correspondence and other writings as authority on the matter, still less connecting him with any particular works. There is no existing piece that we can say with certainty is by him. Amongst the medals and other reliefs which have especial reference to our subject the following are the most important. A medal with a head of Lucretia, bearing the cipher dated 1508, and at one time erroneously called Agnes Dürer : a portrait medal of his master, Wohlgemut, dated 1511, the style of which, it is held, suggests an original in wax : a medal with the portrait of a man, dated 1519, and thought to be the father of the artist : and the famous honestone panel, with the full-length figure of a woman, nude, with her back turned, bearing the cipher and date 1509, which, having passed through the Birkenstock, Brentano, Felix, Stein, and Carmichael collections, is now in that of Mr. Pierpont Morgan, and lent by him to the Victoria and Albert Museum. Erman, one of the earliest authorities on medallic art, and many numismatic critics, have been, and still are, of opinion that these examples should be accepted, but the question is so involved in that which may only connect them with him as the designer, and the signature added with or without his concurrence or consent, that it is impossible to arrive at any definite conclusion. It has been already shown how very much the wood sculptors with whom we have been occupied availed themselves of his designs and of those of the other great engravers and etchers : and certainly his work, both portraits and heraldic compositions, was very much in use by contemporary and later goldsmiths. Interchange between artists was of the commonest occurrence. Marc Antonio

Raimondi is a well-known case in point, and his etched pieces which are absolute copies from Raphael's and other great artists' paintings and sketches.

Hans Daucher was undoubtedly one of the most prominent of the German wood workers of the first half of the sixteenth century, and nothing would be more interesting than, if we could, to name him authoritatively as the author also of the Pierpont Morgan hone-stone Venus. This, Mr. S. Montagu Peartree, in a long and able article in the *Burlington Magazine* for October 1905, has accomplished, to his own satisfaction at least. Without implying that Mr. Peartree's conclusions are irresistible, it may be said that his researches are of considerable interest, with much information concerning Daucher and his work, to which our space will not allow us to allude. Some, perhaps, may think his arguments are hardly convincing and sometimes far-fetched. For example, his comparison of the Morgan plaque with the figures on the left hand of the Limbo panel by Daucher in the Fugger chapel in the church of St. Ulrich at Augsburg, and the Eve herself in the same composition. He compares the features and the folds of the drapery and finds them 'identical' in design and execution. As a matter of fact the identity would seem scarcely nearer than if one were to say that an elbow is more like another elbow than a nose. After all, however, these things are felt, and cannot be argued. Daucher and others were perhaps associated with Dürer in Venice or, may be, in Nürnberg, and allowed by him to translate his drawings into relief, and even permitted to add the cipher as the mark of the designer to whom the chief credit was due, the sculptor effacing himself. This, indeed, would appear to have been the practice with the wood engraver later on : and in etching, to this day, the important part played by the actual printer of the plate is frequently ignored. Various other questions relating to the subject sug-

180

PLATE XXVIII

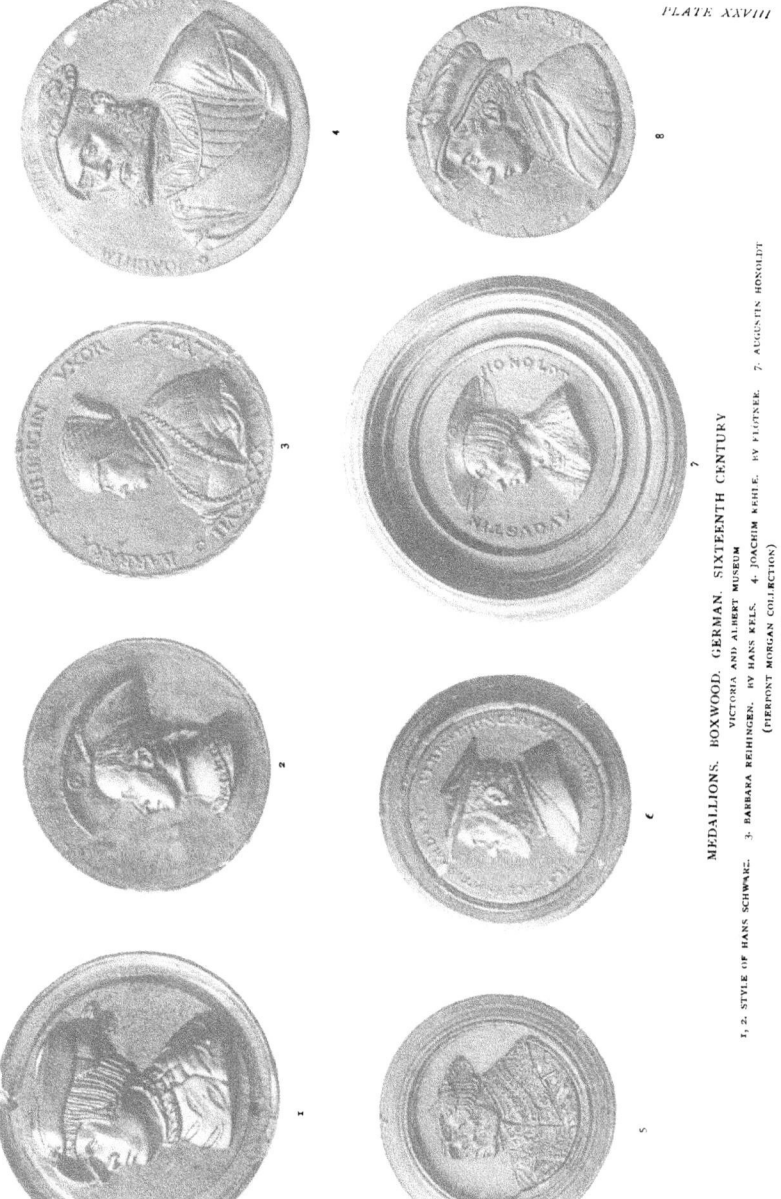

MEDALLIONS. BOXWOOD. GERMAN. SIXTEENTH CENTURY

VICTORIA AND ALBERT MUSEUM

1, 2. STYLE OF HANS SCHWARZ.   3. BARBARA REIHINGEN, BY HANS KELS.   4. JOACHIM KEHLE, BY FLOTSEE.   7. AUGUSTIN HONOLDT

(PIERPONT MORGAN COLLECTION)

PAGE 181

gest themselves, without bringing us any nearer to a definite conclusion.

There has been no attempt, within the limits of a short chapter, to give here either a history of medallions in wood, or even a comprehensive account of the work of Schwarz, of Haguenauer, or of Kels. Nor, even if space permitted, should I make any pretensions to knowledge as a specialist on the subject generally. For such a qualification the study is necessary not only of models in carved wood, but of cast and struck medals in various metals and by various processes, especially in Italy, where the practice of working them in wood was unusual, if used at all. Our national collections are, unfortunately, not rich in examples of this particularly German art. But, indeed, they are nowhere commonly to be found. In the Louvre are about fourteen wood medallions, formerly in the Sauvageot collection, which were described and figured so long ago as 1834 by Lenormant, in his *Trésor de Numismatique*. One of them is, however, a draughtsman. The Victoria and Albert Museum acquired, in 1867, two fine examples, one of which is ascribed to Hans Schwarz, and the other is very much in his manner, and it has possessed also for some time four or five others which are not without interest. Amongst the latter, a portrait of Wolfgang Poemer bears the (added) Dürer cipher. Quite recently the museum has acquired, through the munificence of Mr. Salting, eleven medallions, several of which came from the famous Spitzer collection, which was comparatively rich in examples attributed to Haguenauer. The Pierpont Morgan collection, at present in the same museum, has, with three others, the Barbara Reihingin, by Hans Kels, dated 1538, and the Augustin Honoldt. Several of the above are here illustrated (Plate xxviii.). None have yet been ascribed, with certainty, to a particular master, and it would be out of place, in such a brief notice as the present one, to do more than draw the reader's attention to them. Finally, for our London museums, the Wallace collection has four medallions, including one with the portrait of the Infante Ferdinand of Spain, all of which have this monogram ℗ branded on the backs. Of course it is not to be assumed to be that of the sculptor. Mr. Max Rosenheim's collection, and his reputation as an expert on the subject, are well known. In wood he has a fine example of Kels, with the portraits of Matthew and Anna Raiser on the obverse and reverse respectively. Two or three others from the collection of Sir Julius Wernher were shown at the Exhibition of the Burlington Fine Arts Club, to the catalogue of which the reader is referred.

It will be seen that these specimens of German art are of considerable historical and artistic interest. They differ, also, from medallic art in metal, in that each is in itself the original, and unique, while casts from it may be multiplied. They are artists' proofs; sometimes, also, proofs before all letters, and they are of extreme rarity. Few, indeed, are aware of their high market value. It may be, therefore, interesting to note that the cost to Mr. Salting of the little bit of boxwood, about the diameter of a two-shilling piece, and hardly half the thickness, which forms the Lux Meringer medallion (Plate xxviii.) was no less than £500.

CHAPTER X

MICROSCOPIC OR MINIATURE WOOD SCULPTURE

THERE is a series of undeniable works of art in wood to which the term microscopic sculpture is applicable in default of a better term under which to classify them. The boxwood carvings described in the preceding chapter would seem to form an intermediate class between these very minutely executed works and those which range from statuettes to life-size and even colossal dimensions. If, indeed, the use of a microscope is not absolutely necessary, it is at least an aid which is of considerable use for their appreciation, and they can well stand the test. These curious wood-carvings, on a minute scale, are all of the same character, and though nothing is certain, it is difficult not to imagine that the known examples—of which nearly every collection of importance contains a more or less elaborate specimen—must all be from the same workshop, perhaps even by the same hand. The beautiful examples bequeathed to the nation by Baron F. de Rothschild are so representative of the class that it would be quite sufficient to confine our attention entirely to them. More than one is unequalled elsewhere, and the collection is easy to inspect among the other beautiful surroundings in the Waddesdon room of the museum. Easy to inspect, but not to handle, these precious objects, for so fragile is their nature owing to the extreme tenuity to which some of the carved details have been reduced that it is doubtful if

183

permission will ever again be given to do so for the purpose of photographing them. We are indebted, therefore, for our illustrations to the photographs previously taken for the official publications. Generally speaking, these minute carvings are very clever reductions of monumental Gothic work, or of the altarpieces which were themselves in the architectural style of the period. Even if original to some extent in arrangement, they follow, in common with work of greater proportions, the system, so usual in the minor arts, of copying from paintings, engravings, and sculpture generally. *Chefs-d'œuvre* of technical skill in execution, they are in no way inferior to the altarpieces which have been described in previous chapters. No doubt the fashion was suggested in the first place by some simple ornamentation of the ordinary rosary bead. This became extended, and the beads were increased in size from an inch to three or more in diameter to admit even of figure work and scenes in perspective. These beads — paternosters, grains-de-chapelet, or, as the Germans term them, prayer-nuts—are no doubt the earliest in date. A further extension of the idea are the miniature altarpieces, tabernacles, *memento mori*, and other pious *bibelots*, of which there are charming examples in the Waddesdon and Wallace collections. In course of time the simply-carved beads were made to open on a hinge as a diptych, sometimes even as a polyptych, and were deeply and elaborately carved, within and without, with figures and episodes in sacred history in full relief. Often, again, these precious and fragile carvings were further enclosed in outer cases of delicate open work, and the two hemispheres divided by a thin metal plate engraved and enamelled: after the fashion, in fact, of a pomander box. Naturally, also, in response to the spirit of the time, the idea lent itself to all sorts of quaint conceits. We have the favourite *memento mori* subject repeated in numerous

184

grotesque and terrifying and even repulsive ways. There are strings of grinning skulls and half-decayed heads, or the living head of fashionable beauty in conjunction with the representation of what it was fated to become after death. There was a similar fashion, of course, in the mediæval ivories. Or again, as in this collection, a tiny coffin, with a ridged lid, which opens and discloses a skeleton with its attendant horrors, or a representation of the Last Judgment and the tortures of hell. A natural extension of the idea from the beads, in diptych or polyptych form, would have been the application to other devotional and even secular objects, always on the same minute scale, and always with the same exhibition of dexterity of handiwork and extreme carefulness of execution, with at the same time evidence of a master in art on a level with the most distinguished sculptors of his time. Doubtless this mixture of talent of such a varied kind must have had a considerable reputation, though all trace of the artist, or artists, has been lost.

There is so much similarity in the technical execution of the fairly numerous examples of this microscopic sculpture which still exist, that it would seem evident that they must have been the work of one particular sculptor, or have proceeded from one particular workshop. It is hardly likely that the accomplishment could have been a common one, which astounds us by the apparent impracticability of detaching, without breaking, such details as the hairlike spears of the soldiers in the crucifixion scenes, the multitude of figures carved in the round and standing detached from the background in perspective landscapes (as in the larger retables), and the undercutting in almost inaccessible portions of the subject, always with the same precision and perfection of finish. Of course, as in the case of the well-known Chinese puzzle-balls, the problem would lose its charm if joins of any kind were permitted. There are two most important pieces in the Waddesdon collection : a miniature altarpiece on a richly-carved base ornamented with figures, and a very curious and elaborately contrived structure, mounted on a stand, which the official catalogue describes as a 'tabernacle.' We need not quarrel with this term, for it would be extremely difficult to find an alternative one which should be entirely satisfactory. As an example of this description of work, in which ingenuity and dexterity of handicraft are joined with design from the hand of a master, it is probably unique. It would not be easy to describe, in a few words, the subjects depicted on the central panel and wings of the retable, or the complicated construction and variety of figure work of the second piece. The illustrations here given must speak for themselves (Plates XXIX. and XXX.). In the centre of the altarpiece is the Crucifixion with the three crosses raised on high, the thieves on each side struggling with their bonds : beneath are a multitude of tiny figures, the holy women, priests, soldiers on foot and on horseback, and the people generally, in the manner of the Flemish and German primitives, and the altarpieces copied and adapted from their pictures. Analogies will, of course, present themselves to those who are familiar with these subjects, but the question, however attractive, is not one for which space can here be found. With a magnifying glass, and even without it, one can distinguish the expression of the features admirably portrayed, the minutiæ of the costumes, the harness and accoutrements of the horses, the hairlike ropes binding the thieves, and the equally hairlike spears of the soldiers, completely detached, without any support from the background. One only of the latter shows any injury, being slightly bent, after four hundred years and more of existence. The wings of the triptych are, as usual, in low relief. Beneath, and enclosed with doors, is a

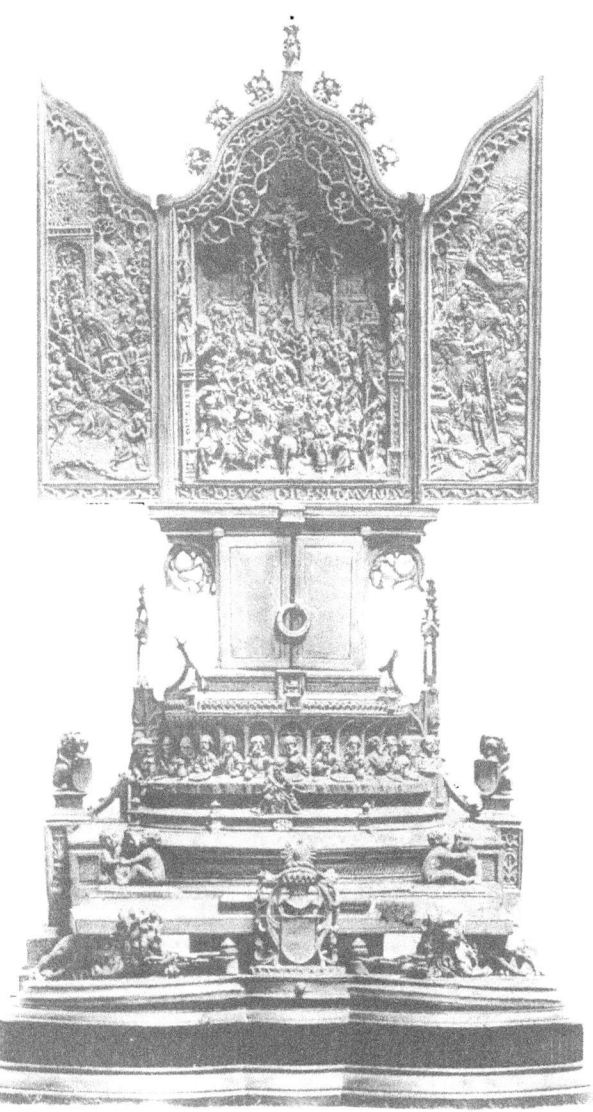

MINIATURE ALTARPIECE. FLEMISH OR NORTH GERMAN. SIXTEENTH CENTURY
BRITISH MUSEUM (WADDESDON ROOM, ROTHSCHILD BEQUEST)
PAGE 166

second, and smaller, triptych with scenes of the Passion carved on the inner side in low relief. Beneath this again, on the semi-circular arcade of steps, is the representation of the Last Supper—the figures of Our Lord and the apostles, in full relief, seated behind the table—and on the base, on the steps of the arcade, and on pillars are cherub figures and lions holding shields in Renaissance style. The whole rests on recumbent lions. There are traces of gilding, and the date 1511 is engraved on a small oval panel. The so-called tabernacle is remarkable, in the first place, for its complicated construction. The *knop*, if it may be so termed, opens and discloses a kind of rosary bead divided into two parts on a hinge, one part having shutters to close as in a triptych. The interiors of the hemispheres are still more minutely carved than in the previous example, with the Crucifixion and other Passion scenes. There is again the same dexterity displayed in the detachment of the spears and other accessories, and all the figures are in full relief. On the top of the bulbous pinnacle which surmounts the whole is a pelican in her piety. If this is removed, the petals forming the bulb itself fall down and, as they fall, cause a charming Madonna statuette to rise out of the bulb beneath. Each petal is itself carved on the inner side with scenes in the life of Christ and of His Mother. Even with this, the ingenuity of the fitting together or displacements of the various parts is not exhausted, and hardly a hair's-breadth of the whole is without its carved subject or ornament.

No Japanese netsuke or medicine-box maker has bestowed more elaborate care on the fitting together, or on the decoration of the exposed or unexposed portions. There are several inscriptions and texts, badges, and coats-of-arms. These, and the character of the lettering, are of importance in the considera-tion of the question of the origin of these boxwood miniature works. Of the coats-of-arms there are two of Charles the Fifth as Emperor and King, and under the foot of the altarpiece is the inscription + DOMINICVS · ACAVALLA · ME · FECIT · AÑ 1562. A more careful examination of the objects themselves and of their cases would be necessary than it is possible for any but their curators to make to warrant any definite opinions which might be deduced. Both the pieces just described have their charming original cases of leather incised with floral scrolls, and set and bordered with gold filigree work. All this points to the high value attached to these objects, and the extreme care with which they were kept. It may be that the base of the altarpiece is of later date than the upper portion, and that the case was made for it at the time of the addition or reconstruction. We may remember that Charles v. was born at Ghent in 1500, was King of Spain and Emperor of Germany in 1516. He would then have been only eleven years of age at the time the dated part was made. He retired into a monastery in 1555, and died in 1558.

To what country are we to ascribe the origin of these curious pieces? The usual opinion, and the official one held at the museum, is that they, and the other known pieces of the same character, are Flemish. Though this is highly probable, something might however be said for a North German origin : in the Westphalian provinces, for example, where, in the sixteenth century, a flourishing school of retable makers existed, under strong Flemish influence. The architectural work, if it may so be called, has nothing peculiar to Flanders, and the branch-work curtain, bordering and hanging from the ogee-shaped canopy of the larger altarpiece, is more in German than in Flemish taste. Many Westphalian and even Lower Rhenish altarpieces might be cited in which analogies would be found. For example, the beautiful early sixteenth-century retable, No. 1336, in

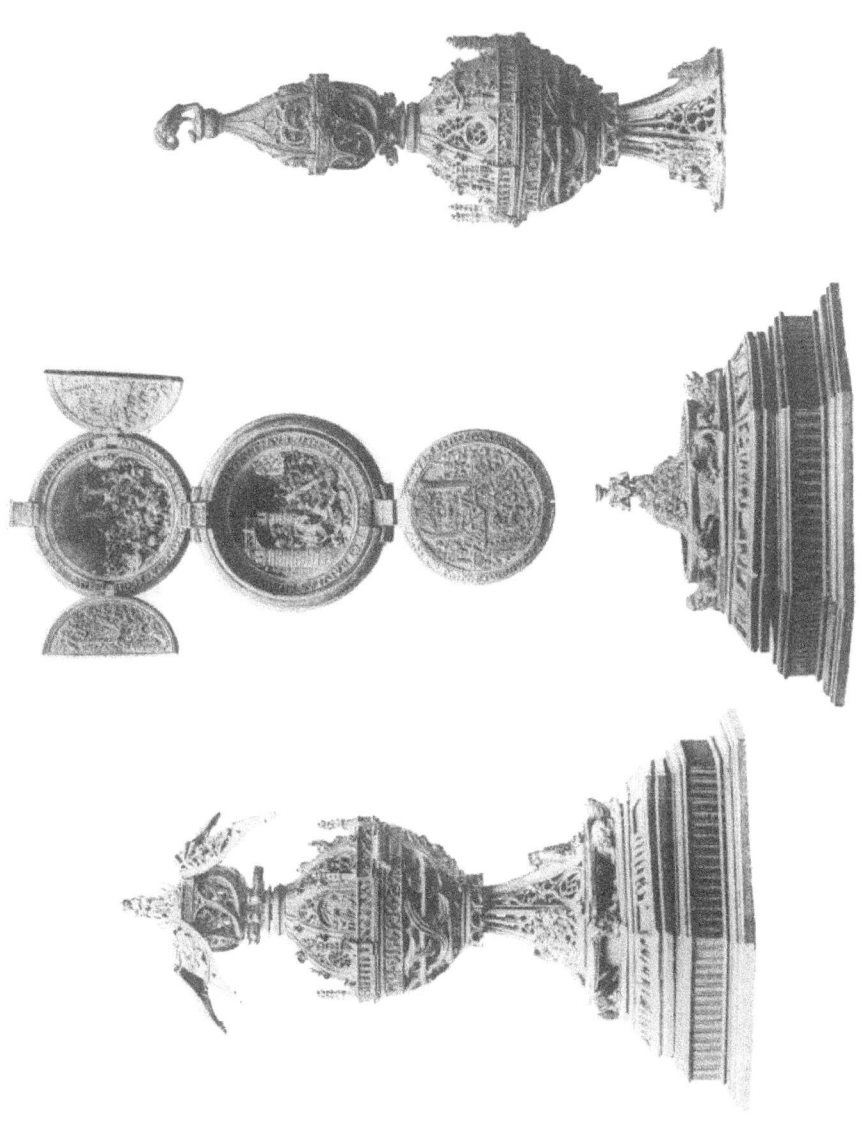

the Bavarian National Museum. In this piece also the pinnacles and the somewhat eccentric open-work ornament of the canopies of the three divisions (whether or no they belong to the original structure) are also strongly suggestive of the flamboyant open-work of the second piece here illustrated. The British Museum miniature altarpiece has been chosen for illustration instead of another extremely fine one in the Wallace collection, because it is perhaps more representative, of extreme delicacy and tenuity in the details and accessories. But it is not to be supposed that the Wallace shrine is less remarkable, and it is apparently from the same *atelier*. The fantastic architectural work forms a further argument in favour of Westphalian, or, at least, North German origin, rather than Flemish.

There is another curious example of microscopic boxwood carving in the Waddesdon collection. It is attached to a gold signet-ring of Italian origin, and according to the museum authorities is probably English work of so early a date as 1340. The style is, of course, of an entirely different character from any of the other pieces, but we need not on that account necessarily assume that it is much earlier in date. Without affirming also that any of these elaborate works, so German or Flemish in character, could by any possibility be English, it may be that the idea of ornamenting rosary beads in this manner originated in our country. The writer of a short paper in the Catholic periodical *The Month* (July 1909) lately brought under notice a curious early sixteenth-century tract by Clement Armstrong, called 'A treatise concerning the staple and commodities of this Realme.' The following passage occurs in it: 'If any Englishman wold stody to devise and invent any new artificial thynges, Londoners, incontynent, is ever redy to destroy it. About a fourteen years past was but a sleyt fantasy devised in Kent of makyng the first bedys with the pater noster holowe like muske balls, made of boxe which in a short time susteynyd a 30 or 40 men, that made theym and sold them to Londoners whereby all parties which occupied them gate lyvyng oon with another: unto a haburdasher that carried a sample into Flaunders and ther causid a gret abundance of theym to be made by young prenters used in all such actyvite ther and brought them into England to the destruction of the seid artificers here.' The tract referred to was first printed and edited by Dr. Pauli in a contribution to the *Göttingen Abhandlungen* for 1878, vol. xxiii., entitled 'Drei Volkwirthschaftliche Denkschriften aus der Zeit Heinrichs VIII. von England.' In this we find all that is known on the subject. The letters appear to have been addressed to Crumwell about the year 1532, the writer calling him 'my maister.' They are a lengthy and elaborately worded complaint concerning the goods and work going out of the country, of foreigners brought to and employed in England, and how to reform the Realm and set people to work. The expression 'young prenters' probably means apprentices.

Before leaving this subject some notice must be taken of two pieces, in a somewhat similar style of minute carving, which involve, in addition, questions of historical interest. They are the letters ⟨M⟩ and F in boxwood or cedar, in the museum of the Louvre. The M is carved with legends of the life and martyrdom of Saint Margaret. The F has on the inside, when opened, religious scenes, such as the crucifixion, mixed with others from the romances of the period, and on the outer sides foliage work and ornament of a Renaissance character. The whole is suggestive of a Franco-Flemish origin, and if these curious objects had any practical use, this would probably have been a method of telling the beads: for thirty round grains, or beads, surmount the edges of the letter M. This carved letter seems first to have been noticed in an account given in a communication by M. Bon to the proceedings of the *Société des Inscriptions et des Belles-Lettres* in 1753. The writer considered it to be of the time of St. Louis, and further conjectured that it belonged to Margaret of Provence, who accompanied him in his first crusade. The F is mentioned by the Abbé Barthélemy in his letters in *L'Esprit des Journaux*, 1779. It is, of course, late fifteenth or early sixteenth century work, and has given occasion for considerable ingenuity in attempting to identify the personages whose initials the letters represent. But the question has not yet been solved. The letter F was bought by M. Debruge Dumenil in 1837 for 120 francs. It afterwards went into the Hope collection for 600 francs, and at the dispersal of the latter was acquired by M. Sauvageot for 2500 francs. Labarte thought that it referred to François 1er and the M to his sister Marguerite d'Angoulême. But a more likely theory is that the letters are the initials of the names of Philibert of Savoy and the Regent Margaret, in whom we have already been much interested. In an inventory of 1523, which has been published in the *Revue Archéologique* for 1850 there is mention of 'une belle lettre M de bois bien taillée à une petite chaîne de bois pendant aux lettres du nom de Jésus.' We may remark the mixture of Italian and Flemish styles and that the subjects in the medallions of the M are still Gothic though the ornamental details are of the Renaissance.

CHAPTER XI

WOOD SCULPTURE IN SPAIN—SOME SPANISH
RETABLES AND THEIR MAKERS

U P to a period as recent as the sixties of last century very little attention had been paid to the arts of Spain, with the exception of the great schools of painting. We knew Velasquez, Cano, or Murillo, but little else. Of archæological research and books on art there was little or nothing in Spanish, or of the sculptural art of Spain in other languages, and very little had been efficiently illustrated. Indeed, to the present day, the *Diccionario de Artistas Españoles*, published at the end of the eighteenth century, is almost the only work of authentic reference in the language of the country. But about 1860 the acquisitions made in the country itself by Sir J. C. Robinson, for the South Kensington Museum, were the means of opening the eyes of a great many hitherto ignorant of the treasures of Spanish sculpture, metal work and textiles, and the interest shown in them culminated in the special exhibition at that museum in 1881. Previously, Sir Richard Ford, in his *Handbook for Spain*, had been the only one amongst us to attempt anything like a systematic account of the arts of the Peninsula. From whatever sources the styles of the great *retablos* or altarpieces, in stone or wood, or the *sillerias* with their elaborately carved stalls, may have been borrowed or inspired, the fact remains that these works have, in common with the treasures of wrought-

192

iron, of the goldsmith's and jeweller's art, or of embroideries, a character of their own which the least experienced critic recognizes at once as Spanish. The neglect and destruction of works of art in Spain that prevailed about the period of the purchases by our museums conduced considerably to the ease of acquirement. It is said that woodwork, and even textiles, were burnt in quantities for the sake of the bullion in the gilding which they contained. The authorities of cathedrals and monasteries were ignorant of their art interest and value, and the opportunities of collectors for a rich harvest were exceedingly great. Nevertheless, so far as wood sculpture is concerned, it cannot be said that our museum at Kensington especially profited, and for a general survey of the art we shall have to go to other museums and to the cathedrals and monasteries of the country itself for what still remains of choir-work, of altarpieces, or of detached figures.

On account of the special character of Spanish art in wood, arising from the national system of polychrome which we call *estofado*, and from other peculiar methods of enrichment, our observations may extend somewhat beyond the period to which, in general, it has been found necessary to restrict the scope of this book. The system of painting, so important with relation to wood-carving, was not, however, a Spanish invention, nor even peculiar to Spain. In this they were merely, according to their custom, imitating methods employed in other countries. In the earlier times, and almost to the end of the Gothic period, the flesh was painted with a single tint and varnished : later on the draperies were decorated by colouring over gold, and tracing upon this surface 'estofado' fine designs. Among the influences which have contributed to form the art of the Peninsula, we need touch but lightly on the most ancient ; that is to say, on the Oriental, or Arab. The effect of the Moorish invasion, and the prolonged occupation of the

country, must have been very great, and they have left
their traces even in comparatively late Gothic times.
Indeed, the earliest choir stalls—those of the convent
of *Gradafes* in the kingdom of Leon, or at least the
remnants of them which still exist in the Archæological
Museum at Madrid—are Arab in style, though of the
thirteenth century. Later still, in the beginning of the
fifteenth, the carver of the stalls of the cathedral of
Huesca bore a Moslem name, Mahomet de Boja. For
the most frequent examples of Moorish art we should,
of course, go to the decorative interior wood-work, the
artesonado ceilings, the doors and other ornamental
details of palaces and municipal buildings, for example
in the Alcazar of Seville. Naturally this is without
figures. Briefly, the influence of Oriental art in Spain
may be summed up under three systems. The first, in
which, from the eighth to the twelfth century, Byzantine
methods prevailed, as they existed in the churches of
the East: the second, the highly decorated style of the
Alhambra and Granada, covering the period between
the thirteenth and the fifteenth century: and the third
the Mudejar, or mixture of Christian and Moorish,
the Hispano-Moresque, due to Christian work carried
on by Moorish artists, or the copying and adapting by
the latter of Moorish styles and designs. During
those times, and indeed for long after the expulsion
of the Moors, the wood most generally used was of the
pine family: pitch pine, cypress, and, in particular,
cedar. The vast forests surrounding the city of
Cuença supplied unlimited quantities of the Cuença
wood so frequently mentioned in inventories as an
accepted term for pine, or deal as we should say. As
late as the middle of the sixteenth century we find in
the contracts for a retable by the *entallador* Diego de
Velasco, and the *imagineros* who assisted him, that the
figures should be in good wood of Cuença, and in
cypress. The Moorish artists kept rigidly to their own

194

style without attempting to imitate that of the Christians with whom they worked. The earlier Gothic work, therefore, is a combination of both, the Moslem confining himself to arabesques, geometrical curves, tracery in inlaid work, pendentives and stylistic foliage of an absolutely Oriental character. This, however, he could accommodate without difficulty to the Gothic style. A fine example, probably the finest of the period in existence, is the painted and gilt reliquary now in the Accademia de la Historia, Madrid. It is a triptych with Gothic arches in relief, dated 1390. The style persisted, and may be followed in several cabinets in, the Victoria and Albert Museum. The whole question, however, belongs more properly to furniture, and is beyond our present purpose.

From the point of view with which we are particularly concerned, wood sculpture in Spain begins to attain a prominent position about the beginning of the thirteenth century, a little later than its early development in France. The sluggish Spanish temperament of the time, the political conditions in the country itself and foreign relations, combined to hinder its rapid progress and the formation of a distinctly national art. As late as the middle of the century the Moors were founding, as their last refuge from the increasing Christian power, their kingdom of Granada, nor were they defeated there till a century later. But there still remain examples of Christian art of the thirteenth century of such interest as the almost life-sized statues in painted wood in the Archæological Museum at Madrid. They are from Oviedo: a seated Madonna figure and a St. John holding a book in the left hand, the head resting on the right arm. The French influence is, of course, evident. In the fourteenth century there was an invasion of Italian, French, and Flemish artists, who made many monuments in stone for the cathedrals of Barcelona, Tarragona, and Leon. The French were indeed the chief, if not the sole foreign artists, to whom is due the sculpture of the cathedrals and churches in the thirteenth and early fourteenth centuries. Leon is absolutely French, and Pampeluna, built by Charles III. of Navarre, is not only French, but in the older parts as fine as anything of the period that France itself could show. Even if a certain number of Tuscan sculptors in marble were imported in the fourteenth century, the dominant note throughout the century is still French, and so continues in the schools of Aragon and Castile, and in the provinces bordering on France, although no French names are to be found in the contracts. In the early part of the fifteenth century we learn from Vasari that Dello Delli, the miniature painter, entered into the service of Juan II., King of Aragon. Delli was famous for the decoration of chests, adorned with paintings in the stucco or gesso style, and one of the first to introduce this Italian manner into Spain. He appears to have abandoned his own country from pique at some supposed affront, and to have devoted his life to Spain, where he died at the age of forty-seven. His influence upon the polychromatic decoration of sculpture must not be left out of account. Then comes the direct influence of Burgundy, of Flanders, and of Germany. The great sculptors of these countries are called in, and combine to establish their master-works in the form of the retables and choir-work, so mixed in character from the various elements from which it is derived, and yet, however strikingly Flemish, Italian, or even Moorish in detail, so overwhelmingly Spanish as a completed structure. Nowhere else are the proportions of a retable on so huge a scale, nowhere else are the materials, whether of alabaster, of painted and gilded wood, of gold and silver and precious stones, of such magnificence, as it stretches from side to side the whole width of the choir, and from floor to roof. All, it may be said, of the hundreds from amongst which it will be possible to select but one or two of the most important to illustrate sculpture in wood, belong to the end of the fifteenth and the beginning of the sixteenth century. About the beginning of the fifteenth century the Italians who had hitherto been employed were replaced by Flemish artists. We find in various archives, such as those of the cathedral of Toledo, the names of maître Rogel, of Juan, and Bernardino of Brussels, of the four brothers Guas, Vas, or Egas, also of Brussels, and numerous 'Aleman' and others, which show that the Fleming was called in to teach and also to establish himself in the country. Thus, the dominating elements in the formation of the sculptural art in wood to be applied to so great an extent in the erection of the peculiar Spanish altarpieces, and in the richly-carved ranges of choir stalls, were, in turn, Burgundian or French, Flemish or German, Italian and again French. From these varied sources was evolved what is called the plateresque style: *estilo platevesco*, a term applied because it has a certain resemblance to the elaborate and delicate ornamentation of silver plate. The expression is somewhat vague, and to some extent misleading, for it by no means indicates anything novel or original, or any settled departure which could properly be termed a style, but simply a general impression of over-richness of decoration: a varied combination of pointed Gothic and Italian Renaissance, to which are often added Mudejar forms. When the whole of Europe revelled a century or two later in the grotesque ornamentation, which at its worst is called *rococo* or *baroque*, it is not surprising that the Spanish temperament should have carried this to the most extreme lengths in that style to which they themselves have given the name of *estilo monstruoso*. It degenerated indeed into a riotous extravagance which, under the architect Churriguera, and connected with his name by the unflattering epithet *churrigueresque*, has not been surpassed or equalled elsewhere. Unfortunately, it is to Spain a subject of national pride. The political conditions prevailing at the end of the fifteenth century naturally contributed to increase the relationships between the courts of Flanders and Spain, from the fact that Philippe le Beau had married the daughter of the Spanish monarch, and early in the century names of artists suggestive of German origin also appear in municipal and cathedral archives. We have, for example, a Juan de Aleman, and the mixture or adaptation to Spanish forms of foreign names is perhaps in many cases almost our sole resource in drawing conclusions, so scanty are the materials for any definite history. A striking example of this is the case of the foremost name on our roll of sculptors, that of Philippe Vigarny, or Felipe de Borgoña, the story of whose origin and life is so uncertain. The Flemish influence and workmanship on numberless retables and stall work of choirs is marked. We find it in the great retable of Burgos, where, on the other hand, the splendid range of choir work of the cathedral is no less distinctively Italian of the Renaissance. These Flemish and German influences continued until early in the sixteenth century, when Spain, with the rest of Europe, succumbed completely to the all-conquering influence of the Italian Renaissance. The infiltration of Renaissance principles and methods was not, however, of sudden application. As in other countries, it made its way first of all tentatively and with hesitation, as it were : certain details were applied to the still dominant Gothic style before being adopted exclusively. Besides the stream of immigrant foreign artists, the Spaniards themselves went to Italy to place themselves under the great masters of Rome and Florence, and the Spanish sovereigns brought to their courts and encouraged in every way the settlement in the country of the best available talent. An example of the transition or mixed style is such a work as the two large doors which were at one time in the Spitzer collection. Although so late as 1541, they are evidence of the slow abandonment of, and still lingering attachment to, the Gothic style, and, indeed, they show distinctly an unsettled purpose in the mind of the artist, uncertain on which side to cast the balance of his affections, and therefore, except in the execution, which is admirable, they cannot be said to be entirely successful. Of a fine, close-grained, and polished walnut, they are an illogical mixture of Gothic motives and panels of the linen pattern with ill-adapted classical Renaissance types. About these times we have more definite information than we have concerning Spanish art of the early mediæval period, where we are left to conjecture and to scanty documentary information. It must be allowed that however great may have been the influence of France and Flanders in the last days of pure Gothic, the imported architects and sculptors were, to a not inconsiderable extent, limited to designing and superintendence, and were ably seconded by the collaboration and admirable execution of the native artists. Whatever may have been the amount of influence applied, especially that resulting from the Italian training of Berruguete, it will be found in *retablos* and *sillerias*, as well as in single figures, to be tempered by the national characteristics of Spanish feeling. If, indeed, the stalls of Leon, for example, may be borrowed or imitated from Germany and Flanders, or those of Burgos from such work as the choir of Perugia, they, or at least innumerable other adaptations, are so overlaid with unmistakable Spanish feeling, so characterized by a profusion of ornament to the extent of congestion, by a lack of restraint in the use of colour and gilding, and by the love of imitative realism which besets Spanish art in general, that, while flattered by the

199

compliment, the Flemish or Italian artist would hardly be contented to acknowledge them.

It is then a heterogeneous mixture which we must expect to find in the retables and choir work of the fifteenth and sixteenth centuries. In the fifteenth it would seem to be the Flemish accent which is predominant : yet not exclusively so, but rather, in general, of Northern Europe, for both Germany and France have largely to do with it; and in the sixteenth it becomes a medley of Italian styles, introduced by French artists who have already gone through the process of adapting them to their own national system ; by Flemish sculptors domiciled in the country, and become naturalized, and by Spaniards themselves, who, without abandoning entirely the national style, so surcharge it with the new Italian methods that it is almost transformed. In point of fact, whether the designs and execution were entirely due to the foreigner or divided between him and the native artist, bred in foreign schools, the Spaniard called the tune, as he was entitled to do. The plan of the present work does not permit of a systematic and inclusive description of the many extraordinary *retablos* in the Peninsula, although a considerable number are in carved and painted wood—in pine, limewood, cedar, or larch, for the most part—wood being more abundant and more easily worked than stone or alabaster. The general remarks in a previous chapter on the origin and development of retables and altarpieces need not be repeated. It is true, perhaps, that although the earlier forms of moderate dimensions became extended into *reredoses* as they are now, unfortunately, generally called, of considerable dimensions, nowhere more than in Spain, at the period with which we are mainly concerned, did they attain such vast proportions together with such exaggerated profuseness of imagery and decoration. Whether of stone or marble or alabaster,

200

of silver or other metal as some are, or of wood as the most usual material, in every case they employed a multitude of artists of nearly every profession. Architects and sculptors, goldsmiths and silversmiths, painters, enamellers, imagineros, entalladores, estofadores, and the innumerable other specialists into which the profession of sculpture-painting was divided, plaster casters and stucco workers were required, and even the stuff-maker was called in to add to the imitative realism in which the Spanish artist delighted. Amongst the host of names of artists, native and foreign, which may be gathered from the pages of Cean Bermudez, it must suffice to confine ourselves to Vigarny, Berruguete, Damian Forment, Pedro da Mena, and Martinez Montañez, with some incidental references to the most distinguished of their co-workers : leaving also the few remarks which it is necessary to make upon Spanish choir stall work to the chapter devoted to that subject. The great epoch of sculpture in Spain, identified, perhaps, more particularly with sculpture in wood than with any other branch of the art, is of the time of Felipe di Borgoña and of Alonso Berruguete, covering in general terms the first half of the sixteenth century.

Damian Forment was born at Valencia in the latter half of the fifteenth century, probably nearly about the same time as Berruguete, than whom he died somewhat earlier, the date of Forment's death being 1533. Martinez Montañez is without the limits to which it has been found advisable to restrict in general the scope of this book, but as it is to him that is due a revival of mediæval methods of painted sculpture in a peculiarly Spanish style, a brief reference to his work will not be entirely out of place. Philippe Vigarny, or, as the Spaniards call him, Felipe de Borgoña, is the most prominent amongst all the sculptors who contributed to form the Spanish Renaissance. Of his early history little is known, but it is generally agreed that he was a Burgundian, a native of Langres, where he was born some time in the last quarter of the fifteenth century. We have our first authentic information concerning his work in an existing document dated 1505, in the archives of Burgos, in which he describes himself as *imaginario*, residing at Burgos, and contracts for the sum of 130,000 maravedis to make with his own hands the figures for the choir of Palencia in fine, smooth, unpainted walnut. It would be out of the question, without numerous illustrations, and within the limits to which it is necessary to confine this chapter, to review in any systematic manner the considerable quantity of wood sculpture in the form of *retablos*, stall work, and single figures attributed to Vigarny. His earlier style suggests a Franco-Flemish influence, yet neither he nor Berruguete were educated in Gothic schools. They were the pioneers of the feeling and methods of the Italian Renaissance, forcing it on their countrymen in the face of considerable opposition. The national temperament was far more inclined to the religious feeling, and the artless expression of devotion fostered by the pictorial methods of Gothic art, than to classical forms and the glorification of human beauty for its own sake. It needed a master mind to impose upon it the elegant formulae which revived the ancient mythology in the guise of the most holy personages, and of canonized saints. Yet, as in default of positive evidence we have to draw our conclusions from the large quantity of work attributed to Vigarny, his sympathies would appear to have been divided, and it is sometimes difficult to distinguish his Gothic from his Italian tendencies. Both he and Berruguete were trained in Italy, but while our information of Vigarny's early years and work is insufficient, Berruguete would seem to have been a more consistent and still more ardent promoter of the Italian style. French and Flemish influence in their early days must have been very strong, for it continued throughout the sixteenth century. Juan de Arphe, the goldsmith, severely reprimanded his fellow-workers who never ceased copying from French and Flemish pictures and engravings. There was also a sculptor of a similar name to Vigarny —Juan Borgoña, also of Langres, and possibly a brother of Felipe, who worked at Burgos between 1522-1540, and it is not unlikely that work attributed to Philippe may, in reality, have been the outcome of various hands during a number of years. There has always been a curious tendency in every country's art to give to the most popularly known master any work of superior quality of whose origin there is no direct evidence. We have seen this already in the cases of Dürer, Riemenschneider, Della Quercia, and others.

Equally with Vigarny we have little record of the actual training and foreign wanderings of Alonso Berruguete, who, in the opinion of some, is given the foremost place amongst all Spanish sculptors. He was certainly acquainted with Michael Angelo, and adopted with enthusiasm the arts of the Renaissance which he studied in Italy at the period of its highest development there. And we may take it that he was the most influential in introducing the new system into his own country. If, however, his style was derived from Italy, he was not contented to follow it blindly in the spirit of a mere copyist. Compared with Vigarny, and better acquainted with Italian, Berruguete showed in his work far more individuality and contributed more to the formation of the national style which, however much indebted to Italy, is still distinctly Spanish. The two men looked at the sources of their inspiration from different points of view, or rather with eyes which had been differently trained. Vigarny was of an older generation, wedded to the Gothic ideas which in his early years in Spain he had found deeply rooted, and still allied to the Mauresque. Berruguete, though the son of a Gothic sculptor of considerable merit, found the ground already prepared and ready to receive the new impressions. Besides this he was in constant communication with Italy, had frequently travelled there and resided at Florence and Rome, was intimately acquainted with the greatest Italian artists, was employed by Michael Angelo and, indeed, had almost become an Italian himself. That he was a follower of Jacopo della Quercia is evident in the fragments now preserved in the museum of Valladolid of the best of his retables — that of San Benito Real. Of the two great Spanish sculptors, therefore, the one, though Spanish by birth, was Italian, and of the Renaissance by education and temperament, the other French and Gothic. Yet on these two stocks, with the peculiarly national system of the use of colour, was engrafted the system of sculpture which is nowhere more unmistakably Spanish than in the case of the retables and single figures in wood with which we are now concerned. Of that system, which later on became still more distinctly national, Berruguete was the principal creator. But however influenced by his association with the greatest Italian artists of the best period of the Renaissance, his style lacks refinement and elegance. It is Italian, Spanishified. We have great work from his hand in marble, stone, and wood : statues and statuettes, choir and stall work in collaboration with Vigarny as at Toledo, or at Salamanca and Granada. We have even Gothic work. Yet with all this, both in sculpture and in painting, he degenerated into the most regrettable mannerisms, for which the tendencies towards or demand for rococo tastes which were rapidly imposing themselves were no doubt responsible.

The names of Vigarny and of Berruguete are the most popular ones in every mouth when there is question of Spanish sculpture of the Renaissance. But of a purer and more elevated—at least of a more religious—style there was one who was a greater artist than either, of the time when Gothic art still held sway, even if its supremacy was already threatened. We hear little of Damian Formente or Forment, and details of his life are again provokingly absent. An architect and sculptor, he was born probably about 1470, and, it would appear, studied in Rome and Florence (not, however, under Donatello, though he was greatly influenced by the work of the Florentine master), whence he must have returned to Spain at an early age, for in 1501 he was at work on a retable in wood for the Gothic church of Gandia in Valencia, his native province: and, but a few years later, on his most famous production, the alabaster retable of the church of Our Lady of the Pillar at Saragossa. His studies in Italy certainly had not the effect of inclining him to Renaissance principles, against which he fought throughout his life with the greatest obstinacy. The retable of the Capilla del Pilar, and the still finer one in a similar style, in wood, of the church of San Pablo, also at Saragossa, are unsurpassed amongst the Spanish late Gothic work of this description of the time. Uninfluenced by Berruguete, and refusing to be enticed by, even though he studied Italian ideas, Forment throughout his life was in the main faithful to Gothic sentiment. The retable of the Capilla del Pilar is in alabaster— now denuded of colour—a material which from its nature is amenable to almost identical treatment with woods of a hard kind. The themes depicted are scenes in the life of the Mother of Christ, the whole composition in arrangement and treatment of the panels, in the ornamental and architectural details, and in the groups and single figures, being certainly more suggestive of Flemish than of Italian teaching. But to whatever sources he may have gone, the work of Forment shows no slavish spirit of imitation, and it is surprising that his genius and individuality should not have been placed on a higher level than that accorded to his more celebrated contemporaries, Berruguete and Vigarny. The retablo of San Pablo, of wood, painted and gilt, and completed in 1517, is again quite Gothic. In general character it is almost identical with the somewhat earlier retable of the Pilar. Yet in the details there are certain differences, and while the spirit is still Gothic, it would be idle to assert that this is true without reservation. Indeed it is evident that the sculptor has gone to various sources. Notwithstanding this, the national type strongly predominates. The Crucifixion group in the upper central panel, the figure of the Apostle beneath, the eight groups of episodes of the Passion, the four scenes in the life of St. Paul, crowded with figures, the canopies of complicated pinnacle work, the innumerable details, with hardly a square inch of the composition undecorated, and the elaborate arabesque foliage work of the borders, identical with those of the alabaster retable, leave an impression which is almost bewildering when we seek to characterize the style. It is Gothic, it is plateresque, it betrays a Flemish love of the dramatic and picturesque, it is markedly oriental, it certainly cannot be quoted as an example of a dislike for Italian teaching and models, or a systematic avoidance of their use; it is Spanish, yet it is not the art of Berruguete. It is, in fine, Damian Forment, and in execution it is a *chef-d'œuvre*.

Notwithstanding the terrible destructions and desecrations which the perverted ideas of Churriguera caused him to work in the latter part of the seventeenth century on decorative art of all kinds, both Gothic and of the Renaissance, there still exists throughout Spain a very large number of magnificent retablos. In the most famous cathedrals also, the *silleria*, by which term is meant the ranges of stalls with their canopies, thrones, and other adjuncts, are additional monuments of wood-carving carried almost to extravagance in their bewildering profusion of details. Although in origin the retable was a simple background to an altar, and in the earliest Spanish examples a light open-worked construction, the tendency, even so early as the second half of the fourteenth century, was towards the gigantic and complicated edifices of which we may consider that of Seville, completed in the early part of the sixteenth century, the type and culminating point. From amongst these, none of which are earlier than the fifteenth century, a choice must be made which may fairly be considered illustrative, if inadequately, of the greater number. For this purpose we may take as an example of an extremely mixed style, yet one which, as a whole, remains Spanish and nothing else, the celebrated retablo of Seville. It has already been sufficiently suggested, and need hardly be further insisted upon, that in this altar work, as well as in the *silleria*, we are to find an art which, although so distinctive in character as to be recognized as Spanish by the least versed in styles, is yet hardly in any case of marked originality, but built up and adapted from various sources of even widely remote periods. The dominating elements which combined to form what we call the plateresque style of the Spanish Renaissance were, as has been stated, French, Flemish, or German and Italian. To these must be added the reminiscences of Oriental influences to which allusion has already been made. Such a distinct feature as the Spanish methods of polychrome or *estofado* will not of course be overlooked.

The retablo of the high altar of the cathedral at Seville, as it exists at present, is in style—if we should accept the decision of Cean Bermudez in his *Descripción de la Catedral de Sevilla*—Gothic. Yet it is a mixture of the most diverse elements, the product of many minds and the work of many hands—

from the time when it was designed and begun by Dancart in 1492, and under the hands of numerous other *entalladores*, *imagineros*, and *estofadores*, whose names and the particulars of their collaboration are extant—until its completion nearly a century later in 1564. Constructed of larchwood, the screen, with its elaborate ornamentation and innumerable groups and single figures, extends the whole width of the choir, and in height to the vaulting of the roof. Ten groups of columns divide the composition into nine spaces, crossed by horizontal bands of complicated carving forming a series of 36 inches in four rows, the borders carved with an elaborate theme of foliage arabesques and bulbous oriental domelike ornaments, each niche or panel containing a scene in the life of Our Lord, and of His prototypes in the Old Testament, starting from the story of the Fall. There is no mistaking the German character of these scenes: they are of the North German schools, and despite the names recorded by Bermudez of some of the earlier *imagineros* and of painters and gilders such as Alejo Fernandez and Andrez de Covarrubias, one can scarcely help wondering whether they and some of the single figures are not of German origin. The whole structure is dominated by a Calvary of colossal style. That is a brief, prosaic description of one of the most important of the Spanish *retablos* in wood. To convey a general idea of these astonishing constructions it would be difficult to surpass the style of the great French descriptive writer Théophile Gautier. Whatever may be thought of his talent as a word-painter, it is certain that the impression which it leaves is a very truthful one. Those who have read his *Moscow* and have seen the building itself will have recognized the actuality and force of his description of the church of Vassili Blagennoi. Equally telling are some passages which I may venture to take from his *Voyage en Espagne*.

PLATE XXXI

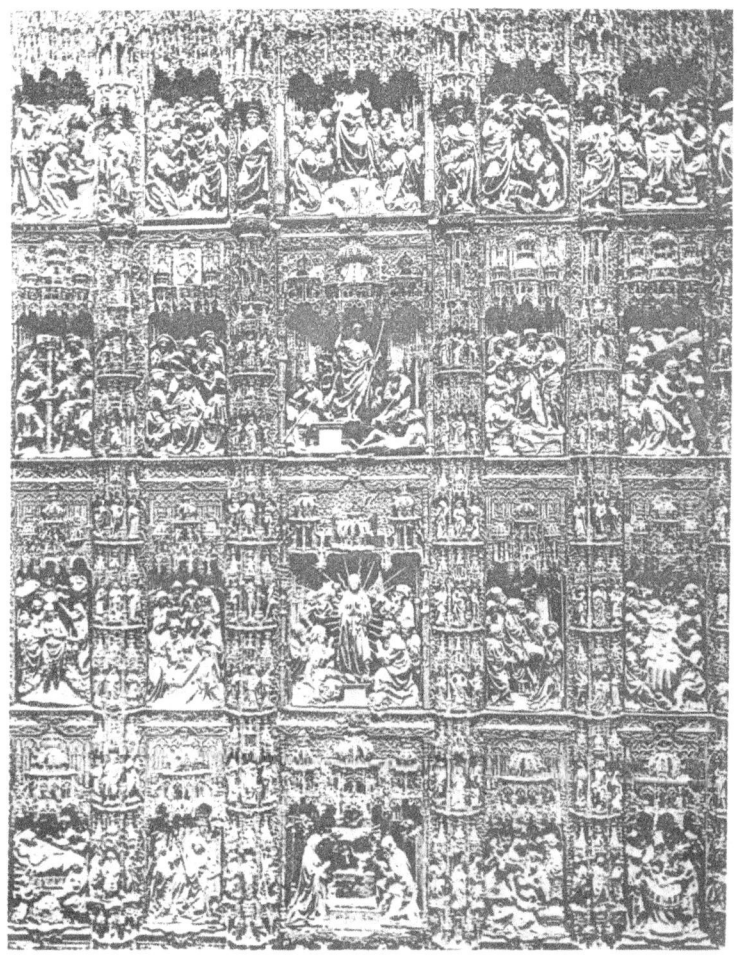

RETABLE OF THE CATHEDRAL OF SEVILLE (1492-1569)
PAGE 209

THE RETABLO OF SEVILLE CATHEDRAL

Inadequate as any translation must be, I shall give them in English freely rendered and somewhat abbreviated. Speaking of the cathedral and of the *retablo* of Seville he says: 'The cathedral chapter which ordered its construction summarizes its scheme in the following phrase: "Let us raise a monument which shall make posterity regard us as insane." The maddest, the most monstrous of Hindo pagodas cannot approach in extravagance the cathedral of Seville. . . . The retablo, or high altar, with its different scenes, its architectural structures superposed one on another, its rows of statuettes stage upon stage is, in itself alone, an immense edifice reaching up to the vaulted roof. The pascal candle is as big as the mast of a ship, and weighs two thousand pounds. Everything is in the same grandiose proportions. The choir, Gothic in style, is enlivened by turrets, by spires, by open-worked niches, by statuettes, by foliage work: it is a bewildering work which confounds our imagination, impossible to understand in these our days . . . a prodigy of talent, of patience, and of genius.' And again : 'The endeavour to describe, one after another, the riches of the cathedral would be madness : a whole year would be required to visit it in detail, and then one would not have seen everything. We feel crushed under the weight of so much magnificence, and know not where to go next. The wish to see everything, and the impossibility of accomplishing one's desire, induces a kind of feverish giddiness. Every style of architecture is represented—Gothic severity, the Renaissance, the plateresco, distinguished by a mad profusion of ornamentation and by arabesques of inconceivable complexity, rococo, Greek, and Roman. It is the sublime uplifting of the soul towards the Infinite expressed in terms of pinnacles, spires, bulbous domes, and ogival arches raising to the skies their arms of stone, joining in prayer their hands of gigantic proportions over the heads of the people prostrate in supplication.' Or again, in the description of the *retablo* of the cathedral at Toledo: 'The high altar, or *retablo*, might itself, alone, pass for a church. It is an enormous assemblage of slender columns, of niches, of statues, of foliage work and arabesques, of which the most minute description could give but a feeble idea. The whole of this architecture, rising to the very roof and surrounding the sanctuary, is painted and gilded in the richest manner imaginable. The dull, warm tone of the ancient gilding is admirably set off by the shimmering streaks of sunshine caught on their passage by the mouldings and reliefs of the ornaments, producing a marvellous effect of the most opulent picturesqueness.' It is indeed piling Pelion on Ossa, and the gilding of gold. In the midst of this excessive richness and profusion of details any ordinary powers of description seem totally to fail. It is all too immense in proportions, too high, too wide: one is confused, one cannot take it all in. One is inclined to be severe, but it is above criticism, for the effect on the senses, compelling admiration, is undeniable. Once more we may have recourse to Théophile Gautier, who finds in such work the richest, the most adorable, the most charming bad taste. 'The object of the sculptor seems to have been to crowd together as much ornament as possible in the least possible space. Here we find truncated columns garlanded with clinging vines, interminable scrolls inextricably convoluted, cherubs' heads furnished with wings, overcharged clouds, blazing and agitated flames, glories spreading out fan-shaped, curly leaf-work in half open bud or full expansion—all this, gilded and painted in nature's richest colours. It is no longer the delicacy and refinement of Gothic, nor has it the classic taste of the Renaissance: instead of purity of line, there is redundance. Yet still it is very fine, as is all that is excessive and complete of its kind.' That

PLATE XXXII

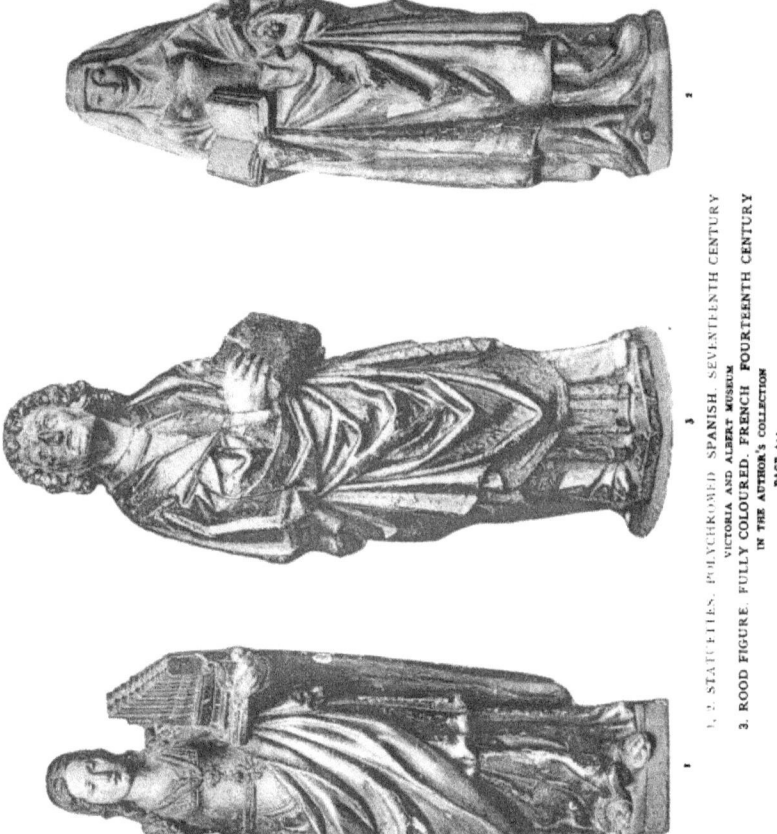

indeed is the impression one receives. Despite of all, one is forced to admire, as ages and millions have admired and praised. The retablo of the high altar of the cathedral of Toledo, again of larchwood, is the work of Enrique de Egas and Pedro Gumiel. Except the statues and the figures of the bas-reliefs, which are of the art of the *encarnador* and the *estofador*, it is fully gilt, and, it may be said, peculiarly typical of the estofado style of Gothic flamboyant which ended in becoming utterly debased in the seventeenth and eighteenth centuries.

We have still to occupy ourselves with the carved choir work and stalls in a succeeding chapter, and a longer consideration of the wood-carving, generally, of the Peninsula would lead us too far into the domain of Spanish art as a whole, and beyond the limits of date within which it is necessary to confine our attention. The subject also is more than ordinarily connected with painting and with sculpture in stone and marble, and would necessitate constant allusions to these. The influence of the Italian Renaissance was irresistible, and, once established, of the most rapid growth, though the process itself may have been slow and tentative in its early stages. Soon, however, we find the Spanish passion for realism overpowering everything else. Such masters of painting as da Mcna and Cano did not disdain to give their aid in the preparation of figures clothed with painted stuffs, with additions of metal work, real chains and cords and the like. Examples may be seen in the solitary case in the Victoria and Albert Museum, which contains in that collection the few contributions to this kind of work. The difference is great between it and that which is exemplified in such beautiful figures as the one of Saint Catherine, elsewhere in the museum, and at one time in the Maskell collection. It is, however, hardly to be regretted that these seventeenth-century painted figures are not more largely represented. One is compelled to ask whether we are to consider such things as paintings or as sculptures, and the question becomes exceedingly complicated. The system was carried to excess. Every one has heard of the crucifix of Burgos with its revolting realism, whether it be true or not that the figure is covered with human skin. Again following the ideas of Théophile Gautier, one cannot but admit that the passion for truth was pushed to its ultimate limits. We are spared not one drop of blood. We are forced to contemplate the severed and contracted nerves, the quivering flesh, the limbs mangled by the executioner, the wounds caused by the stripes. It is all too suggestive of the shambles. However repelling it may be, this craving for realistic horrors is characteristic of Spanish art and of the people, to whom the ideal and the æsthetic are absolutely foreign. Sculpture alone does not suffice. Their statues must be coloured, their madonnas plastered with paint, furnished with eyes of glass, with tears of pearl, and with real clothes. For their tastes, illusion can never be carried far enough. In my *Ivories* of this series, I have already described the crucifix in the church of St. James in Manchester Square. In this, in many ways, it must be admitted, admirable figure, the spirit of imitative realism is carried as far as possible without provoking remonstrance, for it has many beauties. The Victoria and Albert Museum has a crucifix with the figure in boxwood, by Alonso Cano of quite another type, for which, however, little can be said as a work of fine art. The painted bust of a 'Mater Dolorosa' (Plate XXXIII.) in the same museum is a popular and representative work, by an unknown sculptor. Inspired from Italy—one may say by Mino da Fiesole or Nerrochio and the Siena school—it may even have been produced in Italy. Yet it is unmistakably Spanish. There is another such

212

PLATE XXXIII

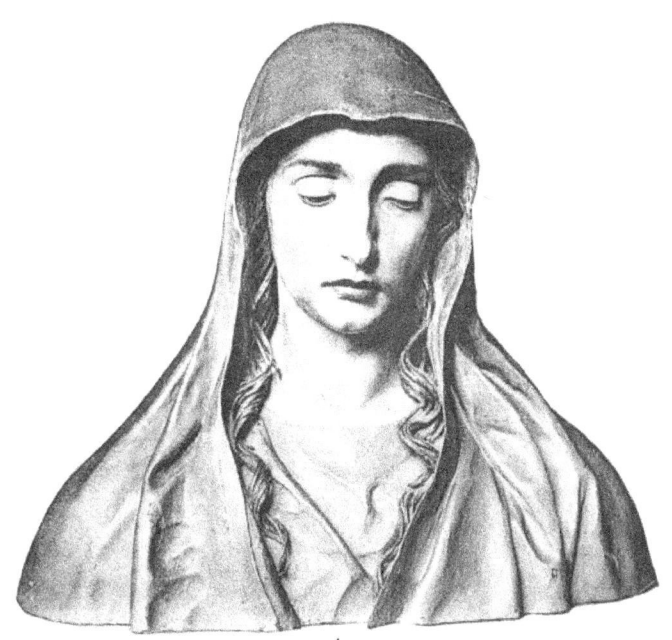

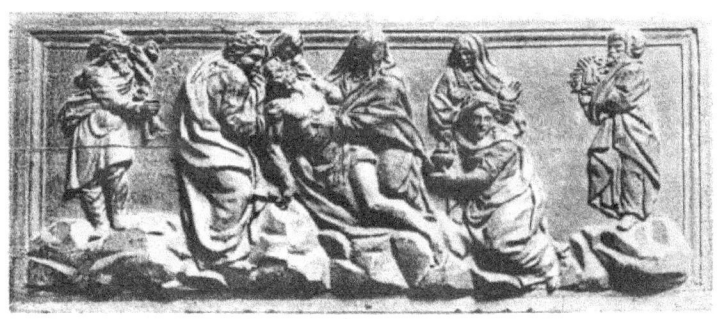

1. BUST *MATER DOLOROSA* FULLY **PAINTED**. SPANISH. SEVENTEENTH CENTURY
2. PORTION OF A PREDELLA. **PAINTED**. SPANISH. SEVENTEENTH CENTURY
VICTORIA **AND** ALBERT MUSEUM

figure in the Berlin Museum, ascribed by Dr. Bode to Montañez. It is still more expressive of grief, with solid tears of crystal upon the painted cheeks. Both are of oak, and painted in oils. It would be impossible to pass by the celebrated statue of St. Francis in the cathedral of Toledo, though we may not agree with the somewhat extravagant praise which has been given to it. At one time attributed to Alonso Cano, it is now generally admitted to be by Pedro da Mena. There is another, at one time in the Odiot collection, with which it has considerable analogy, and, indeed, as it is more generally known and as opportunities for examining it are more favourable, one may be justified in considering it by far the finer of the two. Both are of walnut, fully painted. The saint is represented in his habit, the hood drawn over his head, the waist girdled with a cord, the pale ascetic face, that one sees in the depth of the hood, calm, yet, as it were, in an ecstasy of pious suffering. Of the time there is certainly no other work so fine in painted Spanish sculpture in wood.

CHAPTER XII

CRUCIFIXES AND MADONNA FIGURES

FIGURES for crucifixes, statuettes, and groups of the Virgin and Child, and single figures of various saints, in Gothic and pre-Gothic times, form a very important division of our subject. All art of these periods being religious art, the first named are almost sufficient by themselves to reconstitute the history of sculpture and its development through the Romanesque period and until the Gothic merged into Renaissance methods. But whatever may have been the relative importance of wood sculpture among the other arts, it must not be forgotten that, equally with monumental figure work, it held its place in subordination to architecture. An examination of this class of the figure work of the earlier period would show two different types : the one resulting from carefully transmitted traditions derived from oriental sources, the other the rude efforts of the independent self-taught artist doing his best to copy faithfully from models, which, in one way or another, came into his hands. Some examples are evidently the work of simple country people rather than of trained artists or established workshops, but they are on this account none the less touching and valuable. In previous chapters frequent references have been made to the gradual emancipation of the artist from the hieratic domination which had long prevailed. But our information is vague indeed concerning the practical methods by which this was accomplished. From the designing and erection of buildings and their monumental sculpture, down to the smallest details of artistic work of any description, the impulse and direction were in the hands of the monasteries, but we have no means of knowing what was the actual work of the monks and what of lay artists outside their precincts. There are references to monastic art in the carving of crucifixes in the chronicles of Subiaco of the second half of the eleventh century, which prove their activity in this line, but, as usual, the information is vague. Even with regard to dates we have to be content with such vague ascriptions as the eleventh or twelfth century. Now the lapse of a hundred years is a considerable time, and from the beginning of one century to the end of another involves twice as long. In addition, we have to bear in mind the persistence of types and the copying and adapting which would have gone on for perhaps a century longer. It is unfortunate that our examples of an earlier date than the eleventh century are few indeed. When we reach the twelfth they become, even if still few in number, of the highest importance, not only as connecting links in the evolution of the arts, but also from their own intrinsic beauty. The dark ages, during which all arts had slept except the art of war, had passed. Everything was waking up. It was the age of literature, of chivalry, of devotion, and of a passionate longing for graphic expression. The archaic, squat proportions of the figure sculpture, the total disregard of truth to nature, and a uniform blank stolidity of expression give place to a tendency towards the opposite extreme, and the effort to express elegance of form is sought after in an exaggerated length of limb and straight-flowing draperies in parallel folds. Progress is comparatively rapid, and sculptural art seems to have arrived in the thirteenth century at the point of its highest idealistic expression. Unfortunately we cannot hope to find in our museums and churches many examples of single figures in wood. Even in monumental sculpture what exists are, for the most part, on the façades of famous cathedrals, saved, by their position, from the destructions which a law of nature seems to impose on every country from time to time. In addition, there is the perishable nature of wood.

The crucifix (more strictly, the figures for crucifixes) is one of the most important applications of sculpture to religious purposes ; but examples in any material of an earlier date than the twelfth, or of mid-Gothic type than the fourteenth, century are of extreme rarity. In ivory there exist scarcely any at all earlier than the seventeenth century, but in wood rood figures abound in all countries except in England. It will be unnecessary here to review the history of the representation of the crucifixion. I have referred to it at considerable length in my *Ivories* of this series. Many centuries —five hundred years at least—passed by before the reverential awe which hung about all reference to the sacred event permitted any representation at all in which a human figure should be used, and many more during which the figure was hardly more than a conventional formula. St. Gregory of Tours, about 593, mentions a painting in the church of Narbonne representing Christ on the Cross. He remarks that the Saviour was unclothed, except by a loin-cloth, and that this nudity was a cause of scandal to the faithful. (*In gloria Martyrum*, 22.) It would not be difficult, starting from the doors of Santa Sabina in Rome and continuing up to the crucifix which Brunelleschi made in competition with Donatello, to write from the examples we have in wood alone the story of the evolution of the crucifix as we find it in the universal type of to-day. But it would require more space than we have at our disposal and many illustrations. A

PLATE XXXIV

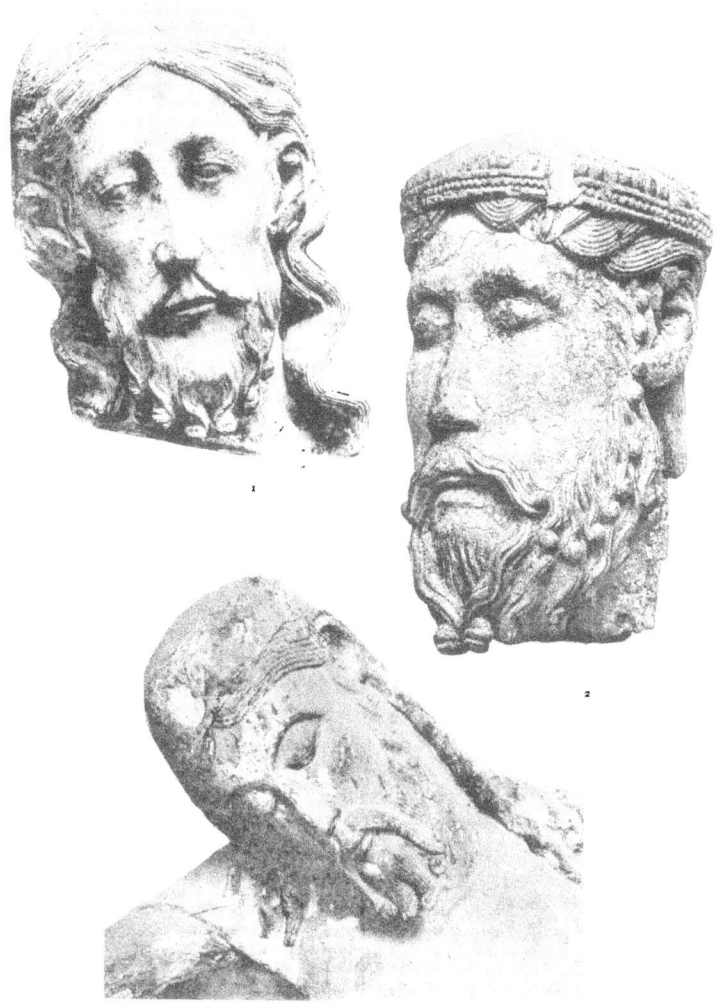

1

2

3

PARTS OF CRUCIFIX FIGURES. FRENCH. TWELFTH CENTURY

1. CLUNY MUSEUM, PARIS. 2. LOUVRE MUSEUM. DOUCET BEQUEST. 3. LOUVRE MUSEUM. COURAJOD BEQUEST

choice of a few only will therefore be made, and the description of them must be brief. I may say at once that it is with the greatest regret that I find it necessary to condense what is, equally with Madonna figures, a most important part of our subject. In the eleventh century the Byzantine formula—archaic, as in the ivory crucifix of Leon, now in the archæological museum, Madrid—was the model throughout the world. The art was primitive, the figure draped in a long skirt, the feet nailed separately, the eyes staring and expressionless. In the Romanesque period, the idea was of a Christ triumphant rather than of suffering Humanity. In the two or three examples presently to be adduced, and in many others, the head of our Lord is of the noblest type. He is represented with the eyes, as a rule, closed, in the moment before death; not as a human being still suffering the most cruel tortures. The tragedy is finished, nothing remains but an impassive serenity. The hair is conventionally treated in a hardly ever varying fashion of regularly curled bands arranged in long channelling streaks, the undulating locks of the moustache and beard each ending in a little curl. Sometimes there is a fillet or diadem, but no crown of thorns, which seems not to have been common before the thirteenth century. A detail that must not be forgotten is that it was usual to add a metal crown set thick with jewels. The expression is full of simplicity; of the nobility of suffering. There is no exaggeration of enduring agony, but as M. Courajod has well said, 'it is a king asleep': or, at least, it is the placid calm which comes after death to those who have suffered violence or some dreadful accident. Yet, if we should take, for example, the twelfth century Christ of the Doucet collection (Plate XXXIV.), or even the fourteenth-century crucifix of Anderlecht, the artist has known how to express, without attempting absolute realism, the sufferings which have been passed through. The head falls, the mouth is slightly open, the eyes closed as if in sleep, the expression calm and resigned. One cannot but think that the sculptor has gone to nature for his inspiration, even if he has respected and continued traditional models in certain features, such as the hair and beard.

To sum up the characteristics which distinguish a crucifix of early Romanesque type from one of Gothic times, the figure hangs straight, and is not contorted, the arms are at right angles, the head erect, the eyes closed or calmly impassive if open, the body somewhat emaciated, the feet nailed separately, and resting on a *scabellum*, the hair falling in serpentine ringlets over the shoulders, the lines of the ribs, and folds of flesh regularly marked in a conventional manner, a short plain skirt from waist to knees. It is a representation of Divinity triumphing over Death. As we approach to and are afterwards in full Gothic times, the body becomes contorted, there is more naturalism in the eyes, the knees are drawn up, the body falls with its own weight, the arms depart more and more from the horizontal, the feet are nailed with one nail, the crown of thorns appears, the drapery is scanty. The artist seeks to give, in every way, an impression of human suffering, and to express it—as when we reach the Italian quattrocento masterpieces—by the display of anatomical knowledge. The body is almost completely nude, or, as we shall find in di Nuto's crucifixes equally as in the paintings of Giotto and others, whom, no doubt, the sculptors followed, the beautiful form is partly covered with a transparent drapery of a thin silky material. The Christ is no longer the King, the Divine conqueror, with regal attributes and emblems. It is the human side, the sacrifice by suffering which is emphasized. To take for example the crucifix—French work of the twelfth

218

century—presented to the museum of the Louvre in 1903 by M. Courajod (Plate xxxiv.). It is interesting to compare this with the beautiful ivory crucifix fragment of the thirteenth century in the Kensington Museum, described and figured in my *Ivories* (p. 257). The character of each is widely different, yet each is the work of a great artist who knew what he was doing, and was under no servile restraint of tradition. Nor have the Courajod, and much less the ivory figure, anything in common with the archaic hieratism of the ivory crucifix of Leon or with the type of the Limoges bronzes of an indeterminate number of years earlier. Romanesque it is, no doubt, but in its truthful naturalness this admirable head of a supernatural beauty, calm, resigned, is fairly comparable to the Gothic figure of Kensington. The artist knew what to observe in nature, knew what to take and what to leave, in his submission to the rules in which he had been trained. He has gone, no doubt, to more ancient models for the treatment of the hair and beard, and for certain general principles, but the individuality of his work is not obscured by this. It is of a type that we should hardly have expected to find developed before the middle of the thirteenth century. In the anatomy we see how nature has been consulted, but without any servile attempt at reproducing it. The artist is impatient of the bonds under which art had so long been held in leash, yearning for freedom, yet obedient to those traditions in which he had been trained that he knew to be good and reasonable in themselves. From the position of one of the arms it may be part of a Deposition group rather than an actual crucifixion : the beginning of the first stage of the taking down from the Cross. The figure is painted after the methods of Theophilus, so often alluded to here. There are some restorations, for example, the whole of the left arm, but the head, if somewhat deteriorated by the ravages of time, is fairly preserved. The art is of the southern districts of France : of Toulouse, or perhaps of the Burgundian provinces. There are other early French examples of almost equal merit; for instance, that of the presbytery of St. Denis d'Amboise, but they cannot now be followed.

A few words must accompany another beautiful fragment here illustrated (Plate xxxiv.). It is the head of a crucifix figure bequeathed to the Louvre by M. Doucet. It is of oak, and, unfortunately, not in good condition. Still, sufficient remains to afford a very fine example of the beginnings of realism, and one may reasonably come to the conclusion that, at so early a period, the artist worked from a living model. Another fragment is the fine life-sized head in chestnut wood in the Cluny Museum (Plate xxxiv.). It is again twelfth-century work, at one time covered with linen or parchment painted to represent the human skin. The expression is full of benevolence, the eyes open, the hair carefully divided, and there is no crown of thorns. Our general observations, which apply to all the figures of the period, need not be repeated. It is impossible to fix a definite date or a place of production for these early examples of crucifixes in wood. Usually of life-size, or even colossal, it is not unlikely that many were made in Auvergne, where the early type both of these and of Madonnas continued into quite late in the thirteenth century : some features, as in the black Christs of Saint-Flour and of Montsalvy to as late, perhaps, as the fifteenth century. The reader may be referred to the work on the Romanesque churches of the Haute, Auvergne, by M. de Rochemonteix, in which several are mentioned (see *Bibliography*). A twelfth-century crucifix at Clermont Ferrand has the eyes enamelled, and the mouth made to move with springs which might be actuated by the preacher's foot. The Christ of the church of Anderlecht, in Brabant, is a work of the end of the fourteenth century of rare merit, yet showing in its somewhat stiff and conventional anatomy, and in the fashion of the long dank hair, in the style of the South Kensington ivory, the persistence of the ancient styles. So also in a fifteenth-century rood group in the same museum (No. 714, 1895) the Saviour's head distinctly follows a much earlier type, at the same time that the figure of St. John has the slimness and all the smirking mannerism of the period. Another interesting early figure is that of the church of Saint-Pierre, Louvain, possibly part of a Deposition group. Westlake, commenting on it, thought it as early as the tenth century. But the feet are nailed together, and this, together with the realistic type, can hardly place it earlier than the end of the twelfth or even into the thirteenth.

A brief mention must suffice to call attention to a Deposition group of the Pisan school in the cathedral of Volterra. It is over life-size, and whether as an example of the system of polychrome in sculpture of the period, or on account of its own intrinsic merits, it must be considered as one of the finest pieces of Italian romanesque or romanesque Gothic in existence. With regard to date, it would be difficult to be more precise than by according the margin of from the first half of the twelfth to the middle of the thirteenth century, the first approximate date being the most likely. The subject of the earlier crucifixes might be pursued to an unlimited extent, and there is ample material for illustration. Of Italian examples of the middle of the fourteenth century it must suffice to note briefly those of Nicolò di Nuto of the Sienese school, of which there are several at Orvieto in the churches of San Francesco and San Domenico, and in the municipal museum. They are life-size and over, painted of course, and of astounding realism in the attention to anatomical detail. (*Figured in Venturi, Storia*, iv. 325.) Italian crucifixes of the fifteenth century are very numerous. Probably all the great sculptors in marble, bronze, the precious metals, and in wood, would have tried their hands at a subject which combined their skill in anatomical expression with the exercise of their imagination and piety. Vasari mentions a large number who worked them in wood : amongst them Verrocchio who, he says, was a universal genius, at once goldsmith, sculptor, painter, engraver, and musician. But it is necessary to confine ourselves to the two famous crucifixes of Brunelleschi (Plate xxxv.) and of Donatello in the churches of Santa Maria Novella and of the Santa Croce at Florence. We may take it, that leaving on one side the question of crucifixions in painting, the first is the ultimate expression of the system evolved from its forerunners from early Christian times, through the archaicism of the tenth and eleventh centuries, and the mannerisms of the Gothic period : the precursor of the type continued to this day. In it we have this method in its purest and best form, imbued with all the new spirit of humanism, perfect in anatomy, touching in expression, yet avoiding anything like the horrors of cruel torment, and the exaggerations of the effect of wounds. The head is simply filleted over the carefully curled hair, the drapery simple without fluttering ends, the arms at a more acute angle than formerly, the emaciated anatomy naturalistic, the expression thoughtful rather than suffering. As a masterpiece of sculpture its own interest is very great, and in addition there is the curious tradition of its origin arising from a contest with Donatello when the two were fellow-pupils in the same studio, Brunelleschi being then twenty-four, and Donatello nine years younger. The story has often been told, and though we may be inclined to doubt the possibility of Brunelleschi having arrived at such

PLATE XXXV

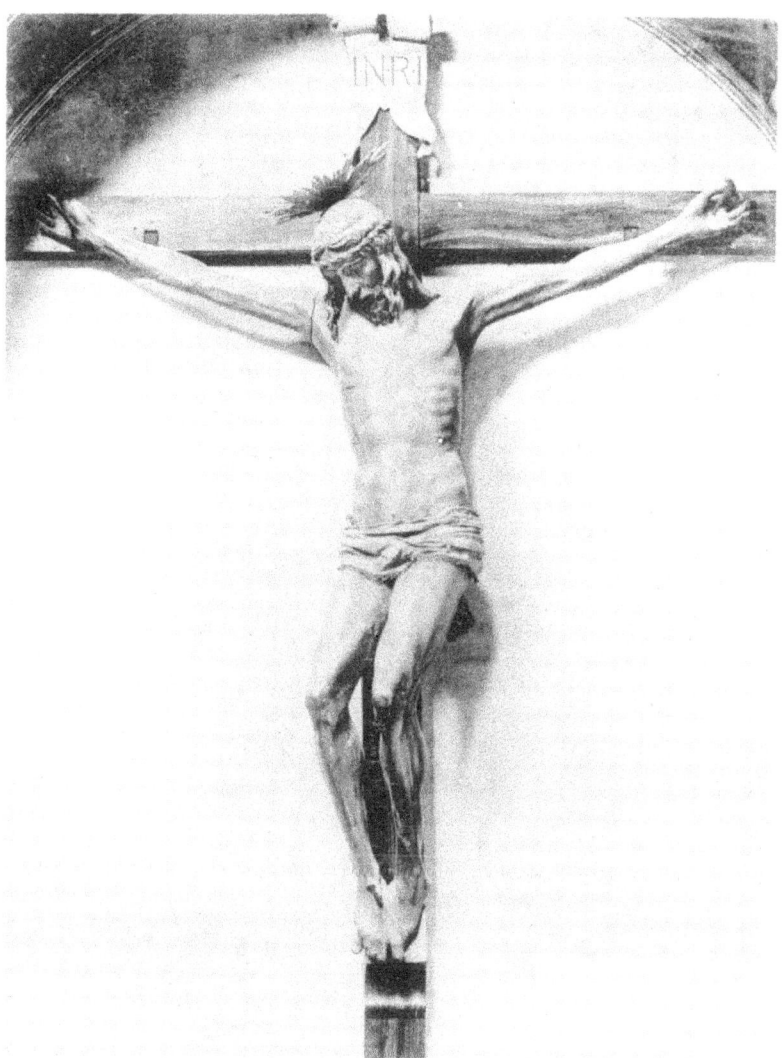

CRUCIFIX. BY BRUNELLESCHI. FIFTEENTH CENTURY

SANTA MARIA NOVELLA, FLORENCE

PAGE 323

masterly perfection at so early an age, it may be given on the authority of Vasari in his own words, as we have them in his *Lives of the Painters*. He says in his *Life of Brunelleschi*: 'Now it happened in those days that Donatello had completed a crucifix in wood which was placed in the church of Santa Croce in Florence, beneath the story of the girl restored to life by St. Francis, a picture painted by Taddeo Gaddi, and he desired to have the opinion of Filippo respecting his work, but he repented of having asked it since Filippo replied that he had placed a clown on the Cross. Donatello answers, "Take wood, then, and make one thyself." Filippo quietly and secretly goes to work and does so, to Donato's so great surprise that, carrying an apron full of eggs the first time it is shown to him, he drops and breaks them all, and not only confesses himself conquered, but declares the work a miracle.' We may briefly dispatch the attempt of Donatello. His fame will rest on the great bronze crucifix in the Santo at Padua, executed many years later. Cicognara, in his *Storia*, thus compares the two: Donatello's crucifix is rigid, ignoble, without abandon and without softness, with neither grace nor elevation of feeling. The other is the eternal glory of Brunelleschi. And indeed Donatello has put on the Cross a powerful, muscular man, whom the stripes and wounds have hardly weakened, and whom Death has not subdued. In the art of Brunelleschi, inspired above all by devotional feeling, he gives us the sufferings and death in the accomplishment of the sacrifice. In regard to the German crucifixes in wood of the fourteenth and early fifteenth centuries, which abound, space will now permit but a brief mention. Reference has already been made to some of those by Veit Stoss and Riemenschneider. The earlier examples follow the type which was universal in Romanesque times. Many of the representations of Calvary in the German retables conform to the schools of the Netherlands, and are evidently inspired, directly or indirectly, by the Flemish and German primitives. We find the same tall crosses with narrow beams, the long thin legs and arms, the same carriage of head and drawing of the feet, the same expressions. In a small fourteenth-century relief in the Kaiser Friedrich Museum we have a following of the system so usual in French Gothic ivories, especially in the pose of the body, and in the knotted anatomy of the arms. And when we come to the life-size and colossal crucifixes of the late German Gothic period, it is evident that Veit Stoss and his contemporaries merely profited by their Italian education, and that the models from which they adapted were those of the schools of Donatello and Brunelleschi. To these they added their own mannerisms and an exaggerated treatment of the drapery which is especially characteristic of German crucifixes. This was made to serve a decorative purpose, and they revelled in twists and curves and floating scrolls which at times verged on the fantastic. It must suffice to mention two well-known crucifixes, attributed to Veit Stoss, which may be taken as typical of many others of more or less merit. The first, at one time in the Spitalkirche, is now in the Germanic Museum of Nürnberg; the other, which presents great similarities, is in the Chiesa d'Ogni Santi at Florence.

Still more instructive than the crucifixes, with regard to the evolution of sculpture in wood up to the end of the Gothic period, are the Madonna figures and groups. These are fairly numerous, and include, besides such pairs of detached figures as the Annunciation statues of Italy, those in which we have the Blessed Virgin standing with the Child in her arms, or seated either alone or with the Infant, in many touching maternal attitudes; as the Mater Dolorosa at the foot of the cross, or weeping over

224

the dead Saviour in the groups known as Pietàs.
Several of the two last-named kinds have already
been noticed. We shall now confine our attention
to the Madonnas as the term is generally used. In
the twelfth century, as in earlier representations, the
Virgin sits throned in majesty, as a great queen or
empress, the chair itself an emblem of authority of the
kind which we find on the consular diptychs. She
herself is the only figure, the centre of homage and
devotion, almost of worship: a figure of majestic
hieratic dignity, noble and queenly, inexpressibly great,
as the one chosen from amongst all by the Almighty.
She is not yet the tender mother, effacing herself and
concentrating attention on the child which she presents
to us for our adoration, emphasizing her maternal
feelings by lavish endearments. Seldom, as soon was
to become the universal style, is her head affectionately
turned towards Him as she holds Him in her arms,
seated in her lap, or standing on her knee. It is but
gradually, as the thirteenth century progresses, that
she becomes the sweet and gentle mother, in the
attitude which was so favourite a one; for example,
in the charming little early Madonna in the gallery at
Perugia, where the Child looks up in her face and
seizes her chin with His hand. But, as in other
paintings, in those of Cimabue or of Guido da Siena,
in the Uffizi, the coming type is still undeveloped.
The Byzantine formula continues to prevail in the
majestic placidity, the solemnity of expression of the
Madonna Gloriosa, and in the treatment of the
draperies. The Romanesque traditions linger long
throughout the earlier Gothic period, even if through a
comparatively slow process of evolution the statuesque
gives place to a more mundane type of nobility, the
solemn majesty of the Odigitria to maternal tenderness
and grace. Instead of an empress enthroned we are
presently to have the courtly lady, or, as Ruskin has

characterized the French thirteenth-century statuettes, the *Picarde soubrette*. To what influences, indeed, of the great masters of the early Middle Ages may we not attribute even Donatello's 'Virgin of Padua,' where she sits, as in the old twelfth-century Madonnas, on a throne which has sphinxlike supports, immovable, a queen presenting a Child King to His people, He Himself, enthroned on her lap with none of the playful suggestiveness of the quattrocento types?

As in the ivories, the twelfth-century Madonna in wood is still the central figure demanding our attention. It is to her that the sculptor addresses all he knows of art. The Holy Child is, as it were, left to more conventional treatment as if beyond his power of expression. He is grave beyond His apparent years, having with the form of a child a much older look, as He raises His hand in blessing. Unfortunately, what examples we have in wood in this country, such as the two in the Victoria and Albert Museum (Plate XXXVI.), can hardly be said to be the work of great masters, though it cannot be doubted that sculptors as well as painters would have devoted the highest talent to such a subject. Such figures as these would seem to be rather from the hands of simple country people. As in the ivories, by the beginning of the thirteenth century there came about in the smaller figure work a more general assimilation with the monumental sculpture of the period. France is foremost in setting the fashion, and the dominant type is the sweet-smiling mother affectionately toying with her child ; the attitudes are of the most studied grace pushed to extremes, which become mannerism ; the pose is affected, at least in the 'ivory' twist or bend of the figure ; the draperies rich and voluminous. Compared with the feeling of the previous period, it is as if we were transported from heavenly to earthly regions. The

PLATE XXXVI

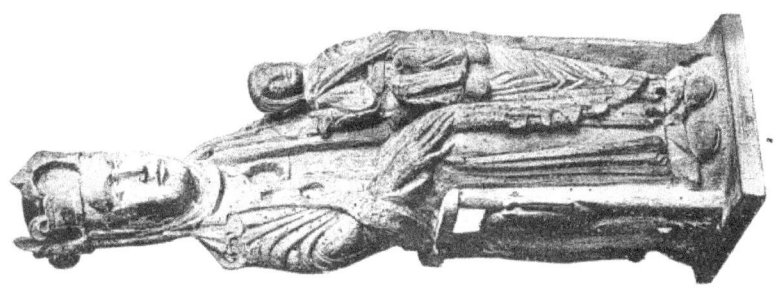

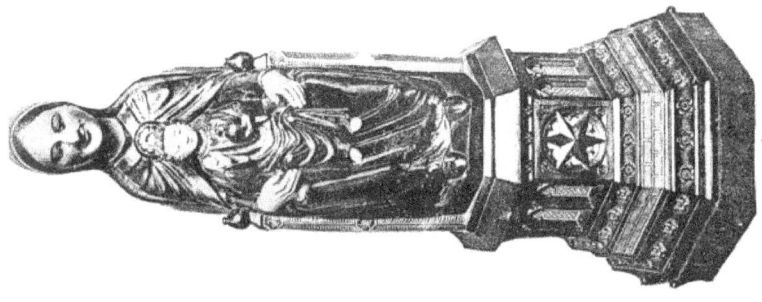

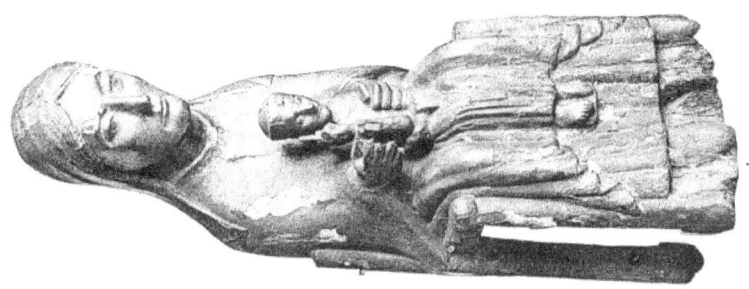

1, 2. EARLY MADONNAS. TWELFTH CENTURY
VICTORIA AND ALBERT MUSEUM

3. MADONNA OF ALSEMBERG. THIRTEENTH CENTURY
ALSEMBERG, BELGIUM

PAGES 226, 230

Mother of God becomes the mother of our own race, smiling, playing, coquetting with the Child as He amuses Himself with a flower, a fruit, or a bird, or affectionately entwines His arm round her neck. They are courtly figures, made for the delight of courts, and it is indeed hardly surprising that not in a single instance have figures of this type been endowed by the populace with miraculous gifts as in the case of the homely Flemish madonnas to which reference will presently be made. There is in fact almost a stereotyped pattern, a repetition of a similar smile, the same candid expression, fashion of hair and veil, and pointed shoe peeping out beneath the multifolded draperies. Yet, notwithstanding this family resemblance, how sweet is this series : always the same, yet always with differences as we find them in ivory and wood, leaving out of consideration painting and other branches of sculpture ! The Child is almost always clothed. The earliest examples unclothed to the waist, are not till the second quarter of the fourteenth century. Later on, He is quite naked, and it is about mid-fourteenth century that we first find giving the breast which afterwards became very usual, especially —if we may judge from few examples—in England. With the advance of the fourteenth century there is again a change of feeling : a wholly different type. As in the representations of the crucifixion we had put before us Christ triumphant, crowned with a royal crown instead of one of thorns, and as this gave way to an insistence on His suffering humanity, so now in the Madonnas the brightness and cheerfulness associated with the life of the Virgin changed into the tendency of emphasizing and continually presenting to the devotion of the people her sufferings as a mother bereaved of her son. Especially in Flemish art the Holy Virgin is represented as fainting in the arms of her attendants, weeping at the foot of the cross or over the body of our Lord extended on her lap. It was the result of the devotional mysticism of the time, inspired by the teachings and writings of St. Francis of Assisi in the latter part of the twelfth century, of St. Gertrude, and by the paintings and illuminations founded upon these. Yet it would be difficult to lay down any rigid type, and, as in painting and in other sculptures national characteristics asserted themselves. We may note, however, the extreme contrasts presented between what may be called — without denying its infinite charm—the smart simpering type of the thirteenth century and the nobility of such a group as the polychromed Madonna in wood in the Maignan collection, or of the one in the Louvre presented by M. Albert Bossy—both French art of the fourteenth century, which will presently be noticed.

Madonna statuettes in wood of so early a period as the eleventh and twelfth centuries are of course of considerable rarity, as indeed they are also among the ivories. Probably they were numerous enough, and we must judge their general character from the few still existing; from bronze and enamel figures and from the early mosaics. We are fortunate in possessing two examples in the museum at Kensington. It is interesting to compare these with an ivory group of somewhat later date in the Louvre from the Dutuit collection, with which they are clearly connected, and there are others in the Cluny Museum (No. 1037) and in the Basilewsky collection of the Hermitage, St. Petersburg. Both the wood and the ivory statuettes are characterized by the archaic and stony attitudes peculiar to the age. In the ivories there is certainly a tendency to the realism which became more marked in the succeeding century. Evidently the artists were not of the same class. In the wood examples, particularly, the disproportions of the too long busts, the too large heads and the clumsy execution are marked.

228

MADONNAS

The impression first conveyed is that they are hardly in advance of the south sea islands type of fetish image. But we must remember that they were intended to be, and were at one time, coloured and set with stones and gems. These are rude works no doubt, but let us put against them the superb Madonna in wood of the church of Sta. Maria Maggiore at Alatri ; central, or southern Italian work of the twelfth century. It is the finest of all existing Madonnas of the early mediæval ages, formerly polychromed, now entirely gilded. The Child is almost a smaller repetition of the figure of the mother, having the same long face, the same expression and arrangement of the hair. It is a proof that at that early time a great school of sculpture in the round must have existed in central Italy, and that the art was not confined to ornament alone. Although scarce, there are other still existing figures in various churches and museums. Amongst notable ones are a seated Madonna in the Nürnberg Museum, another in the minster church of Essen (figured in Ausm' Weerth, Plate xxiv.) which has eyes of enamel, and two similar ones in the treasury of Hildesheim. Nor must we forget the Madonna in the Berlin Museum, made in 1139 by the priest Martino, nor the *Odigitria*, entirely gilt, known as the Madonna of Constantinople. But there is a whole series of Flemish Madonnas in wood of the thirteenth century which are still strongly marked with the archaic type of the Romanesque formulæ, yet show at the same time the existence of a realistic school and an independent observation of nature on the part of the artist. That he was self-taught is, in some cases, evident. At any rate, he followed freely his own bent, released from hieratic conventions both in the type which he chose for his model, in the expression of the features, and in the arrangement of the accessories. In general, the influence of France at the beginning of the century is not to be contested. The formula is similar. The Virgin is seated on a thronelike chair or low bench, as, for example, in the ivories of the Cluny or the Hamburg Museum which are in certain ways analogous. The Child either sits or stands on the left knee, or on the lap, instead of being held in the arms as was, later on, the universal practice, and raises His hand in blessing. She presents to us with pride, as it were, her son. The draperies fall in long straight folds. The chief distinctions from the French formulæ are in national characteristics or preferences, for which, as elsewhere, it is not always easy to account. For example, whence did we English derive the type of head and expression of features distinguished by the high forehead and almond eyes of our ivory and alabaster figures of the fourteenth century? Except when the inspiration would appear to come directly from some classical source, the Flemish Madonna is of the womanly rather than of the queenly or noble type.

These early Flemish Madonnas are, then, evidence of the growing feeling for realism, whatever may have been the extent to which it was reacted upon by the increasing influence of French idealism. A few of these interesting—and certainly important— figures may be briefly noted. Unfortunately it is extremely difficult to obtain adequate photographs of them. The original of the one here given suffers also from modern restoration and repainting. The figure of the Child is entirely new. The miraculous Madonna of Alsemberg — a small village in the neighbourhood of Brussels—(Plate xxxvi.) presents features which are a combination of deeply-rooted traditional motives with an evident endeavour to substitute for them a more natural type directly drawn from living models with which the artist was familiar. Naive though the representation may be, there is poetry in this young mother calling for attention to herself and for adoration of her divine Child. It is not surprising that it should appeal to homely instincts and even to all classes, and thus become qualified, with many of the others, for miraculous powers. The curious smile in the small half-moon conformation of the mouth is characteristic of several Flemish Madonnas of this period. It is, in fact, a stereotyped fashion confined to this school; a reminiscence of, perhaps, and attempt to reproduce, the mincing affectation of the French. Another image, of the same period, also reputed miraculous, and of similar advanced tendencies is that of the church of Saint Sulpice, Diest. A third, the Madonna of Laeken, again among the miraculous, presents the same solemn and stiff attitudes and traditional draperies, the Child held up high on one knee. It is, however, less archaic, and the expression of the Virgin is more refined. Of the same school is the Madonna of Hal. Unfortunately much damaged, it is of a most remarkable type. The Holy Child, after having received Its nourishment, reposes on the mother's knee. The physiognomy of the Virgin has a pure Greek profile of peculiar beauty. The image known as Notre-Dame du chant d'Oiseaux—*Onze lieve Vrouw in Vogelzang*—in the church of the Pères-Conventuels of Brussels, is of the second half of the century and, naturally, is even more affected by French influence, though the type of face, and somewhat squat figure are still national. As an example of the persistence of traditions and mixture of styles, we may take the interesting Madonna—*Virgo sedes Sapientiæ*—of the church of St. Pierre, Louvain. Here, we are in full fifteenth century (1442), yet the attitude and the arrangement and style of the draperies are in accord with the ancient traditions, while the head of the Virgin is decidedly realistic, and the Child sits playing with a bird in the French fashion of the time. Yet one more may be cited in the large Madonna figure, fully coloured, of the church of St. Jacques, Louvain, one of the finest existing of Flemish work of the first half of the fourteenth century. What is most noticeable is the unusual arrangement of the drapery. The Child, naked to the waist, is thence covered with the mother's veil, except the left leg from the knee. The whole treatment of this drapery, the oblique line from the shoulder across the breast, the folds which follow and do not conceal the form, the indication of some soft silky texture, the rich, jewelled ornamentation—all this is charming, and due not to the polychrome decoration alone, but to the art of the sculptor, as consummate as in any French figure work of a similar kind and period. We have here also the fashionable bend or twist so much affected in the thirteenth century, which has been attributed to various causes, amongst them that it was simply following the curve of an ivory tusk. Personal influence in the matter of costume probably had more to do with it. A homely figure in the church of N. D. de la Dyle at Malines derives its name—*Onze lieve Vrouw van Schewe* —from this peculiarity. The references to these Flemish Madonnas, of which a few have been cited, have necessarily been brief. They are none the less of considerable importance in the history of wood sculpture, and the student will do well to refer to the erudite articles in the *Annales de la Société archéologique de Bruxelles* (toms. viii., ix., x.), by M. Destrées, who photographed several of them before they were restored and repainted.

French Madonna statuettes in wood of the fourteenth century are comparatively rare. The type followed to a considerable extent, and often preserved entirely, the traditions of the previous century. The drapery alters somewhat and becomes more complicated, displaying itself in voluminous folds and

PLATE XXXVII

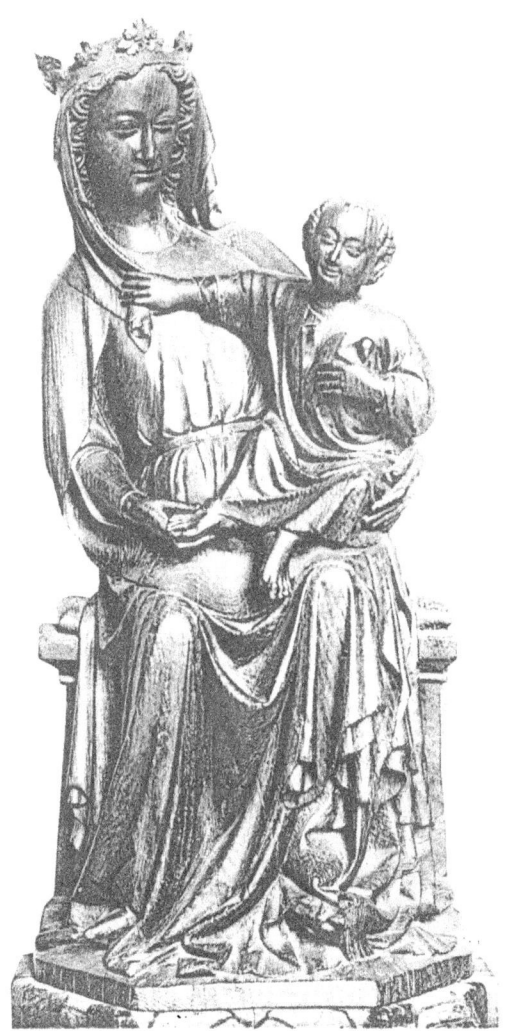

MADONNA. FRENCH. FOURTEENTH CENTURY
LOUVRE (BOSSY COLLECTION)
PAGE 232

stiffly defined angles and zig-zags. If we do not lose completely the sweetly smiling expression, amounting sometimes to affectation and coquetry, there is a tendency, at any rate, to greater nobility, more striving after distinction, less simpering coquettishness, less suggestion of worldly fascination. What greater contrast could there be than between the almost frivolous type of the thirteenth century as we have it in so many charming ivories, and the nobility of such a group as the one in wood of the Maignan collection, of another of similar yet still finer character bequeathed to the Louvre by M. Albert Bossy, or of that in the FitzHenry collection in the Victoria and Albert Museum. For all that, in such figures, to use the trite French phrase, the more the changes, the more it is always the same thing. The ancient formulæ cannot be got rid of. The feeling, the attitude in general, the draperies of the twelfth century are with us still, two hundred years later, and if the Virgin sits no longer in enthroned majesty, but with a happy mother's smiling face, the ideal is still there under the more real. The figures are, as yet, from no human model. It is merely another phase of the evolution towards the complete change which a little more than a century was to bring forth. May we not bear in mind the hieratic Madonna of Donatello made for the altar of the Cappella del Santo at Padua, that solemn figure of an antique matron rising from the richly decorated chair supported by sphinxes, and still holding in her lap the Child Who blesses in this rather awkward position? It is hardly too much to say that of the whole of the Gothic period there is no finer group in wood or ivory—to go no farther—than the Madonna of the Bossy collection, now in the Louvre (Plate XXXVII.). Almost life-size, that is, about four feet in height, it is of oak, and now in the bare purity of the wax-polished wood. In it we may recognize a *chef-d'œuvre*, the ultimate realization of refined idealism resulting by slow and measured steps from the archaic hieratism of the twelfth century through the charming aberrations of the thirteenth. There is nothing here of the courtly type, made for the luxury of kings and nobles rather than for churches, there is nothing of the coquetry of the *grande dame*, yet there is no sacrifice of the ideal in its appeal to the most humble also. We may remark the unaffected pose, the fall of the drapery concealing, yet outlining the figure, the cushion indented by the weight of the body, the foot resting on the head of a basilisk, the Child dressed in a simple tunic playing and laughing as He turns away from His mother, holding the end of her veil, toying—after the favourite fashion—with a bird. If we might criticise His figure, it is, perhaps, prematurely old, almost too clever: a sharp youngster, even a little tiresome. Yet it is the accepted type of the time, from which the sculptor had no escape. We may remark also the masterly treatment of the wrist of the Virgin as she holds the Child's foot, and the long, thin, delicate fingers; the feet of the Child, the crown of natural foliage instead of a jewelled one. It is no doubt northern work, probably of the Ile de France. In fine condition, the restorations are confined to the right wrist of the Virgin, and the fingers of the right hand of the Child. If there is anything to regret, it is that it is a *figure d'applique*, but in a front view this is not noticeable. The FitzHenry collection in the Victoria and Albert Museum has a somewhat similar, though smaller and not so well executed, group; the drapery is more summary, the hands not well modelled. But if at Kensington we have no seated group in wood so admirable, there is a charming standing figure in oak, also French, of the same period (No. 746, 1895) (Plate XXXVIII.). It is simply coloured, the under-dress red, the veil blue, as was usual. The expression of the Virgin's face has all the sweet French charm, and the

PLATE XXXVIII

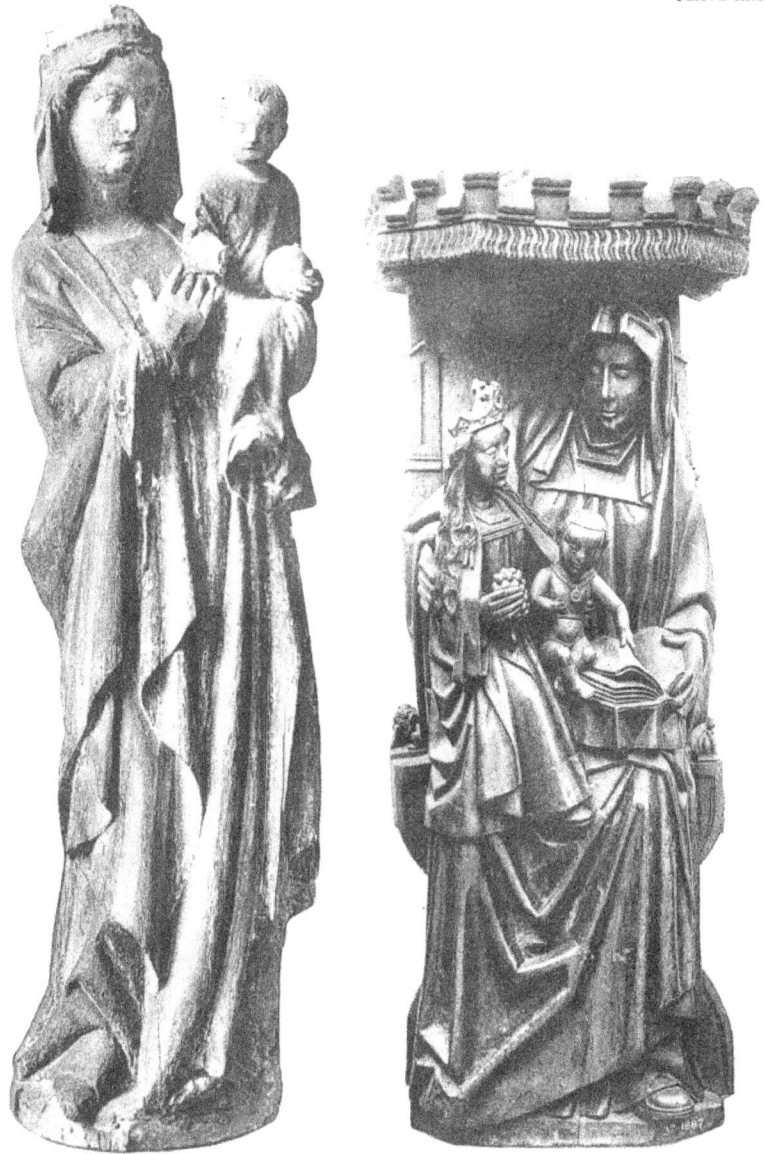

1. MADONNA FRENCH. FOURTEENTH CENTURY
VICTORIA AND ALBERT MUSEUM.
2. ANNA SELBDRITT GROUP. FLEMISH OR GERMAN. FIFTEENTH CENTURY
VICTORIA AND ALBERT MUSEUM (MASKELL COLLECTION)
PAGES 116-234

drapery is admirably simple. The Child, with a solemn expression beyond his years, holds a gilt globe. A painted standing Madonna in walnut, French of the early sixteenth century (No. 735, 1895), no doubt a rood figure, recalls, in attitude, the Nürnberg Madonna. A passing reference may be made to the number of twelfth-century Madonnas in wood in the churches of Auvergne. There was doubtless in this province a long-continued industry, usually in oak, in this class of wood sculpture, and of crucifixes. The type continued quite into the fifteenth century; for example in the *Vierge noire* of Molompize. M. de Rochemonteix's work on the Romanesque churches of Auvergne may again be referred to, on the subject of these images.

Noticing incidentally an extremely fine fourteenth-century statuette of German origin in the Carrand collection of the Bargello in order to remark how little, except the type of face, there is to distinguish some Flemish and German Madonnas of the period from the French by which they were inspired, we may take next one or two examples of the Italian trecento, and quattrocento. We must be contented with a bare mention of a standing figure of the Virgin and Child in the Berlin Museum. It is of the school of Giovanni Pisano, and, bearing a remarkable resemblance to his ivory Madonna in the cathedral of Pisa, is perhaps by his pupil Andrea, father of Nino, whose Annunciation figures will presently occupy our attention. The reader will appreciate the importance of these two statuettes in the history of sculpture, and of the evolution of ideas which connect the pioneers of the Italian Renaissance with its later developments. One of the earliest examples we have of wood sculpture from the hand of a great master is the life-size Madonna and Child, now in the museum of the Louvre, which, if it cannot be with absolute certainty attributed to Jacopo della Quercia himself, is nevertheless so connected by its

style and by the system of drapery to others of his
known works that it will be sufficient to note that the
opinions of such critics as Bode, Fabriczy, or Schubring
leave the question still unsettled (Plate XXXIX.). Continuing the great traditions of the school which we
connect with Niccola, Giovanni, and Andrea da Pisa,
it is certain that amongst all the great names of those
who disdained not to handle wood as well as marble
for great sculpture, none stands more prominently
forward than Jacopo della Quercia. The group here
illustrated is of walnut, the Virgin seated and clasp-
ing the Child, who is almost entirely naked, on her lap.
The somewhat long oval contour of her face, the tender,
almost melancholy, expression, the narrow forehead,
slightly protuberant, the drawing of the eyelids and
eyebrows, the eyes themselves, the formation of the
lips, the setting on of the neck, and the style of the
draperies are details which demand careful comparison
with other works of the Sienese sculptor. Amongst
these, the most nearly related would seem to be the
Madonna of the central doors of San Petronio, Bologna,
and the Virgin of San Martino, which is entirely gilt.
There are, it is true, some not inconsiderable differences in the shape of the head, in the veil, and
especially in the arrangement of the drapery, and
some may feel inclined to depreciate our group in
wood as not good enough for the master himself,
and that it is, at best, by a very clever pupil. The
naked Child is thick-set, solidly built and muscular.
In both figures there is evidence of the rapidly increasing tendency towards naturalism, towards working from the living model and the introduction of
portraiture in religious subjects. The group, as in
the case of many others of like character, was at one
time over an altar. It is fully coloured, the painting
excellent and, happily, in fair condition; for we have
here an admirable example of the method of colouring

PLATE XXXIX

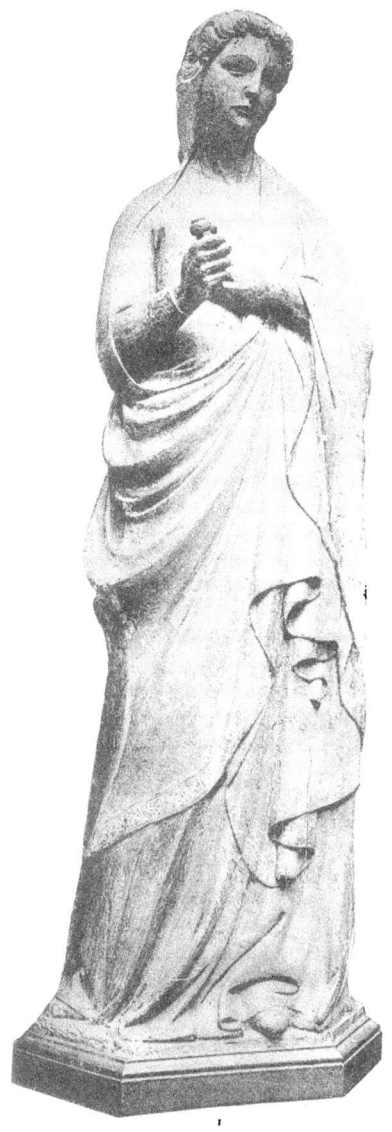 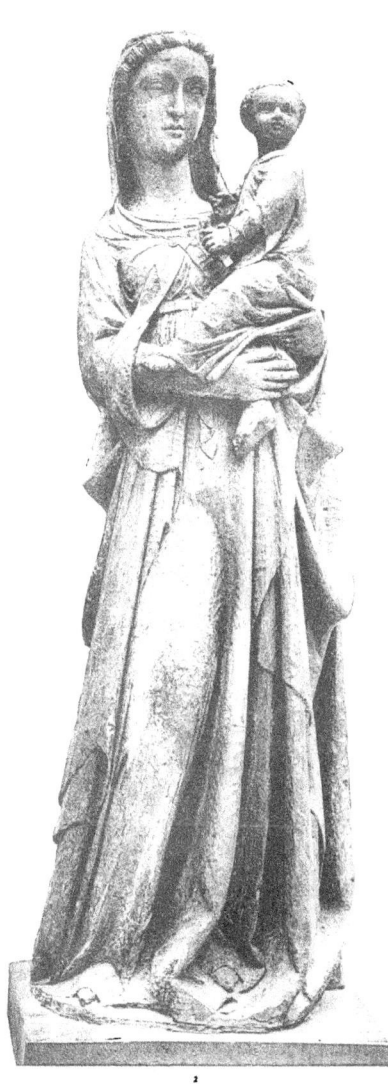

1. ANGEL OF THE ANNUNCIATION. PISAN SCHOOL. FOURTEENTH CENTURY
CLUNY MUSEUM, PARIS
2. MADONNA ITALIAN. FOURTEENTH CENTURY
VICTORIA AND ALBERT MUSEUM
PAGES 237, 252

sculpture taught by the twelfth-century monk Theophilus, and given to the world by Cennino Cennini in 1437, not long after the probable date of this group. The robe of the Virgin is a deep rich red, lined with green, the upper drapery and veil of a yellowish or light amber tint, the hair of both figures gilded, and the orphreys and other ornaments also gilded and tooled. The wood itself, in the accustomed manner, has fine linen stretched over it fixed with a lacteous cement upon which is the plaster coating for the reception of the colour. Possessing all the fresh and delicate features and the unaffected simplicity of the Sienese school of the first quarter of the fifteenth century, this group, with the earlier French group of the Louvre, is alone sufficient to place sculpture in wood of the finest mediæval period on a level with that in any other material whatsoever. The Madonna of Jacopo della Quercia is an evidence also not only of his following of the Pisan schools of Niccola and Andrea, and of Giotto, but also in common with other Tuscan artists of his time, of the influence of the more northern Gothic schools of the Netherlands and of Burgundy, then dominant everywhere. The Madonna and Child of the Victoria and Albert Museum (No. 5892), again life-size and of a somewhat later date, is one of the earliest acquisitions made in Italy for the South Kensington Museum by Sir J. C. Robinson. He himself, in the catalogue published in 1862, describes it as by a master unknown of about 1400-1440, having much of the manner of Jacopo della Quercia, the gesso priming and painting all disappeared or removed (Plate XL.).

There are several other fine examples of wood sculpture by Jacopo della Quercia, or of his school in the churches and public institutions of Siena and the neighbourhood. Amongst them are a standing group of the Virgin and Child and some figures of SS.

Peter, Paul, John the Baptist, and St. Antony in the church of San Martino. They are all completely gilded. But though the Madonna figure may be said to be in the style of that of the Louvre, or, rather, of the Madonna of the church of San Petronio, these figures are not likely to be by the hand of the Master himself. Born in the last quarter of the fourteenth century, and working during the first half of the fifteenth, the art of Jacopo della Quercia is distinguished by its singleness of purpose, straightforward simplicity and elegant refinement, without a trace of artificiality. He was strongly influenced by the school of Niccola Pisano and the Gothic tradition, following no doubt the methods of the Flemish and Burgundian masters whose authority in his early days was everywhere paramount. And, indeed, his style would connect him rather with the trecentists than with the more florid and overcharged tendencies of sentiment which characterize the fifteenth century. But, of course, all through the first half of the fifteenth century the Florentine schools were still very much influenced by Gothic methods however modified by the naturalistic feeling which Niccola of Pisa had been the first to borrow from other sources.

PLATE XL

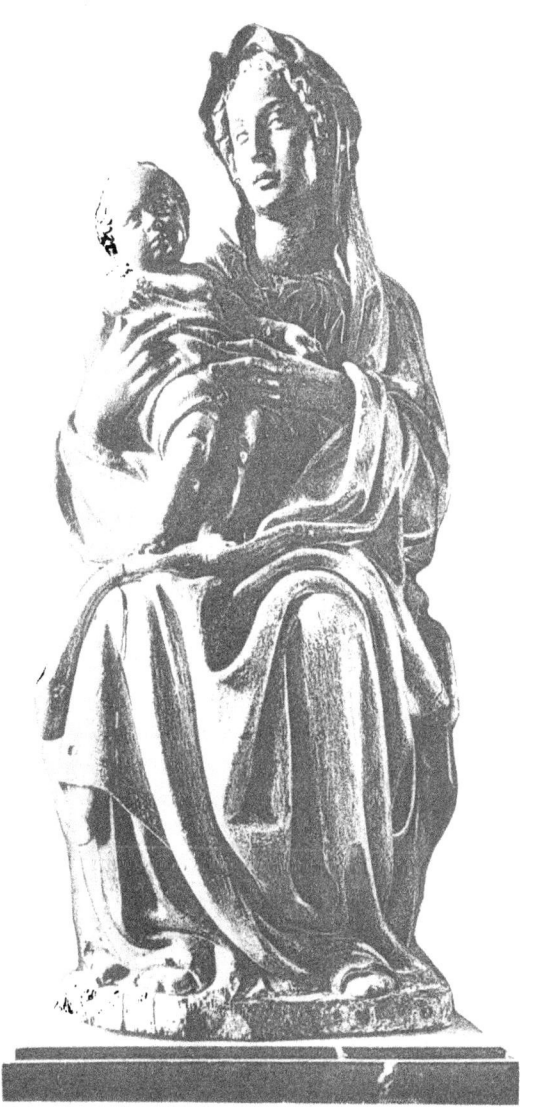

MADONNA AND CHILD, BY JACOPO DELLA QUERCIA
LOUVRE MUSEUM
PAGE 236

CHAPTER XIII

ON SOME EXAMPLES OF WOOD SCULPTURE OF THE TRECENTO AND QUATTROCENTO IN ITALY

I T would be impossible to approach, without the greatest diffidence, the task of attempting to describe Italian art in wood within the limits of a few pages. The period to which we have to go for the best examples is one which is intimately connected with the revival of art in which Italy played so overwhelmingly prominent a part. Italian sculpture in wood has been hitherto little known and little studied, at any rate by English writers. There are certain museums, such as the *Museo Civico* of Pisa, where a fair amount of fine examples is to be found, but much is distributed in various cathedrals or hidden away in village churches where it has often suffered from neglect, from unskilful restorations, and from additions of tawdry drapery. It is but recently, in 1905, that a considerable number of interesting examples of the art of wood-carving in the Abruzzi were gathered together at a special exhibition. Contrary to a formerly received opinion (it may be noted that Molinier, in his *Histoire de l'Art*, treats the subject very summarily, and confines his attention almost entirely to tarsia work), the art has always been popular in Italy, and as elsewhere has followed on the lines of the more important sculptures in stone, marble, and bronze. The story of sculpture in Italy is evidence of a wide-reaching effect on the art of other countries from the dawn of the Renaissance to its full development in the days of Michael Angelo, but in the examples which will be selected we shall find ourselves in an atmosphere entirely different from that in which we have been living in the case of those of the period of Gothic art in France, in the Netherlands, and in other more northern countries of Europe. We shall be confronted at every step with the greatest names of the early Renaissance—indeed, it may be said, with all the great names—so that comparisons with their work as sculptors in other materials—in marble and stone, in terra cotta, bronze, and even in majolica, would be constantly arising. To embrace the subject with any completeness would imply an incursus into the whole history of Italian art of the period. It would involve such questions as the influences exercised by the study of antique models on the trecento schools, or, again, the measure of inspiration from French art to be accorded to those of the quattrocento. We might have to discuss the position of Gothic art in Italy, how far it was congenial to the character of the people, and what were its relations to the older systems in the work of Niccola, of Giovanni, and of Andrea Pisani, who added to it the poetical naturalism which laid the foundations of the great change which we know under the name of Renaissance. For, as in this book we are dealing almost exclusively with Gothic art, we must remember that the early Renaissance was but a development of Gothic feeling, passing by slow degrees into an appreciation of humanism and realism.

Owing to the quantity of available matter and to the impossibility of treating in one chapter the whole subject of wood sculpture in Italy, it is necessary to make a selection, and to confine attention for the most part to certain figure work belonging to the trecento and quattrocento schools of Pisa, Florence, and Siena.

These are life-sized statues representing the Annunciation by means of detached figures of the Virgin Mary and the archangel Gabriel. In their general character they find no parallel elsewhere, and for poetic beauty and unaffected naturalism many of them are unsurpassed in the history of mediæval carvings in any other countries. They may indeed claim to rank as great sculpture, and in addition combine the arts of sculptors and painters of the highest rank. Some few other examples of figure work of the same period will also be noted, and, for the rest, the crucifixes and Madonnas of Italian origin have already been included in the section devoted to that part of our subject. In earlier days and throughout the Carlovingian period, art in Italy remained steadfastly attached to Byzantine methods and traditions, and was always coy of the influence of the north and consequently of Gothic ideas. Wood sculpture was especially cultivated in the monasteries of the south of the peninsula and some ancient doors of the twelfth century, besides the well-known ones of Santa Sabina still exist: for example, those carved with scenes in the life of the Virgin of the church of Santa Maria in Cellis at Carsoli, the similar ones of San Pietro, Alba Fucense, and the panels with like scenes of Sta. Maria Maggiore at Alatri. In Romanesque times sculpture in wood had produced also in Tuscany one of its finest efforts— the 'Deposition' of the cathedral of Volterra, already noticed. The Victoria and Albert Museum possesses four interesting columns (No. 269, 1886) each about eight feet high, which may have been supports of a pulpit, or as the museum label suggests, for organs. The capitals are carved with foliage, amongst which are human and animal figures: rude work after decidedly oriental models, the surfaces of the wood flat, so that the carving is in the fashion of *entaille* or *champlevé*. They are described as south Italian work of the thirteenth century, but the fashion and designs must surely be of at least a hundred years earlier.

Of the oldest Gothic work in wood, little is known. Vasari, in the sixteenth century, was the first to characterize the great change in the systems of art of which the earliest manifestations were made more than three hundred years before his time under the influence of Niccola Pisano. That influence marks the first great movement in the rebirth of the plastic arts. It was, in the terms which Vasari was the first to apply, the *Rinascità*, the *Rinascimento*, the *Resorgimento*, the Renaissance, as is now the accepted expression. It was the rejuvenation of taste, and the appreciation in the human mind of the study of the antique; the awakening of ideas which had long remained dormant and stagnant throughout the protracted period of ignorance which we call the dark ages. Under the restraints of Byzantine mannerisms, sculpture had suffered more than any other expression of art, and had fallen very low indeed. By a return to classical principles, and by a systematic study of the antique, it was destined to differentiate itself from the almost wildly independent system by which the purely Gothic is characterized. The picturesque and the natural took the place of the ideal which had so long exclusively prevailed, borrowing the classical formulæ and adapting them to Christian religious feeling. The great name which we associate with these beginnings in the middle and second half of the thirteenth century is that of Niccola of Pisa, whom we know best perhaps by his pulpit of the cathedral of Siena, or by the bas-reliefs of that of Lucca, among so many more of his marvellous productions. It may be, indeed, that he derived his inspiration from the old Christian sarcophagi rather than direct from classical antiquity, for the bas-reliefs of the Gothic pulpit of the Baptistery of Pisa are obvious imitations of these. And it may

242

be that the great sculptures of Chartres, of Paris, of Amiens, or of Strassburg, are entitled to an earlier date. We shall find their influence in such figures as the angel from the Timbal collection in the Cluny Museum, which will presently be noticed. However this may be, so far as our immediate subject is concerned, Italian sculpture before the impulse given to it by Niccola calls for little consideration. Giovanni, his son and pupil, of whom is recorded on the pulpit of Pisa, '*sculpens in petro, ligno auro*,' carries us into the trecento period. Another of the same patronymic, perhaps even a greater artist than his master Giovanni, is the famous bronzist, maker of the first great gates of the Baptistery of Florence, and we have already noticed a Madonna in wood which is probably his work. Finally, and still of the trecento, we have Nino Pisano, son of Andrea, to whom and to his school we owe the beautiful Annunciation figures that will presently occupy our attention. Andrea Pisano has been called the creator of the Florentine school of sculpture. Nino worked with him, and after his father's death took his place as architect of the cathedral of Orvieto. The art of sculpture in wood in Romanesque times had probably occupied no important position, though we possess such interesting examples as the ' Deposition ' of Volterra, but towards the middle of the trecento it had become important and popular, and in 1349 the Society of St. Luke had founded at Florence special schools under its protection.

Tuscan sculpture, then, begins with Niccola Pisano, at a time when the increasing tranquillity and prosperity of the country found people capable of appreciating ideas of refinement and nobility of expression. The turn of Siena was not to be till somewhat later, while that of Florence, destined to be greatest of all, was to await for the culminating point

of its distinction in the arts, the full quattrocento—
the fifteenth century. For it was not until the close
of the fourteenth that the great names appear of
Donatello, of Brunelleschi, of Desiderio da Settignano,
or of Ghiberti, all of whom did so much to spread
pictorial fashions in sculpture, and all of whom—if, as
is probable, we may include the last named—with such
another famous sculptor as Jacopo della Quercia of
Siena, render illustrious the art of wood-carving. Our
space will not permit us to follow the work of every
artist in detail. If it did so, we should find in the
company of those just named some others hardly less
distinguished. We should be able to illustrate by
existing examples the work of Matteo Civitali, of
Andrea and Simone Ferrucci, Baccio da Montelupo,
Niccolo Baroncelli, Michelozzo, Andrea della Robbia,
Benedetto da Majano, Neroccio, Giuliano da Sangallo,
Nanni Unghero, Giacomo Cozzarelli, Il Vecchietta,
Caradosso, the Barili, Leonardo del Tasso, Andrea
Sansovino, and Andrea del Verrocchio, for the most
part Florentine of the fifteenth and early sixteenth
century, and of others of lesser note. There are, of
course, amongst these, many carvers of crucifixes, and
of Madonnas there is a wealth also. Baccio da Montelupo's fine crucifix, made for the monks of San Marco,
still exists in their refectory. Many others made by
him and mentioned by Vasari cannot now be traced.
From Vasari we learn that Margaritone of Arezzo
(1236-1313) carved a large crucifix in wood for the
Santa, which was 'painted in the Greek manner,' and
four other figures in the parish church of Arezzo, and
even Giotto is credited by tradition with one in the
church of Santa Maria Sopra Minerva, in Rome.
Finally, Vasari himself, followed by others, has attributed a crucifix in wood, in the Santo Spirito, Florence,
as a youthful work of Michael Angelo. At Ferrara, in
the fifteenth century, wood sculpture was represented

by Arrigo da Brabant, and by a numerous colony of German, Flemish, and French artists. At Modena we find such names as da Basio, da Lendmara, and the Canozzi. It would seem that in certain districts, as in the Abruzzi for instance, owing no doubt to the considerable number of religious houses which flourished there from the twelfth to the sixteenth century, there was great activity in the art of wood-carving. Examples of figure work of considerable merit are still numerous in the churches at Chieti and at Aquila. Many were shown at the exhibition of the art of the Abruzzi in 1905.

The resuscitation of the sculptural arts in Italy at the time of the great awakening in the thirteenth century, and afterwards, was aided by several circumstances. The new spirit ran parallel with that of the revival of literature in the age of Dante, with a popular impulse towards mysticism which had been fostered by the teaching of St. Francis of Assisi, with general prosperity and increasing luxury, and with the more free study and observation of nature, leading to a greater refinement of æsthetic ideals, to which reference has already several times here been made. About the middle of the fourteenth century the new ideas had triumphed all along the line. We see this exemplified in the charming Annunciation figures of the school of Nino Pisano. We may reasonably assume that some of these delicate works, so full of poetic feeling, are by Nino himself. Most admirable among them are those of the museums of Pisa and of the Cluny of Paris: most charming of all, those which the museum of Lyon was so fortunate as to procure. We shall not stay to inquire how far such things as these imply a triumph of humanism over the symbolism and mystical ideas which had hitherto governed art in the church, and whether religious fervour and devotion suffered in

245

consequence. We shall take these beautiful Madonnas and groups as we find them, purely as works of art: sweet-smiling women of the time, in the very garments of the age, youthful attendants or messengers suggestive of the Court, babes with the chubby features and plump soft limbs that we associate with them. It must be left to individual feeling to discriminate between the devotional sentiment and an appeal to the sensual and the materialist. The time was fast approaching when the most sacred figures were used as a mere pretext for the portraits of anything but saintly people, and a classically draped figure did duty as this or that holy personage. What is unfortunately impossible is to give in our monotone illustrations an idea of the polychrome decoration in view of which these figures were first of all prepared by the sculptor. Allowances must be made, for here the photograph fails. In thus confining our attention for the most part to a certain class of figures we have also to leave on one side the glorious choir and stall work with which the churches of Italy abound. It would be pleasant at least to notice such Gothic work as that of Santa Maria dei Frari at Venice, and, even if somewhat later than our limits in date, the charm and perfection of the choir of San Pietro, Perugia, or the exquisite carving in walnut of the church of St. Severinus at Naples. But it would be difficult to consider the subject apart from that of the art of colouring and inlaying wood which we call *tarsia* or even *certosina* work, in which Benedetto da Majano, Giovanni da Verona, Damiani da Bergamo, and Davido da Pistoja are, among many others, cited by Vasari.

In Tuscany especially, in Siena and Pisa, it became the custom, about the second half of the fourteenth century, to represent the Annunciation by the two figures of the Virgin and the angel Gabriel, which were not necessarily grouped together, but placed on

246

PLATE XLI

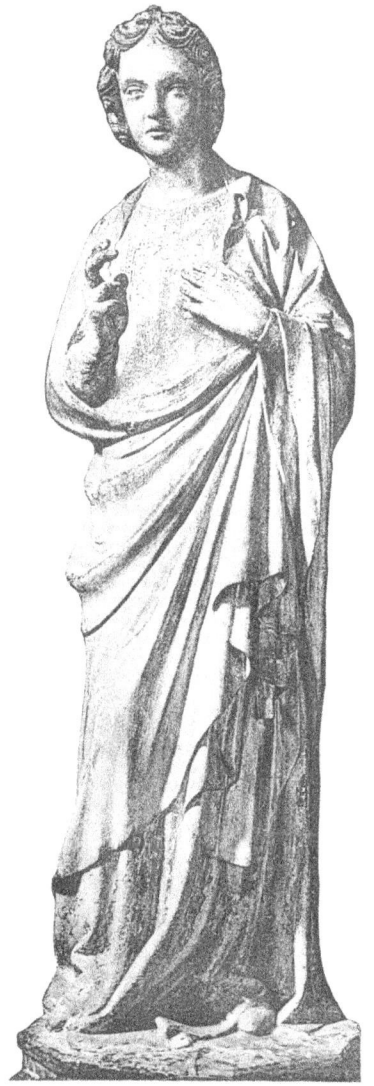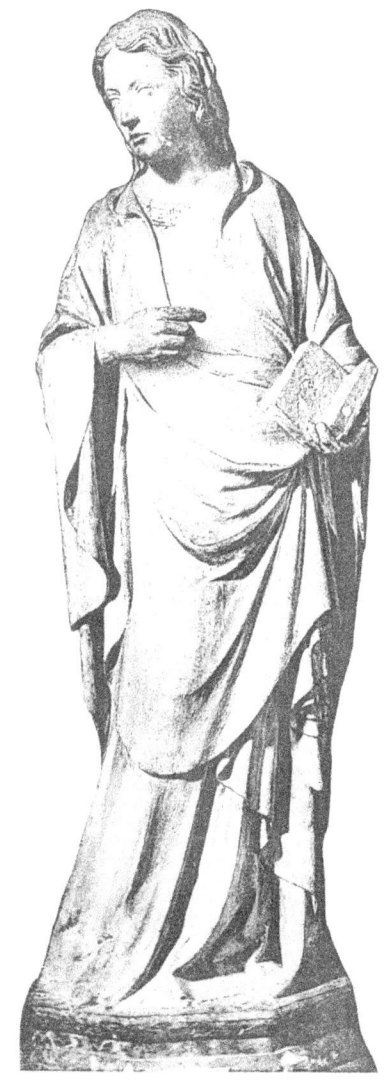

ANNUNCIATION FIGURES. ATTRIBUTED TO NINO PISANO. FOURTEENTH CENTURY
MUSEO CIVICO, PISA
PAGE 248

consoles as separate statues. It would appear to have been an entirely new idea, corresponding with nothing else in the plastic arts of any country, and, especially also in their treatment, they are examples of an art of which little, besides themselves, remains. In general they indicate the following of the early school of Giovanni da Pisa, and the motive and method of expression undoubtedly speedily became favourite ones. It is, however, especially to the influence of Nino Pisano, son of Andrea, who—as we know only the date of his death in 1368—worked probably for the most part throughout the second quarter of the trecento, that we owe the chief impulse in the carving of the pairs of Annunciation figures, of which some amongst the most important will now be cited. They are, with one exception, life or nearly life-size figures of the same general type. The Virgin is represented standing, simply clad, usually with a prayer-book in her hand, as if disturbed by the summons of the angel : the heavenly messenger also standing, one hand raised to call attention, the mouth open as in the act of speaking. In accordance with the universal practice in sculpture of the period, they are fully coloured. The question how far they are from Nino's own hand, and how far they correspond with known Madonna figures by him, is not one for which much space can now be found. It may, perhaps, after all, suffice to say that the best among them are strongly influenced by him, and that they are of his school. We have no certain knowledge that Nino himself worked in wood, though if we consider the customs of the time and the roll of sculptors already cited, it is hardly likely that at one time or other in his career every great sculptor would not have exercised his genius in this material ; at any rate, up to the time—perhaps late in the fifteenth century—when, under the new system of art, wood sculpture would have given place entirely to marble. The most enlightening reference that can be made towards establishing Nino's participation in at least the group of the Pisa Museum, with which others are closely connected, is a comparison with the figures in marble of the Saltarelli monument in the church of Santa Caterina at Pisa. These have always been considered as the finest creations of this refined and sympathetic master. The tomb itself of the archbishop is his greatest work, and according to Vasari was executed about the year 1370. But Nino was then no longer living, and the more correct date is 1342. The Madonna at the top has considerable relationship with the same artist's Madonna of Santa Maria Novella. In the chapel of the Rosary in that church are other two Annunciation figures closely identical with the pair of the Museo Civico. Supino, in his *Arte Pisana*, says they are without doubt by the same hand, and illustrates them side by side. The style is, indeed, similar, especially in the figure of the Virgin, the drapery alike in arrangement and feeling.

In these Annunciation figures and Madonnas we find an entirely new type of the Virgin. It is the un-affected sweet girl—almost a schoolgirl—who receives the salutation of the angel. Confining ourselves to the wood examples, I can see nothing that would justify the suggestion of the French critic, M. Michel, that Nino was inspired in any way by the small French groups in ivory of the subject, and that he modified these and enlarged them in marble and wood. Their striking characteristic is their girlishness. On the other hand the analogies with such sculptures as those of Reims or Chartres is marked, in the attitude, the expression, the quite classical draperies, and the general sentiment of the Gabriel of the Cluny Museum and the others with which it is related. What is so notice-able in nearly all the figures of this category is the intense emotional feeling, the full story told by two

248

separate figures without any scenic adjuncts, the dramatic aspect, the angel in the act of speaking, the Virgin answering as it were—or, rather, expressing by her attitude, by her whole demeanour, her carriage, features, even such a detail as the book of prayers in her hand, as if hastily closed—all that is passing in her mind. Very simple, yet elegant, is the attitude in which she stands, the shape of the head and transcript of the features expressive of almost extreme youth, the costume unusual yet most refined in its lines of simple drapery falling lightly, and covering the form down to the feet. There is little or none of the undulating Gothic bend of French fourteenth-century work, except, perhaps, and that but slightly, in the Gabriel of the Cluny and the Madonna of the Museo Civico. The style of costume of such figures as the Madonnas of the Lyon, Pisa, or Asciano groups is peculiar, in the long straight falling robe, without waistband or girdle, and with very few straight folds : perfectly plain, and with plain tight sleeves : no ornaments or overmantle, no veil, and the hair very neatly arranged. If other influences are to be traced, they would seem to be from the refined idealism, the almost enervated grace of Giottesque traditions, with at the same time a suggestion of realism and portrait-like fidelity to nature. For these figures are still truly Gothic. The reproductions given here will dispense with more than general descriptions. The photographs must speak for themselves, regretting only that the charm of the original colouring must be left to the imagination. Yet this colouring is of so great importance that it is almost impossible to estimate the true value of the art from monochrome reproductions. These figures represent, indeed, sculpture painted, or paintings differing from those on plane surfaces, and if we could imagine them as they left the hands of their creator, we should find them to be the work of great artists in

both lines of art. It is true that the surface of
the sculptured wood was destined entirely to disappear, yet it does not follow that sculpture takes
a secondary place. The colouring throughout of
the faces and hands, and of the patterns and orna-
mentations of the drapery, was of extraordinary
delicacy, the former painted with a light carnation, the
cheeks rose-tinted, the lips deepened with cinnabar,
the draperies richly ornamented with gilded orphreys
and edgings, sometimes raised with impasto and tool-
ings. In short, even in their present condition, except in
those cases where in later times they have been wholly
bedaubed with a uniform colour, these figures, and
other French and Italian madonnas described in an
earlier chapter, are amongst the most distinctive remaining of the methods taught by Theophilus and
Cennini.

In the first half of the fourteenth century, sculpture
had not attained a high position and was not held in
great esteem in Florence. Nino Pisano therefore, and
his brother Tommaso, also a sculptor, but of whose work
there is nothing of importance, had installed themselves
at Pisa and later on at Orvieto. Among the Annunciation figures there are three which are usually
attributed to Nino himself. They are the beautiful
pair in the museum of Lyon, and a figure of the archangel—the companion figure is missing—in the Museo
Civico of Pisa. We may take first the Annunciation
figure, and the accompanying angel, of the Lyon
collection, both of which present many points of interest
and originality entirely different from any of the other
groups, and indeed from any other known sculpture.
The group appears to have been acquired in 1887; it is
said, from the church of Santa Caterina. The figures
measure each almost five feet in height, are fully
coloured, and preserve to a great degree the original
colouring. The charming head of the Virgin, youth-

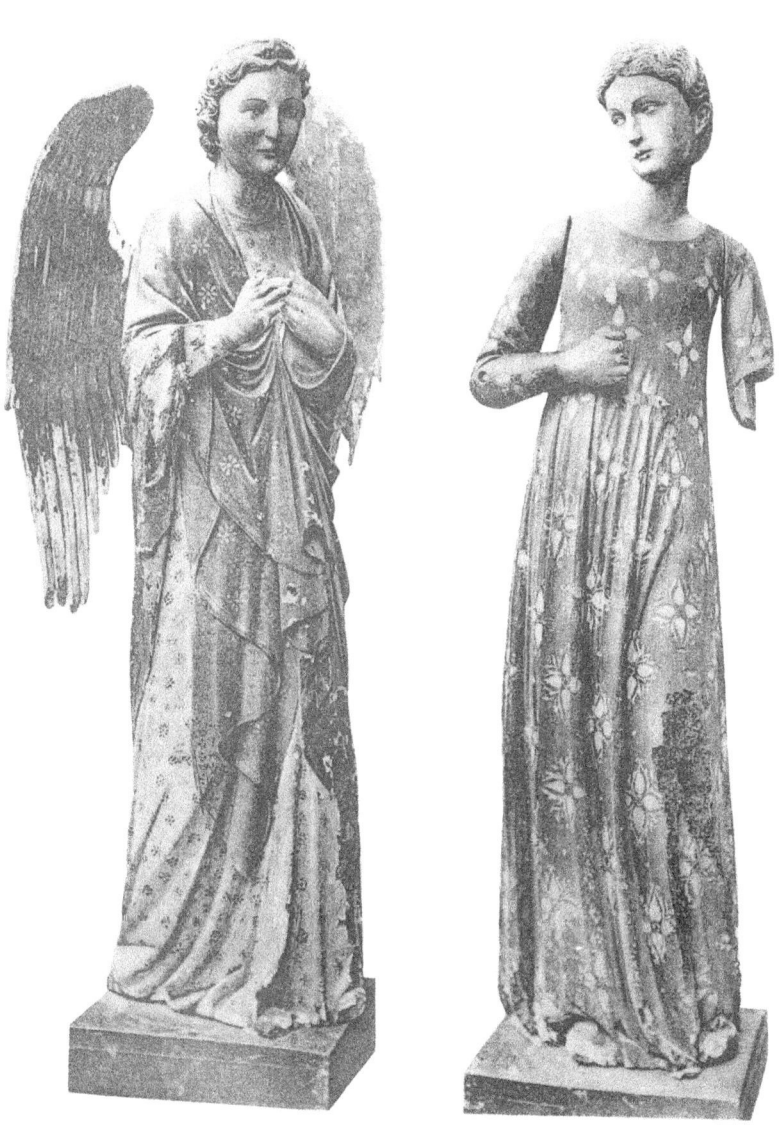

ANNUNCIATION FIGURES. PISAN SCHOOL. FOURTEENTH CENTURY
LYON MUSEUM
PAGE 230

ful as a girl of sixteen, is turned to right and slightly inclined over the shoulder, the face bearing a listening expression of anticipation. She wears a long loose robe without any waistband or girdle. An unusual peculiarity is that the arms of the figure—one is unfortunately broken and partly missing—are jointed and movable, as in a lay figure. This, it has been thought, was to facilitate the clothing with real stuffs. Certainly the dress, as it is, suggests an under-garment or *negligé*, which with great skill indicates the full form beneath. Yet such a complete figure, so elaborately decorated a dress, could not have been intended to be ignominiously concealed by the addition of draperies. Admitting the possibility of a mantle being added, it is in itself the finished production not only of a great sculptor but also of a great painter. It would be impossible not to recognize the master hand in the consummate treatment of the carnations of the face and hands, and in the rich decoration of the dress. The Virgin of the Annunciation in the Municipal Museum—at one time in the convent of St. Domenico, has much in common with that of Lyon. It is somewhat taller, measuring quite five feet six inches in height, and unfortunately has at some later time been completely bedaubed with a new red colour. The modelling of the head, the treatment of the hair, and the style generally, are strikingly similar to the marble Madonna by Nino in the museum of Orvieto. The figure has the same feeling as that of Lyon, a like elegance of pose, and similar proportions, though the head is older and not nearly so fascinating in expression. Possibly the missing angel is the one now in the museum of the Louvre, to which also is wanting the accompanying Madonna. The arms are again jointed and movable. The Pisa Museum also possesses a complete and more dramatic group, attributed to the master of the works just mentioned. The figures measure, respectively, five

251

feet nine, and five feet six in height, and though there are traces of the original coloration it is now almost entirely hidden beneath a coat of dirty white paint. Undoubtedly the original face tints, and the patterns and other decorations of the simple drapery which falls in graceful folds to the feet, was as rich as in the Lyon example. The hair, as was the universal practice, was gilded. The attitudes have the French feeling of the fourteenth century, with the Gothic bend in the figure of the Virgin which was so common at that period, but is here not at all exaggerated. Again these figures invite comparison with those in the chapel of the church of Santa Caterina, with the Madonna of Santa Maria della Spina and others by Nino, and by his father, whose art he continued.

We may take next the angel of the Cluny Museum at Paris, at one time in the Timbal collection. Closely related, perhaps, especially in the character of the head, to the Pisan angel last noted, it has perhaps more affinity still with the marble angel of Santa Caterina. Nor can we help thinking of the statuary of Chartres. With regard to the connexion of any of these figures—not excepting those of Lyon —with Nino Pisano himself, it would be hazardous indeed to express a decided opinion. The most that can be said is that they must have been executed under his immediate influence, and that, if by one of his most talented followers, there may have been added to the style of the master other graceful motives which, some may think, would have contributed to his own fame. The group of the museum of Orvieto is of another type which has several interesting features. As it is not illustrated here, it will suffice to remark the long oval head with high forehead of the Virgin, the curious way in which the angel holds up a fold of his mantle, his mild and sedate expression, and the mouth not open in the act of speaking. It is the type

252

PLATE XLIII

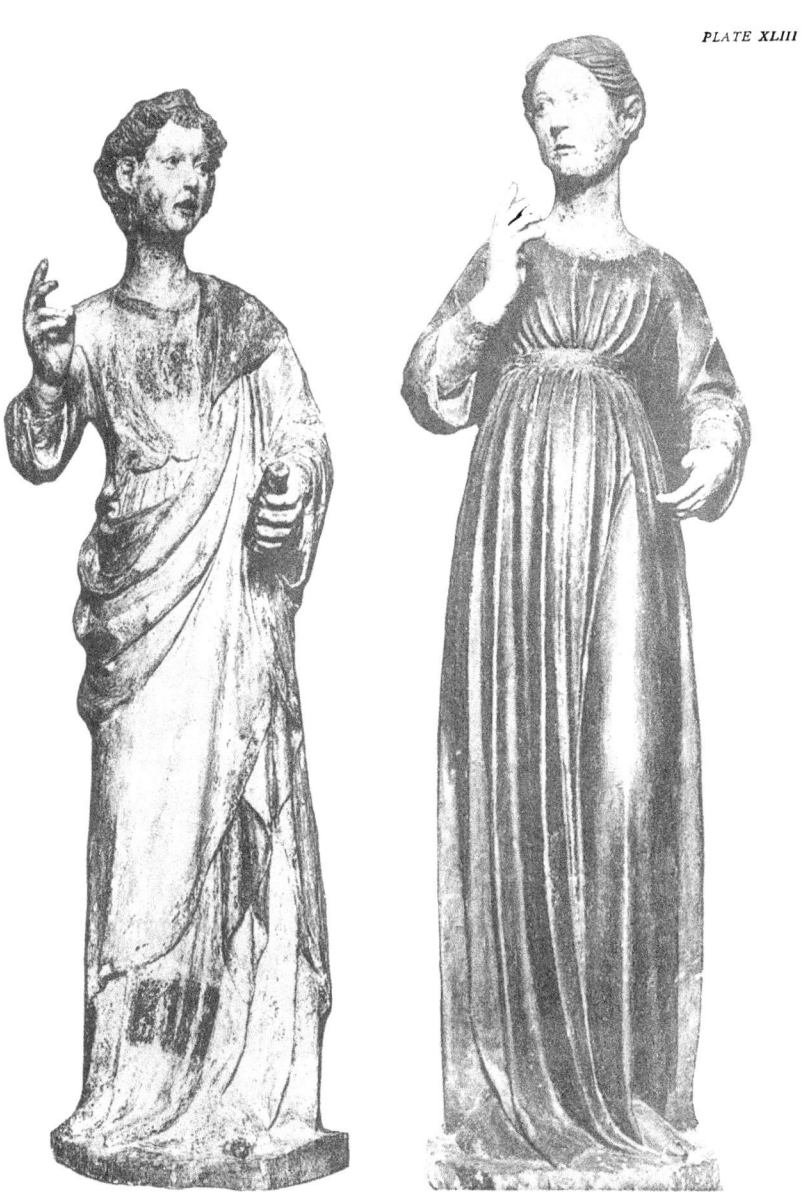

ANNUNCIATION FIGURES. PISAN SCHOOL. FOURTEENTH CENTURY
LOUVRE MUSEUM
PAGE 254

found frequently on the façade of the cathedral of Orvieto. There are other Annunciation figures and other statues in wood in the Pisan Museum, evidences of the long-continued influence of the school of Nino throughout the fourteenth century, and until the Pisan school itself fell into decadence and that of Florence became flourishing. Sometimes there is a reminiscence of the thirteenth century in the simple straight-folded drapery and of the influence of the school of Siena. The Victoria and Albert Museum has an interesting figure of the angel of an Annunciation group, standing six feet high, of the end of the fourteenth or beginning of the fifteenth century. It was acquired in Florence as long ago as 1861, and might almost be the pendant of the Annunciation Virgin, formerly in the Goldschmidt collection of the Louvre. Sir J. C. Robinson's catalogue of 1862 states that both this and the companion figure had, it was said, been recently sold, for some unaccountable reason to a country priest who took them to his own parish church. Here, being found too tall for the niche for which they were destined, the statue of the Virgin was summarily shortened by several inches, and attempts made to convert the Angel into another Virgin. Resold to a Florentine Jew, Robinson acquired the Gabriel for fifty francs. It is now entirely denuded of the original colouring. The Louvre possesses also a complete Annunciation pair, coming from the Bardini collection, which has some affinity with the figures of the Lyon Museum, and at Pescia there is the so-called Madonna dell' Acquavino, probably of Nino's atelier. It is figured by Stiavelli, who attributes it to Matteo Civitali, in his *L'Arte in Val di Nievole*.

Of the Florentine and Sienese schools are other Annunciation figures after the Pisan model. Foremost among them all is the group of the church of San Francesco at Asciano, for here the figure of the

253

Virgin in its charming simplicity is sweetest above any of this type of Madonnas. Her demeanour is not that to which we are accustomed in most of the others. There is movement in her attitude as she stands as if entering a room, one hand upraised in astonishment at the apparition which meets her eyes. It is again an instance of a whole dramatic story told by two simple figures without any scenic adjuncts. The sentiment differs from that ordinarily expressed. It is not one of humility and resignation, but rather of the youthful face lit up with glad surprise. The position of the gracefully executed hands of the figures is most expressive, both of the delivery of the message and of its reception. The original colouring is almost intact, and charmingly delicate are the carnations, and the hair gilded as usual. The angel wears a white alb with apparels and a stole over the left shoulder, lightly knotted under his right arm, the Virgin a red and green dress with a gold girdle. Unfortunately his face has been repainted. Schubring thinks these two childlike figures to be the work of Martino di Bartolommeo of Siena who is credited, on account of the inscription on the base, with an Annunciation pair in the Collegiate Church of San Gemignano. But we know nothing of him as a sculptor, and, in any case, nothing could be more dissimilar in style than these fifteenth-century figures of Asciano which have all the Gothic feeling and grace of the fourteenth century or even earlier, and the possibly elegant and classical, but almost pagan group of San Gemignano. The Annunciation pair of the church of Corpus Domini, Montalcino, of the Siena school of the fourteenth century, though not without defects, and the far finer pair of the Abbey Church of Sant' Antonio, at the same place, are of interest amongst the series. The first two bear inscriptions stating that they were made for the shoemakers' guild in 1368 and 1370.

PLATE XLIV

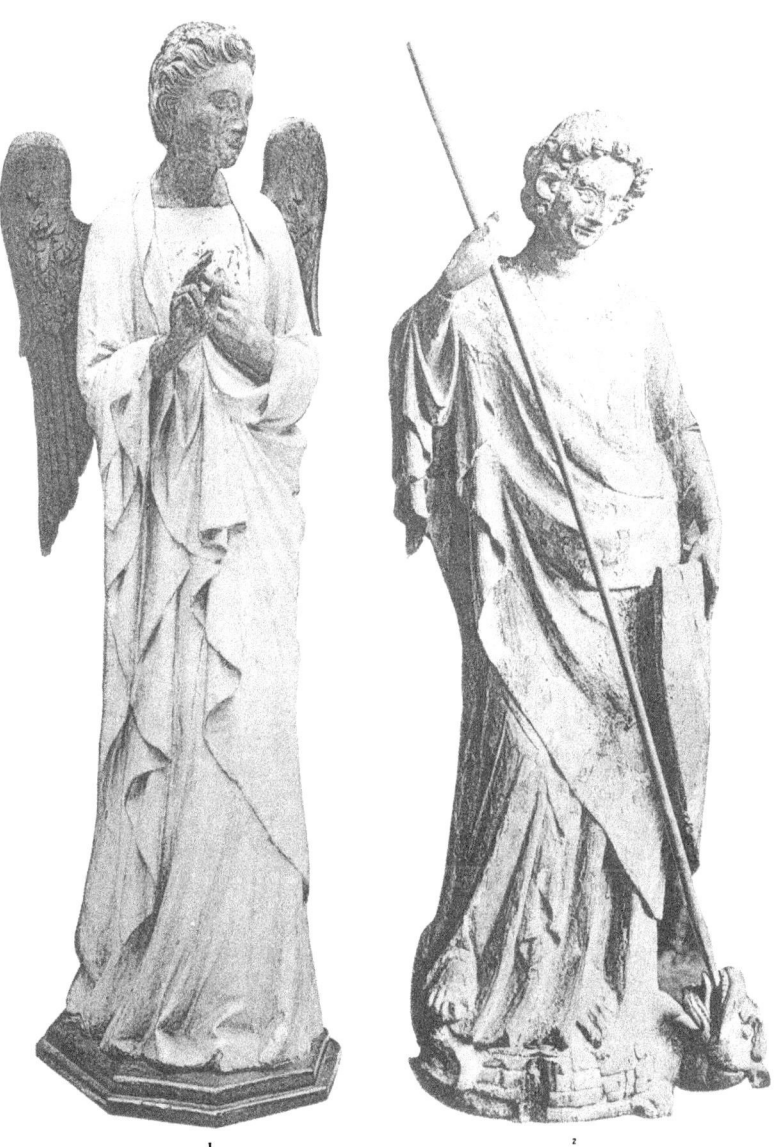

1. ANGEL OF AN ANNUNCIATION GROUP. ITALIAN. 2. ARCHANGEL MICHAEL. FRENCH.
FOURTEENTH CENTURY. VICTORIA AND ALBERT MUSEUM

ANNUNCIATION FIGURES

We come now to a smaller and highly interesting group in the museum of Berlin of an entirely different character from those we have hitherto been considering (Plate XLV.). It is the product of the mixture of the Pisan and Sienese and Florentine schools, of an art which has profited by many influences, and carries us into the fifteenth century, while preserving the Gothic feeling and much of the characteristics of the preceding one. The two figures, measuring each about eighteen inches in height, are clearly—and this is most noticeable in that of the angel—due to the school of Nino Pisano, though hardly to be immediately connected with one of his pupils. The name of Tommaso, brother of Nino, might even be mentioned. Differing from most of the others of this class of the subject the Virgin is seated, the angel kneels on one knee, the right hand upraised, as he delivers his message. Her attitude is as if the apparition were a sudden one disturbing her reading, and she puts down her book on her knee and waits expectantly. The angel is half in profile, the open hand raised to call attention, not perhaps, as some think, holding at one time a lily now missing. Yet there is evidence of inspiration by the trecento schools of painting, and comparisons may also be made with many sculptures of that period such as the Annunciation of the tabernacle of Orcagna or the figures of the façade of Orvieto. But it would be impossible to ascribe the group definitely either to the school of Siena, which was an offshoot of the Pisan, or of Florence, which followed this. Some hold one opinion, some another : some would refer it back to the mid-fourteenth, others place it in the first quarter of the fifteenth ; some even give it to a more northern school, perhaps Piedmontese. On the whole, we may come to the conclusion that it is the work of a Florentine sculptor strongly influenced by Ghiberti, and a follower of the Pisan school of Nino ;

255

and although at first sight one might be inclined to give it an earlier origin, the influences discernible, which are very various, lead us to decide rather on the early part of the fifteenth century. A seated Madonna in wood, fully painted, of unusual type, of the Siena school of the fifteenth century, in the church of Sant' Agostino, has analogies with the drapery of the Berlin figure. The Child, in this group dressed in a belted frock, stands in a half-running attitude on His mother's lap, His back turned to the spectator as He plays affectionately, one hand on her neck.

It is necessary to pass rapidly over a few amongst a large number of Italian sculptures of the fifteenth century which might be cited. The first two are the work of no less a master than Donatello, whose crucifix at Santa Croce has already been noticed. Vasari mentions the statue of St. John, which was in his time in the Chiesa dei Frari at Venice, and is there to this day. Although probably executed between the years 1453-1466, when Donatello had completed his work at Padua and was in the full vigour of his art, this is not a piece which attracts greatly at first sight. The head resembles, rather, a head of our Lord at the pillar, crowned with thorns. Yet the expression is an appealing one. It is 'the voice of one crying in the wilderness,' the beckoning hand upraised. The body is clothed to the knees with skins, with some drapery over the shoulders and arms. The limbs are admirably chiselled, but—allowing for the qualities of two different methods and materials—not so finely modelled, perhaps, as in the bronze St. John of the Baptistery of Siena. Both exhibit the same style, both are dramatic to a degree, telling a whole story in a single figure. So also with that most touching and powerful, if at the same time almost repellent figure of the Magdalen of the same Baptistery. It is reproduced here in con-

PLATE XLV

ANNUNCIATION FIGURES. FLORENTINE SCHOOL. FIFTEENTH CENTURY

BERLIN MUSEUM

PAGE 256

trast with the German conception of Riemenschneider (Plate XII.), a conception which, after all, is strongly indebted to Italian precedents, however filtered and adapted to other temperaments. Very different indeed is Donatello's Magdalen from the later pagan nudities with which we are familiar : the beautiful sinner reading in a cave. What is insisted on here is penitence and renunciation. It is true that the figure is horrifying in its realism. The Magdalen, clothed in long unkempt hair, is reduced almost to a skeleton. Premature old age has disfigured the once beautiful body. The expression of the face is almost repulsive. Yet if art is entitled to teach, it cannot be denied that a great moral lesson is taught in such a figure, and whatever may have been said against it by some art critics, we may be permitted to class it among the great sculptor's highest efforts.

An interesting figure of St. Christopher, standing about five feet in height, was acquired by M. Eugène Piot at Siena, and bequeathed by him to the Louvre. At one time in the Church of Sant' Agostino, Vasari mentions it in his life of Signorelli. The saint is represented as a youngish-looking man, leaning with both hands on a long stick, or pole, after having carried the Christ-child across the river. The bambino is missing. Analogies with the character and style of the well-known Signorelli monument have led to the attribution of this figure to Jacopo della Quercia, or Jacopo della Fonte, but—though it is almost a pure matter of conjecture on the part of M. Piot and others—a more likely name is that of Il Vecchietta, who was a pupil of Quercia. He was above all a bronzist, and this certainly fine figure is really after that method. A writer in *L'Arte* (*anno x. fasc. iii.* 1907) considers it to be not at all in his style, nor in that of Jacopo della Fonte, and proposes Francesco di Giorgio, although few pieces of the latter's work are known. There are two angels in bronze of the high altar of Siena Cathedral, in which he sees analogies. Francesco's style is of the school of Il Vecchietta, of whom also Urbano da Cortona was a pupil. Something might be said of the treatment of the hands in Il Vecchietta's style, or of analogies with his 'Resurrection' and his tomb of Marino Soccino at Siena. But nothing is more unsatisfactory than deductions from comparisons of style in two such widely differing materials.

Though of full sixteenth century, and perhaps beyond our limits of date, some notice must be given here to a beautiful statue of St. Sebastian in the Salting collection of the Kensington Museum, which found no place in the chapter devoted to boxwood work of this class. It is of fig wood, standing about three feet high, and is here reproduced (Plate xv.). Although on a comparatively large scale, the impression conveyed is that it is goldsmith's work of a high character, and whether or not there is absolute evidence in its favour, it is not surprising that it should be attributed to Ambrogio Foppa, called Il Caradosso, generally considered next to, or even rivalling, Cellini amongst the goldsmiths of Milan. We have beautiful things in the shape of paxes and inkstands and other decorative objects from his hand, but I do not know that there is any large figure work in bronze which can be given to him with certainty.

Should we attribute a fine statue in limewood, of St. Roch, in the church of the Annunziata at Florence to Italian, German, or French art? The question has received numerous answers from the time of Vasari to our own day. But it is not really difficult of solution. This figure is now in a niche in the wall of the second chapel on the left as one goes up the church. Painted white, to imitate marble, it escapes general notice as a figure of wood. Vasari, in his work on *Technique*, of which the first edition was published about 1550, describes it as a miracle of wood-carving by the hand of a Frenchman whom he calls Maestro Janni, living, he says, in Florence, who had adopted the Italian manner. He says of it that it is a figure of San Rocco in limewood, life-size, with soft and undercut draperies, preserved to his own day in the church of the Annunziata, free from any covering of colour, and beautiful beyond all other figures carved in wood. We do not, of course, always take Vasari *au pied de la lettre*. Granted that there is something of the Italian *maniera* (it is interesting and instructive that Vasari should notice this), iconographically we have a treatment hardly in accord with Italian tradition. St. Roch was a favourite figure in Germany as well as in France. The drapery, with its sharp angles, the bare knees and long turned-over boots, the downcast eyes, the down-pointing fingers, the large close-fitting skull-cap as in Peter Vischer's portrait of himself, all are distinctly German. We must remember the constant flow of German artists into Italy during their wander-years in the late fifteenth and early sixteenth centuries. Many also settled and worked there. The name Janni might indeed be the Italianized form of a stranger artist—by name John—from almost any country. The figure certainly points to the Nürnberg school, and has in fact been ascribed to Veit Stoss. It is known, also, that Stoss sent many figures to Italy. M. Marcel Reymond, however, says that in the over-elaborated costume, the excess of reliefs and the 'agitation' of the draperies, it is connected with French art of the fourteenth to the sixteenth centuries, notably that of Burgundy.

Though late, an extremely interesting altarpiece, with many detached figures showing Flemish or German influence in Italy, if indeed it is not a work of one of their sculptors domiciled in the country, is in the Victoria and Albert Museum [No. 137, 1891].

It is of the pictorial kind, with figures in the round, of plain uncoloured wood, measuring about 5 feet high by 5 feet in width. In it we have, principally, the crucifixion with numerous figures and groups, soldiers on foot and on horseback, the Jews and other traditional personages, in costumes and armour of the early sixteenth century. Nothing more is known of it, or of its supposed author, than some particulars in a letter from the Italian vendor in 1891. He says:—
'This carving in wood, representing the nativity and the death of Jesus Christ, was formerly in the church of S. Agostino at Piacenza, and is attributed to a certain Giovanni, or Lucio, Ottivetono of the end of the fifteenth to the beginning of the sixteenth century.'
I do not know that the name Ottivetono is elsewhere to be heard of, nor does it sound very Italian. The church of St. Augustine was suppressed by Napoleon I., and the carving presented by the Pope to a duke of the Farnese family. There was at one time a frame all round it, which, it is said, has been transformed into a bookcase in England.

In this comparatively brief notice there has been by no means any pretension to a general study of Italian art in wood of the periods included. Such a task would involve many other considerations, and could not be confined to art in one particular material only. I have desired only to call the attention of those—and they are many I think—who are not already familiar with them, to some examples of a particular kind which, generally speaking, do not find their analogies elsewhere. Considerations of space compel also the leaving on one side such architectural work with figures as the splendid retable of the cathedral of Piacenza, late Gothic work of Antonio Burlenghi, many other fine examples of Venetian sculptors in wood, and those Gothic choirs which would otherwise form a portion of our subject, if within our limits of style or date.

CHAPTER XIV

ON THE COLOURING OF WOOD SCULPTURE

THE extreme lengths, already alluded to in a previous chapter, to which the practice of colouring sculpture of all kinds was carried in Spain, and continued there longer than elsewhere, lead us to some general consideration of the subject. When we remember that, as there has been occasion also more than once to remark, it was the universal custom in the Middle Ages to colour every description of sculpture, and especially sculpture in wood, it is evident that the question demands more than ordinary attention. We have seen the practice exemplified in the retables of the Netherlands and Germany, in the single figures and groups for roods, the Madonna statuettes and crucifixes, and in the beautiful Italian Annunciation figures of the quattrocento and earlier. As everything else in art, polychromatic decoration comes to us from the East. Long ago Owen Jones wrote in his *Grammar of Ornament*: 'The architecture of the Egyptians is thoroughly polychromatic: they painted everything. They dealt in flat tints, and used neither shade nor shadow. The colours used by the Egyptians were probably red, blue, and yellow, with black and white to define and give distinctness to the various colours: with green used generally, though not universally, as a local colour, such as the green leaves of the lotus.' The statues and bas-reliefs in limestone, basalt, wood, and even granite were coloured

261

to life, with differences distinguishing those of men from women, the latter having always a higher complexion. Even the mummy cases were gorgeously coloured and thickly gilded. Numerous are the references to the practice in Holy Writ. In the Book of the Wisdom of Solomon we find : ' For neither did the mischievous invention deceive us, nor an image spotted with divers colours, the painter's fruitless labour, the sight whereof enticeth fools to lust after it, and so they desire the form of a dead image that hath no breath ' (xv. 4, 5).

It would be interesting, if our space allowed, to follow the question through the times of ancient Greece and Rome, to discuss the Parthenon, the Temple of Minerva at Athens, the colossal statues of Pheidias and Praxiteles, the polychromatic decoration of buildings, and of statues, at Herculaneum and at Pompeii. Socrates is reported by Plato, in his Fourth Book of the *Republic*, as remonstrating with those who blamed the painters of statues with not being contented to leave the eyes black instead of enriching them with the most beautiful colours. The sage remarked : ' Pray, sir, do not suppose that we ought to make the eyes so beautiful as not to look like eyes, nor the other parts in like manner, but observe whether, by giving to every part what properly belongs to it, we make the whole beautiful ' (*Republic, Eng. transl., Cam.*, 1866). Undoubtedly the use of colour in architecture and sculpture in marble was much more common than is generally thought. The Elgin marbles have been proved to have been painted : the great ivory and gold statues of Minerva and Jupiter Olympius were fully coloured. Sometimes the hair alone was gilded, or painted yellow, and ornaments were frequently added, the ears, for example, being pierced for rings. Very applicable to our subject is the interesting account by Callistratus of a bronze statue of a boy. He says:

'His cheeks were tinged ruddy colour like a rose. We marvelled to see bronze imitate nature: for though metal it blushed.'

In early Christian times the evidence of the catacombs is alone sufficient to show that the same feeling prevailed. Though we have few examples to guide us, we may gather that in early mediæval times, down to the twelfth century, statuary, following the most ancient principles, was painted in a most conventional manner, the prevailing colour being an ochre-tinted white. About the middle of the century the colouring of architecture and sculpture became general both within and without the buildings. There was a universal call for brightness and cheerfulness in decoration, not only appealing to the senses as a mere gratification of them, but a use of art as a teaching medium, compelling attention: as it were, the advertising method of the day. And so the succeeding centuries, until the change of ideas in the sixteenth, were essentially ages of colour and opposed to the cold monotony of white which is the absence of colour. The note of joyousness was abroad, and amongst innumerable signs of this, surely it would be sufficient to compare an archaic, grave Madonna of the eleventh century, clad in sombre garments of a dull uniform tint, with the sweet smiling, almost coquettish, figure that an ivory statuette of the Virgin, of the thirteenth century, presents to us, the draperies and ornaments decorated with bright and lively colours enriched with gilding.

The colour of statuary, and of all the sculptured ornament, pervaded the whole interior of sacred edifices. To understand properly the spirit of the Middle Ages it is necessary to picture these great creations as glowing with painting and gilding from top to bottom. Even the light was subdued and tinted, the sun's rays entering through stained windows of glass, of which the secret of producing the richest tones has been lost. If we bear this picture in mind it is impossible to imagine that mediæval feeling could tolerate the white marble statuary which forms such glaring contrasts with its surroundings in the Abbey Church of Westminster, or the chill regularity of the Madeleine at Paris. Above all it must not be forgotten that the colouring of the statue or other piece of sculpture is not to be considered for itself alone. Everything was studied with regard to its effect in the general scheme. Marble and alabaster, metal and wood, were used also for sepulchral monuments, and for these, too, polychrome was the rule. Yet they were not treated as separate creations and placed haphazard. In our modern Gothic it would seem to be too much the rule to build and decorate piecemeal with no governing plan. Things are accepted as they come in and a place found for them somewhere.

In mediæval times, as a general principle—perhaps in the earlier days arising from a want of more extended knowledge—the colours applied both to statuary and smaller sculpture were limited to the three primary ones: a dark red, yellow, and blue. The great sculptures of Reims were, for example, painted in this way. Many, indeed, were simply partially or wholly gilded. Black was of course used, and, later on, browns, purples, and violets were added. In viewing them, as we do to-day, we must remember how the reds, for example, lose their original strength and brilliancy, and other colours are toned down, by atmospheric influences. In France, as elsewhere, the colouring of sculpture was long held in high honour. For the three centuries during which we can point to names—the fourteenth, fifteenth, and sixteenth—those of André Beauneveu, of Michel Colombe, and of Germain Pilon may well serve to illustrate this side of polychrome art. It was long before oil colours were used, the medium, in general, being prepared from gums, albumen, or other colloids. Existing documents are numerous relating to the painting of such monuments as the chartreuse of Dijon, its tombs, retables, and single figures. From these much information may be gathered regarding the methods, materials, and prices paid. Nor is information wanting in respect to the colouring of sculpture in the neighbouring provinces of Flanders and France, which were in close relationship with, or dependence on, the courts of Burgundy. Not the least interesting fact that we can gather is that Jan Van Eyck himself painted six statues for the façade of the Hotel de Ville at Bruges, and the names of many others of the most famous Flemish painters, employed in a similar way, are known. The question of their participation in the work of the carved wood retables has already received attention in these pages. This is a matter of considerable interest, but, together with the subject, generally, of the polychrome decoration of these works in Flanders and Germany, is one which it would be impossible to treat adequately within the limits of a single chapter and without the aid of coloured illustrations. When coloured at all, no portion of the surface of the wood remained visible. Thick gold was used also as a means of accentuation, the backgrounds almost invariably richly gilded or diapered, and the gildings burnished. It was a common practice also to gild the hair and beards of the figures.

The colouring of Madonna figures and groups and of crucifixes has also been noticed in their several places, and the system being everywhere identical need not again be considered at any length. Gold was the dominant in the scheme which blended the colours into harmony. So general and universal was the practice that the natural colours of wood were not permitted to assert themselves. Bronze, and even the precious metals, did not escape, and we know how beautiful was the colouring of mediæval ivories. In general terms it is impossible not to recognize the immense influence in these times of the art of the Netherlands through its painters. In the fifteenth century they seem to have given the word of command to the whole of the rest of Europe. Not even Italy can be excepted, and if Italy is mentioned in this connexion it is with a full recollection of the Annunciation groups of Pisa, of Florence, and of Siena, which have been noticed in a previous chapter, and of much else also that it has been found necessary to pass over. The application of colour to other materials, such as the terra-cotta reliefs and busts of the period, must not be forgotten, and even the majolica *chefs-d'œuvre* have their relation to our subject. In common with all these the great names of Brunelleschi, of Donatello, of Benedetto da Majano, of Nino Pisano, of Jacopo della Quercia—to name no others—are equally connected with the colouring of wood sculpture.

Painting on reliefs differs, of course, from painting on plane surfaces. It has rules of its own. There is always the natural play of light and shade of which advantage can be taken. Thus, two colours, or tones of equal value, can be placed side by side ; for example, a blue and a purple. In the thirteenth century art of all kinds tended towards naturalism. Conventional methods gave way before increased knowledge and powers of observation. Painters learnt to make use of such aids as reflected half-tones, or processes such as we now call scumbling, and other methods of giving brilliancy to their scheme of coloration.

Later on they were not afraid of stronger contrasts ; for instance, a rosy tint against a deep blue, a light green and dark purple. But there was always the danger of commonplace trickery, and the colouring of sculpture generally, in the later days of Gothic art, losing the quality of the earlier methods, became in some countries—in our own for example, as certain rood-screens will testify — garish and vulgar. But degeneration in taste in this respect was universal when the intervention of great artists was no longer so easily obtainable. For, if allowable at all, it must be admitted that the polychromatic decoration of sculpture is a branch of art which demands a special training and the highest talent.

So great have been the changes in the interior of churches and in the disposition of the ornaments and sculpture of all kinds which we still possess in them that it is not easy to imagine the effect produced when the edifices were first completed and adorned, when every detail from a vestment or even a censer, to the light which filtered through the storied or jewelled windows, had a studied effect in the general harmony. Possibly all was not due to design alone, and some allowance must be made for the natural good taste of the time. Yet the mediæval master of the works had doubtless more supreme authority than the architect of modern times, and his aim was to accentuate the lines of the building, and to give special prominence to those portions which were richest in sculpture. He used his flat surfaces in general harmony with the rest, filling them with painted histories for the instruction of the people who could read in no other way. And as time went on, he learnt to know the value of materials, such as the different woods and their varying tones which have a colour of their own, contributing without additions to the polychromatic scheme. The modern architect is satisfied with the introduction of pictures in glass admitting as much light as possible, and indeed we can hardly feel certain that in our northern climate the effect produced by the marble facings, inlays, and mosaics of such an edifice as the cathedral at Westminster is not as far as we can go. Yet the climate was the same in the Middle Ages, and therefore it is possible that we do not realize completely how the polychromatic decoration of exteriors, as well as of interiors, was actually carried out.

It may be objected that the choirs of Amiens, Ulm, and so many others of the great cathedrals, with their stalls and canopies, thrones and sedilia, were left uncoloured and in the purity of the unstained wood. It may have been so in general, perhaps, but we see them to-day after the lapse of centuries and among altered surroundings. Nor do we know for certain how the wood was treated. Certainly such great expanses of newly carved surfaces would not have been tolerated. No doubt a considerable amount of relief was obtained by colour and gilding. The carved screens and fronts which remain of the rood-lofts which abound in Devonshire and the West Country were elaborately painted and gilded, so that not the smallest part of the surface of the wood was left clear. Traces of colour still remain on some bench-ends, and even on misericords in England. Of recent years many of the restored screens have been repainted and gilded, though not in all cases, perhaps, judiciously. But, as a rule, this has been done in accordance with the remains of colour still happily left. The mediæval practice may have been abused, but the remedy under the classical Renaissance was worse. With the departure of colour went also the joyousness of life amongst the simple inhabitants of the villages, the fervour of the devotion and the attachment to their churches. And whatever may have been the other contributory causes, it would seem that the period of the Renaissance synchronized with the loss of the good taste possessed by the people which had hitherto made of every man an artist and a craftsman. Art was henceforth for the learned and the wealthy.

In mid-fourteenth century and during the first

quarter of the fifteenth the polychromatic decoration of sculpture was general in Germany as elsewhere, but less the absolute rule in certain districts than in others. At the end of the fifteenth, in the flourishing times of the schools of Nürnberg, Würzburg, and Suabia to which so much of our attention has been directed, it would seem probable that a considerable number of the great retables were never intended to receive decoration in colour. And when we consider the perfection of finish in such a group as the fragment in the Victoria and Albert Museum, with the figures of SS. Anne and Joachim, it is difficult to imagine that the aid of the painter could have been called in for an addition which would completely change its character. We may sincerely hope that it was not, for the sculptor's art of the time was on an immeasurably higher level than that of the painter—whether identical with him or not —employed to colour such work. At any rate the taste of to-day will be more than satisfied to find it in its present condition. So again with the Nürnberg Madonna. This and the Pietà in the Marienkirche have for many years been covered with a uniform coating of a dull olive colour which is not altogether unpleasing. The artist's intention may have been to complete these figures in polychrome, but we have no means of determining whether this was carried out or not. Modern copies of this Madonna are frequently coloured with the most deplorable and disastrous results. The coloured statues in stone and wood in Catholic churches are, indeed, as a rule, beneath criticism. Happily, exceptions occur which show that a careful attention has been paid to the delicacy of treatment which characterizes the best feeling of the thirteenth century. That the colouring of figure sculpture is not altogether a lost art, an instance may be given in the stone statuettes of the altarpiece in the Hammond chapel of the Abbey church of Downside.

WOOD SCULPTURE

Some mention will be made in a succeeding chapter of the sepulchral effigies in wood, of which we still possess in England nearly a hundred examples. Dating from the thirteenth to the seventeenth century, the aid of the painter and illuminator was, in every case, called in, in accordance with the general practice. Monochrome was, as has been shown, disliked. Sculptor and painter worked together, nor would it be easy to say which was subsidiary to the other. In the wooden effigies the groundwork was first of all prepared by cementing linen over any cracks or faults there might be in the wood, applying a coating of size, and next a pretty thick layer of a composition of parchment, glue, and whiting, forming a smooth surface for the reception of the colour and gilding. The coating was sufficiently thick in places, where required, to admit of modelling, after the manner of gesso work, and capable of being impressed or tooled with dies and stamps and raised for gilding and jewelling. As was the practice elsewhere, the grounds for gilding were also often first of all treated with bole Armenian. This has the effect of giving transparency to the gold, which was liberally applied, mixed with white of egg; left matt, or burnished with an agate. In this manner the details and ornaments of the armour, the crowns, sceptres, sword - hilts, spurs, orphreys of vestments, jewels, and other accessories were raised, chiselled and goffered with the richest effect. How fine this painting was in some of the English effigies may be gathered—to offer but one or two examples—from the figure in stone of John de Sheppy, Bishop of Rochester, in Rochester Cathedral. He lies with precious mitre on his head, the hands covered with the embroidered episcopal gloves, in full Gothic red chasuble, and maniple, of rich design, lined with green, and bordered with a gold orphrey, the thinner dalmatic of an equally beautiful pattern, and

270

under it the silken tunicle, and alb with embroidered apparels, the sandals, and finally, beneath his head, the two cushions of rich pattern and colouring. Or, again, there is the effigy of Bishop Bronescombe (1280 A.D.) in Exeter Cathedral. Unfortunately, in the case of the greater number of the wooden effigies, the merest traces only of the original polychromy remain, and many have suffered the degradation of successive coatings of whitewash or paint—sometimes sanded, with the idea of imitating stone or marble, and of bringing them into accordance with the singular taste in ecclesiastical art of the last century.

In our own country we can find innumerable instances of the prevalent practice of colouring sculpture both in stone and wood. We can point as examples, among many others, to the minstrel gallery of Exeter, to the Lady Chapel of Ely, the chantries of Salisbury, of York, of Gloucester, or of Winchester, and for exterior sculpture, to the west front of Wells; and the restoration of the numerous village churches which has been undertaken in recent years shows how they glowed with colour and gilding from the angels supporting the hammer-beams of the roofs to the elaborately carved wood screens and rood-lofts. Not unfrequently—perhaps as a rule—the removal of the horrible ochre wash on the walls has revealed gigantic pictures of St. Christopher and other legendary figures. This has recently occurred at the village church of Poughill in Cornwall. Undoubtedly the whole of the interiors was a blaze of coloured illustration, the walls themselves a *Biblia Pauperum* in the most attractive form.

In the fifteenth century, especially, the polychroming of sculpture reached its utmost limit. It may not be without importance to notice that at the famous château of Gaillon, of which we still possess such remarkable remains of sculpture not only in marble

271

and stone, but also in wood, French and Italian artists worked together for the Cardinal d'Amboise. There is documentary evidence that, so lately as the beginning of the nineteenth century, the carved wood-work of the château still retained its original colouring. Nor was the practice less general in France throughout the reign of Francis i., despite the strong influence of Michael Angelo. For it was in measure owing to this great sculptor—as later on in our own country the influence of our most renowned architect contributed to the destruction of the Gothic which he detested—that is due the definite disuse of the poly-chromatic decoration of sculpture. And it was the restorers of churches of Wren's time who first started the practice of whitewashing them. With the Renais-sance—at any rate after the sixteenth century—the colouring of sculpture was practically a prescribed art. It was considered vulgar, and imagined—but wrongly—to be opposed to the canons and practice of the classical art then so much admired.

Nearly all Italian marble sculpture is, as we now find it, uncoloured. But close examination would show that originally in very many—perhaps in the majority of cases—the contrary was the case. The statues and statuettes, busts, and bas-reliefs in marble, wood, and terra cotta of Donatello, of Rossellino, of Verrocchio, of Desiderio, and of other great names of the Florentine and Sienese schools, were, in countless numbers, coloured and gilded, in parts if not wholly. In wood we have already considered many Annunciation figures and crucifixes. There is, indeed, little occasion to labour the question. What is necessary to insist upon is that the practice, up to a period which might be definitely stated, almost amounted to a rule without exception. The French critic, M. Courajod, has not hesitated to say that, in the first half of the fifteenth century, in Italy, the two arts of painting and sculpture so jostled each other, so trod on each other's toes, that in a number of instances painting was sculpture painted, and sculpture was painting sculptured. In general, the system was followed which had been so elaborately and quaintly laid down in the treatises of Theophilus or of Cennino Cennini, so that we can verify the processes from the *Schedula diversarum Artium* of the twelfth century work to the *Libro d'Arte* of the fifteenth. The general preparation was for centuries the same as that which was therein taught. The wood was covered entirely or in places, and principally in the draperies, with linen prepared with a cement made from boiled shreds of parchment or from cheese. Over this was applied a layer of fine plaster of a fairly thick consistency, well smoothed and made still thicker, and raised where required, for modelling in details of ornaments. The rest was the work of the painter, often, as in the case of such figures as the Annunciation groups of Pisa and Lyon, a great artist. Tools were used, dies in circles, nail-heads, stars, and other devices for the diaperings and other ornaments. Sometimes a particular artist may be recognized from these: for example 'the master of the tulip,' whose name is not known. In the condition in which we now find these beautiful figures the action of time has harmonized and softened down the original brilliancy of the colours, especially the reds, and subdued, perhaps, the over-gilding. Sometimes, as in many Italian, Flemish, and Spanish figures—for example the St. Stephen in the museum at Kensington—the whole figure is thickly gilded on a ground of bole Armenian, except the flesh-tints, and perhaps the linings of the draperies, which were usually blue or green. Often the edgings and orphreys of vestments had inscriptions running down their lengths, or thick pastes in imitation of brocade, and the gilding diapered in *pointillé*. Or, instead of gilding, silver leaf would be laid on the wood covered with a transparent layer of varnish, coloured pink, blue, or green, with an effect of translucent enamel.

Nowhere more than in Spain has the colouring of sculpture been carried to greater lengths, and nowhere else is to be found so remarkable a history of the development of the system, its spread at the time of the Spanish Renaissance, and its degradation in the days of decadence. The story can be taken up at a comparatively early period if we may accept, for example, the painting of the sculpture of the cathedral of Santiago de Compostella as contemporary with the completion of the building in 1188. The rage for colouring every description of sculpture was extended even to such things as the great silver-gilt and enamelled reliquaries, of which the one containing the head of St. Valerius, made in 1397, is an example, or the silver statuette of St. George in the chapel of the *Palacio de la Diputación Provincial,* at Barcelona. For the polychroming of retables, and the statuettes and groups appertaining to them, a numerous body of workers was employed under the direction of the master builder. There were the *imagineros*, or figure sculptors, the *encarnadores* or flesh painters, *estofadores* or painters of stuffs, gilders, damasceners, and other assistants. Amongst these the director, or principal artist, was the *encarnador*. Some coloured statues in stone of the end of the thirteenth century, now in the museum at Leon, are evidence of the influence in the northern provinces of France and her schools on architecture and figure sculpture which continued to be dominant until the middle of the fifteenth century. Not yet, however, had French artists been introduced. In the fourteenth century the peculiarly Spanish system of colouring begins to assert itself strongly : a system which is characteristic for many centuries. The seventeenth-century statuette of St. Catherine from the Maskell collection, now in the museum at Kensington, is a fine example of these methods, difficult to explain, in which the grounds of the draperies are prepared by fine alternating bands of gold, yellow ochre, Indian brown, and indigo, modifying the prominence of the gilding, yet without losing any of its rich effect. Undoubtedly the Spanish colourists borrowed freely from the practice of their Mussulman conquerors in the arrangement of tones and colorations in the Moorish faience, and from such monuments as the third *mirhâb* of the cathedral of Cordova.

The process termed *estofado* may, generally speaking, be taken to mean the preparation of the surfaces to be treated before painting and gilding, especially in its application to draperies by the laying of colour on a gilt ground and tracing on it ' *estofado*,' fine designs. In wood figures the carving is executed in a somewhat summary manner, for though the decorator must have a perfectly smooth surface to work upon, the wood itself is destined to disappear under successive layers of white and varnishes. The *estofador* worked with the *dorador* : gold on colour, colour on gold, the patterns applied to the metal with roulettes, punches, and other tools of the kind, giving to the representation of stuffs and tissues, in this manner, the shimmering, scintillating effect of rich damasks. The southern temperament of the Spaniard, still further influenced by oriental associations, revelled in such rich displays. In the early days the *ensamblador* or *trazador* was the architect in chief, and had under him sculptors, draughtsmen, decorators, master carpenter, and master mason, but not the painters, gilders, and *estofadores*. The *imagineros* were the sculptors, who worked from the designs supplied them by the *trazador*, the *encarnadores* were the flesh painters, the *estofadores* the painters of stuffs or draperies ; the *encarnadores* ranking higher than the last named. The *doradores* were the gilders. With the proper tools the layer of colour on the ground of gold was traced through so as to expose the metal in parts, thus forming the designs of the stuffs to be imitated, at the same time that divers effects of tonality could be produced. Reliefs were also applied on the dead gold ground, the term *estofar* implying the method of representing rich stuffs and damasks, so that the saintly personages should be clothed in the most magnificent garments. Francisco Pacheco, in his *Arte de la pintura* (1649), gives long details of all the methods of polychroming sculpture, with recipes for colours, varnishes, gilding, and the rest, and almost a treatise on the then vexed question of the respective merits of highly polished and matt effects.

In the seventeenth century, when painting in Spain acquired a national and individual character, the system changed. Draperies were copied from nature, and real stuffs used instead of painting, pushing the practice of imitative realism to the last extreme. Figures of the latter kind are known as *imagines de vestir*, and no doubt the practice, common to this day, had an early origin. An image, said to have been given by St. Louis of France, is in the Capilla Real of the cathedral of Seville. Jointed limbs and mechanism to move them are frequently to be found. Yet although the artist had sometimes little more to do than the painting of the face and hands, the greatest ones did not disdain giving their assistance, and the colouring of the flesh received as much care in details as a miniature portrait. If the chisel were wielded by a Montañez, a Roldan, or a Nuñez, an Alonso Cano, a Pedro da Mena, or a Pacheco, the talent of the sculptor was supplemented by his skill as a painter. The painter Geronimo Garcia collaborated with the sculptor Miguel Garcia, nor are the names of Murillo or Valdez Leal, amongst others in the first rank, to be omitted. Of
276

Cano, as a sculptor, we possess fewer examples in wood than in stone. Amongst the former are the life-sized crucifix of the high altar at Valencia, a little St. Antony in the church of St. Nicholas, at Murcia, a St. Bruno in the Cartuja of Granada, and a seated figure of Elijah sleeping, his head resting on his hand, in the church of Santo Thome at Toledo. The last named is more probably by Becerra. In the Victoria and Albert Museum there is a group in painted terra cotta attributed to the school of Cano, which is much in the style of the Elijah. Whatever may be the measure of our admiration for this style, concerning which there is room for difference of opinion, we may take the group as very fairly illustrative of Cano as a wood sculptor.

Pasos are the groups of figures representing scenes in the Passion, often larger than life, which, to this day, are favourites in Spain and carried in processions. They are frequently of the exaggerated realistic type, with real stuffs glued on, and eyes of glass and enamel: horrible pieces of anatomy, with gaping wounds and other evidences of torments, in which the passion for realism and of truth in art is pushed to its ultimate limits. Yet many still existing are the work of Montañez, who made several for the different churches of Seville, which are still used in the Holy Week ceremonies. Others, at Valladolid, are by Gregorio Hernandez (1566-1636) and Juan de Juni (d. 1586), at Murcia by Salcillo. There is one in the Victoria and Albert Museum by Risueño, a pupil of Cano. Some dispute seems to have arisen in the seventeenth century with regard to the relative merits of the painting of sculpture in general, and on the question of matt or polished surfaces. Pacheco, the father-in-law and master of Velasquez, in his *Arte de la pintura*, abuses the 'vulgar enamellers.' 'What audacity,' says he, ' have those who say that painting on a plane surface is

the culminating point of the arts, and that, as to painting the flesh of a statue, they could do it better with
their feet than the specialists could with their hands!'

Though of late date, a short mention must be made
of Gregorio Hernandez. Born in 1566, he is considered, by M. Paul Lafond, as one of the purest glories
of Spanish sculptural art. There is a *Mater Dolorosa*
by him in the chapel of La Cruz, Valladolid (not mentioned, however, by Lafond), which in the opinion of
many is his *chef-d'œuvre*. Unfortunately, as in the case
of so much other church statuary in Spain, it is made
ridiculous by the additions of monstrous crowns and
draperies. We may not like, perhaps, the tears of glass
encrusted in the wood, but, after all, such methods
have ancient authority, and from the accounts which
have come down to us, were practised by Pheidias
or Antenor. Amongst the very few examples of the
work of Spanish wood sculptors in the Victoria and
Albert Museum, is a curious small relief attributed to
Berruguete, representing St. Sebastian. The whole
of the exposed parts of the body of the martyr, and of
the little angel who accompanies him, is covered with
seed pearls arranged and tinted so as to suggest actual
flesh. The drapery and other adjuncts are sprinkled
with powdered glass and minute fragments of coral and
tinsel. It cannot be denied that in this work, which
shows great labour and ingenuity, there is also art
of a kind—indeed, of considerable merit. But one
hardly knows how to characterize it or what to think
of it.

CHAPTER XV

IF we look at a map of the English dioceses in the twelfth century, such as Mr. Edmund Prior gives us in his *History of Gothic Art in England*, it is impossible to help being struck by the astounding activity displayed in the building of cathedrals, of abbeys, and of magnificent parish churches in those early days of the revival of the arts. Starting from the south and progressing towards the north we find—to name but a few only—Salisbury (1130), Ford Abbey and Wimborne (1145), Bristol (1150), Wells (1170), Glastonbury (1185), Gloster (1170), Lichfield (1190), Shrewsbury (1180), Canter- bury (1175), St. Albans (1200); and, in the north, York, Kirkstall, Fountains, and many more. The succeeding century was the golden age of English Gothic. Henry III., on his accession in 1216, rebuilds Westminster Abbey, Lincoln is completed, Wells and Salisbury also. To add to our astonishment we may remember that the whole population of England at that time amounted to less than three millions. Doubtless these magnificent edifices became treasure- houses of sculpture of all kinds. The fabrics them- selves, so far as the architectural sculpture in stone is concerned, are still open to our admiration. But of the wonders of gold and silversmiths' work, of enamelled and jewelled shrines, of embroidered vestments, and all the profusion of ecclesiastical ornaments which the inventories we possess testify to have existed, hardly a trace remains even in our museums and private collections. After the great period of unexampled activity there may have been one of quiescence. When we remember the scanty population of England, and the consequences of such inflictions of plague as the Black Death of 1368, we must take into account also the unquiet state of the kingdom, which called many to arms. There were the Crusades, and the troubles with Scotland, the invasions of France, and finally, in mid-fifteenth century, the Wars of the Roses, at the termination of which, thirty years later, under Henry VII., tranquillity was restored. Prosperity reigned again, and the king, bringing over Torrigiano and other foreign artists, gave a fresh impulse to church decoration. And, notwithstanding the destructions and alterations they have undergone, the choirs and stall-work of numberless of our churches can still show, also, that there were native carvers of excellent skill and taste. The later designs were perhaps furnished by the introducers of the new fashions, but in deviations here and there, and in special national characteristics, there is manifold evidence of English workmanship. We shall note this when we come to consider the screen-work of the West of England.

Other nations have suffered from invasions and from the horrors and impieties of revolutions, but none more than ourselves from iconoclasm in the name of religion. The small number, then, of existing examples of images and of decorative work of all kinds in such a perishable and intrinsically valueless material as wood is hardly to be wondered at. For English figure-sculpture we are left very much to conjecture. No doubt the art of wood-carving followed the same lines in England as in France and elsewhere, and we may safely conclude that at a period when Gothic art had reached its highest development, and was characterized by extreme refinement, England was capable of holding its own with any other country. The invasion, in force, of foreign artists was not until later. For if the stone-carvers could design and execute such richness of arch and pillar, niche and gable as we find, for one instance only, in the west front of Wells, and could cover them with admirable statuary, it would not be surprising that equally in wood they should fill with figures the elaborate choir-work and rood-screens which adorned every cathedral and parish church. Yet in a general way it is not, perhaps, improbable that the English mediæval craftsman in wood was more distinguished as a hucher than as an image maker, and that either the foreigner was called in to work, and perhaps to settle in this country, or that considerable importations were ordered from abroad.

In the few examples which remain to us there must be always some little difficulty in distinguishing original native work from the imported, from that copied from other sources, or made in the country by foreign artists, themselves influenced by the surroundings in which they found themselves. There must always be a distinct difference between the work which such imported labour produces from its own genius and that which it forms under the direction of native artists or to suit the tastes of its employers. There was, of course, much copying. Designs from foreign examples were repeated over and over again, modified or slightly varied, making it difficult to be accurate as to dates or origin : for example, in the microscopic piece of wood-carving in the Waddesdon collection of the British Museum, which is there labelled as English of the thirteenth century. The striking characteristic of

English work is its solidity and thoroughness, suggestive of the national character—contented with what is sufficient, correct, plain-speaking, with a certain severity and heaviness of structure, and timid of giving an impression of showing off. As in other sculpture there would probably have been more analogy in the thirteenth and early fourteenth centuries to the French than in the fifteenth, when a misapplication of Flemish, and a multitude of other foreign influences, brought about a more expansive style, tending to the extravagant and even vulgar. There is a want of invention—a fondness for repetition as in the rows of similar figures of angels, or of other figures under canopies. Yet Gothic art was peculiarly adaptable to English sentiment, and predominated amongst us long after its absolute disappearance everywhere on the Continent, except, perhaps, in Germany.

Unfortunately, with the exception of the rood-screens, bench-ends, and font-covers; of the wooden sepulchral effigies, and of some isolated chests and fewer images, which escaped the searching destruction of probably innumerable fine examples, the material with which we have to deal is meagre indeed. We have to gather what light we can from old chronicles and inventories, and in these there is often ample evidence of a wealth of carved work in wood. In the *Rites of Durham* we read of the 'Nine Altars' in the cathedral, and are told that 'all the foresaid nine altars had their several shrines and covers of wainscot overhead . . . having likewise between every altar a very fair and large partition of wainscot with fine branches and flowers and other imagery-work most finely and artificially pictured and gilded, containing the several lockers or aumbres for the safe keeping of the vestments and ornaments.' There was the great shrine of St. Cuthbert also, 'the cover which drew up being of wainscote, having on the top from end to end most fine carved work cut out with dragons and other beasts most artificially wrought.' There are references again to many other 'almeries of fine wainscot with little images, very seemly and beautiful to behold.' And, once more, we are told of the monks' pews or *carrells* in the cloisters, 'very close, all but the forepart which had carved work which gave light in at their carrell doors of wainscot.' We may take it that the term 'wainscot' refers also to tabernacle work in the fashion of the Flemish and German retables, and that these also, either of native work or imported, abounded in our cathedral and parish churches. From the same interesting book we learn also of the 'picture of our Lady, so called the Lady of Boulton, made to open with gymells from her breast downward. And within the image was wrought the image of our Saviour, marvelous finely gilted, holding betwixt his hands a fair and large crucifix all of gold, the which crucifix was to be taken forth every Good Friday, and every man did creep into it that was in that church as that day.' The image was of the kind which we now call *Vierge ouvrante*. A few examples in wood still exist on the Continent.

The destruction of images in England in the sixteenth century was so complete that in all probability not a single saintly figure of importance in carved wood could now be found throughout the length and breadth of the land. In order to understand the character of the finer work which must have existed, we have little to guide us except a reference to the images in stone which, for the most part in a mutilated state, still cover the west fronts and gateways of our cathedrals and collegiate buildings. Here and there also, in a niche on a country church tower, there may be a Madonna figure which has escaped complete destruction through being almost out of reach. Of the better class in wood there is one example in the fourteenth-century *Pietà* which was found a few years ago at Battlefield, Shrewsbury. Unfortunately it is in an extremely dilapidated condition. Still we may gather sufficiently to make sure that in its polychromed state it was no doubt not only a noble group, but absolutely English in style and execution. There still remain, on some benches in parish churches, such as the magnificent set at Wiggenhall in Norfolk, or the somewhat similar ones at Walsoken, Cambridgeshire, several unmutilated figures in the panels of the ends or supporting on either side the massive poppy-heads. And, indeed, it is to the poppy-heads of bench-ends, though they are but too frequently defaced and mutilated, that we have to look for the most interesting remnants of English figure sculpture. For example, at Chesterton, a monk bearing a scourge stands in the centre of the foliage work ; at Stowlangtoft it is a preacher in surplice and skull-cap, with his open book on the desk before him ; at Chesterton, again, a man in tunic and characteristic headdress of the time of Richard II. ; at Gresford a charming Madonna figure, and in very many cases Annunciation groups or figures of angels, archangels, and seraphs. We may be helped also by the ivory statuettes of the Virgin and Child, of which there are several beautiful examples in the Victoria and Albert Museum and in continental collections. More, indeed, of these are probably of English origin than has yet been recognized. In addition there are many figures in alabaster which are known to be English, and are, perhaps, more representative of English style in figure work than anything else we possess. The exhibition of alabaster work organized in the present year by the Society of Antiquaries is especially enlightening. Many are magnificent not only as sculpture, but for their polychrome decoration. Amongst them, the beautiful Annunciation figure of the tomb of Thomas Boleyn at Wells (A.D. 1450) is of the truly English type of face, strongly influenced by the art of the Netherlands. Documentary evidence is abundant also of the wealth of carved figure work in stone and wood which must have existed throughout the land. To take but one case, the instructions for the adornment of Eton College Chapel, the details of which are fully set out in the ' Kynges own avyse,' or so called will, preserved at Eton. The reredos of the high altar was to consist of figures in full relief, carved and coloured, 'a grate ymage of our Savyoure with the xij Apostles y sett on every syde of the same ymage, with synes and tokenes of here passion and martirdome,' and there are particulars of many other figures. The roodloft was to be made 'in like manner and fourme as be the stalls and rodeloft in the chapell of Saint Stephen atte Westminster,' which was itself copied from Winchester. This loft is expressly stated to be used 'for redying and syngying and for the organs and other manere observance there to be had after the Rewles of the churche of Salisbury.' We may read, too, of the stately shrine of 'Our Ladye of Walsingham,' which drew multitudes of pilgrims from all parts : the image of wood, as Erasmus describes it, 'a little image remarkable neither for size, material, nor execution.' In the privy purse expenses of Henry VIII. is an entry in 1511 of an offering made at the shrine, at the king's visit, of £1, 3s. 4d. In 1538, by the same king's orders, the image was brought to London and there burnt at Chelsea, with others, as notable, from Ipswich, Worcester, and Willesden, in the presence of Crumwell.

Or, we may turn to but one of our many magnificent cathedrals and parish churches whose choirs, after many vicissitudes, show us now, through the more reverent care of recent times, something of the semblance of that which they presented in the days of their full glory. In the cathedral of Lincoln there are, besides the magnificent architectural work of the canopies and other adjuncts of the stalls themselves, the misericords beneath the seats, than which, for design and execution, no finer set exists in England : or, it might even be said, in any other country. Amongst them, and most remarkable indeed for spirited drawing and equally capable talent of the carver, one represents a knight in armour who, struck by an arrow which still sticks in his back, falls headlong from his horse. On another corbel-bracket a knight, completely unhorsed, lies prostrate on the ground. In both cases it was no mean artist who designed and executed the figures of the men and their steeds, which afford us also such valuable information regarding the habits and costumes of the time. On again another misericord, incomparable are the truly English angels who swing their censers as they stand on the foliaged volutes which spread out on either side of the central subject. Not less remarkable, indeed, are the designs and handling of these volutes, or supporters, when confined to purely foliage work without the addition of any figures or storied imagery. And when we consider the dearth of imagery which confronts us, we may congratulate ourselves on still possessing the charming series of panels which, equally with those in the spandrels of the architectural work, entitle the choir of Lincoln to its well-known appellation. On these are ten or a dozen large figures, in rather high relief, playing on musical instruments : on harps, on various kinds of lutes, on a zither, on a fiddle of quite modern form, on a portable pipe organ, on a drum and the rest. They sit on low seats each beneath a pointed arch, their serious faces sweet in expression under the flowing hair carefully arranged and bound with a fillet, the well-modelled bare feet showing in every case, the draperies admirably disposed, with no sign of mannerism or exaggeration of the folds, the attitudes elegant and in perfect conformity with their several occupations. They are indeed simple *chefs-*

286

d'œuvre. Other panels bear figures of kings seated and crowned, of a similar style, and no less fine in drawing and workmanship. Finally, we have in this same choir a series of quatrefoils enclosing figures of saints, grotesques, weird Bestiary animals and little scenes, such as a knight creeping stealthily along with drawn short sword and shield for his defence, amongst other figure work equally deserving of individual attention. If even we omit to add to the above, detailed mention of the variety and imagination displayed in the massive carved bosses of the groinings, and in the poppy-heads of the stalls, all characterized by the same excellence of design and execution, it may be said that in this one cathedral alone these remains are the pathetic testimony that our country could not have been behind others in the arts of the hucher and imaginator in wood sculpture, and that Lincoln, in the time of its glory and of the almost inconceivable richness of its treasures of which we have evidence in its inventories, must have been distinguished above all for the excellence of its woodwork.

The story of the insensate destruction, the contempt and hatred of things previously held sacred, has often been told. A few references will suffice to recall attention to this. Parish registers and churchwardens' accounts give us the history pretty plainly, especially in the twenty years from 1550 to 1570. One record of the county of Lincoln sums up the enumeration as 'the rest of the trash and tromperie wch appertaynid to the popish service.' Altarstones, fonts, and other pieces of stonework were broken and defaced, turned into cistern bottoms, set into fire-hearths, or used for mending walls, or laid in the highways 'to sarve as bridges for sheepe and cattall to go on,' books and illuminated manuscripts were torn up and the vellum used for haberdashers' measures; 'some to serve their jaykes, some to scoure their candlesticks, some to rubbe their bootes : sold to grossers and sopesellers, whole ships-full sent over the seas. I know a merchant man bought two noble libraries for 40s. : kept him in gray paper ten years' (*Whitaker's Cath. Com.*, II. p. 355). What wonder that an ample provision for firewood was welcomed in numberless images and screenwork of wood! In Worcester Cathedral candles and ashes were still hallowed till 1547, but in the same year the first step was made, in the order to destroy all images. In the following year, 'creeping' to the cross is abolished, and the old books burned. In 1551 the high altar was removed in accordance with the injunction to have plain tables of wood everywhere. Under Edward VI. all images which had been abused with pilgrimages were ordered to be taken down and destroyed. On 17th November ' at nyghte was pullyd downe the Rode in Powles with Mary and John with all the ymages in the churche. Item, also, at that time was pullyd downe thorow alle the Kynges domynion in every churche alle Roddes with alle images and every precher preched in their sermons agayne alle images.' Archbishops and bishops made strict inquiries. Thus Archbishop Grindall in 1576, ' whether your roodlofts be taken down and altered, so that the upper part thereof with the soller or loft be quite taken down unto the crossbeam and that the said beam have some convenient crest put upon the same.' In the ' Rites of Durham,' we read that ' two holy water stones were taken away by Dean Whitingham, and carried into his kitchen, in which stones they did steep their beef and salt fish.' And in 1650 that ' when the Scots were sent prisoners from Dunbar and put prisoners into the church they burnt up all the woodwork, in regard they had no coals allowed them.' In the first year of Elizabeth the high altar, roodloft, and images were again taken down, and ' on the eve of St. Bartholomew the day and morrow after were burned in

Paules churchyard, and in some places the copes, vestments, and altarclothes, books, banners, sepulchres,
and roodlofts were likewise committed to the fire and
so consumed to ashes.' Under the Commonwealth
soldiers were quartered in Westminster Abbey, where
'they brake down the rails about the altar and burnt
it : they brake doun the organ and pawned the pipes
for ale : they put on some of the singing men's surplices,
and in contempt of the canonical habit ran up and
down the church : he that wore the surplice was the
hare, the rest the hounds.' In the churchwardens'
accounts of 1566 of the parish of Belton, near Grant-
ham, we find 'Imprimis a roodloft taken doun and
part of it given to poor folkes and other parte occupied
about the mending of the pinfold yeates and the
churchyard yeates.' At Croxby 'Roode Marie & John
were burned the last yere (1565) to make a plummer
fire which mended ye churche leades.' In other cases
'to make barres and railes for a bridge': to 'make
window frames,' 'a weaver's loom,' 'a well poste and
such like things,' 'doors and chests,' 'a joyce tree for
a chamber' and 'bed ceilings': of a sacring bell they
made 'a horse belle to hang at a horse's head': 'of a
holy water vat of stone our vicaire hathe made a
swines' trough of.'

In quite recent times, that is, in the nineteenth
century, vandalism, neglect, and bad taste worked still
more havoc on what remained. Mr. Waller, writing in
1845, says that the Horkesley wooden effigies were
recently displaced and put out of sight in a corner near
the porch. In Quarendon Chapel, near Aylesbury, in
the chancel among a heap of rubbish, lay the fragments
of the alabaster effigies of Sir Henry Lee of Ditchley
and his lady. Brasses were torn up and allowed to lie
about. In 1839 St. Margaret's, Westminster, was
rotting with damp and neglect. These are but samples
of a state of things which might be multiplied to any

289

extent. Then came what was called 'restoration,' which worked worse havoc still, for the effects are still before our eyes. We might indeed think better of some architects, with distinguished names, of those days, if there had remained no ancient material at all.

There is one division of the art of working in wood in which England excelled above all other countries. This is in the magnificent timber roofs which still adorn many of our country churches and some of our cathedrals. But it is a subject which would require special and lengthy treatment. There are very fine examples throughout England. To recall but a few haphazard, we have St. Stephen's at Norwich, St. Mary's at Devizes, Westminster Hall, St. Mary's at Bury St. Edmunds with its many figures of prophets, apostles, saints, and whole length figures of angels, Warmington (Northants), Lincoln, with its elaborate bosses, Selby, Crosby Hall, Hampton Court, the painted wood groining of the choir of St. Albans, or the magnificent roof in Irish bog-oak of St. David's—even a list would fill pages if we should mention but the parish churches of the counties of Devon and Somerset. From mid-thirteenth century, and in the reign of Edward III. and his successors, the use of wood for roofs became more general owing to the greater security of the times and the disuse of fortresses. They were, as in the case of other work in wood, imitative of stone sculpture. In the thirteenth century Henry III. ordered for St. George's Chapel, Windsor, a wooden roof, 'like the new work at Lichfield, to appear like stonework with good ceiling and painting.' Carpenter's work was, in fact, to continue long dependent on the mason. Roofs and screens were imitations in wood of existing stonework, with its vaultings, groinings, and traceried fenestrages. And we must not forget the painted panels of honour over the roods in Devon : usually a blue ground with elaborately carved ribs, and bosses of stars picked out

PLATE XLVI

1, 2, 3. ANGEL AND SERAPHIM. EWELME CHURCH, OXON
4, 5. ANGELS. FROM ROOF OF HATHERLEIGH CHURCH. DEVON ENGLISH. FIFTEENTH CENTURY

in gold and colour : or the entire ceilings of a similar kind, which abound in the churches of small provincial towns, as for example at Shepton Mallet. Besides the more elaborate ones, very numerous are those of the simple parish churches such as we find throughout Devon, with their cofferdams of the waggon roofs, brilliant with colour, and the angels of the hammer-beams and wall-plates, sometimes rudely carved, and roughly painted in white albs and bearing shields. Most curious and richly carved and painted were the bosses at the intersections. There are dozens of them of large size and ponderous weight, thrown in a heap at St. Saviour's Cathedral, Southwark. We may class and compare them with the misericords of the choir stalls. And, again, everywhere abound the typically English angels, sometimes simple village work, at others, of real merit as sculpture, as at Cullompton and Ewelme (Plate XLVI.) or at Lincoln : bearing shields with emblems of the Passion, or in later times, with coats of arms.

No doubt such figures as the angels were to a great extent a commercial production, turned out to pattern by the hundred. But the motive is characteristic of fifteenth-century English art, and patterns ordered from some famous workshop or renowned sculptor of the towns were probably copied more or less intelligently and well by the untrained village artist in the building of his own church in which so much pride was taken. So it is that we find them frequently hovering, as it were, among the roof timbers, or capping in rows the cornices of parcloses and screens, as, for example, in the charming series of crowned ones bearing scrolls in St. George's Chapel, Windsor, along a cornice at Exeter, or along the top of the parclose screen at Cullompton. At Cawston and Wymondham in Norfolk the angels are of large size, spreading their broad wings eight or ten feet across. Best known,

perhaps, of all are the angels in the spandrels of the
'Angel choir' of Lincoln. But they may not properly
be called English, nor are they of wood. Stone carving
apart, if the English carvers in wood loved this angel
motive, what they could do in the way of demons is
illustrated by those of the bench-ends of Ashcombe to
which reference is made in a succeeding chapter.

The angel figures at Ewelme, Oxfordshire, are twelve
in number, attired in tunics or cassocks with collars
and girdled surplices. Their wings are spread, and all
are crowned with fleur-de-lis crowns. But among them
four are seraphs, in the close-fitting costume of feathers,
resembling tights, which—coming from the East—
seems to have been a representation especially favoured
in England. Seraphs or angels of this kind are
frequent on bench-ends, either on the panels or among
the foliage of the poppy-heads. Angels figure upon
those of South Brent and Swavesey, amongst numerous
others which might be cited. At Southwold a pair of
very beautiful angels support on their outstretched
wings a small projecting gallery. A stall-end in
Chester Cathedral has on it a quaint Annunciation
group, in which the Virgin and an angel in the tight-
fitting feather dress kneel on each side of a vase holding lilies. On bench-ends at Warkworth and at
East Brent, the angel is attired in a similar fashion in
Annunciation groups, and on a fine bench-end at
St. Mary's, Haverfordwest, the archangel, so clothed,
with uplifted sword stands on the dragon. An example
of pure village work, from Hatherleigh, is included in
our illustrations. But the whole subject is one which,
as regards England alone, would well repay a lengthened
study.

Coffers and parish chests belong, strictly speaking,
rather to furniture than to that divison of woodwork to
which our attention has been especially directed. To
appreciate properly their value as specimens of carving

would entail, also, more space than it is possible now to devote to them. Although we should find on them from time to time very interesting examples of figure work and of bas-reliefs of a similar character to those of the *jouées* and stalls, and the like, still, as a rule, we should have to consider them as panels and panelling generally, and, from the point of view of the mullioned architectural tracery and flamboyant fenestrages, which are so frequently used, we should be led into side paths further than our present limits will allow. There are also the questions of their form, construction, and origins, and of the variety of the patterns of the panels amongst which that known as the *linen* pattern is not one of the least interesting. Our remarks, therefore, must be confined to a few considerations, only, to accompany the two illustrations here given. The chest or coffer was the principal object of domestic furniture of the early Middle Ages, and was made to serve all kinds of purposes: as a coffer for storing garments or valuables, a table, chair, bench, and even bedstead; sometimes, when of large size, a standing wardrobe. *Bahut*, or *huche*, is the frequently recurring French term in old documents, whence we have the trade of the *hucher*— furniture-makers who separated as a corporation from the master carpenters of architectural work about the end of the fourteenth century.

Without taking into account ancient Egyptian coffers of which specimens in sycamore, acacia, tamarisk, cedar, and other fragrant woods abound, the oldest existing examples of this piece of furniture are a sort of long trough or box with a lid, roughly chipped out of the trunk of a tree—the dug-out class of hutch as we may call them. Examples are not lacking in most museums, and, indeed, are to be found of dates so late as the fourteenth century. Of this hollowed tree-trunk kind, often bound and clamped with iron, we have in English country churches not a few still existing specimens. They are not seldom of considerable dimensions (the one at Cudworth, Warwickshire, is ten feet long and of great thickness), the cavity itself very small, and there are frequently slits for money. In an inventory of goods belonging to St. Mary's, Warwick (A.D. 1464), there is a quaint reference to their cumbrous form : ' Item, in the vestrye, 1 grete olde arke to put in vestments, 1 olde irebounde cofre.' An early example, carved with subjects—amongst others, birds, beasts, and human figures—is in the cathedral of Terracina, and has been ascribed to the ninth, or even eighth century. It is probably a much later copy of some Oriental models.

As there has already been occasion to remark, most furniture of the Romanesque and Romanesque-Gothic period was decorated in low relief, incised in the champlevé manner. But, for our chests, there is little to go by, as there is no existing piece earlier than the twelfth century. The scarcity of any kind of Gothic-English work in wood has already been noted, although, doubtless, much was made, for statutes exist of the time of Richard III., prohibiting, in the interests of the native industry, importations from abroad. Of the thirteenth century it is not surprising, for reasons that have already been shown, that there should be a penury of examples of decorated work. On this account the specimens of this most useful—and, for that reason, longer preserved—article of furniture of the period named, which still remain in our cathedrals and churches to the number of over a hundred, are the more valuable. Of these, with regard to the construction and method of attaching the lid, we may distinguish two groups—the pin-hinge style and the strap-hinge, and these peculiarities are useful to note in cases of dating. Shortly stated, in the pin-hinge method the top bars attached to the ends of the lid, and rising with it, are fastened by pins passing through tenons to slots in the back posts, the tops of the latter being rounded so that the lid-rails slide easily over them. It is not found in English examples later than the thirteenth century, and not in any of those with panel fronts decorated with tracery. Sometimes the chests have a false bottom, or secret compartments with lids, as in sailors' or old-fashioned school chests. Of these early English chests made for church purposes, one of the best known, and probably the earliest, is the one at Stoke d'Abernon. As was usual, it is of oak, of very plain and somewhat unusual form (something like a pedestal writing-table), with a simple incised decoration of three circular ornaments of a geometrical pattern. These curious whorls or roundels of chip-carving, with starlike or geometrical patterns, are found, again, in the fine fourteenth-century chest of Faversham Church in Kent. The motive is, of course, derived from the East, and from the intercourse with Syria at the time of the Crusades. The six-pointed star, so often met with in the ruins of the magnificent religious edifices of that province, and in small work, such as the ivory caskets of the Veroli kind, is itself derived from still further east. The Stoke d'Abernon chest has an ingenious secret cavity. The date is probably from 1200 to 1220.

It was not until the fourteenth century that the practice began of forming the fronts of chests by a framework enclosing a number of panels, carved as a rule with traceried fenestrages, or with the linen pattern. Others, as in the case of the fine Alnwick chest, have no traceried decoration, but are carved with hunting subjects, all of a secular character. Or, again, there is that most beautiful oak coffer at Brancepeth Church, Northumberland, of the perpendicular period carved with tracery, foliage, and chimeras. May not this, however, be due to a Flemish hand or importation? Other English chests, however French in inspiration, are undoubtedly of English execution.

Chests of the thirteenth century with figure subjects are, of any country, excessively scarce. The famous coffer of the Cluny Museum, formerly in the Gerente collection, is doubly interesting on this account, and if not of the thirteenth it is certainly not later than the first quarter of the fourteenth century, if the shoulder pieces of the armour, which went out of fashion about that time, are a criterion. On the front panels are twelve armed knights standing in niches beneath early ogival canopies. One bears on his shield the leopards of England. The subjects on the end are of rather a free character. English chests of the fourteenth century are to be found in many of our churches. They are, naturally, of the florid style of the time. Among fine examples are those of Alnwick, Brancepeth, Hacconby, Huttoft, St. Peter's at Derby, Wath, St. Mary Magdalen at Oxford, Chevington, Faversham, and Rainham. The term 'Flanders chest' is one which frequently occurs in wills and inventories prior to the fifteenth century. There is no space now to discuss particular instances, or in what cases so many of our parish church chests may be of Flemish origin. The fine example at Dersingham, Norfolk, with the angels and emblems of the Evangelists is a typical one of which the English workmanship cannot be doubtful. A more difficult question is involved in the origin of the chest in York Minster and the panel of similar style (Plate XLVII.) in the Victoria and Albert Museum. In other cases may we not consider the fact of so many Flemish artists having become domiciled amongst us? The district around Southwold appears to have been particularly favoured by them in the fourteenth century. But in the two just mentioned we may reasonably see a Flemish origin. There is a similar design on the chest at Ypres, a similar story,

PLATE XLVII

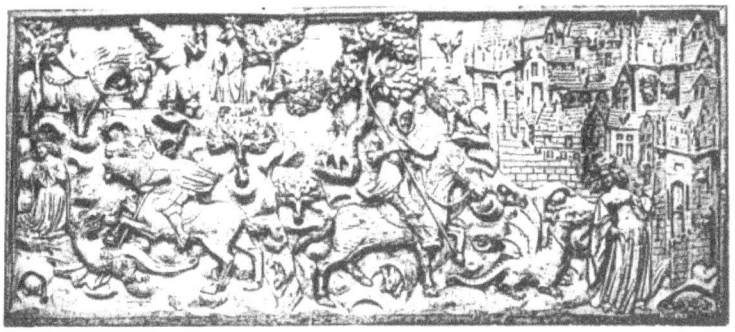

1

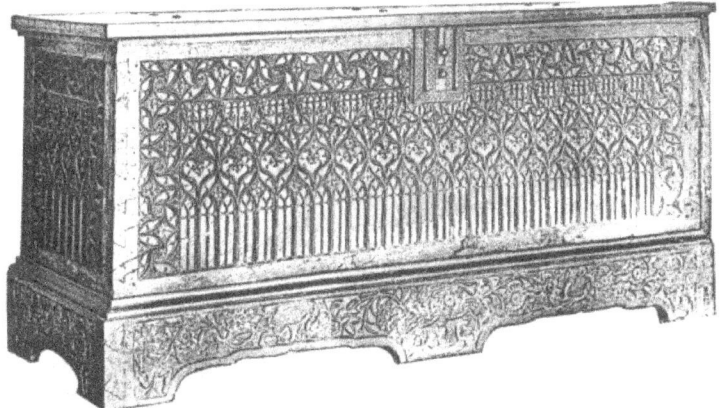

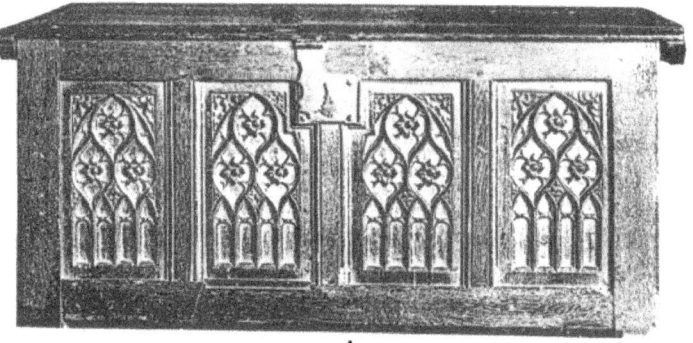

3

1. PANEL OF CHEST, ENGLISH OR FLEMISH. **FOURTEENTH CENTURY**. VICTORIA AND ALBERT MUSEUM
2. CHEST. FRENCH. **FIFTEENTH CENTURY**. VICTORIA AND ALBERT MUSEUM
3. CHEST. FRENCH ? **FIFTEENTH CENTURY**. IN THE AUTHOR'S POSSESSION

spiritedly treated, yet almost childish in perspective:
and, as in the York and Kensington chests, the same
tumbledown Gothic buildings, conventional trees re-
calling those of early Christian sculptures, the same
naïve representations of many episodes in the story of
St. George and the Princess all in one picture, the
horrible dragon being slain or captured in one portion
and in another docilely following the princess with
quite an engaging smile on its face; the same little
animals scurrying into their holes in fright, and the
kings and queens, with their crowns on, looking out
of the windows in true miniature style. We may
note that in the Kensington panel the subject is
exactly reversed from that of the York chest. What
may be the reason of this, what might be deduced
from the circumstance, which is the earliest in date,
and whether either or both are English, are questions
not easy to determine with certainty. Mr. Roe in his
Ancient Coffers and Cupboards is persuaded that they,
with the Ypres chest, are English in design and
execution. Judging from the large number of
mediæval examples of this most useful article of
furniture, which still exist in churches and in public
and private collections, there must have been an
enormous output of worked panels, decorated with
figure subjects, with window tracery, linen pattern,
and every other known description of ornament—
intended to be worked up into choir-stall panels,
panelling of rooms, coffers, dressers, wardrobes, beds,
alcoves, sedilia and for innumerable other purposes.
Doubtless, many that we now find on the fronts of
chests and elsewhere had already been used under
other conditions.

The beautiful linen or napkin pattern, which was
so much a favourite on chests and coffers and for
panelling generally from the early fifteenth century
and for perhaps three centuries afterwards, lent itself

to an almost indefinite number of variations. Of French, or Flemish origin, it came to England about the year 1500. The conception of the idea has been variously accounted for. According to Viollet-le-Duc it was often the practice before the fifteenth century to cover wood panels with parchment or with linen stiffened with glue. As this covering got old and torn it shrunk and became unstuck in parts, and the edges crumpled up. The wood-carvers from this accident evolved the idea of an ornamental motive and a method of thickening portions of the panels. The earliest example known to him was in a small fourteenth-century armoire in the church at Mortain. Others see in it a suggestion from mullions flattened out: others, again, that it was developed from simple champfered lines and that it went on developing with all sorts of exaggerated complications and differences till it was metamorphosed out of existence. It is more than likely that the first idea proceeded simply from the folding of a length of cloth, such as a tablecloth or other linen which the chests themselves were made to contain, backwards and forwards without allowing the different folds actually to meet and overlap. In this manner they form a number of ridges and furrows or grooves suggesting ogee mouldings, the upper and lower edges indicating the arrangement of the pleats with a certain symmetrical regularity. In its simpler forms no more charming and refined design for ornament could be imagined, resulting in a restful play of light and shade alternating and undulating in swell and hollow, which is not the least of its attractive qualities. There is, perhaps, no special English variety, but we meet in old houses numberless specimens of every kind. In the case of our own country the subject is one which would be more properly considered in dealing with the fine examples of English panelling of Tudor and Jacobean times.

298

Amongst them would be conspicuous those of such great houses as Aldermaston Court, Abington Hall, Crowhurst Place, the Vyne at Basingstoke, Knebworth, and Haddon Hall, and literally hundreds of others could be named. But Aldermaston alone would require a book to itself.

Chests and coffers are attractive also in other ways. Many, besides their own simple elegance, are remarkable for the charming forged ironwork of the bands and lockplates, and are examples of the arts of the smith, of workers in engraved and embossed leather, and of the painter. Finally there is their historical interest and the thought that these venerable objects have for centuries been the receptacles of the most treasured archives. And, again, the early ones especially, testify to their use as offertory chests for the collection of alms for special purposes such as the Crusades. In the year 1200, under Pope Innocent III., a general mandate was issued for setting up these offertory chests. 'To this end we command that in every church there shall be placed a hollow trunk, fastened with three keys, the first to be kept by the bishop, the second by the priest of the church, and the third by some religious layman, and that the faithful shall be exhorted to deposit in it as God shall move their hearts their alms for the remission of their sins, and that once in the week in all churches mass shall be publicly sung for the remission of sins, and especially of those who shall thus contribute.'

There is a class of figure sculpture in wood which until recently has received very little attention. Few people are aware that there still exist in England nearly a hundred sepulchral effigies for altar, or table tombs of a similar character to those in stone, marble, alabaster, and bronze. A list of early references to the subject will be found under *Sepulchral Monuments* in the Bibliography appended to this volume. An account of

299

these effigies, considerably longer than pressure on our space now permits, had originally been prepared for the present work. In the meanwhile an admirable monograph by Mr. A. C. Fryer,[1] who has collected all the available information on the subject, has appeared, and the reader may now be referred to this for details of the various figures. These effigies are scattered amongst various counties from Yorkshire in the north to Devonshire in the south, the most prolific districts being in Northamptonshire and the eastern counties. The identification of the personages represented is, in a large number of cases, by no means certain, nor can we be sure of dates or even periods. Roughly speaking, if we exclude the figure at Gloucester, which has been supposed to represent Robert Courthose, there are perhaps ten or a dozen dating from the thirteenth century and about forty of the fourteenth. Then, with the exception of two or three which may possibly belong to the fifteenth, the remainder are all later than the early sixteenth, at any rate they did not again become common until about 1550, when the exhaustion of the Derbyshire and Northamptonshire alabaster quarries probably caused a recourse to a less expensive material. The last of all are the Oglander effigies in the parish church of Brading, Isle of Wight, which date from the second half of the seventeenth century.

In accordance with the universal practice the mediæval sculptures were coloured, and, as the traces of the old colouring show, where still remaining, often in a most beautiful style. The remarks in other parts of this book upon the polychroming of statuary apply equally to these and need not now be repeated. Particular references to the subject generally and to those which have been repainted in later times will be found in Mr. Fryer's work. One of the earliest effigies

---

[1] *Wooden Monumental Effigies in England and Wales.* By A. C. Fryer. 1910.

—a priest in a chasuble, at Clifford, Hertfordshire—
of the thirteenth century (Plate XLVIII.), is extremely
valuable as an example of ecclesiastical costume and of
the treatment of drapery in sculpture of the period, and
a very beautiful one is the early fifteenth-century figure
of Catherine, Countess of Stafford, in Wingfield church,
Suffolk.

The thirteenth century in England, as elsewhere,
had been a period of the highest refinement in the
cultivation and practice of the plastic arts, and of a
lavish display of magnificence and of material wealth.
Sepulchral figures were of marble or alabaster, the
draperies simple and usually gilded only in the
orphreys and other decorative portions. The same
elegance and simplicity would have applied to those in
wood. Then there succeeded a mixture of materials
and a lavish use of colour. These composite figures
were painted and gilded and even completely covered
with plates of silver and bronze, with rich enamelling,
on a core or carved model of oak, as we find in the
effigy of William de Valence at Westminster. Effigies
of wood, alone, then appear to have become common,
and these also were covered with gesso and elaborately
painted and gilded.

As in sepulchral monuments in other materials our
wooden effigies comprise not only figures of knightly
personages, but of their wives also. Of the latter
there are, in all, perhaps about a score examples of no
small value in regard to the costumes of the period.
There are priests and bishops and secular ecclesiastical
dignitaries at Canterbury, at Greatham in Durham, at
Little Leighs, Essex, and at All Saints, Derby. The
single example of the law is the effigy at West Down,
Devon, whether it be that of William Donne, chief
baron of the exchequer in the nineteenth year of
Edward III., as was long supposed, or of his brother
judge and contemporary, Sir John Stowford, who died

about 1372. In the sixteenth century not only the effigies themselves but the whole monument, with a canopy and other decoration, were made of wood as in the case—a very beautiful one—of Sir Alexander Culpeper at Goudhurst in Kent. Oak was, naturally, the wood in general use, but we find elm and chestnut also. An examination of the figures shows that it was the practice to make them lighter by hollowing them out; and to dry the wood and perhaps to dry the colouring also, they were filled with burning, or partially burnt, coal. Remains of this still exist in some cases. In accordance with universal practice the whole work was elaborately painted and gilded, the gesso raised in parts for tooling and jewelling, the colours thin and flatted, and the gilding deadened and usually on an ochreous base. Many of these figures have since been painted white to imitate marble or alabaster. For this reason the fact that they are of wood frequently escapes attention : for example, in the case of the effigy in St. Saviour's, Southwark. Notwithstanding the carelessness and impiety of succeeding ages, we are fortunate in possessing as many as we do (about ninety or a hundred) of these figures, no less interesting than their companions in other materials. And we may remember that the neglect which has overcome some of them, and the destruction of many more, are due to events and causes subsequent to the Reformation, for a proclamation of Elizabeth in 1560 expressly forbade the 'breaking and defacing of tombs, and the effigies of kings, princes, nobles, or of any others set up for the memory of them to their posterity.' Here are records, each in his own village church, of the knight who fell fighting in battle in the Crusades, or—yet always in his knightly armour—who died peacefully at home. Here, inscribed, is handed down to posterity the story of their deeds of valour, or of honours, of their ambitions, of their charities. Here is the simple prayer in always the same set terms addressed to the passer-by to pray for the soul of the person represented. Perhaps there is hardly anywhere else in England so late an example as in the effigies of the fifth Earl of Westmoreland and his three wives at Staindrop (the last being his deceased wife's sister). He died in 1564, but the tomb was made in 1560, and bears inscribed round the edge: 'All you who come to the churche to pray a Paternoster and a Crede for to have mercy of us and all our progeny.' In the case of Sir John Savile at Thornhill, Yorks, who died 1529, the knight lies between his two wives on a wooden altar-tomb bearing shields of arms, and this curious inscription in Gothic characters: 'Bonys emong stonys lys here ful styl— Qwylste the sawle wanderis were that God wyl. In Anno D.M. millesimo quingentissimo vigesimo nono.' Here are men and women dressed in the costumes of times long past, with their jewels and ornaments upon them. These are valuable details in the history of costume. They are not always free from anachronisms. In some cases, it may have been before, in others some years after death, that the monument was set up. It can scarcely be doubted, also, that in all figures of this kind, of whatever material, there was wholesale shop-work, kept in stock and ordered from London, York, and other great centres. There would, again, have been copying, and perhaps using figures made at an earlier date, though none would have been ordered from abroad as is the case with brasses. The wooden effigies before us are unfortunately almost completely restricted to the noble and ecclesiastical class. Of lesser personages, of the yeoman who worshipped in the village church, and of his dame, of the wealthy woolstapler or other prosperous merchant we have but three examples, but they are interesting ones. The first is at Eaton under Haywood, Shropshire, in civilian costume, wearing a long gown and close-fitting hood. The second at Much Marcle, Herefordshire, has a long, tight-buttoned tunic to the knees, a hooded cape over the shoulders, is cross-legged, and the feet rest upon a lion, the tail of which curls round the left foot. The figure, Mr. Fryer tells us, is considered by Mr. James Wood, who had access to the manuscript histories of Herefordshire in the library of the Benedictine cathedral priory at Belmont, to be the effigy of Sir Hugh Helyon, removed from Ashperton, to the new chantry chapel about 1414. The identification is, however, extremely doubtful. The third is a civilian, with his wife, at Little Baddow, Essex.

There is always in these as in similar effigies in other materials a pathetic interest and even a kind of universally recognized symbolism. The knight, in the fashion which is peculiarly English, often lies not absolutely still, but as if in life, one leg bent, the hand unsheathing the sword, ready, as it were, to start up. We have a particularly strong example of this in the effigy at Chew Magna (Plate XLVIII.). In the case of ladies there is something homely in the dog which lies at his mistress's feet, often an obvious pet dog which even yet looks up into her face. Neglect, restorations, and repainting have, unfortunately, worked havoc amongst these figures. Even when—as there is evidence to show—the original polychroming still remained fairly intact, it was considered that they would look far better masquerading as stone or alabaster. At Banham the effigy of a knight of the early fourteenth century was painted and sanded so successfully that a writer in *Notes and Queries* says that it ' now looks almost as well as stone.' In the beginning of the nineteenth century the splendid tomb with the effigies of three members of the family of Games of Aberbrain and their wives, on three tiers of oaken beds elaborately carved, painted and gilded, in the church of St. John the

PLATE XLVIII

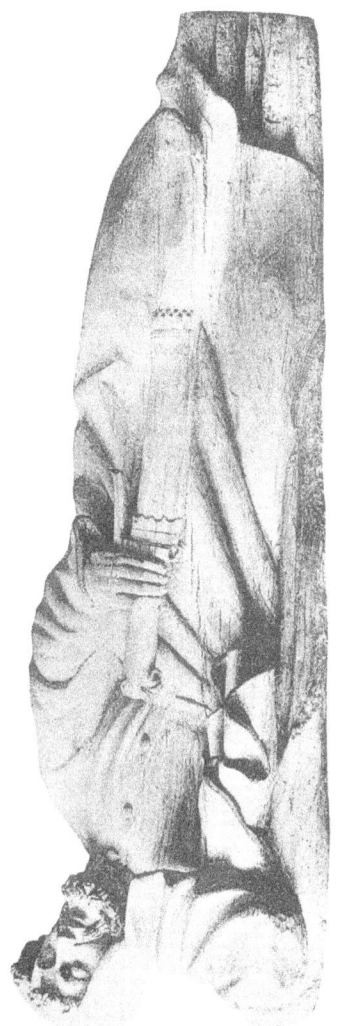

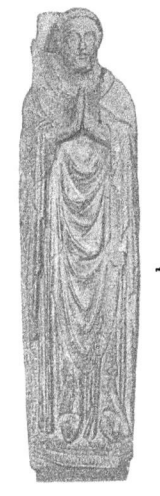

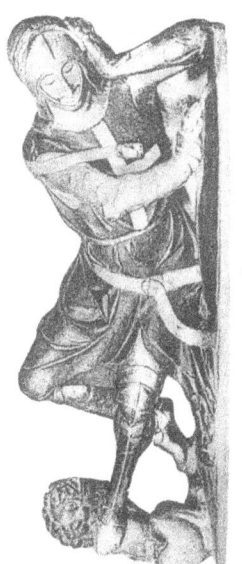

SEPULCHRAL EFFIGIES

1. ITALIAN. MUSÉE DES ARTS DÉCORATIFS. 2. ENGLISH. CHEW MAGNA CHURCH, SOMERSET. 3. ENGLISH, CLIFFORD CHURCH, HERTS

PAGES 301 TO 305

Evangelist at Brecknock, was removed. The well-known and indefatigable antiquary, Theophilus Jones, speaking of this monument in his *History of the County of Brecknock* (1809) says : 'Only one female figure remained when this vile incumbrance was removed ; the rest were burnt by the Commonwealth soldiers ; much as I deplore the outrages they committed, I have often lamented while it continued that they did not destroy the whole of it. Lord Camden has, however, with great propriety, lately caused it to be taken down and the chancel decently and uniformly painted.' The mutilated figure of Elinor, wife of Thomas Games, now alone remains. Churchyard, in his poetic description of *The Worthiness of Wales* (1587), after noticing the tomb of the family of Walters, goes on :

> 'Cross-legged by him, as was the auncient trade
> Debreos lyes, in picture as I troe
> Of most hard wood, which wood as divers say
> No worms can eat, or time can wear away.
> A couching hound, as harrolds thought full meete
> In wood likewise lyes underneath his feete.'

It would be difficult to say whether the practice of making monumental effigies in wood was peculiarly English. I know no references to the subject in any foreign publications. We have it on Mr. Albert Hartshorne's authority that in reply to his inquiry, Mr. Hefner von Alteneck, whose name carries such weight, informed him that not one now exists in Germany. Mr. Fryer says that there is a wood effigy to an ecclesiastic of Hildesheim, and one to an English priest in the cathedral of Burgos. The fine figure in wood in the museum of the Louvre, and called there a *figure tombale d'un moine chevalier* is here reproduced (Plate XLVIII.). And, in the Museé des Arts Décoratifs, Paris, there is a very beautiful life-size figure of a girl, fully coloured and gilt. It has been placed on the top of a Florentine *cassone*, with which it has no relationship. At one time in the Bardini collection, it is said to have been bought at Faenza. Of the first half of the quattrocento, it would appear to be the work of an artist of considerable talent—perhaps of the Sienese school—inspired by the beautiful figure of Jacopo della Quercia's *Ilaria del Carretto* monument in the cathedral of Lucca.[1]

We may now take, as further illustrations of English mediæval figure work—deficient though they may be in numbers and importance—the few examples to be found in our national museum at Kensington, which are there labelled as English. The first is a half life-size late fifteenth-century group of the curious Holy Family kind so common in Germany and Flanders, and known as *Anna selbdritt* (No. 37, 1887) (Plate xxxviii.). At one time in Mr. William Maskell's private chapel at Bude, the principal figure, seated on a faldstool under a canopy, is some thirty-six inches high. The Virgin holds the Child, who in the usual way turns over the leaves of a book on her knee with one hand: in the other is a bunch of grapes. She herself is seated on St. Anne's knee. The whole group is extremely difficult to characterize, and to assign an origin with any confidence. The St. Anne, in pose, in breadth of handling of the draperies, and in expression is noble and inspiring. But the Infant, weakly and unintelligent,

---

[1] M. Koechlin, the well-known French writer on art, was kind enough to give me the following information in response to my inquiries concerning effigies in wood on the continent. He says: 'Sepulchral figures in wood are very rare in France. For my part I only know one, of the fourteenth century, which was shown at the exhibition of French Primitives in 1904. It is an effigy of a lady, in very low relief, which had never been placed on a tomb, but, I think, stood upright, something after the manner of certain brasses in Italy or Germany, on a wall, the body interred beneath. As to the effigy in the *Musée des Arts Décoratifs*, the young girl is Italian. This and another French recumbent figure, evidently a fragment of a monument, are reproduced in our catalogue *Le Bois*, 1ᵉʳᵉ *partie. Planches* 19 *et* 10. As to the " Moine chevalier" that you ask about, it is no doubt Italian, but it is very difficult to say whether it is a sepulchral effigy, or some other kind of figure. In any case the piece is not French.'

is puzzling. We must remember, however, that the figures lack now the colouring in view of which they were probably sculptured. I hesitate to accept the ascription of the museum authorities to England, even allowing for close following of Netherlandish or German models, for we have no authority for the probability that the fashion of *Anna selbdritt* was followed in England. On the other hand it would not be difficult to find in Flemish or German art analogies with the face of the Virgin. The Infant, small and rickety as it seems to be, has not a little resemblance, in form and pose, to some fifteenth-century Suabian wood sculpture. I would cite, for instance, a painted Madonna group in the Berlin Museum: Mary seated, holding a large ball or globe, the Child facing and blessing. Yet if we take the figure of St. Anne by itself, it must, I think, be given to the Low Countries. At the same time I hold it to be a question not easy to settle with any certainty. The principal difficulty is that we have here an unfinished work.

There is a curious panel in high relief in the same museum which we may feel pretty sure is English, of mid-thirteenth century, and an exceedingly interesting example. The Almighty—so says the label—seated in a recess holds a cross between His knees. But the face, with the parted hair, flowing locks, and type of beard is not suggestive of God the Father, but, rather, of the Saviour, although it was unusual thus to represent Him. Neither is there any figure on the cross, but a plain circle or aureole and a cross within it at the intersection of the arms of the larger cross. The panel is of oak, in its present condition almost black oak, but of course at one time painted, as the linen substratum and priming remaining show. Six of a set of English figures of the Apostles (No. 411, 1589), formerly in the Maskell collection, and given by Mr.

Maskell, are here reproduced on the same plate as a set by Riemenschneider (Plate XLIX.), but one can find in them no resemblance to the Lower Frankish school. The draperies are entirely different, without any exaggerated angular folds. I think them to be late fourteenth rather than fifteenth century as the museum label describes them. They are of fairly early style, with something of the stolidity of the Lewis ivory chessmen. The faces and general character are of the type of the Saviour figure just described. But the inspiration is various: partly French, and, if in any way German, would be of the Low German or Suabian type of the early fifteenth century. It is not unlikely that the destination of figures such as these was to flank the poppy-heads of some elaborately carved benchends. A fifteenth-century Madonna statuette, also from the Maskell collection, is interesting (though in bad condition) on account of the scarcity of English examples. It is not a fine work, certainly, with the fat heavy cheeks which even the colouring would not alter. A standing figure of St. Andrew in oak, unpainted, and an appliqué group of the Blessed Virgin and St. Joseph adoring the Infant—interesting on account of the costumes—and an early sixteenth-century figure in a flat doctor's cap almost exhaust the list of English figure work of Gothic times in the museum.

There still exist in various churches in the country a few lecterns, of wood, which come more properly under the head of furniture. Among them may be cited those of Detling in Kent, Ramsey and Bury in Hunts, Lingfield, Wells, and Norwich. In Labarte's *Handbook of the Arts of the Middle Ages*, published in 1847, is figured a carved saddleback or cantle of wood, which, judging from the engraving, seems of extremely fine character. It was formerly in the Debruge collection. The subjects are a knight and a

PLATE XLIX

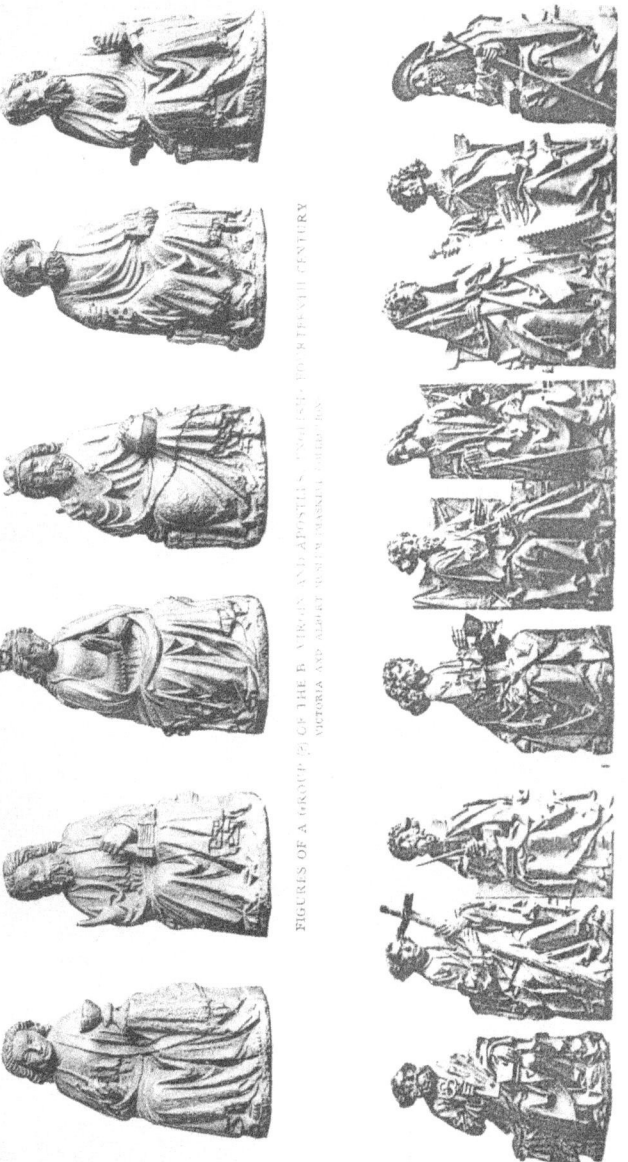

FIGURES OF THE B.... VIRGIN AND APOSTLES.... COLUST.... By R.... FIFTEENTH CENTURY

VICTORIA AND ALBERT MUSEUM (SALTING COLLECTION)

FIGURES OF A GROUP OF THE APOSTLES. BY RIEMENSCHNEIDER. FIFTEENTH CENTURY

BAVARIAN NATIONAL MUSEUM, MUNICH

PAGE 308, 110

wodehouse or wild man of the woods fighting wild animals, and other small figures hunting. There is an edging of rosettes, and the character of the carving generally is in the style of English ivories. I cannot help remarking how often in the case of ivories which at first glance suggest an English origin, one finds, next, that characteristic border of rosettes. It is not, of course, intended to say that these by themselves prove English workmanship, for one finds them equally in French ivories. I have no information where this saddle cantle now is—perhaps in the Louvre. In default of examples in wood, I have long held the opinion that very many mediæval ivories usually ascribed to France should testify to the excellence of English art, and the difficulties in the way may one day be elucidated.

The question is asked in a succeeding chapter—'Who, then, did this village work?' For a reply we are almost entirely dependent on parish accounts. There are few of these earlier than the fifteenth century, and the names of carvers are hardly ever mentioned in them. We may take it that the master carpenters of the Middle Ages were not only architects and contractors for work, but were the designers also. Some information may be gleaned, with the names of carpenters in the thirteenth century, from Smith's *Antiquities of Westminster*, and Brayley and Neales' account of the abbey; and in the accounts of the Carpenters Company are some mentions of the panellings of the halls of the City Companies, but few names of carvers. In an issue roll, we find that William de Lyndesay, of London, a carver of wood images, was paid in 1307 for a table (retable) with wood images for St. George's Chapel, Windsor. Other names of imagers appear, such as Alexander of Abingdon, 1305, but we cannot distinguish those who worked only in wood   In or about 1506 Laurence Imber, Drawswerd, and others, made estimates for patterns in wood for the images for the tomb of Henry the Seventh. The 'patrones to be made as well as can be done.' Laurence Imber, who died in 1529, was of a famous family of carvers, and came to be sheriff and mayor. No doubt these pattern makers such as *le imaginator*, John Hales, who made one for a bronze effigy at Ormskirk, were sculptors of general figure work also. The bill of the king's goldsmith for the Coronation Chair at Westminster includes '*pro duobus leopardis parvis de ligno, faciendis, depingendis et deaurandis*' to be made by Master Walter, who was also the king's painter, A.D. 1299. In the Fabric rolls of Exeter we find the charge for timber for the bishop's seat brought from Newton Abbot and Chudleigh : four pounds to Robert de Galmeton for making it, also for six statues. The accounts for Somersetshire and Devon parishes are referred to in another chapter of this book. At Yatton in 1446 Crosse, the carpenter, is conspicuous in the making of the roodloft, and there are payments to John Balwe and J. Hikke *pro factura sedilium*, probably of wood, for the cost for nails follows, and we find also the names of John Wakelyn, R. Kew, and J. Mey, carvers and gilders, Hyllman and Maskall being churchwardens in 1408. In 1535 'to Sperark ye carver, ernest pense iij^d.' At Tintinhull in 1451 occurs the name of Thomas Dayfote, carpenter, for making the roode '*ut in meremiis ligneis ex conventione,*' and to ' uno peynter for peynting de la rodeloft.' But most frequently there are no names, but only entries, such as in the Stamford accounts, that the churchwardens go to Abingdon 'to speke for ymages, vij^d : item for three images, the Rode, Mary, and John, xxij^s. iij^d.' The records and documents belonging to the dean and chapter of Worcester afford some information. Amongst them is Prior Moore's most interesting journal of 1518. In this are many particulars of payments: nearly twelve pounds (a large sum) to Thomas Stilgo for 'gylding and peynting of y⁰ ymags Ch'us and or Lady in y⁰ mydd. of y⁰ awtur in Seynt Cecili's chapel.' In the accounts of St. Mary at Hill, in the city of London, in 1496: 'Item to Sir John Plumer for making of the fygyres of the Roode, xxᵈ; item to the Karvare for making of iij dyadems and of oon of the evangelystes, and for mending the roode, the crosse, the Mary and John, the Crown of Thorn, with all odyr fawtes, summa 10ˢ.' 'Paid to Undirwood for paynting and gyldyng of the iij diadems, with the ij nobillas that I owe to him in moneye summa vli xjˢ xᵈ.' Among sepulchral effigies on the Neville monument at Staindrop is recorded on the edge the name of the artist, John Starbottom.

Meagre though these entries may be, they might be extended to a considerable extent, and the quaint language and spelling add not a little to their interest; sometimes, even, to our information. In any case they show that there was considerable activity in the craft of woodcarving in England in the centuries immediately preceding the Reformation to which they refer. But in but one instance can we identify by record or by mark on the piece itself any English sculpture with the name of the artist. Nor have we any sign of guildmarks and their regulations such as those to which reference has been made in the case of Flanders. In all probability the English mediæval imager was not an artist of great consideration. His identity was sunk in his craft. Even in stone, in the thirteenth century, we hear only vaguely of imagers who made the Eleanor crosses: of William of Colchester, of William de Torell, or of the masters in bronze or in gold and silver whom Matthew Paris mentions. How much less account, then, must we expect of the wood chippers! The master carpenter was everything, the others his tools. He was the arranger of the picture, and it was the decorative whole rather than the individual units which told. Yet of the master builder himself, his name and methods of organization, our information up to the revival in Italy, and then for a further considerable period in that country only, is vaguely indefinite.

CHAPTER XVI

CHOIRS AND CHOIR STALLS

THROUGHOUT the history of woodcarving and of the innumerable uses to which the material has been applied in decoration, nothing is more prominent than the furnishing and ornamenting of the choirs and chancels of churches. Even if we should consider only the quantity of material employed this has been enormous, and despite destructions it still continues to beautify innumerable churches, great and small, throughout the land. Necessarily, of course, woodwork, more or less carved, is used in the architectural construction of these edifices. It is not, however, with the timbered roofs, which still exist in considerable numbers, and in no country more than in England, of such incomparable beauty, or with the other details of the main structure that we shall now be occupied. The choirs and chancels with their canopied stall work, the episcopal thrones, the sedilia for the officiating clergy, the rood and other screens dividing the choir from the rest of the church and—in England especially—the interesting bench-ends, form a subject which is almost endless in variety and interest. Each and every one of the divisions just mentioned might again be subdivided, and is of sufficient importance to require a monograph surpassing the dimensions of the present book. As a matter of fact such monographs already exist, not only on each subject generally, but on each as applied to some particular instance. For example, amongst others, the choirs of Amiens and of Ulm have had their special chroniclers; misericords, and the countless number of themes which they illustrate, have been specially described over and over again in the proceedings of provincial societies in every country and—to refer to England alone—the subject of screens and roodlofts has received special attention in quite recent years. But even this division of the subject, so far as our own country is concerned, is of so extensive a nature, and involves so many general considerations, that in no one book can it be said to have progressed further—broadly speaking—than as regards the west of England. In a volume such as the present one, therefore, it would be hardly possible to attempt more than a general outline of the use of wood sculpture in the decoration of choir and stall work, and of the screens forming the enclosures, or separation from the rest of the church, together with a slight survey of the history of the symbolism so extensively used in the carving of the under parts of the stall seats, known as misericords, of the statuary, and of the elaborate, pictorial, and ornamental sculpture which is so remarkable a feature of Amiens, of Ulm, and of many other great choirs of the later days of Gothic.

We know very little indeed regarding any precise date at which we may place the introduction of a choir, such as we understand it to-day, with its places for the clergy and assistants in the form of ranges of stalls having arm-rests and seats which turn up in order to afford a kind of rest to a position which is neither sitting nor standing. In ancient times churches were entirely without any seating for the faithful, as, indeed, they are now in those of the Oriental rites. The attitude for prayer, in which may be included any part of the assistance at the holy offices, was standing. The arrangement of the choir permitted a view of the altar and the priests, and it was not until about the ninth century that screens forming enclosures rendered the officiating clergy invisible from the body of the church. There would certainly appear to have been no kind of seats before the eighth century. From that time to the eleventh all kinds of attempts were made to introduce them. That they existed in England in a movable form in the eleventh century is certain, for Lanfranc prescribes their removal on Good Friday at the ancient ceremony of creeping to the cross (*Decretum pro ord. S. Ben.*). The early history of the construction of choirs need not, however, be followed here in detail. It will be sufficient to name, for the needs of the student, such works as those of De Fleury, Guénébault, Ducange, the encyclopædia of Cabrol and Leclercq, and the researches from which we continue to profit, of Mr. Edmund Bishop.

Until, roughly speaking, the eleventh century, the chancel was separated from the body of the church by a low screen or balustrade—the *cancelli*, whence the name of this part is derived. Within these rails stood the altar, and beyond this and facing it was a range of seats against the wall of the apse, and in the centre of them the throne or seat of the bishop. In those days —or when this arrangement was altered and the monks took their places in rows on each side of the choir, in front instead of behind the altar—the long offices and ceremonies at which they assisted necessitated some indulgence or relaxation from the standing position. The earliest practice was the use of a kind of crutch, the head often curiously carved and decorated. Some of these in ivory, wood, and metal, still remain, and are sometimes confounded with the similarly tau-shaped staff, used by a bishop, which became later the crosier as we now know it. Ancient regulations and constitutions show that the use of this support was general. Sometimes protested against, it was disallowed, from time to time, according as a more or less severe rule prevailed, and it is certain that its use was not confined to the old or infirm. Even the laity availed themselves of it, and there are liturgical instructions regulating when it must be laid down—for instance, during the reading of the gospel.

The origin of the term stall would seem to be from the *standing* place, or division, in which persons, or, in the case of a stable, animals, are separated one from another. It is impossible to say at what date the form of choir stall with the arm-rest fulfilling the earlier function of the crutch, and the upturned seat, with its support against which the body could rest, became general. Certain it is that from the thirteenth century to the present day no kind of church furniture has altered so little in form. If not the earliest, a very early mention of stalls is in the statutes of the church of Maestricht in the year 1088. The annals of Amiens Cathedral have, at the end of the twelfth century, an order that new canons should have each his stall (*stallum*) in choir. In the thirteenth the custom is fully established, so that it is hardly necessary to refer to the allusions to stalls which we find in the *Historia major* of our own Matthew Paris. At Wells there would seem to have been stalls in Bishop Jocelyn's time, according to the register of his election in 1206, now in the library of the dean and chapter. They were removed in 1325 when new ones were ordered, and as they are then termed *ruinosi et difformes*, we may take it that they had already existed some considerable time. The misericord, or something which seems to correspond with it, is mentioned in several documents of the twelfth century. The actual term itself appears in the constitutions of the abbey of Hirsaugh in Germany, in the first quarter of the twelfth century (Const. Hirs. seu Gengembach ex MSS. Einsiedln), and it will suffice for further early references to quote

316

the following from a Cottonian MS. containing the rules of the Carthusian order : '*Item, tunc stent in sedibus suis versa facie ad altare donec ad misericordias vel super famulas prout tempus postulat inclinent a laudibus enim vigiliae natalis Domini usque in crastinum octabarum apparitionis et a Pasca in crastinum octabarum Pentecostes et infra octabas Corporis Christi assumptionis et natalis beate Mariae et in festis xii lectionum ad misericordias inclinamus omni vero alio tempore procumbimus super formulas*' (*Monasticon.* vi. 5). A little bit of monkish humour is inscribed on a fragment of a choir stall in the museum of St. Andrew's Church at Freising. It is dated 1423 :—

> ' Cantet in choro, sicut asellus in foro
> Hic locus est horum qui cantant, non aliorum.'

A habit seems to have grown up in England of late years of using the term *miserere* instead of *misericord* for this kind of console beneath the movable seat. It is quite inappropriate and without authority. If any other term besides the Latin *misericordia, subsellia* or *sedicula* might be suggested, the French *patience* or *indulgence* would be expressive. But we may be very well content with *misericord*, which is happily replacing, in literature at least, the incorrect *miserere*. Incidentally it may be noted that the name *misericord* was also given to a portion of an abbey where the indulgence of eating meat was allowed to the old or infirm.

Stalls were assigned to dignitaries and choir monks in a certain order, and one uniform system seems to have been in vogue in pre-Reformation times in England. Here the Benedictine custom was that the stall of the highest in dignity was the first one on the south side, farthest from the altar, on entering the choir : the others followed from side to side, the lowest in rank nearest the altar, the stall of the claustral prior on the north side, opposite that of the abbot. In cathedral

317

priories the bishop had his throne on the south side in the chancel. This fashion is still followed in the English cathedrals and in the college chapels of Oxford and Cambridge. At Ely the bishop, who has no throne, and whose abbey became a bishopric in 1109, occupies the abbot's stall. According to the *Ordinatio clericorum* of Wells (Creighton MS. in the library of the dean and chapter) the dean's place was the first returned stall on the south side at the entrance of the choir, the bishop's at the extreme east end on the same side. 'The English Benedictine arrangement just described seems to be followed at the present day in only two of the many Benedictine monasteries in this country, and those, curiously enough, are not of English origin. They are St. Augustine's Monastery, Ramsgate, and St. Mary's Abbey, Buckfastleigh—both belonging to the Cassinese congregation. But in the monasteries of the English congregation—Downside,[1] Ampleforth, Douai, and Belmont—and also in those of the Beuron congregation at Erdington and of the Gallican (Solesmes) congregation at Farnborough and Appuldurcombe, the plan followed is just the reverse, *i.e.* the stall occupied by the abbot is that nearest the altar on the north side of the choir, and the western-most stalls are those of the lowest in the community (*Downside Review*, vol. iv. 181).

No traces are left of the ancient arrangement of the bishop's place in the apse, and, so far as we know, no stalls remain of an earlier date than the thirteenth century. Viollet-Le-Duc quotes de Verneilh to show that Hugues de Toucy, bishop of Sens from 1143 to 1168, had had constructed some stalls of oak. But the chronicler responsible for this statement lived in 1294. Still, accepting as we do the thirteenth century as the date of the misericords and stalls of Exeter and Poitiers, for example, it is evident that the system was at that

[1] Downside has lately reverted to the earlier English plan.

time firmly established and no novelty. Briefly stated, the arrangement of the choir fittings which has obtained almost without change from their earliest introduction to the present day, consists of rows of seats raised on steps one behind the other, in number according to requirements, on each side of the choir from east to west, with spaces at intervals to give access to the higher rows. The separation between any two stalls is termed the parclose, the top of this the *museau*, and the woodwork at each end of a set, where the carving is usually richer, the *jouée*. The elbow rests are slightly sloped, so as to prevent the slipping of the arms, and the ends enlarged in spatula form to allow two neighbouring persons to rest their elbows without inconvenience. The upper part of each row forms a kind of *prie-Dieu* for the set above, and the rows as a whole are usually *returned* at the western extremities so that a certain number on each side face the east. The whole is enclosed by woodwork richly carved and rising sometimes almost to the roof. This enclosure, which perhaps was not fully evolved before the fourteenth century, serves as a protection against the cold of northern climates, during the recitation of the offices through the hours of the night, and may possibly be an adaptation of the Oriental iconostasis separating the portion destined for the celebration of the holy mysteries from the rest of the sacred edifice. The imposing mass of screen, the richest in carving and the most brilliant accessory of the choir decoration, served also to carry the canopy or dais which, as it were, separately roofed in this part of the building. Glorious above all, a forest of imagery and ornament, this towering mass of architectural work is carved into vaultings, arches, pinnacles, pendentives, *culs-de-lampe* and every fancy and vagary derived from sculpture in stone, supplemented by all that gives distinction and grace to the peculiar characteristics of wood, and affording ground for every description of pictorial sculpture in panels and statuary, in low and in high relief.

Coming to the stalls themselves we find them composed of seats which can be turned up, bearing on their under sides a projection from which some support, when standing, may be obtained. This is the misericord, or patience, which in course of time gave opportunities for carving on it all manner of decorative and pictorial themes. Far from being confined to sacred imagery these indeed display very often, after the joyous fashion of mediæval times, what may almost be called albums of quaint conceits, of fun and humour, degenerating at times—at least according to modern ideas or squeamishness — into a certain coarseness and exaggeration of the grotesque and a twisting of symbolism, of which it is by no means easy nowadays always to discover the meaning or application. Nothing is more difficult of explanation than the fact that wherever we find these things—abounding in almost countless hundreds in every western country—not only do the general character, choice of subject, and the treatment of it differ but slightly, but even the execution is such that—with a certain allowance for changes in costume and manners during a period of three centuries —it would be hardly an exaggeration to say that all might have issued from the same workshop.

To complete the stall there are, besides the parcloses and *jouées* already mentioned, the projecting elbow rests, or *accoudoirs*, and the knobs on which the hands may be placed as an assistance on rising: the latter very frequently carved with heads—grotesque or otherwise—or perhaps an entire animal or a subject of some kind. Probably, at first, the *jouées* were openworked volutes as in the examples given in the sketchbook of Wilars de Honecourt. Later on, and in the fourteenth century especially, birds, animals, figures of holy personages and incidents in their lives, and a diversity of ornament were added to the openwork, as well as to the closed portion beneath. At Amiens especially, this figuring of entire scenes in relief was carried to an extent hardly equalled elsewhere.

Almost every country possesses in its cathedral and collegiate churches examples of decorative choir-work in which wood sculpture forms the most prominent feature. They are in such numbers, and they vie with each other to such an extent in the richness and elaboration of detail, that to attempt anything like a full description of any one of the most important would require a volume and innumerable illustrations. It is, therefore, impossible, within our limits, to do more than select a few typical examples and endeavour to summarize their general aspect. For this purpose we must be content with Amiens in France, Ulm in Germany, Windsor in England, and a short notice for Spain. The choir-work of Italy comes more under the head of post-Renaissance art with which, for the present, with some exceptions, it has not been proposed to deal. The stalls themselves, with their misericords, must also be treated as a whole, with a few references to the most striking features.

The records of Amiens seem to show that from the earliest times of which we have precise documents the choir of the cathedral was furnished with rows of stalls in two categories : a higher range for the greater dignitaries, and a lower one for those of inferior rank. Ancient regulations, which go back as far as the eleventh century, assign them thus to the bishop, deans, precentors, and minor clergy. But they were evidently of a provisional character, and the troublous times of the fourteenth and fifteenth centuries prevented the accomplishment of a greater scheme which had long been contemplated. Until the thirteenth century, furniture of the kind—indeed, furniture of all kinds, if we may judge from the few examples which have come down to us—was the work of the ordinary carpenter. The hucher or huchier had little or no pretensions as a carver or figure worker. The time had hardly arrived when a more important part was to be given to sculpture in the fittings of churches, and when the architect was to determine the general lines of the edifice and to assign to the hucher his particular share in the work. It is still quite uncertain to what extent art work of all kinds should be attributed to monks. As we are, for the moment, concerned with France, it may be observed that Molinier held strongly the opinion that the idea that they were so greatly responsible has been much overdone. He says that though in Italy the religious orders furnished woodcarving to a considerable extent, there is no documentary evidence, in France, at least, to prove it : not even that illuminated MSS. proceeded habitually from that source. However this may be, it was not until the last years of the thirteenth century that the hucher began to enrich his work with sculptures in relief and with figures in the round. We have then, of course, such characteristic pieces as the coffer of the Cluny Museum.

We are beginning, it is true, in this woodcarving of the cathedral of Amiens, an account of choir-work at almost the latest period of its full development. It is of the early years of the sixteenth century, but although the influence of the Italian Renaissance is marked, here and there, in some ornamental details, it is still Gothic in general, and the evidence is apparent how very strongly influenced the architects and sculptors were by the architecture and glorious imagery of the doorways, screens, and other parts of the great edifice, the work of those who had preceded them three centuries before. The sculpture of the choir of Amiens is a résumé of Gothic art at its culminating point, at a period when it was slowly flickering out and destined soon to be abandoned in favour of the advancing Italian style.

Without quitting the cathedral we are enabled to read the whole story of Gothic architecture in the country of its birth, and not far distant from its birth-place. We may read also, perhaps, the influences brought to bear by the political conditions of centuries ; from the days, at least, of the first quarter of the fourteenth when the kings of France and England met within these walls, with all the pomp and state of the time ; when our Edward iii. rendered solemn homage therein for his French duchies to Philip vi., until at the end of that century the flamboyant style became dominant.

We have been accustomed to see in the small sculpture of the thirteenth and fourteenth centuries—for example in ivories—an inspiration from the greater sculptural work, not only in architectural details, but also in the figure work. But comparing these with the method of imitation used by the woodcarvers of Amiens, the same comparison no longer applies. In the one case they were in many instances rudely counter-feiting a general effect by the introduction of a decorative framework of an impossible architecture that never existed, and that was not intended to be other-wise. In the wood it is true architectural work. No longer do we have these little scenes, each under its arch, in a kind of symbolical shorthand, or like little cinematographs, but a broadened out conception of statuary tableaux analogous to the retables already described. We shall see, also, how it was the comple-tion of a new system of ornamentation, led up to by slow and timid steps, during the fourteenth and fifteenth centuries. No longer were these decorators contented with a conventional arrangement, borrowed from a restricted number of elements in the flora of the country, interspersed with representations of fabulous animals drawn from the bestiaries. They go now to the everyday life around them and reproduce it faithfully, adapting it even to the most sacred subjects.

In the tendency which is so marked, towards the mingling of sacred subjects and ideas with the surroundings, costumes, manners, and customs of contemporary life, one cannot help recognizing the influence of Flanders and of its great schools of painting. Nothing, of course, would have been more natural, when we consider the political conditions of the two countries, the near neighbourhood of the Burgundian provinces under a common sovereign with the Netherlands, and the considerable commercial relations. All this conduced to a spirit of artistic brotherhood working on the same lines and governed by similar principles. Contemporary records show also that the assistance of Flemish artists was frequently called in, as well as those engaged in the building and decorations of other cathedrals and churches in the north of France and the bordering provinces. But whatever other influences may have contributed, and however strong that of Flanders may have been, the work at Amiens is entirely French and by French artists.

It was early in the sixteenth century that the chapter of the cathedral decided to reconstruct the choir and stalls. In the city itself was Arnoul Boulin, *maître menuisier*, to whom the order was given to make 120 richly carved stalls, and with him were associated, for the storied parts, the *tailleurs a'images*, Antoine Avernier and, later on, Alexandre Huet. The canons of the cathedral sat as a permanent committee, and decided every important detail. Before, however, the plans were definitely fixed the *maîtres menuisiers* made prolonged visits to the cathedrals of Rouen, Beauvais, and St. Riquier. The stalls of Rouen still exist, and it must suffice to refer to their important connexion

324

with the works at Amiens, our artists having taken ample notes during their journeys. Meanwhile, great quantities of oak and chestnut had been collected at considerable expense from the forests of Abbeville and Saint Valery, and especially from that of Neuville-en-Hez, near Clermont. The finest, which was used for the bas-reliefs, was brought from Holland. Huge pieces, almost entire trees, were required for certain portions, such as the throne. There are still to be seen single blocks measuring 30 feet and more in length. We have the names of the principal workers or contractors, but information is wanting regarding the actual carvers of the astonishing series of figure work and decorative sculpture in wood with which we are confronted. Boulin is generally named as the principal carver. How far this may be true would involve more space than can be spared for the investigation. We may be content to accept his name as a representative one. Doubtless the practice of a wood-carving establishment, under the direction of its owner, was not very different from that of the present day. Begun in 1508, it is not until eight years later that we find carved on a stall-end the name and inscription JAN · TRVPIN · DIEV · TE · POVRVOIE ·, and not for three years more was the work completed.

Those who are already well acquainted with the astonishing variety to be found in such works as the choirs of Amiens, of Ulm, or of Auch—and there are many more in the same category—will not be surprised that one renounces at once, in such a book as the present one, the task of a detailed description. A French writer has said of the first that its study is the whole study of religion. It is this and more. It is a study also, within a limited area, of the domestic history of the period, of the architecture, manners and customs, trades and occupations, costumes, life and character of a city and of a people at a time when almost a revolution in thoughts and habits was taking place throughout the Western world: a revolution outwardly expressed by the transition from Gothic mediævalism to everything which may be implied by the term Renaissance. On the one hand we have the pictorial Bible in its countless figures and episodes drawn from the whole of the Old and New Testaments, as it had been exhibited for three hundred years at least for the instruction of the people: on the other a freer and more natural rendering of it, by bringing these episodes, as it were, down to the period of the then living citizens of Amiens, and connecting it with the domestic life, the luxury, costumes, occupations, virtues, and failings with which they were familiar.

The sculpture which covers the vast extent of surface of the screen-work, parcloses, *jouées*, and dais, leaving hardly a square inch unoccupied, is in three distinct series, comprising Old and New Testament scenes, episodes in the life of the Blessed Virgin, and endless subjects drawn from history, allegory, and morality, including some entirely profane. We begin with the Creation, the story of the Fall, and the other events narrated in Genesis, everywhere meeting with the prophetical and mystical interpretations connecting them with the Blessed Virgin. So vividly are these things expressed that we hardly seem to notice the daring poetic licence with which they are treated. The buildings and accessories are those of the time: the coiffures and costumes of the richest in the case of important personages, for example, in the up-to-date elegance of Potiphar's wife. Or there is the execution of a malefactor, the butler of Pharaoh's household, the gibbet, and the executioner in the official dress familiar to the people. Or, again, an illustration of table manners of the period. Moses sits at the banquet, richly dressed, the king's daughter near him, in a long, close-fitting dress, with jewelled girdle hanging loosely in front, and wearing the elaborate steeple headdress known as the *hennin*. In every detail there is something to be learnt : in the architecture of the palaces and streets, the furniture, beds, chests with their iron-work and locks, couches, chairs, tables, sideboards, cradles, or funeral paraphernalia. On the principal stalls we have the whole history, scriptural and legendary, of the Virgin Mary ; her attributes, and the prophecies and symbols connected with her. We have, for example, amongst others, for which legendary lore has been ransacked and exhausted, the unicorn pursued by four greyhounds taking refuge in the lap of a pure Virgin ; allegories connecting her with the Incarnation, the earthly life, culminating with the crucifixion, resurrection, and ascension, and finally her death, the Assumption, and the Coronation. As Ruskin wrote of it : ' The people of Scripture go about their daily affairs as the sculptor saw the people of Amiens go about theirs.' Throughout, of course, the costumes of the holiest personages are according to hagiographic conventions.

From another point of view it seems a repetition, yet an unavoidable one, to insist that we may find in these scenes a complete treatise on the architecture of a city of the sixteenth century, a guide to every detail of domestic life and of the habits of every class of society in those days. The costumes are of the time of Louis XII. : we remark the extravagantly pointed footgear, or the fashions termed *en guimbarde* or *en bec de canne* which supplanted that *à la poulaine*. The ladies of quality wear the hennin, the turban, or the stuffed headdress known as the *bourrelet*—the fashions of Anne de Bretagne. Every class is represented : the clergy, episcopally vested, or in chasuble for mass, in long sleeved surplice or in almuces as canons, the acolyte, and every grade of the minor orders—even the long-haired giver of holy water : the apothecary in the costume and with the accessories of his profession; the butcher, the baker, the schoolmaster, the itinerant musician ; scribe, money-changer, banker, merchant, *huchier* or cabinetmaker and carver—and we remark that the last named is richly dressed, showing the importance of his position ; tradesmen and tradesmen's wives, ladies of easy virtue, shoemakers, tailors, and craftsmen of all kinds ; monks, nuns, soldiers ; the confessional, with a confessor and his penitent, the other sacraments of the church ; nurses and babies, pilgrims, doctors and their patients ; dances and games and drinking scenes, dances of death, mystery plays ; scolds and scandalmongers, usurers, fools, money-lenders, children with their toys and hobby-horses ; public baths and people bathing, a woman beating her husband, a coiner making coins— the list is inexhaustible. Every phase of virtue and vice is shown. It is the *Summa* of St. Thomas illustrated : it is humanity, in fact.

One special figure must be mentioned. It is that of Master Jehan Trupin, richly dressed, working with chisel and mallet on a statue, by his side a pot of some refreshing drink. But whether, and to what extent, we may recognize in him the creator of this great work is not absolutely certain. Late investigations would seem to show that far from being the principal sculptor and designer he was merely an ordinary workman ; perhaps not even a *huchier*. It is hard to destroy the legend that the figure is that of the Jean Trupin who for some reason or other has been immortalized by the inscription of his name on the elbow-rest of stall 85, but there is nothing positive to support it. Again, Antoine Avernier may have been the architect and designer, or, on the other hand, only the contractor. The registers show that Boulin and Alexandre Huet went to Beauvais and St. Riquier to see the *chaires*

PLATE L

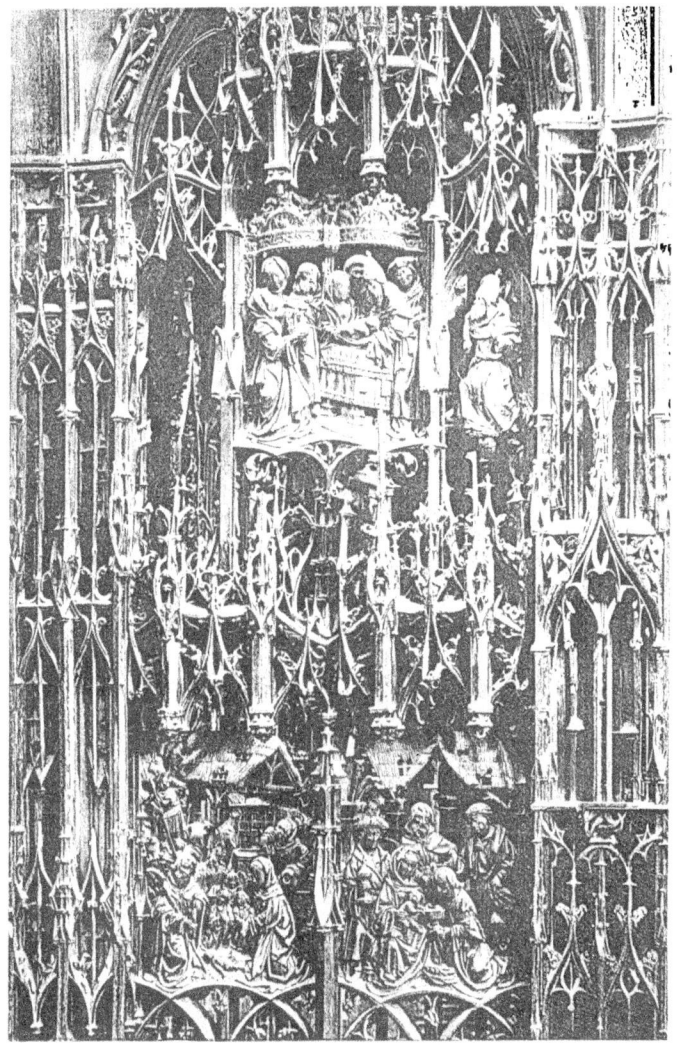

AMIENS CATHEDRAL. PART OF THE SCULPTURED WORK ON THE *JOUÉE* OF STALL 31.
EARLY SIXTEENTH CENTURY

there, and to Rouen, whose stalls date from 1457, but judging from results, they made little use of their notes. It is interesting to observe that at first the misericords were to be '*garnis de feuillage ou manne-quins et petits bestiaux et autre chose a plaisance.*' Later on, it was decided to make a '*suite de sujets bibliques*,' which was a novelty. The following additional names are known, whatever their part in the work may have been : Linard le Clerc, Guillaume Quentin, Pierre Meurisse, and two lay-brothers, '*deux frères convers Cordeliers, habiles menuisiers d'Abbeville*,' who were engaged in 1510, '*pour tra-vailler aux chaires et conduire l'ouvrage.*'

It is said that the task of counting the figures to be found in the scenes and decoration of the work has been attempted, and that they amount to 3650. Gothic in its sentiment throughout—in the attitudes and expressions, for instance, of the holy women at the foot of the cross—mingled with the mystical art of the ages of Faith as it was nearing its decline in the first decade of the sixteenth century, we have in other parts of the decorative details an evidence of an acceptance— if with reluctance—of the spreading teachings of the Renaissance. But if Arnoul Boulin, in the pendentives and *culs-de-lampe* which are probably by his hand, was unable to resist these advancing principles, he took from them only what was sufficient to brighten the monotony which long continued association with the older system had no doubt begun to make felt. Here and there are columns, here and there are the *putti* of Italy, singly or dancing in a garlanded chain, exquisite foliage work, cartouches, heads in medallions, cornu-copiae, and vases. What we have of this character is of fine execution, but in low relief : almost, as it were, apologizing for its presence and unobtrusive. It is interesting also to notice that although we find this influence of the Renaissance amongst the more strictly

329

decorative portions of the work, and subordinate to the generally flamboyant Gothic character, it is entirely absent in the treatment of the historical and domestic scenes. Here there is nothing conventional but the faithful realism of fashions, manners, and customs at Amiens in 1508. In considering the work as a whole, we must remember also the horrors of the Revolutionary period, and, worse still perhaps, here, as elsewhere, the deplorable taste of the eighteenth century. All this contributed to considerable alterations. A row of fleurs-de-lis formerly ornamented the panelling at the back of the stalls. This was removed at the Revolution, restored in 1814, and finally taken away in 1831. A great deal of the original work was destroyed in 1755 at the time when the new high altar of carved wood was erected. This still remains, its huge and vulgar glory and other adornments, in the worst possible taste of the time, continuing to disfigure the Gothic *chef-d'œuvre*. Marvellous it is that so much should be left, despite even the desecrations at the time of the celebration in the cathedral—as at Paris— of the Feast of Reason.

It was Ruskin who said, with truth, that few have written quite calmly who have written of Amiens at all. No one better than he could appreciate, also, the technical excellences of the work, the masterly chiselling, boldly executed by practised hands, the last almost of the race of artists by instinct, of workers by tradition. He has given us *The Bible of Amiens*, in which he writes : 'Aisles and porches, lancet windows, and roses you can see elsewhere as here, but such carpenter's work you cannot. Woodcarving was the Picard's joy from his youth up, and, so far as I know, there is nothing else so beautiful cut out of the goodly trees of the wood. Sweet and young-grained wood it is: oak *trained* and chosen for such work, sound now as four hundred years since. Under the carver's hand it seems to cut like clay, to fold like silk, to grow like living branches, to leap like living flame. Canopy crowning canopy, pinnacle piercing pinnacle, it shoots and wreaths itself into an enchanted glade, inextricable, imperishable, fuller of leafage than any forest, and fuller of story than any book.' The Frenchman Didron was not so enthusiastic. The stalls of Amiens were not to his taste. Wonderful, then, as may be the beauty of this great work, there may still be room for differences in appreciation. No one can pretend to compare it with those parts of the cathedral designed and executed at the earlier and purest epoch of architecture and statuary: with the pictures in stone throughout the exterior and interior. To take the great west front alone, there are no more beautiful figures than the Virgin of the south door, the Virgin of the Annunciation and the Virgin of the Visitation. And for those to whom the imagery of still earlier times appeal, need one call to mind the *Beau-Dieu* of Amiens ?

Whatever the cause, whether from the approaching Reformation or from some other, Germany is less rich in stall- and choir-work than France, although the practice and love of carved wood in the fifteenth century was so strong. But there is one, at least, remarkable exception. This is Ulm, the glories of whose cathedral choir have been sung over and over again. Once more, in the series of ninety-two stalls in carved oak with their accessories of screen and dais, throne and sedilia, we meet with, as it were, an enchanted forest peopled with innumerable figures : great moral lessons drawn, for the sake of teaching by the eye, not only from sacred history, but also from ancient records of pre-Christian times : illustrated by great heroes, by writers, poets, philosophers, and rulers. It is an imposing company, the men and women figures separated : the men in three lines on the right-hand side of the choir, the women, similarly, in three lines on the left. Pagans, Jews, and Christians, philosophers, prophets, saints and martyrs, form together a grave assembly, an universal council. On the one side Socrates, Seneca, Pliny, Terence, Pythagoras, Cicero, Moses, David, and the Jewish kings of the Old and New Testaments. On the other the sibyls: Jael, Ruth, Rebecca, Naomi, Martha, Magdalen, Ursula, Elizabeth, Agnes—to name no more. All these, and the stalls beneath with their misericords, are set in a rich framework of elegant tracery, in great part openworked: a profusion of ornament under charmingly crocketed ogee arches, the crockets themselves formed of trailing vine leaves and grotesque animals. The eye is everywhere bewildered by masses of luxuriant vegetation, amongst which innumerable animals and human figures, more or less fantastic or natural, climb and disport themselves. Dragons crawl and raise their terrible heads, lions crouch and prepare to spring, dogs of the chase run hither and thither, squirrels, apes, marmosets, and the smaller denizens of the woods, snakes and snails and every creeping thing, mix in endless numbers with birds of all kinds—eagles, owls, doves, domestic fowls, the inhabitants of sea and river; with all zoology, known and fabulous, and with man himself under every natural and grotesque aspect.

All this is repeated and, it may be said, summed up in the finest part, for design and execution, of the whole work; that is in the principal stall, or sedilia of three places, for the priest, deacon, and subdeacon at mass. This, the earliest executed of all the sculptured masterpiece, is the work of the elder Jörg Syrlin, father of Master Georg Syrlin, who has carved his own portrait figure, in the round, on the *jouée* of one of the stalls. Here he sits, his hat on his head, leaning over and contemplating this great work of his creation. And amongst the crowd of Jewesses, prophetesses, sibyls, and saints, he has placed also the portrait figure of his wife. That so much should have been done in so short a time is recorded in the inscriptions added by him: '*Georgius Surlin*, 1469, *Incepit hoc opus*'.: and '*Jeorg Syrlin*, 1474, *complevit hoc opus.*' This German *chef-d'œuvre* of elaborate choir-work was then completed thirty-five years before that of Amiens was contemplated. Molinier was of opinion that it does not deserve the extravagant praise which has been lavished upon it, and King in his *Study Book of Mediaeval Architecture*, refers to it as a medley of subjects due to the unsettled mind of artists of those days. On the other hand, many will still continue to see, notwithstanding its intricacy and elaboration, a wonderful balance and, withal, a certain restraint so far as was compatible with so comprehensive a scheme; and in the sedilia, taken alone, a masterpiece.

Details of the family of Syrlin, or Sürlen, are unfortunately almost completely wanting. The name first appears in the list of master carpenters of the city of Ulm in 1427—that of Jorg Syrlin the elder in 1458, and of the younger, to whom is attributed, with much other work, the stalls of Blaubeuren and of Geislingen, in 1512. Little else is known. In fact we must consider the 'Master' of this name to be the one who executed the sculptures of the choir of Ulm. Of the other work, which is unequal in merit, it is not easy to be precise. The family name may even have been continued as a trade-mark or corporation. In any case, the one who has left us his self-portrait and that of his wife amongst the innumerable other busts and figure work of the famous choir was a great artist, and amongst those who worked in wood, an incomparable sculptor. In his own portrait he represents himself as Virgil. It is a striking head, forcibly reminding us of the style of an Italian quattrocento terra-cotta bust. Throughout the series Syrlin shows an immense talent as a portraitist, and this is the more remarkable when we consider the age and country in which he lived. Gothic feeling still almost exclusively prevailed, and his absolute realism distinguishes him from his immediate predecessor Multscher. Certainly, also, the sculptor of such a group as the 'Entombment' of the Zweifalten Monastery, of which a cast may be seen in the Kensington Museum, was a greater artist than his Franconian successor Stoss, or even than Riemenschneider, if we should judge the latter only by the work attributed to him which is authenticated.

One more example from among the fine choir-works in wood of extreme elaborateness must be referred to in general terms. It is that of Auch in the Toulousain district of France. Here the whole choir area is quite closed in with a mass of carved oak, which separates it from the rest of the building as effectually as if it were a small church by itself. The date of its construction, 1529, is little later than that of Amiens, yet although the Gothic style is still apparent in the stalls themselves and in the pinnacle and canopy work, it is dominated by the pure paganism of the Renaissance, which characterizes the beautiful figure work in low relief of the panels which form the principal feature. The architect, to whose imagination the general conception is due, was content to leave the greater part of the flat surfaces at the disposition of the sculptor. But the reign of the animal and vegetable world, so dear to the principles upon which the Gothic decorator worked, was not yet entirely abandoned. It still imposes itself and flows over the magnificent traceried details of the parcloses and *jouées*, finding, too, full scope for the exercise of a fertile imagination in the misericords of the stalls. Above these, and surrounding the whole of the choir, runs a noble row of figures of saints and warriors and allegorical full-length statues on *culs-de-lampe* pedestals. These with the dividing

334

PLATE LI

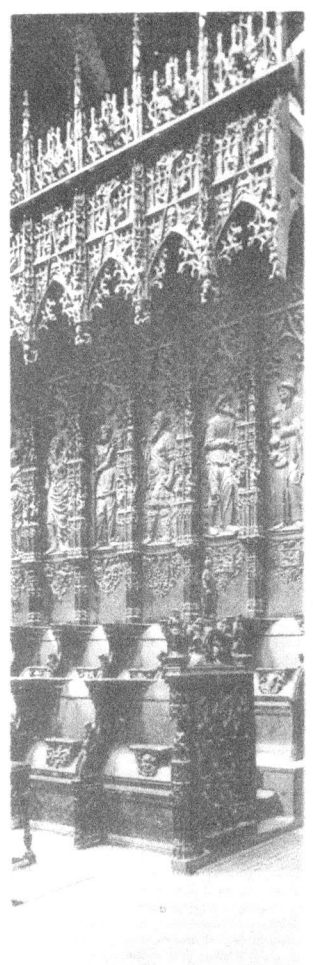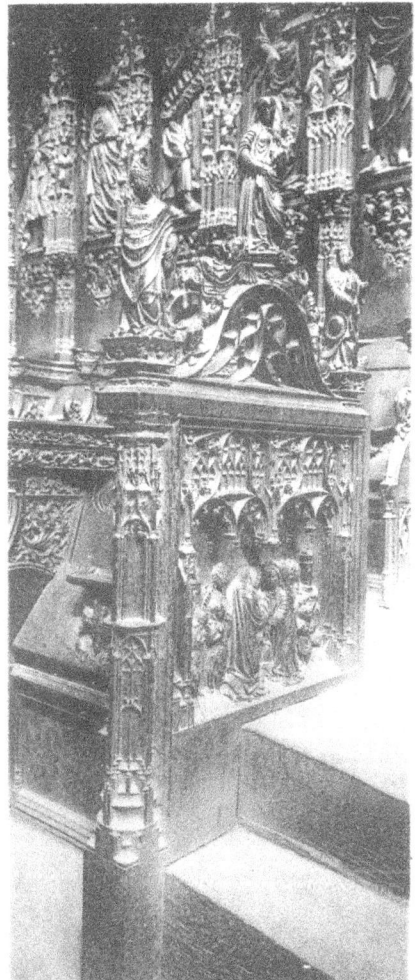

Negatives by Fredk. H. Evans

PORTIONS OF THE CHOIR. CATHEDRAL OF AUCH

columns, the strings of dancing *putti* and the *culs-de-lampe* themselves, show the strong Renaissance influence in this district at the time. The artist's name is unknown. A Pyrenean, he was no doubt strongly impressed with the art of the Peninsula on the other side of the mountains, which he here endeavours to imitate. But he was at least a master of his craft, and has treated the oak with as much ease of touch as if it had been the softer walnut which later on supplanted it in these districts.

CHAPTER XVII

SYMBOLISM IN CHURCH WOODWORK—MISERICORDS—
BENCH-ENDS

IT is necessary to leave the general consideration of choirs, and to restrict ourselves to those parts only which—though as a rule hidden from view—possess, nevertheless, a peculiar interest of their own. These are the misericords of the stall-seats, and their charm is not only, if principally, on account of the subjects represented upon them. In all countries they are not infrequently examples, also, of the art of wood-carving as it was practised not only by sculptors by profession and training, but also by the mechanic of the workshop, the villager, or the inhabitant of a monastery—the amateur artist, as we might say. The same will hold good — especially in England — with regard to the bench-ends of village churches, and even, in some cases, the rood-screens.

Despite the destructions and degradations which have fallen to the lot of religious edifices in all countries, despite also the changes of taste by which Gothic art had been overpowered by that of the Renaissance, and supplanted frequently by the rococo and the sham antique, and despite the perishable nature and small intrinsic value of wood, these misericords still remain in almost numberless quantities. It is obviously impossible to treat the subject here in detail or with any completeness. Thousands of examples of misericords are noticed in the transactions of the provincial archæo-

336

logical societies of every country, yet many more, no doubt, have escaped especial attention.

As may be gathered from the general description of those which will be presently noticed, the real meaning of the subjects which they offer still affords material for investigation and conjecture. Every now and again the key to these cryptograms appears to suggest itself. As an instance, there is the subject, so frequently found, of the woman clothed only in a net, riding on a goat, which will presently be described. There is evident symbolism of a certain kind everywhere employed in these carvings, but symbolism which after a time became so distorted that its original meaning and place among folk-lore were lost, and the subject was used only from its comic aspect and suggestion. A symbol has been defined as a figure or image employed to represent something else : that is to say, something other than at first sight would appear to be obvious ; something in which our ingenuity or experience of the science is to discover a deeper hidden meaning. A misericord with Reynard the fox carrying off his spoils of the poultry-yard does not merely refer to that animal's natural propensities, but, especially if he walks on two legs and wears a hood over his head, is a satire on vices which are to be found even in a monastery. This is still symbolism, even if degenerated into mere ridicule. A signification of symbolism, as expressed by Hugues de Saint Victor, is the allegorical representation of a Christian principle under a material form that may be seized by the senses. From the earliest times and in all ages symbolism has had an attraction for mankind. In the first chapter of Genesis we are confronted with the Tree of Knowledge, and the last book of Scripture is an allegory from beginning to end. At least we are left to discover hidden meanings clothed in poetic imagery, expressed in terms suited to our limited human knowledge. Those, then, who constructed these books of imagery, whether in picture, in sculptured stone or in wood, addressed themselves to the illiterate or, at anyrate, to the mediæval mind, whose knowledge extended no further than to imagine as possible the existence of a dragon, a griffin, or a creature half human, half animal. The intention was to instruct the ignorant in the sacred Scriptures, in moral theology, and in some part also in natural history and in the habits of plants and animals. It is certain that human nature has ever delighted in representing animals, or half-human, half-animal creatures, performing human functions, and endowed with human virtues and vices. More than this, our nature, from earliest infancy, takes a morbid pleasure in the horrible and in the distortion of nature. The child, as a rule, prefers the wicked giant to Jack who slays him, and turns to the Yahoo in Gulliver with more eagerness than to the gentle Houyhnhnm. And when, as we know, the most elderly amongst us can, for the moment, seriously believe in the reality of the strange inhabitants of Alice's Wonderland, there is little necessity to insist further on this aspect of the subject.

A systematic examination of the symbolical or satyrical representations to be found on our misericords would show that many of them are to be found with precisely the same significations or train of thought on the monuments of the earliest times of old Egypt, and continued throughout her civilization. We have, for example, on a papyrus of the nineteenth dynasty, an ass and a lion singing to the accompaniment of a lyre and of a harp on which they are playing; a flock of geese attacking and vanquishing a cat (as, on the misericords, a cat is so frequently hanged by the geese); a lion playing draughts with an antelope; an army of rats led by their general in a chariot, assaulting and taking a fortress held by cats—and so on. We find this same satire of the rats reversing the order of nature by taking

338

the offensive, in a psalter of the thirteenth century, attributed to Gui de Dampierre, in the Brussels library; and, in our day, in the hare going shooting, in 'Shock-Headed Peter.' Nothing appeals more strongly to us than a mocking of the foibles and miseries of human life. And of all the animals, the one which has longest in this way held our imagination is Reynard the fox, who, on Egyptian papyrus, on the frescoes of Pompeii and Herculaneum, in stall and on column, in painted glass or pictured manuscript, stands for the embodiment of cunning, duplicity, and hypocrisy. Nothing, of course, is more natural than this comparison of the good qualities and defects of man with the instincts and habits of the lower animals. We assign to man in the figure of the latter the courage of the lion, the innocence and gentleness of the lamb, the dog's fidelity, the suspicious and tricky fox, the silly goose, the dirty pig. But the fantastic, the outrageously deformed and impossible creatures, with eyes in the foreheads, with head in the middle of their bodies, with arms or legs of excessive disproportion, or the most monstrous mixtures of parts placed anyhow; had these also lessons to teach, or was it only the ingenuity of the draughtsman, exercised to the utmost in devising something hitherto unthought of which could be twisted into allegory, or made merely to serve a purpose of decoration?

The earlier illuminated manuscripts, generally speaking, confine the decoration to the intricate interlacement of the capital letters and borders of the pages. With the greater pictorial illustrations come also, in the margins, figures with satirical applications, animals and birds among the foliage, with no other intention than beauty of ornament, groups and hunting subjects, and a certain amount of coarseness for which the different manners of those times must account. The grotesque began to be frequent about the tenth century, and especially in the eleventh, when the fashion was pushed to the utmost extreme of mingling, amongst the floral and foliage ornament, the most impossible figures of beings, neither human nor animal, composed of limbs contorted and misplaced in every possible way that a fanciful and often morbid imagination could suggest. Assuredly this was not always for any teaching value, but with a sheer purpose of distraction and amusement.

In wood sculpture, the symbolical, other than that which we associate generally with a Celtic origin, is comparatively of late introduction. It is not until the fifteenth century, perhaps, that we meet in it such extravagances as those which became but too common, such as the representation of the Almighty as an old man, or as, on some misericords, an allusion to the Trinity in a head with three faces, three heads crowned with one crown, or three heads within one hood. Primitive Christianity was undoubtedly still restrained by a fear of infringement of the commandment against the making of images. Lactantius, St. Clement of Alexandria, St. Augustine, and, in later times, St. Bernard, have all inveighed against abuses which may result from a want of perfect understanding. Fearful of these abuses, the East, whence so much of our imagery proceeds, hunted it out, and sent it to us.[1]

In the Middle Ages, the association of animal and vegetable life with the expression of mystical ideas became an absolute rage. The artist of those days, in illuminated manuscript and in sculpture, was ever on the lookout for methods of combining quaint imagery with some underlying teaching. He twisted and adapted pagan traditions to Christian dogmas, and ransacked classical writings, such as those of Aristotle and Pliny, for ideas and semi-fabulous stories which would serve

---

[1] 'Nec ideo tamen quasi humana forma. . . . Tale enim simulacrum Deo nefas est christiano in templo collocare.'—St. Augustine, *De Fide et Symbolo.*

his purpose. In the course of the thousands of years during which animal imagery had been used, this method had become a science. It had its rules and interpretations, the meaning of which has since, to a great extent, become lost, or overladen, from century to century, with fresh accretions and adaptations. The animal imagery of this science, which so frequently meets us in the stalls, misericords, and bench-ends, is to be found in the extensive literature which is known under the name of *Bestiary.* If we desire to find the hidden meaning and subtlety of the pictorial symbols we must search these mediæval encyclopediæ. We must go to such works also as the *Speculum Universale* of Vincent de Beauvais, the *Speculum Naturale*, the *Speculum Doctrinale* or *Morale*, the *Speculum Historiale* (or History of the World from the Creation to the Last Judgment), the *Bestiaire d'Amours* of Richard de Furnival, the *Speculum Ecclesiæ* of Honorius of Antun. To name but a few amongst them; The 'Mirror of the World,' of the thirteenth-century Dominican Vincent de Beauvais, written by order of St. Louis of France, is divided into four parts, the Mirrors of Nature, of Science, of Morals, and of History. Earlier still, in the beginning of the twelfth century, Philip of Thaon had written, in England, a bestiary from which much may be gathered. He explains and illustrates the signification of the unicorn and the trick by which it was to be caught. The unicorn is the Almighty, the maid the Blessed Virgin, her lap the Church. So also the favourite imagery of the siren, which is frequent on misericords—the equivalent of the mermaid, less intelligently used, up to quite late times in England. The siren had the form of a woman, a falcon's feet, a fish's tail: as a mermaid, with long hair, a mirror and a comb, weeping in fine weather, singing in a storm and deceiving the mariner, she represents earthly treasures. The sea is the world, the ship, man's body; the steersman, the soul. The rich man oppresses the poor, and causes murders and ruin and at this the siren rejoices, but if the rich man does good she laments, and—as in fine weather—loses her prey. At the same time, the mermaid was not invariably a symbol of earthly things, or the allurements of the flesh. Certainly, in Cornwall in the fourteenth century, we find in it an allusion to the double nature of Christ. We must not forget also such other mediæval literature as the *Lapidaries*, in which the properties and virtues attached to classical cameos and precious stones or gems, and the subjects engraved on them, are set forth.

Works of this kind were popular both from the religious or secular aspect. Thus, in these treatises— for example, in the *Speculum Naturale*—we are taught by beautiful descriptions of country life and the occupations of the Christian year the reasons for choosing the signs of the Zodiac and the mystical interpretations to be derived from them. We learn how the seed is the Word of God; the harvest, the end of the world; the threshing, the tribulation which visits the sins of mankind. All the joyousness, too, of life is expressed: the singing of birds, the whisperings of trees, the sports and feastings, the pleasures of the chase, and so on. It is the history of man fulfilling his destiny. The symbolical representation of the months and seasons is frequent in our choir sculpture. A very common subject on misericords is winter. A man—labourer, or perhaps a monk—warming his hands by the fireside. Such a symbol is plain enough to read. On the other hand, a more intimate acquaintance with the hieroglyphic language is often called for. A drinking horn held upright, horizontally, or upside down, represents the beginning, middle, or end of January. March is a barrel, or a leg and a shuttle for stocking-weaving time; July, a bunch of fruit;

August, a hop-pole. Or, again, we may find these indications scattered over a greater subject, so that our ingenuity may always be on the stretch to discover fresh clues towards unravelling the whole story or teaching, hidden under what, at first sight, is no more than a commonplace representation. Of all subjects, that of the seasons is the favourite and most universal. But the symbols employed vary considerably. In France, January is indicated by a seated figure with two heads; July, a lion lashing his tail; August, a woman brushing out her long hair; November, a hunter with bow and arrow; December, a winged goat The origins of course are obvious. On a marble bas-relief of the thirteenth century of the doorway of St. Mark's, Venice, we have all the seasons expressed by figures of men engaged in country occupations, amongst foliage work, birds, vases, and the like. Another illustration of this subject will be found in the wooden watching-loft of the feretory of St. Albans, carved with similar imagery. At the same time, it is evident that while every possible occupation might be twisted into this particular symbolism, it is not necessary always to do so, unless in the case of a consecutive series.

There was no doubt a considerable amount of unintelligent copying without any particular intention, and the attempt to attach a symbolical meaning to every detail of church imagery may be easily exaggerated. Even when apparently obvious, as in the case of the bishop's crook, the real origin is so commonplace that *post hoc* does not necessarily imply *propter hoc*. The older carvings exhibit considerably more decent gravity than the later ones. The tendency, as time went on, towards an abuse of punning conceits and humorous incidents without other meaning than pure fun and a desire to amuse, and towards jokes which are by no means in the most refined taste, is no more than the freedom of manners of the time would lead us to expect. With the changed ideas of propriety of the present day, we must transport ourselves entirely to mediæval times before we can understand how the taste for the satirical and grotesque originated, and pervaded everything, even the sanctuary of the Church. We must remember that the Church was the centre of the life of the age in the smallest village as in the greater cities. Towards it tended even the amusements of the people. The Feast of Fools, with its irreverent buffoonery, is an instance. It would be otherwise difficult to imagine the frame of mind which permitted the pages of pious books to be bordered with pictures and figures of fabulous subjects, or, as is so often the case, the subjects on misericords to be ironical satires on the ministers of religion and even on the mysteries of religion itself.

The Bestiary writers and, through them, the carvers of misericords, went also to the fables of classical antiquity for inspiration. In these they found typified the strength and courage of the lion, the corrupting viciousness of the hyena, the spotless purity and healing influence of the plover *caladrius*, the wakefulness of the basilisk, and that every living beast or bird could be transformed and adapted to some human attribute. On a door of the cathedral of Puy-en-Velay is a carved and painted tiger with a movable tongue, which works by a counterpoise as the door is opened. As a work of art it is admirable, but for a moral application, could there be any? Often, no doubt, as in the illuminated MSS., the seeming satires were purely gratuitous, and for the sake of ornament. The artist followed, without knowledge, perhaps, of symbolism, those who had preceded him. One thing grew out of another. In initial letters it was easy to distort the curves and other lines by a stroke or two of the pen, a dot here and there, an eye or a mouth which by some chance suggestion had a kind of resemblance to the human or the animal. The Trinity with three heads might have originated in such casual distractions. Certainly the nondescript figures, such as those all heads and legs, or a head on one leg, as on a misericord in the Tufton Street collection, could have had no spiritual teaching.

From these early suggestions of animal or human life, derived from chance combinations of lines, the carver of stone and wood opened up, when the idea reached him—which it seems not to have done before the thirteenth century—a much larger and more public field for the display of imagination. And still the favourite subject on gargoyle or console, or partly hidden beneath the choir-stall's movable seat is the satire on the hypocrisy of the ill-regulated life of the insincere religious : it may be intended to show that the monk is, after all, but human and subject to the same temptations and lapses as the man of the world. But it was not only the dissolute priest, the debauched or gormandizing monk, that was attacked ; in their turn the feudal lord, oppressor of his serfs, the venal judges, the sordid usurer, the dishonest tradesman or innkeeper, come in for a more keen yet good-humoured and tolerant castigation than the most outspoken press of any age has ventured upon. And, underlying it all, there is evidence of a struggle between the classes and a hatred of the rich. Naturally the lady of fashion and the exaggerations of feminine costume do not escape the lash. A very common caricature to be found on misericords in every country is the fine lady in the guise of a sow, dressed in the latest fashion, steeple head-dress and all, mounted on high stilts and playing a harp. Another subject, dear to the artist and to the sculptor of misericords, from the fifteenth century at least, is the fight for the breeches—that is, between man and wife, which of the two should prevail. It is the story of Sire Hain and Dame Anieuse from the romances of Hugues Piancelles. Or, again from the romances, the history of Aristotle, so common on ivory caskets and mirror cases; the philosopher, on all fours, ridden whip in hand by the offended beauty, pointing the moral that *tant com cis siècles durera*—there is no fool like an old fool. Or, once more from the classics, where Virgil is left hanging in his basket from the lady's window, treated as the tales of Boccaccio love to recount of frisky dames. But the most favourite subject of all is the wily hypocrite, Reynard, attired as a bishop, or as a hooded friar preaching to a congregation of silly geese, ducks, fowls, or hares—up to as many tricks as Tyll Owlglass. Yet none was more full of varied moral teaching, as we learn from many Bestiaries: for example from that of Philip de Thaon, where he explains that ' Gulpilz' (Vulpus) signifies the devil in this life. When he finds people leading carnal lives, he pretends to be dead and observing nothing till they enter his evil mouth, when he slays and devours them : so acts a real fox in attracting a bird.

What is absolutely incomprehensible to the modern mind is to understand how the authorities in charge of the religious edifices could have allowed to exist, always before their eyes, representations of a kind, of which not a few remain to this day, which outrage the most elementary notions of decency. These are simply disgusting, and could have served no moral purpose whatever. It is indeed difficult to conceive what was the real object aimed at in these caricatures. Was it not often nothing more than a superabundance of imagination, the delirious ravings of depraved minds, with no other intention than to pander to the crowd? Nothing is more surprising in all the arts of the Middle Ages than the taste for the horrible and the unnatural side by side with the most refined appreciation of all that is most beautiful in the real and in the ideal. As

346

OBSCENITIES

Victor Hugo has said in his preface to Cromwell: 'They surrounded religion with a thousand original superstitions, they invested piety with a thousand picturesque imaginings.' Our stalls and misericords show us the most tender feelings which nature inspires, and as if to prevent our minds being always too highly strung, or always in the same key, near by are depicted the evil propensities of mankind, the hideous forms of demons and of monstrous creations, a witches' Sabbath of eccentric revels and a fearless exposure of the most revolting obscenities. The misericord forms so important a part of our subject that it is necessary to allude to these things without, however, going into details. Every country can produce examples, but the greatest offender—if we may judge from the number of still existing specimens to be seen at such places as Walcourt or Hoogstraeten, would seem to be the Netherlands, and the student who is curious on the subject may be referred to the recently published works on the grotesque in Church art by Maeterlinck and Witkouski.

In other ways nothing is more instructive than the part played by Flemish art in caricature and the satirical. The fifteenth and early sixteenth centuries abound in names, both in Flanders and in France, which are common property in the world of fantastic and extravagant satire—on monks and popes, on priests and pedants, from Rabelais and the sayings of Gargantua and Pantagruel, from Sebastian Brandt and 'the Ship of Fools,' or Jerôme Bosch, to the elder Breughel whose method we find also imitated by our own Hogarth. That our English misericords are closely related to the Flemish can hardly be questioned. Not infrequently the carvers themselves were probably Flemish. The Flemings themselves undoubtedly drew the inspiration for their misericords from manuscripts of much earlier date: for example, the eighth-century gospel book of Maesych, itself inspired from more ancient Gallo-Belgic sources. As other origins, we have, among the old Flemish and French romances, the Enid of Henri Van Veldeke of the twelfth century, the Romance of Troy, the Quest of the San Graal, the Gestes d'Alexandre (thirteenth century), the Chanson d'Antioche of Richard of Flanders, the stories of Tristan, of Lancelot, of Merlin, and the Mirror of Wisdom : all these, and many other *dits* and *contes*, and hundreds of similar mixtures of didactic satire and mysticism, in prose and verse, the joy of our mediæval forefathers, were laid under contribution and must be borne in mind in the study of misericords. The same ideas persisted until quite into the sixteenth century. In the choir of the church of St. Sebaldus at Nürnberg there is a frieze in wood attributed to Veit Stoss, in which we have a dispute between the devil and one of the blessed for a human soul. It is a procession of naked figures, representing popes, cardinals, and bishops, to the gates of Heaven, where St. Peter receives them ; and in another part of the composition a naked figure is being dragged by demons to the mediæval representation of hell as an open-mouthed monster.

In our more prosaic age, for the proper understanding of these things, it is necessary to throw ourselves completely into the spirit of the Middle Ages, when, if the chief idea of the master builder was beauty of form and proportion, the controlling powers of the Church compelled him to carry them out in accordance with the teaching idea. Everything must have a didactic end : the crucial disposition of the nave and transepts, the vaulted roof, the towers and steeples, and the thousand other details of every part of the edifice. The field is still open for a comprehensive treatise on misericords : that is to say, on the whole subject taken by itself, and its story as told in various countries. It has, necessarily, the closest connexion with wood sculpture, but as, notwithstanding destructions and restorations, these carvings still abound everywhere in infinite variety, it would be out of the question, within our limits, to do more than to refer to it in general terms.

It has already been pointed out that the origin of stall-work is obscure, and even if we may connect it, roughly speaking, with the date of our earliest examples, there are few remains of the work of the thirteenth century, and fewer still of the fourteenth: none, I think, of the latter period in France. In the fifteenth they become frequent enough, and in the sixteenth, the Renaissance introduces an entirely new system of ornament with which it is not, for the present, proposed to deal. Stall-work of the thirteenth century is rare in any country. In France the only existing examples are those of Poitiers, of Saint-Andoche de Saulieu, of N. D. de la Roche, near Chéveuse, in the department of Seine-et-Oise, and possibly of Lisieux. Germany has some remains in the church of Saint Gereon at Cologne, and at Xanten ; Flanders, at Celles and Hastière near Dinant, and in the churches of Saint Jacques and Sainte Croix at Liége ; and in Switzerland there are some extremely interesting remains at Lausanne. This early stall-work is all, to a certain extent, fragmentary, and has been subject to alterations and additions. The same remark applies to that of our English choirs attributed to the thirteenth century. In England, especially, the devastations at the time of the Reformation, and the neglect and bad taste of later times, have left us little else but the misericords. Of these we have, in the first place, the fine set at Exeter which, if we may accept the date which it is usual to assign to them, may rank possibly as the most ancient in existence. Besides these, there are early examples at Chichester, and at Hemingborough, Yorks, a few at Fordham in

Cambridgeshire, three at Christchurch, Hants, and one at Westminster amongst the others of much later date, and three at Sutton Courteney, Berks.

The stalls of Poitiers, numbering seventy, as they exist at present, are of oak, the ornamentation in general characterized by the simplicity and refinement of the golden age of Gothic art. They are usually supposed to date from the year 1239, and ascribed to Jean de Moléon, or de Melun, the bishop of the diocese then reigning, but if he died in that year they would be in that case still earlier. Those of Notre Dame de la Roche, again seventy in number, are of the same character, but unfortunately in a mutilated and badly restored condition, and were made, it is supposed, by the same Bishop Jean de Melun, of whose death, the date just given is quite uncertain. The workmanship is again somewhat rudimentary, but the simple design of slender columns, plain fenestrations, and purity of style give them the highest historical interest in connexion with the early forms and decoration of choir stalls. The same applies to the fragments remaining at Saint-Andoche de Saulieu. They are of the last years of the thirteenth century, a period of transition, when the huchier was beginning to work on more independent lines. He was no longer contented to use only the charming window tracery, of which he had become a master, in the furniture of the period, in his panelling and in the chests and coffers already referred to and illustrated. He was beginning, as we find here, to enrich his work with figures in low relief and with statues and statuettes and scenes from the Old and New Testaments on the outer sides of his stall-ends, the other surfaces covered with foliage work and imaginary animals. Yet throughout it all was a note of restraint and simplicity distinguishing it from the over profusion of detail which reigned in the following century. The same system continues to prevail in the

350

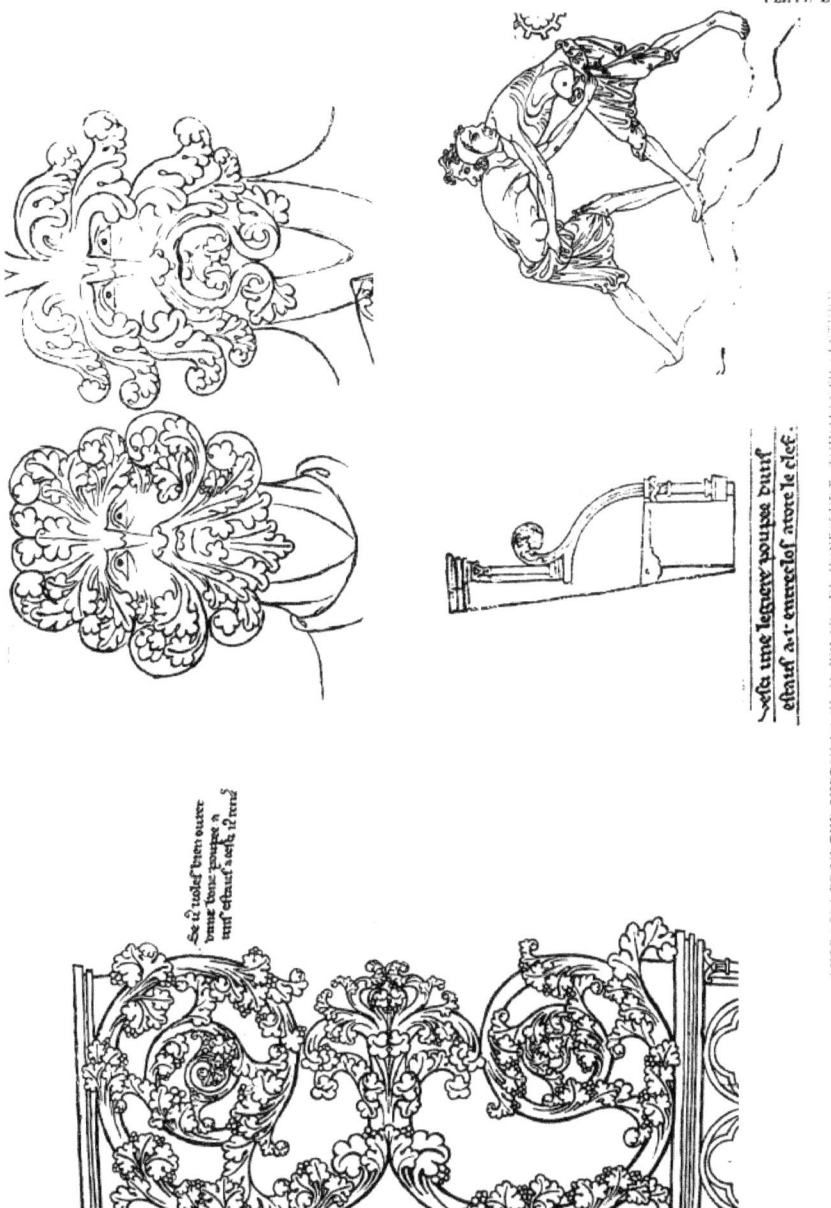

PLATE LII

eſta une legare poupee buiſ
eſtauſ a·r enrrelof avore le eleſ.

Se ũ uolef bien euret
vma tone poupee a
unf eftauf woft i? tme

EXTRACT FROM THE SKETCH BOOK OF WILARS DE HONECORT · THIRTEENTH CENTURY

PAGE 321

stall-work of Lisieux—a similar refined ornamentation in the end-panels of openworked foliage and of animals' heads in the misericords.

With these two early examples of choir stalls we may connect those of St. Gereon at Cologne and the early stalls, now removed and replaced by later ones, of the cathedral of Lausanne. To go no further than these two churches, we have in that most delightful sketchbook of Wilars de Honecourt, designs for and a description of the terminating standard of a range of stalls of similar design to the stalls of St. Gereon, and a sketch of two men wrestling, which has so much analogy with a bas-relief on a *poupée* standard at Lausanne that the connexion with the thirteenth-century architect seems evident. What would be of importance to determine is the part which the designs of Wilars played in connexion with the stalls of Lausanne, or whether, on the other hand, the sketches were made from, or from recollection of, the already existing stalls. The subject cannot here be followed in detail. It must suffice to refer the reader to the dissertations on the Sketch-Book by MM. Quicherat, Lassus, Darcel, and Willis, the last of whom published it in 1859 in facsimile, with an English translation of the notes of Lassus and references to the others. Our illustrations are taken from the facsimiles. On the *verso* of the twenty-seventh leaf we have: '*Vesci une legière poupée d'uns estans a 1 entreclos a tote le clef.*' That is, 'Here is an easily made *poupée* for a stall with one partition with the clef.' The drawing represents the carved high standard which terminates a range of stalls and the ordinary partition, or *parclose*, which separates every stall from its neighbour. On the twenty-ninth leaf is another and richer design to which the word *poupée* is applied. This shows that, in the descriptive title just quoted, the word *poupée* designates the standard, and consequently *entreclos* is the partition. From this we may deduce that the florid ornament to which, in England, the terms 'poppy' and 'poppy head' have been applied, can only claim the latter as being the head of the former. The *clef* of the *entreclos* is the richly moulded cap which receives and supports it, and is curved backwards to form a convenient elbow and leaning place—in modern French joinery terms the *museau* or nosing. Lassus remarks that this *poupée* is of the same form as in the stalls of St. Gereon with only the difference that in the latter a statue is added in front of the double volutes (Wilson). The recto of the twenty-ninth leaf on which is the drawing of a more elaborate *poupée* has: '*Si vus volez bien ovrer dune bone poupée pour une estaule a cesti vus tenes*'; that is—'If you wish to make a very fine *poupée* for a stall you may take this design.' We have here, then, examples of a *legière poupée* easy to make and of a *bone poupée* which means one in which nothing is spared in the way of elaboration of design and of workmanship. It is to such an example as the latter that those of Lisieux and N. D. de la Roche have analogy.

The ancient stalls of Lausanne, after having suffered much neglect for many years, are now reduced to ten and, without their misericords, preserved in the château of Chillon. There are many large figures on the panels of the parcloses, besides the wrestlers, and these, together with the foliage openwork, though boldly designed and vigorously executed in oak, and inspired by French models of the thirteenth century, lack their spirit and grace. What may have been due to Wilars it is impossible to say. 'I have been in many lands, as this book shows,' he writes in his album, and he was certainly at Lausanne, for it contains a sketch of the rose window of the cathedral. He may, then, have sketched also the wrestlers of the stalls.

352

GERMAN STALL WORK

A few words only can be given to the stall work of Germany, although this is in many ways of considerable importance. Otte, in his *Handbuch der Kirchlichen Kunstarchäologie* (see Bibliography), gives a very long list of that still existing, amongst which the stalls of Xanten, Cologne, and Marburg may date back, perhaps, to the thirteenth century. At Xanten we find on the *jouées* a similar system of simple conventional foliage work to that of the example of a *bone poupée* in the album of Wilars de Honecourt, which has already been noticed and illustrated. At Cologne two *jouées* are terminated by full-length figures of St. Gereon and St. Ursula. Didron (*Ann. archéol.* ix. 130)—very unjustly, I think—compares these figures most unfavourably with the work of the sculptor of the stalls of Poitiers. He condemns the drapery broken up into folds, and as if rudely chopped out with a knife, the wooden-doll-like limbs, the coarse heads, and so on. There are excellent reproductions in the gallery of casts in the Kensington Museum, and judging even from these—admitting the French inspiration, and that the German artist may not have completely caught the French feeling of the period in all its elegance—it should be impossible to deny their general charm, the sweetness of the head of St. Ursula, the grace of the attitudes and the whole spirit, entirely of the period.

Long after almost every description of sculpture was beginning to abandon itself with docility to the influence of the Renaissance, wood-carving in Germany, as we have seen, and especially for stall work, still remained faithful to Gothic traditions. The great influx of German sculptors into Italy, and their residence there, could not have failed to have considerable influence. So it is, perhaps, that even there, so late as 1464, the stalls of Pienza are still Gothic, and at Assisi we find the same foliage-volute *poupées* as those to which attention has just been drawn.

The stall work of the Netherlands, however interesting, must give way to considerations of space, of which other classes of its wood-carving have already occupied a considerable proportion. Amongst the finest examples of the fifteenth century are those of Diest (1491), and above all the admirable, but unfortunately incomplete, set of the church of Saint Pierre, at Louvain. But, everywhere, a good deal of the fine panelling of the choirs with the canopied dais has been removed in compliance with the new taste of the seventeenth, eighteenth, and early nineteenth centuries. Aerschot formerly possessed some marvellously fine Gothic stalls, but about 1833 the upper parts were taken off and sold. Those who are acquainted with the little church of Gatton in Surrey will remember the panelling filling it, which is of the finest period of pointed tertiary. This, with the stalls, is said to have been acquired in Belgium in the early part of last century. Possibly it might be traced to Aerschot. The very fine choir and stall work of Holland can also, for the present, be briefly mentioned only. A great deal is late fifteenth and sixteenth century Gothic. Such, for example, is the splendid carving of the stalls of the Broederkerk at Bolsward, of the Hervormdekerk of Breda (the *joueés* especially), of the Grootekerk of Dordrecht, and, of the late transitional style, of the Grootekerk at Haarlem, with its fine figure sculpture, grotesques, foliage and flower-work, and the great and elaborately carved churchwardens' pew of twelve seats.

It seems generally to be agreed nowadays to apply the term misericord to the carved subjects or ornaments beneath the supplementary support of the seat of a choir stall. Were it not that the expression has become accepted, a more correct one, perhaps, would be the corbel, or bracket, for their function is to support the misericord itself. From the very beginning of the system they have been taken over and over again from the stone sculpture of the period, or of earlier dates—from the capitals of pillars, from busts, *culs-de-lampe*, or brackets with parallel sides. If not always directly derived from these—for there is equally to be observed a remarkable originality—they are identical in feeling, in variety, and in execution, and in the case of grotesques and moral lessons the resemblance is absolute. There is one very striking difference between the style or form of the ornamentation in England and on the Continent. In England, instead of being so essentially in bracket form, the subjects are spread out on either side, and these extensions have been given the name of supporters, side lobes, cusps, or volutes. I do not know that this difference in style between our own and the Continental practice has been before alluded to by writers on the subject. So far as my own observation goes, though we have examples in England of misericords without such supporters (Mr. E. S. Prior says that it was not until about 1330 that the practice came in), abroad they are not found at all, or at least only in such elementary forms as in a misericord at Albi, where there is no central subject but only heads or masks at the extremities of the scrolled edge. The Victoria and Albert Museum has until quite recently been, with the exception of one small fragment, entirely destitute of any example of a misericord, either English or foreign. In 1910, however, some sixteen specimens, of one character or set, were presented by Mr. FitzHenry. Their previous history, or, as we may say, *état civil*, is entirely unknown. They are at present officially described as English, fifteenth-century work. We have in them, at least, examples of the bracket, or corbel-form of misericord ornament, without supporters or ornamental side lobes. Without, however, taking this factor into account at all, there would seem to be little to support such an ascription as an English origin. The shape of the seats themselves, in plan, does not

355

correspond with the systems followed in England, and something also might be said of the form of the hinges. As to the subjects, the style and treatment are inferior and wanting in the feeling and didactic applications which were usual. On the whole, notwithstanding the venerable and much worm-eaten appearance, there must still remain grave reason to doubt the genuineness. In default of documentary evidence and bearing in mind a prevailing habit of copying from already existing sculpture, the dates of our earliest misericords —such, for example, as those of Exeter—are so uncertain that the question of the addition of the volutes is not without considerable importance. Types or ornament, and even costumes and armour form no infallible criteria. There was doubtless a persistence in their use, and anachronisms, especially in remote districts, would not perhaps have been considered of importance. It is neither called for, nor would it be possible to follow these subjects, here, in a systematic or exhaustive way. It will suffice to summarize a few of the most striking amongst them. As might naturally be expected from the position which these carvings occupy, sacred scenes or figures of holy personages are unusual. Still, they are to be found, and some of this class may first of all receive attention :—

Scriptural and other sacred subjects.—At Gayton there are many, including Adam and Eve, Noah and the Ark, the decollation of St. John, St. Ursula, the three Maries at the Sepulchre, the Last Judgment. At Gloucester, the Shepherds and the Star in the East. At Chester, the Coronation of the B.V.M. At Lincoln, the Ascension, the Visit of the Magi, the Resurrection, the Assumption. At Ely, the Temptation in the Wilderness. At other places the above are repeated, together with others : Worcester holding the record, perhaps, for scriptural, chiefly Old Testament, subjects, and Lincoln for legends of the B.V.M. Three faces or heads joined together, or within the same hood, as in the Collegiate Church of Champeaux in France, are fairly frequent, and may have some connexion with the doctrine of the Trinity. At Cockington we find the Evangelists with their emblems, on misericords which are of high interest as typical of English figure work of the time. St. George, of course, occurs, and the legend of the dragon; St. Margaret, St. Martin dividing his cloak, St. Giles and his hind, St. Werburgh, St. Mildred, and, without pretending to complete the list, St. Veronica and the miraculously imprinted handkerchief.

Trades and occupations.—These subjects are very common, and many of them similarly treated in all countries, especially that of the hucher or *menuisier* carving or working at his bench, as on the very early misericords at Poitiers, or the carver's own portrait as at Amiens and Ulm. At All Saints, Wellingborough (14th century), he wears a tippet fastened with a rose-like brooch, the sleeves of his doublet puffed at the shoulders. A table is in front of him, and he is carving a rose. To name but a few others, we have the carver or carpenter at the church of Saint Martial, Bordeaux, and at Presles (Seine-et-Oise), at Brampton a carver and a tailor, at Great Malvern a physician and a sick man, at St. David's boatbuilders at work, at Corbeil and Rouen a cobbler.

Fox preaching and satires against the clergy.—This very favourite satirical subject, with Reynard as a monk, a bishop, or a preacher, in endless variety, is common everywhere. At Windsor we find him with stolen geese in his hood (in his *cowl*, it is but too frequently the custom wrongly to call it); at Beverley, Nantwych, and other places, the stolen geese again; at Boston, as a bishop preaching to poultry and rabbits; at Bristol an ape, serving as clerk, has caught one of the fowls, while a number of geese in the back row are asleep as the sermon proceeds; at Windsor, an ape, wearing a stole, is blessing a dog; at Saint Exupère, Corbeil, there is, or was, a bishop with a fool's bauble; at Kempen, a peasant is smashing a quantity of eggs with a flail—a satire against the mendicant friars. Retaliation frequently occurs, as at Sherborne, where the fowls hang the fox, or the rats the cat. Satire in connexion with religion was naturally embittered in Reformation times. At Toulouse, on a misericord of 1566, Calvin is represented as a pig preaching.

Saracen's head.—This reminiscence of the Crusaders persisted long after the last of these was concluded. At Rothwell, late in the fifteenth century, we find the turbaned Paynim with the flowing locks and curly beards which are usual : also at Tilney and Bishops Stortford of the same period. At Lingfield nearly all the eight remaining stalls have some connexion with the Saracen. One is of the foliated-face type. In another the ends of the turban flow out behind the stars with which the stalks of the volutes end. The Wodehouse, or Wildman, is also frequently met with ; for example, in the mid-fourteenth century stalls of Lincoln.

The zodiacal signs, or emblems of the month, occur at Brampton, Huntingdon (1400), where amongst those remaining, we have hay-cutting and corn-harvesting ; at Exeter, with *Sagittarius*: the two heads in a hood at Worle, a man emptying two huge jugs for rainy January, and sitting over the fire for February, and emblems of the rest of the months at Ripple, and innumerable others both in England and throughout the Continent.

Grotesques and human headed birds.—We find the latter frequently in all countries—in England, at Exeter and at Lingfield, for example. Their classical origin can scarcely be doubtful ; evolved perhaps from a suggestion such as we find in a Tanagra figure, where a naked child sitting on the ground holds a goose by the head under his arm, giving the effect that the child's smiling head is that of the goose. As a matter of fact, no other compound of human and animal figures is more naturally convincing and suggestive than the human head on a bird's body. Other monstrous anomalies abound everywhere.

Games and the school are, of course, illustrated by many examples of chess and draughts, by blindman's buff (Bristol), by hot cockles, by schoolboys playing at ball (Glo'ster), and so on ; and condign punishment is meted out to unruly boys in many ways, amusingly treated, as at Sherborne or Rouen.

Dancing and posturing.—At All Souls College, Oxford (1442), where the work is unusually good, we have examples of contortionists, and in many other places the acrobat, or the elastic-faced man appears, the latter, for instance, at Ulm. Or again, there is "Our Lady's tumbler," the poor monk, once a posturer, who, having no other talent, was found displaying his art, as the best thing he had, before her image.

358

MISERICORDS

Costume.—The information with regard to costume is end-less and full of interest. As, however, in other cases, such as the armour on sepulchral effigies, it is not always to be im-plicitly relied on as evidence for dating. We find the horned headdress at Saint Mary's Minster in the Isle of Thanet, and at Ludlow ; the hair in nets of the time of Richard ii., and at Beverley the scalloped sleeves of the men's costume of the time of Jack Cade's insurrection. The stalls at Ely were, according to some authorities, erected by Bishop Alan de Walsingham in 1332, but in the misericord with the story of Herodias we have a style of ladies' hairdressing which did not come in till early fifteenth century : no doubt a later addition. It is not to be forgotten also that fashions were frequently exaggerated and caricatured.

Furniture and objects of domestic interest.—These, together with scenes in the life of the middle classes, of the villager, or of the monk, are no less fascinating than the illustrations of the court, the chase, the tournament and military affairs which also abound. It is true that on misericords they are usually single figures and on a small scale. There is not the space for such perspective scenes as are to be found on the parcloses and *jouées* of Amiens, which constitute a complete encyclopædia of illustra-tion of the ordinary *bourgeois* life at the end of the mediæval period : architecture, within and without, chairs, tables, benches, sideboards, plate and crockery, buffets, wardrobes, *prie-Dieu*, mirrors, altarpieces, kitchen utensils, costumes, implements of trade and occupations of all kinds. The designers and carvers seem to have done for us what the bas-reliefs of ancient Egypt and the custom of sealing up in tombs objects of daily use have done to assist our knowledge of far-off days.

There is, of course, any amount of fun and humour in these carvings. For those who possessed no printed and illuminated books, for whom even a *Biblia Pauperum* was a rarity to be inspected occasionally, they answered several purposes. They were the Punchs and Charivaris and even the Pasquinades of those days, and the satirical lash fell heavily at times. For pure fun we have such things as the devil carrying off the dis-honest alewife (St. David's, 1470) ; the three men in a boat—one of them, a monk, very sick ; family quarrels—a woman chastis-ing her husband with a ladle ; the fight for the breeches, the symbol of domestic authority, as in the story of Sire Hain and

Dame Anieuse at Rouen; innumerable instances of animals turning the tables on men and subduing instead of being governed by them; and moral lessons conveyed by jest and caricature over and over again. The manners of the age were coarser than they are now, but beyond coarseness (and there is not very much even of that) in England, at any rate, there is no longer any existing example of absolute obscenity. Our humour in that way goes no farther than a suggestion, as at Malvern or Hereford (1409), where a man appears to be making rather free with a cook.

Foliage faces.—In the fifth leaf of the album of Wilars de Honecourt there are some sketches of a fantastic application of foliage to the human face, which was much in favour in sculpture of the period, and afterwards frequently found on misericords. A *foliage head* is simply a human head in full face, the hair, eyebrows, and beard transformed into leaves, or, sometimes, flamelike additions. The elementary forms of foliage are adapted from natural types into a curly, hirsute resemblance—in Wilar's sketches from a fig-leaf [Plate LII.]. The fashion has, no doubt, a pagan origin. There are several interesting examples at Lingfield, Surrey. On one the beard is leaf-shaped, and from the eyes proceed some fanciful additions, tressed like an ear of corn. And again, in the early misericords of St. Mary's Hospital at Chichester we have flamelike leaves curving upwards from beneath the eyes, with a small 'supporter' on each side in the form of a sunflower with a human face for the centre. This conceit continued to be a favourite one until late Renaissance times, as we find, for instance, in the woodwork of about 1580 in the Benedictine abbey of Ochsenhausen.

If we consider the sources from which so much of the wood-carving was inspired, and the crystallizing in the course of ages of the popular stories of all times, we shall be prepared to find that the Folklore is also profusely illustrated. It is not easy, in all cases, to trace these sources, or to be quite certain of the real meaning of some which still seem to present insoluble enigmas. One of the many which occur—too numerous to specify more particularly—may serve as an example. Among the very fine series of misericords of

360

the stalls of Worcester there is a subject which, with variations, is found frequently also in all countries. It is that of a woman riding on a ram, with one foot on the ground, naked, except for a net over her shoulders, a rabbit under her arm. Until recently, this has usually been understood as an ancient punishment for incontinence, a woman being compelled to ride thus through the streets. But the real story is drawn from Folklore, as is shown by Mr. D. S. MacColl in a paper in the *Burlington Magazine* for October 1907. It is variously applied in different countries. In Scottish folklore it is the story of ' Diarmid and Graine '—a riddle contest, the wit game so common in early times (see *Popular Tales of the West Highlands*, by J. F. Campbell, vol. i. No. 60). The gist of the riddle, under its many variations, is that the woman is to be not clothed, not naked, not riding, not walking, not in the road, and not out of the road. So she strips, wraps herself in a fishing-net and ties herself to a donkey's tail, which drags her through the ruts of the road with one foot on the ground. We find the woman and the goat in a sculpture in the cathedral of Lyon. But here she has not one foot on the ground, the goat has a human face and she is whirling a dog or a cat with one hand. The rabbit has still to be explained. At Amiens the ' Fine Lady ' of one of the stalls is petting a rabbit in her arms. This has been thought to typify the frivolity and frolicsomeness of women of her class.

For beauty of design the volutes of misericords, peculiar to England, have more character than the principal subjects themselves. In many cases the execution is masterly, and exhibits an understanding of the qualities of wood as distinguished from the technique of stone sculpture, and, in general, it is finest in foliage work. The origin of thus adding ornamental supporters is still open to conjecture. In the earliest misericords it seems to have begun with a head, or a simple flower or

leaf on a short stalk, as we find at Chichester or Exeter.
It was only natural that the idea should be extended,
sometimes, indeed, in an extravagant way. It is, after
all, merely a decorative addition to the simple console.
Still it is puzzling that the practice should have originated and have been adopted only in England. The
form of the rest tablet itself varies considerably in
length, depth, and outline. In England it is much
wider and altogether larger than on the Continent,
where, for example, at Ulm, Auch, Saumur or Xanten,
the bracket is quite small and compact, with often only
a single figure, bust, or small ornament. Sometimes
the corbel subject is (as at Winchester Cathedral) about
the same size, or smaller, than those in the volutes,
and as the latter are frequently the better executed of
the two, we may suppose that they represent the work
of more than one artist. In some cases the subjects
are independent of each other, but, as a rule, the side
ones have some reference to the central and principal
one. Shields of arms, medallions, cyphers, monograms,
and rebuses are common. More rarely, but still to be
met with (as at New College, Oxford), there are whole-
length figures at the terminations of the volutes. A
commonly found bracket to the patience rest is a man,
grotesquely figured and attired in a girded tunic.
Sometimes, as at St. Mary's Hospital, or at Wells,
he is head downwards, his hands spread out, his back
upholding the tablet, his legs merged into the leaf-
scrolls of the volutes. Or, for a foreign example, as at
Saumur, where, with arms and legs spread-eagle
fashion, and head thrown back, he supports the misericord on his chin. Or, again, at Chichester, it is a
merman, in a crouching position, holding his tail in
one hand. In the Victoria and Albert Museum there
is a corbel or bracket-like carving in wood from the
Maskell collection, no doubt at one time a misericord.
It is of the fourteenth or fifteenth century; English

work representing the Assumption, the Virgin in an aureole or vesica-shaped border, borne up by angels, and beneath, a kneeling monk. Said to have come from Malmesbury Abbey, it is crude, untaught work, an example of monks' amateur efforts, the artist having evidently been inspired in the details from older sources which he found to hand : for example, in the style of the trees, which go back to early Christian methods. It is interesting to observe that, if a misericord, it is painted. Few of these retain even traces of colour, but this will be found, for example, on the very interesting ones at Cockington in Devon. For some reason or another, our museum at Kensington has never acquired a specimen of a misericord, English or foreign. Nor are there any examples of the carved woodwork of the English rood-screens, although in mid-nineteenth century and later still they might have been had for the asking. There are a few misericords of considerable interest in the architectural museum at Tufton Street, but these have long been left kicking about on the floor of the gallery and exposed to great neglect, from which it is high time they were rescued.

There remains space for a few summary remarks on stalls in France, which present points of special interest :—

Poitiers, *c.* 1239 to 1257. There are seventy stalls, for the most part foliage work of fine character ; many fantastic animals ; a carver measuring with a compass ; moralities symbolized as at Amiens.

N. D. de la Roche (near Chevreuse). Perhaps the most ancient ; very plain slender columns ; charming simplicity of the foliage work.

Saint-Andoche de Saulieu. Last years of thirteenth century ; epoch of transition ; but continuing to be a model of elegant simplicity.

N. D. de Brou (Ain). A fine series with innumerable figures of patriarchs, prophets, apostles, saints. Strong Flemish influence, but the work of French sculptors.

Pontigny (Yonne). Remarkable for variety of natural history illustration : flowers, fruit, vegetables, insects.

Anellan. Fifteenth century. Elegant simplicity.

Chaise-Dieu (Auvergne). Early fifteenth century; rich and naturalistic; grotesques with much irreverence; a donkey playing the organ; astonishing variety. Attributed to the monks of Chaise-Dieu.

Saint-Claude (Jura, 1455). Monstrous animals, scenes and tableaux; some obscenities; by Jean de Viéry.

Rouen (1457–1469). There were eighty-six stalls: now mostly destroyed; here, probably, was the beginning of the fashion of elaborate scenes and grotesques which culminated in many great series of choir stalls at the beginning of the sixteenth century. Paul Mosselmen was working at Bourges on the monument of the Duc de Berri when called to Rouen for this work. The style may be called Flemish Burgundian (see Langlois, F. H., *Stalles de la cath. de Rouen*, 1838).

Lisieux. Fourteenth century. Fifty-six stalls. *Cf.* Wilars de Honecourt.

Auch (1529). Very rich and fine example of transition period.

Others to be noticed are Rodez, Saint Bertrand de Comminges (Renaiss.), Champeaux, Salins, Orbais, Solesmes. Toulouse. Saint-Martin au Bois, Châteaudun, Vendôme, Andelys. Trôo. Saint - Benôit - sur - Loire, Reims, Lyon, Alençon, Mantes, Alby, Mortain, Toul.

It is impossible to go further and to make a choice amongst so many throughout the country.

The choirs and stall work of Italy are so intimately associated with the rise and progress of the Renaissance that the consideration of them must remain for special treatment in that connexion. This must be said, of course, without prejudice to the fact that certain choir work—for example, that of Santa Maria Gloriosa dei Frari at Venice, by Marco da Vicenza, and so late as 1468—may be entirely Gothic. We have to avoid also for the present the extensive subject of tarsia work and its mixture with the fine carved stalls by the sculptors of northern Italy, as we find it at Perugia or at Siena.

Names of sculptors, also, would be found more frequently in Italy: for instance, the Da Basio in the late fourteenth century at Ferrara; the Majano, the Barili and many others. Italy is, indeed, impossible to condense in a chapter. In a general way, also, the influence exerted by a centre to which the artists of every other country gravitated, and from which they returned home laden with ideas, is over and over again apparent.

Spain, on the other hand, has been a borrower only and never a teacher. France, Flanders, Germany, Italy were all laid under contribution. This is not to say that the magnificent *silleria* of her cathedrals and collegiate churches do not call for attention, and are not worthy of our admiration. The retables of Seville, of Toledo, of Burgos, of Palencia, of Saragossa have their complements in the stall work of Vigarny, of Berruguete, Becerra, Dancart, Doncel, of Martin and Nufrio Sanchez, of Hernández, or of Juan de Juni; at Palencia, Granada, Toledo, San Marcos of Leon, or Plasencia; in that of the Cartuja of Burgos, of the Seo of Saragossa and of numbers more besides. Of many of these, indeed, it may be said again, in the picturesque language of Théophile Gautier, which in this case we need not attempt to translate, that they show " une verve inépuisable, une abondance inouïe, une invention perpetuelle dans l'idée et dans la forme; un monde nouveau, une création à part, où les hommes fleurissent, où le rameau se termine par une main et la jambe par un feuillage, où la chimère à l'œil surnois ouvre ses ailes ongleés, où le dauphin monstrueux souffle l'eau par ses fosses. C'est un enlacement inextricable de fleurons, de rinçeaux, d'acanthes, de lotus, de fleurs aux calices ornés d'aigrettes et de vrilles, de feuillages dentelés et couronnés d'oiseaux fabuleux, de poissons impossibles, de sirènes et de dragons extravagants, dont aucune langue ne peut donner l'idée. C'est le genre païen de la renaissance—ces enfants qui jouent avec des masques, femmes qui dansent, gladiateurs qui luttent, paysan en vendange, jeunes filles tourmentant ou caressant un monstre fantastique, petits mannekens-pisse."

There is no doubt a certain amount of exaggeration and invention in this description. Yet it is strongly suggestive, and might be applied not only to work of this kind in Spain, but also to much with which we have just been occupied in France, in Germany and elsewhere. Was the intense richness and variety of this kind of work overdone? It is not altogether improbable that the same rich superabundance characterized our English choir ornament of the fifteenth century. But mainly, perhaps, as the result of the iconoclastic destructions which accompanied the accomplishment of the Reformation, our choirs of to-day are reduced to the correct sobriety of the pinnacled and canopied architecture, with the misericords hidden away when the seats are turned down, some grotesque *museaux*, here and there, and the absence of any but the most simple *jouées* or parcloses. There is no impression now of a riotous imagination in sculptured detail, no realistic or fanciful reconstruction of the animal and vegetable worlds, no panoramas of mediæval civil and domestic life. Yet who will deny the grandeur of the simplicity which an apparently ruthless destruction has left us in such typical examples as we may find at Exeter, at Windsor, at Lincoln or at Chester?

As Mr. E. S. Prior has pointed out, 'the home of the wood-carver lay doubtless in the woodland centre of England where a carpenter's craft of oak-building had grown to maturity on the borders of the great forests of Sherwood, Charnwood and Rockingham.' As in other countries this carpenter's craft in the first half of the thirteenth century was still but a reflection of the art of the stone cutter. Nor could we afford to be dependent only on our own resources.

The foreigner had to be called in, and, in particular, numbers of Flemish artists came over and settled amongst us in the reign of King Edward III.

The arrangement of choir stalls, as we find them to-day, differs from that adopted on the Continent, the lower range being simply benches without divisions into stalls. This is no doubt due to rearrangements in post-Reformation times for the accommodation of choir boys, and to the provision of seats for vicars-choral in receipt of stall wages when their masters, by whom they were engaged as understudies, occupied their stalls themselves. It would seem, also, that in the last Gothic times of the fifteenth century it was more usual to support the canopies by a system of slender columns than to leave them unsupported as abroad. But both systems existed in Tudor times: for example, at Chester, where the magnificently complicated work of light and airy pinnacled tabernacles has canopies, unsupported, over each stall. On the other hand, Windsor, Lincoln, Westminster, Ripon, and many others are of the columnar type. The famous chapel of King's College, Cambridge, is remarkable as an example of Tudor Gothic in which the earlier system of small columns supporting the canopies of the upper ranges of stalls was replaced in 1530 by baluster supports of pure Renaissance style, all exactly similar, and the canopy work was altered, to be still further altered in the last quarter of the seventeenth century. And, indeed, what still remains of the native Gothic is overpowered and killed by the parasitic overgrowth of the exotic elements. The alterations in all our great cathedrals and churches have been, of course, considerable. When, indeed, we examine such records as we may find in the illustrations to the descriptive works, of which so many were published early in the last century, and compare the condition of these edifices in those days with the present time, it is difficult to connect them as they are now with their mediæval completeness. Harrod, in his notice of the stalls of Norwich, says that he can just remember them *painted in the style of the seventeenth century.*

Exeter. Fifty of the stalls have misericords. These are generally accepted as of the thirteenth century, dating from 1255 to 1279. The character of some is certainly derived from much earlier stone sculpture. These are the open-worked ones of interlaced foliage and grotesques of a similar character to the earliest at Christchurch, Hants. There is indeed more than a reminiscence of the art which we find on many eleventh-century Norman stone fonts and capitals. It will be noticed that these early examples have no volutes, and that the "patience" itself is of a different form, as seen in plan. Among the subjects at Exeter is the famous "elephant," the oldest example in England, with his hocks, however, bent the wrong way, or rather it should be said that an elephant, properly speaking, has none. The volute ends are mostly foliage of simple character, and are highly interesting as early examples of an adjunct afterwards developed and carried to extravagant lengths. The "restorations" by Sir Gilbert Scott were, as is well known, equivalent to reconstructions, but the fine canopy work of the bishop's throne remains.

Christchurch, Hants. Here there are three misericords, probably contemporary with the earliest of Exeter, amongst others of the sixteenth century. One is of the simplest kind, the "patience" merely supported by three brackets in the form of curled foliage of excellent character and execution. The later transitional and Renaissance work is of a poor, imitative character, probably by English artists, and differing in this respect from that at King's College, where the hand of some great Italian master, or perhaps Holbein, is evident.

Hemingborough (Yorkshire) possesses also a misericord of thirteenth-century character, somewhat in the style of the early Christchurch ones.

Sutton Courtenay, Berks. Three, of thirteenth century, remaining. Very simple. Corbel, or bracket form. Ball-flower ornament: perhaps the only example of this in wood.

368

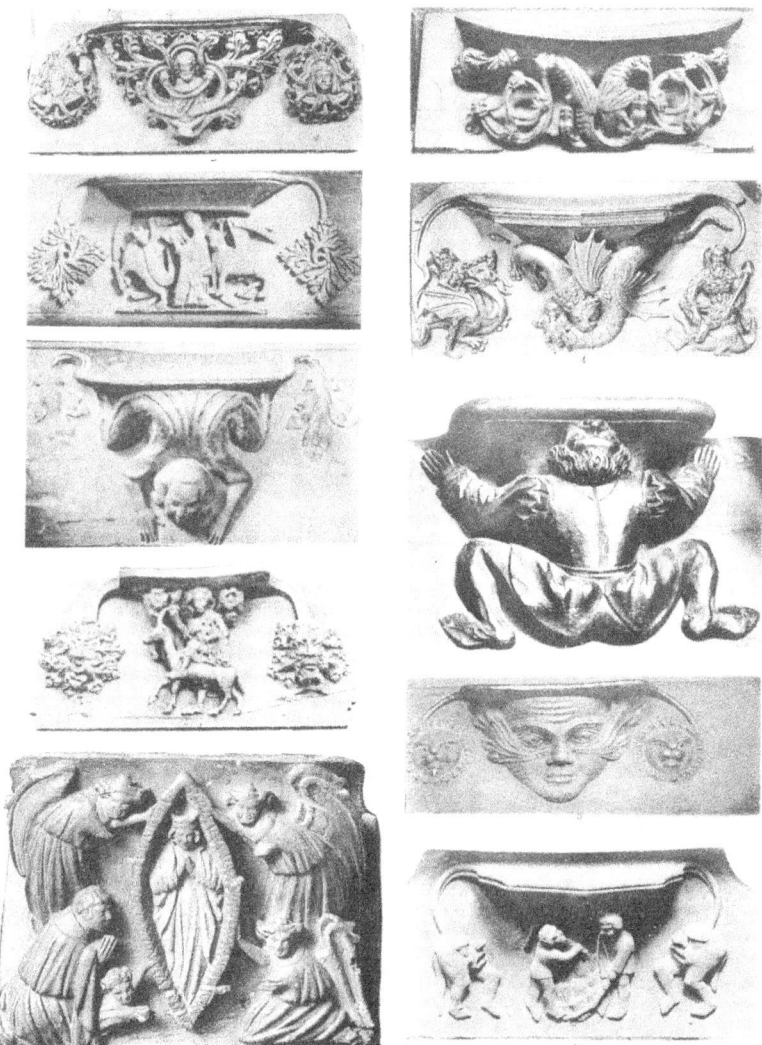

MISERICORDS. ENGLISH AND FRENCH

1. EXETER.   2. CHRISTCHURCH, HANTS.   3. COCKINGTON, DEVON.   4. CHESTER.   5. ST. MARY'S HOSPITAL, CHICHESTER.   6. SAUMUR.
7. WORCESTER.   8. ST. MARY'S HOSPITAL, CHICHESTER.   9. VICTORIA AND ALBERT MUSEUM (MASKELL COLLECTION)
10. LYNN ST. NICHOLAS

PAGE 368

Chichester. Same general character as Exeter. Destruction and defacement in Puritan times.

Fordham (Cambs.). Thirteenth or early fourteenth century. Mask centres; foliage supports.

Winchester Cathedral. Most beautiful thirteenth-century foliage and fruit work in the spandrels and arches of the dossals of the stalls; a true conception of the power of expression in wood, and rightly used. Neither France nor Germany could show anything finer of the kind.

Worcester (the earliest, 1397). One of the finest sets in England. Largely natural history, bestiaries, travellers' tales. Figure work less good than the decorative, but wonderful natural aptitude of evidently untrained artist, following good models. (See Aldis, *Carvings and Sculptures of Worcester Cathedral*, the whole series reproduced in excellent photographs.)

Lincoln (1370). Very varied. Figure work by an artist; for example, the knight thrown from his horse; full of spirit and movement, and good in execution. Glorious pinnacled canopy work; panels with bas-reliefs of kings, and angels playing musical instruments.

Winchester Coll. Chapel (1390). The subjects are amongst the most varied we have. A curious one is a man, haunted by goblins, seated on a cusp of the volutes.

Wells (1330). An extremely fine series of the highest interest, intimately connected with the expansion of Gothic sculpture in England. Comparatively early, these misericords are not to be surpassed elsewhere in England. They are peculiarly English in character, and very many of them, especially with regard to the bosses of the volutes, are specimens of wood-carving which would hold its own with any of the same kind elsewhere. Nor are several of the central subjects of birds and beasts, natural or monstrous, of which there are forty-two, less remarkable for refinement of character and perfection of execution. Note also amongst the human figure work the charming head of a lady with her hair in a caul on each side, covered with a veil confined by a fillet. The whole of the leaf-work may no doubt be found elsewhere in stone, but this does not lessen the value of its arrangement and treatment in another material. We find here, besides other frequently used plant-forms, the maple, vine, marsh mallow, ivy, wild rose and beech, which

2 A

the West Country carvers loved so much to use, as the Somerset and Devon screens and bench-ends also abundantly testify.

Beverley Minster (1520). The misericord with the Fox preaching has inscribed in the volutes " Johannis Syerke Clericus Fabrici."

The carving on the bench-ends which still exist to the number of many thousands throughout the country and are especially characteristic in Devon, Somerset and Cornwall, has frequently much analogy in subject and technical treatment with that on the misericords. The space at our disposal having already been very fully occupied with other important divisions of our subject, I propose now to refer very briefly to these interesting examples of English work. To do more than this would require numerous illustrations. The whole subject will be fully treated and illustrated in another book which I have now in preparation.

The general impression which one gathers from the bench-ends, of which we find examples in nearly every village church throughout Devon and Cornwall, is, in the first place, of their massive character and deeply cut carving. They are seldom less than three or four inches thick, of solid oak. For their subjects, we may take those of such churches as Kilkhampton, Launcells, Poughill or Abbotsham, as typical of many others still existing, and of thousands which have been destroyed or turned to other uses. In very many cases we find the emblems of the Passion—the nails, ladder, crown of thorns, pierced hands, spear, garments and dice—to be the favourite theme, and these, with other pious devices, testify to the spirit of simple devotion which still lingered in the West of England up to the very eve of the Reformation, against which, to the very last, protests were stronger here than elsewhere. In other parts of England, additional interest is to be found in the stories on the panels, and in the elaborate nature of

370

the poppy-heads in which busts and other figure work in the round are frequently mingled.

The somewhat neglected church of Launcells, almost hidden in a depression in the hills which surround the little town of Stratton, on the borders of Devon and Cornwall, possesses what even in their present condition is, perhaps, the finest and most interesting set of bench-ends of the West Country style. Unfortunately they have never, I believe, been photographed as a whole. The designs are excellent, the carving bold and deeply cut in the massive blocks of timber. There can be little doubt that, as in other cases, the work is due to local talent, but we have no means of determining the position, lay or monastic, the artist may have held in the community. We find here the frequent short-hand notes, as it were, usual in small carved work of the period, calling our attention to the Passion of our Lord : a plain cross with a crown of thorns hanging on it, the sponge, rows of money, the pincers and cord, spices in vases, the nails, a sword and a human ear cut off, the winding-sheet, the Veronica handkerchief, and so on. Further than these, there are the feet of the Saviour disappearing in a cloud at the Ascension, and the footmarks left on the ground below ; the tomb as an early Christian basilica with a tree and spade near it ; hell-mouth as the wide-open mouth of a monstrous animal ; the large Gothic M crowned, monogram of the Blessed Virgin ; the fleur-de-lis ; an Annunciation lily in a vase ; the emblem of the Sacred Heart and a hand pointing to it ; and others. Of a later date in the same set are some helmeted and profile heads in Renaissance style, shields with initials or coats of arms, such as that of Sir Bevil Grenville, the Tudor rose, and panels of the linen pattern. At Abbotsham the bench-ends are narrower and of less thickness than usual. As in the case of other churches they have their own individual interest. We have, again, the Passion emblems, the

Veronica face on the napkin, the Sacred Feet, Hands and Heart, the lantern, and the crucifixion itself with the rood figures on either side. The builder is represented by his compass and square, and the Founder in a full-length mitred figure, holding in one hand a model of the church. On another panel is his shield of arms surmounted by a mitre.

As the subject of bench - ends is but summarily treated here I have not thought it necessary to give illustrations. But on account of their interesting relation to mediæval figure-sculpture generally, the panels on the backs of some benches in the choir of the parish church of North Cray, Kent, are here reproduced. They are carved in low relief and represent the seven corporal works of mercy : the feeding of the hungry, giving drink to the thirsty, clothing the naked, harbouring the harbourless, visiting the sick and in prison, and burying the dead. The carving is most excellent and spirited, and, though on a larger scale, one is reminded, at the first glance, of the style and technique of the mirror cases, caskets and panels in ivory of the same period. The panels are said to have been acquired in Belgium a few years ago.

NOTE.—Through an unfortunate accident occurring when this book was ready for press it has not been found possible to include an illustration of the Annunciation group at Asciano, described p. 254. Advantage has been taken to introduce instead the accompanying English figure of St. Catherine, now in the collection of Dunstan Powell, Esq., of Birmingham (Plate LV.). Although it may be considered by some critics somewhat bold to ascribe an English origin to this piece, the author has no hesitation in so doing. He is of opinion that there are not a few works of art, especially among the ivories, generally ascribed to France or the Netherlands, which should be restored to England. At the same time, it is a question for which space could not at present be found in this book. There are many examples, throughout the country, of carved woodwork, such as—to name but one only—the fine roof of the church of Mildenhall in Suffolk, with which comparisons would have to be made ; and, indeed, the character of the more or less perfect figures in stone and alabaster, and of English mediæval sculpture, generally, would call for attention at considerable length.

PLATE LIV

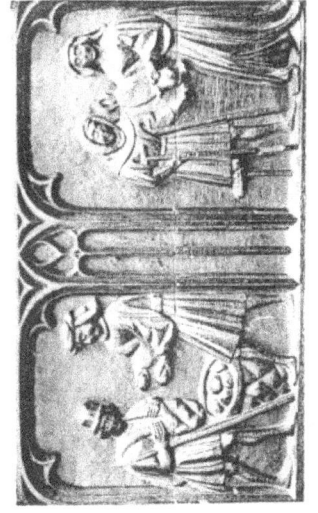
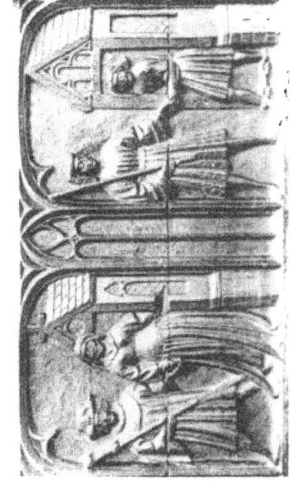
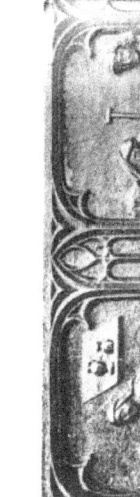
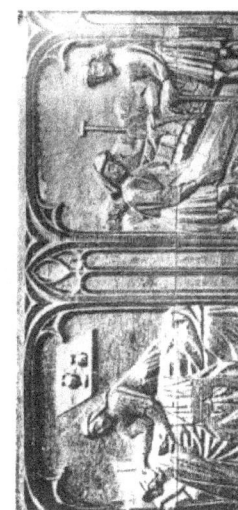

PANELS ON THE BACKS OF BENCHES. FLEMISH (?) SIXTEENTH CENTURY
PARISH CHURCH, NORTH CRAY, KENT
PAGE 372

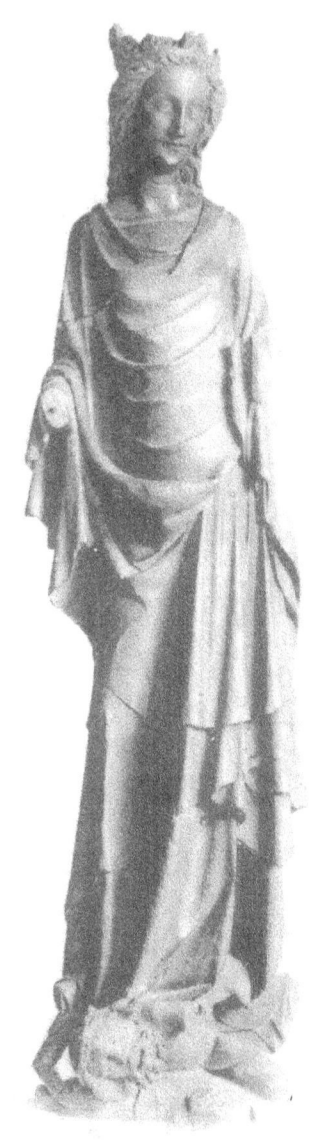

STATUETTE. ST. CATHERINE. THE EMPEROR MAXENTIUS UNDER HER FEET.
ENGLISH. FOURTEENTH CENTURY
IN THE COLLECTION OF DUNSTAN POWELL, ESQ.
PAGE 172

CHAPTER XVIII

CHANCEL SCREENS AND OTHER CARVED WOODWORK IN PARISH CHURCHES IN THE WEST OF ENGLAND

ALLUSION has already been made more than once to the paucity of remains of mediæval wood sculpture in England, due to the wholesale destructions at the Reformation and in Puritan times. But if, in figure work, little indeed has been spared for us besides the misericords and the somewhat cognate bench-ends, together with some scattered remnants here and there, and a number of angels on hammer-beams of roofs, we have in what remains of the carved wood rood-screens examples of native art workmanship of which we have every reason to be proud. For many years neglected and unappreciated, and entirely ignored by foreign critics, they have recently attracted, in our own country at least, not a little attention and admiration.

When we consider that at one time the rood-screen and the choir-screen or *pulpitum*, were to be found, in conformity with canon law, in every cathedral, collegiate and monastic church throughout the country, that no parish church was without its rood-screen at least, and that this was usually of wood more or less richly carved and decorated, it will be admitted that the subject is too large a one to be treated in detail within the limits of the present volume. Besides this, the usual character of the ornamentation—in the main architectural, enriched with foliage work—is only partially included in the scheme or plan which we have attempted to follow. These beautiful specimens

373

of the wood-carver's craft, together with bench-ends, chests and panellings generally, must therefore await another opportunity when—if it should be called for —the character of the ornament and its technical treatment may be given the special attention they deserve.

The question of the early history of the rood-loft may be dismissed in a few words, the more so because the screen, as we find it now, is but a fragment of its former self. It is chiefly interesting from the point of view of the often elaborate carving of its foliage work, the elegant series of fenestrations, the real merit of the refined and delicate craftsmanship, and, above all, from the fact that it is essentially English in arrangement and treatment, however much the motives may have been borrowed from foreign sources. In the early days of the Church, before the choir system was fully developed, it was to the altar alone that a screening off was applied, and this, to speak generally, was done by an arrangement of curtains during the celebration of the sacred mysteries. In the basilica the screen assumed the form of a low wall—still surviving in our altar rails—and on either side were raised the ambons or pulpits, for the reading of the epistles and gospels. As time went on the seats of the bishops and other ministers were no longer behind the altar, the choir occupied a larger space in front of it, and a higher screen divided this sanctuary from the main body of the edifice. A loft, or gallery, to which access was gained by a staircase in the wall, was supported by this screen, and took the place of the ambons, serving also as a passage across the building. This gallery supported the organs, gave accommodation to the choir, and was at times even furnished with an altar at which mass was said.

It is unnecessary to do more than allude to other uses to which it was put. Some of them still form matter for discussion and dispute. It will be sufficient to bear in mind that in the greater churches there were two screens, the *pulpitum* and the rood-screen. It may be said that the chief object of the latter, besides displaying the Holy Rood and its attendant figures, was its use for what we now call the organ-loft, that is, as a place for the organs and as a singing gallery. From the *jubé*, or *pulpitum*, were sung the epistles and gospels and other offices, which, as at present—at compline, for example—were prefaced by the reader's request, "*Jube domne benedicere*." In churches where there were two screens the rood-screen stood at some little distance west of the *pulpitum*, and carried, or had suspended over it, the great crucifix or rood, with its attendant figures of Our Lady and St. John, while below it stood the rood-altar, where the parish mass was daily said. In some cases mass was celebrated in the loft itself, and we still find traces of the rood-lights kept burning there. In parish churches the two screens were combined, and this combination may properly be termed the rood-screen.

It is uncertain when the practice began of placing a rood, or Calvary, on the loft of the chancel-screen. There is probably no existing complete rood with its three figures earlier than the thirteenth century. Two examples of this date arc in the museum at Dresden. In those cases where a still earlier origin has been assigned, it is more than likely that they are merely copies made as late as the fourteenth or even the fifteenth century. They are, however, still interesting, for the older style was faithfully imitated. An early mention of a rood-beam occurs in a MS. of the monk Gervasius, who, in describing the work of Lanfranc in Canterbury Cathedral before the fire in 1174, says that above the *pulpitum*, and placed across the choir, was a beam (*trabes erat*) which sustained a great cross, two cherubim, and the images of St. Mary and St. John the Apostle (Willis, *Canter. Cath.*, p. 37). At the suppression of the monasteries many rich rood-lofts were removed to the neighbouring parish churches. The fine rood-screen and loft at Atherington, in Devon, is probably an instance, and no doubt numbers were destroyed, for few remain of an earlier date than the fifteenth century.

The general subject of crucifix figures is one that demands special treatment in the story of wood sculpture and, so far as considerations of space allow, has been already alluded to in other parts of this book. The iconoclasm of Reformation times, the hatred of the Puritans, and the irreverence towards, and curious dislike of, a representation of our Lord on the cross—especially if sculptured — which was still rampant in early Victorian days, have reduced the number of English rood-figures probably to no more than two or three fragments. That is, if we leave out of account the crucifix and attendant figures rudely carved in low relief on a panel now placed over the communion table in the little church of Gwerful Goch, near Corwen, in North Wales, which is sometimes referred to as a rood. About the year 1876 the visit of the local antiquarian society brought to light a fragment of a crucifix figure standing in a corner of the vestry of St. Antony's Chapel at Cartmel Fel, Lancashire—'like an old umbrella,' as the *Transactions* relate—which for some time had been used as a poker for the vestry fire. So far as can be judged from its present condition, as illustrated by a photograph, the figure was a large and extremely fine one, evidently English work, about 2 feet 6 inches long, of oak prepared with a ground, as described in a previous chapter, and coloured and gilded. The arms are missing, and the wound, from which stream gouts of blood, is seen on the right side. It is now preserved in the local museum. In 1886 the remains of a rood figure of the fourteenth century, found

376

about 1856 in the blocked-up staircase of the church of Kemeys Inferior, were exhibited at the Society of Antiquaries. From the account in the *Proceedings* we gather that the legs from the knees are now missing, the long hair bound with a fillet, the face thin with curly beard and moustache, and that there are remains of colour. Besides the fragments which have just been described, there are also two remains of rood figures from Mochdre Church, Monmouthshire, now in the Powysland Museum. They had been hidden, or stowed away at one time or another, on the top of the wallplate, where they were found at the time the church was restored in 1867. The figure of our Lord measures, in its present condition, 19 inches in length, but the arms and feet are gone. There is a crown of thorns over the full-flowing hair, and the brow is deeply furrowed. The work is rude, but of course was at one time painted. The attendant figure of the Virgin is 15½ inches in length, the face of elongated type, and a long veil covers the robe. Native work of the fifteenth century, it seems to have been copied roughly from some Flemish model. It is remarkably like the type of some of the English alabaster figures : short, with a certain stiffness, large head, long hands, prominent eyes and cheeks. There is such a one in the museum at Ghent ; a Saint Cathcrine of alabaster painted. It may be compared also with a Madonna figure on the west front of Sleaford Church. These figures would, of course, be rather small for a rood. The dimensions of some great roods must have been very imposing. At Cullompton there are still to be seen the remains of the Golgotha, or rockwork, from which the Crucifixion group sprung. It is constructed from the butts of two oaks measuring 9 feet 6 inches by 1 foot 6 inches, carved to represent rocks, on which lie skulls and cross-bones, with mortices for the figures of Mary and John. In England it is unique. At Causton Church, Norfolk, are four medallions fixed to

377

the roof, which seem to have been the end of a rood-cross, and, standing on the first hammer-beam on the north side is a large image of Our Lady, probably one of the usual accompanying figures. A few other attendant figures are, or were not long ago, in existence : for example, Our Lady at Etchingham, Sussex, and a St. John at Lapford, Devon. The latter was found hidden in the north wall of the church in 1889. It has a typical long narrow face, and well-treated drapery in long folds confined by a belt. Some few examples of representations of the Crucifixion with the attendant rood figures remain, also on bench-ends ; for example, at Littleham, North Devon.

The subject of the erections and destructions of the roods which, up to the time of the Reformation, must have existed on rood-screens alone to the number of many thousands, is sufficiently interesting to justify a slight digression. A systematic account compiled from the many quaint entries in the churchwardens' accounts of the centuries concerned would assist in making us acquainted with important details regarding the contracts for the making of the screens and their images, the methods of raising funds, the employment of master carpenters and imagers and, in a few cases, even the names of the sculptors. We find also details of the painting and gilding and their cost, records of the first ruthless wave of iconoclastic destruction, the short-lived replacements followed by a second " plucking down " and reduction to decent order, and, finally, material for amazement at the taste which so lately as last century condemned the much despoiled, but still beautiful, screen-work to the stable-loft of the vicarage or a bonfire. They were not suited to the æsthetic ideas of the Victorian age, and when not utterly destroyed might have been had for the asking. Happily, there has been a revulsion of feeling, and in the West Country especially, the work of restoration has, in recent years, been undertaken almost everywhere, and, in most cases, this has been well done.

Materials abound in such churchwardens' accounts as we still possess, with regard to pre-Reformation village life, and unfortunately, more as to the work of destruction so gaily carried on by the orders of the reforming sovereigns. A parish meant the community living within limits defined by the Church, with its organizations instituted by, and under, ecclesiastical authority. The Church was its meeting-place, and it was the bounden duty of the church council to furnish the House of God. The name 'Vestry' nowhere occurs. In every will the testator bequeathed something for a purpose connected with the fabric. Over and over again the keeping up of the 'rode-loft' and its decoration is a favourite object of devotion. Not only was money lavished on great cathedrals, but the smallest and most remote of the village churches, seemingly of little importance, was often most richly endowed and furnished. How else can we account for the evidence of former magnificence in out-of-the-way Devonshire villages, even to-day difficult of access, nestling among the combes and valleys, or scattered about the desolate wastes of Dartmoor?

We read in the accounts for 1530 of the small parish of Morebath of the monies devoted to various altars, of the guilds of young men and maidens, and how the funds for pious purposes were in the hands of the people and administered by them. It is always the same picture of church life, whether in town or village. As examples which may illustrate the whole, none is more instructive than the Tintinhull Records, collected in 1883 by Bishop Hobhouse, and published by the Somersetshire Record Society. Over and over again in these and in other churchwardens' accounts we come across such information as the following, which is here briefly summarized. The accounts of

Tintinhull give a surprising picture of village life. The church fabric and services were not maintained by the neighbouring priory, but by the people, the 'parish' being a purely religious organization, distinct from the manor or the tything, though composed of the same personnel, man for man. The bishop at his visitation *orders* things to be done, such as the repair of the roof, and the parish has to do it. The great rood-screen at Yatton was all executed by Crosse, a carver, in Cleeve within the parish, the oak being bought by the wardens in standing trees, which they selected, felled, and seasoned for this work and for the fine bench-ends at Tintinhull. There are interesting details of the payments to Crosse, large sums for the rood-loft and solario, for 'divers colours to the aler, for trussing of the hyde and the crosse with the Maries, for painting oyle for the crosse, for gold to peynt the angel, for vernaysche, glew and divers colers for the loffte, for the chandeler in the roodlofte, for the images to the rodelofte yn number lxix, for ernest peny to the ymage maker, for ale given to Crosse yn certeyn timis yn his worke to make hym wel welled, to the peynter to peynt oure Lady, to peynt the Crystofer, for amendyng of the vyne in the rodeloft, for gylting of Saynt James and oure Lady,' and so on, and so on, items of the most suggestive interest. And amongst other records of a similar kind there are few more instructive than those of the parish of Stratton, on the borders of Devon and Cornwall. These were at one time in the possession of the father of the present writer, obtained by him when it was easy to acquire such things. They have been partly published by the Society of Antiquaries, and are now safely housed in the British Museum.

As it would be impossible within a limited space even to summarize the character of the decoration of the carved wood-screens throughout the country, our

380

attention may be confined to the West of England, and principally to Devonshire. We may omit, also, the construction of the screens themselves and their purely architectural features. In general the type is characterized by the beauty of the foliage work which covers the cornices, and by the decoration of the fillings of the elaborately coved and richly decorated groinings. In these features we have fair grounds upon which to form an idea of the condition of wood-carving at the close of the Gothic period, apart from that of figure sculpture, of which some few examples still remain also in the screens, in the bench-ends, beams and other portions of the structures of the roofs. But for figure work in wood, either bas-relief or in the round, it can hardly be said that English artists were particularly distinguished, though we may find here and there examples of rare merit, as at Lincoln or Worcester, or in certain misericords. Doubtless the foreigner was frequently called in for any fine work. What there is of native origin in the West of England is generally but a rude copying from Flemish and Italian models or—as in the case of such figures as those of the Dartmouth communion table—from German sources. The Italian style is, naturally, of a late date, and bearing in mind the amount of destruction which has taken place, it is but fair to say that our materials for forming an opinion are but scanty. The recent exhibition by the Society of Antiquaries of English sculpture in alabaster is evidence that in this material at any rate this country could produce work in the round capable of holding its own with any other of the period.

If the rood-screen, with its figures and with the elaborately canopied work of the front of the loft, no longer exists, we may at least be thankful that the beautiful substructure and the delicately carved cornices and traceried vaultings, which at one time supported the gallery flooring, have in a large number of cases throughout the country, and especially in Devonshire, been at last rescued from the neglect and devastation to which the bad taste of the nineteenth century, far more than the Elizabethan regulations, had reduced them. Still, as not one single example exists in its original form, as we have virtually one only (at Atherington) retaining part of the original gallery front and not a solitary instance of a rood, what we have to deal with are fragments only, and these also, in many cases, misplaced and worked up with odds and ends. The screen, as we know it now, is simply a screen and nothing more. It accords with Elizabeth's injunctions, 'a comely partition between the chancel and the church.' In Devon hardly a scrap of woodwork remains earlier than the fifteenth century. The most characteristic we have are of quite the end of that epoch. The reign of Henry VII. inaugurated a new era of peace and prosperity, in Devon especially, inducing a marvellous activity in the building and decoration of churches. There were great tracts of country where the troubles excited by the Wars of the Roses were scarcely felt at all. The middle classes and the farmers were rich and prosperous, and they gave freely of their riches for the needs of the Church. It may be said, then, that Devonshire screens are all much about the same date.

Most of the pre-Reformation examples seem to belong to the time of Henry VII. and later, when Gothic art was merging into that of the Renaissance, passing through the iconoclastic havoc of the change of religion, profiting by a short period of restoration, and being again 'plucked down' and shorn of their principal features during the second half of the sixteenth century. Mr. Bligh Bond, in his monumental work on Rood-screens and Rood-lofts, dates back one Devonshire wood-screen, that at Stoke-in-Teignhead, to the last quarter of the fourteenth century (1380–1390). However this may be—and such an early ascription is more than doubtful—we are more concerned with those which retain their original ribbed vaulting and fanwork filled with Perpendicular tracery, complex feathering, heavily foliated cusps and richly ornamented inter-spaces. These fill a period of, roughly speaking, about a hundred years; that is, from about 1420 to 1520, the time of greatest activity having been probably during the last half of the fifteenth century. The system of groined covings began, perhaps, in the previous one. But although we may seem to be guided from time to time by certain indications—such as shields of arms, devices of families and royal emblems such as the pomegranate of Aragon—these may not always be absolutely reliable, for undoubtedly there was a certain amount of exchange and alteration, as in the case of Atherington. Documentary evidence is almost, if not entirely, wanting.

The carved wood-screens of the West Country are still distinguished by the solidity and massive character which are characteristic of English decorative work. The cornice beams are huge baulks of timber selected with the greatest care from native oaks, hard as iron, as that wood grows to be in the course of centuries. But the screen as now existing bears but a slight pro-portion of the dimensions of the great structure which was originally raised. The order of 1561 (3 Elizabeth) had been but too faithfully obeyed. This was that in every parish church 'the rood-lofts shall be so altered that the upper part of the same with the soller be quite taken down unto the upper parts of the vautes by putting some convenient crest upon the said beam towards the church,' etc. But not even the 'vautes' were spared in numberless cases, and so we find these now replaced by a flat surface with, very often, scraps and odds and ends of the old carvings stuck on in the most meaningless manner.

The admirable foliage work which covers the beams

follows, and of course was often copied from stone sculpture. Instances might be multiplied of that taken from the capitals of pillars and other places : oak and other leaf-work and vines and bunches of grapes. It is analogous to the stone models, but treated with greater breadth on the larger surface of the spread out bressummer. The species of foliage used was in general limited to the flora familiar to the county. The vine, of course, from its symbolism and beauty of form was bound to take the first place, and next the oak. The hedgerow also furnishes its contribution, the tangled 'traveller's joy,' the wild poppy with its seed vessels, the prickly holly, acorns, rows of filberts and the poisonous berries of the deadly nightshade—we should be led too far were we to attempt to follow them all. It is strange, however, to find that the fern is rarely used. The vine-leaf is treated in a variety of ways : with bulbous centres, as are, also, the leaves of the maple, marsh mallow or beech, or, most characteristic of all—stylistic to a degree, in the research for decorative application—lengthened out till we hardly recognize it, and would take it to be, rather, a fern leaf of the hart's tongue variety. The screen at Atherington especially exemplifies this feature ; and we find it prominent also at Pinhoe and Burrington, to name but two others, though it is by no means confined to the county of Devon. The pomegranate figures frequently with its decorative foliage, the fruit either in its ordinary condition or cut open and showing the seeds. It has, of course, its special signification as the badge of Katharine of Aragon, and we find it—at Colyton, for instance—beautifully figured in conjunction with Henry the Eighth's Tudor rose.

Foliage-work is certainly the most striking feature of·the carving on the cornices of these West Country rood-screens. Than wood no material could be more appropriate. The system followed is, of course, derived from the earlier forms in stone which for five hundred years at least had abounded in every country. It was perhaps about the twelfth century that the native flora first began to replace the acanthus and other classical formulæ of Romanesque times. That the earliest inspiration was from Syria can hardly be doubted : not necessarily always a copy, but adapted and perhaps improved upon. Fern leaf and lily forms were tentatively used, and at last the vine, with its symbolism, and the oak in many varieties, predominate. But there is always a process of evolution going on. The vine, for example, as we find it in the thirteenth-century sculptures of Exeter, differs in many ways from the same leaf in the cornices of Atherington or of Kenton. In the latter, and in other similar cases, the treatment is sometimes fanciful to a degree which, while it is not lacking in attractiveness, leaves us in doubt as to the kind of plant which is intended. In the best work we may conclude that the sculptor had his models before him, freshly gathered perhaps from the neighbouring woods and enclosures. He would have sought for those possessing the greatest decorative value, and in their arrangement for his preliminary sketch he would have availed himself principally of the general outlines of their foliage, not troubling to keep with any exactness to the quality of the dentellations or serrated edges and minor details. He would have beaten up, waved, folded or moulded portions of a vine-leaf here and there, and using both back and front would have given special value to the lines of the ribs and veinings, enlarging, diminishing or varying the natural forms as his fancy might suggest. The result would not have been a copy of nature. Such leaves and stalks and fruit may never have existed : at least, they are often difficult to identify. Yet we are deceived into imagining their reality, and in the general effect of luxuriant vegetation we are not concerned to detect anomalies. It is true art which, in such cases, confronts us. At the same time it is of a different nature from the art of the Bestiaries in which we are deluded into imagining forms to be possible which are but creations of phantasy.

A classification of all the flora employed in the West Country and other screens of wood remains yet to be made. A strict research would probably reveal that besides the vine and oak, which are the most prominent, many of the most homely and commonplace plants would be found: for example, the wild orchid, the coltsfoot, trefoil and its varieties, celandine, fig, ivy, hop, chicory, wild parsnip, rosewort, chervil, convolvulus, holly, poppy, blackthorn, the nut tribe, parsley, briony, nightshade, or hemlock; with the leafage of chestnut, beech, elm, sycamore, yew and other trees, and much else besides. We cannot fail to remark the almost total absence of flower, though fruit is used constantly. It is the foliage which appeals: neatly arranged or thickly matted together with the tendrils and branch-work, slender or coarse and gnarled as the case may be, bound together in a mass, or opened up by delicate undercutting—a seemingly orderly arrangement of a wilderness of growing plant-forms.

The subject of the varieties of flower, foliage and fruit on these screens, or bench-ends, and their treatment is one, however, which would carry us to indefinite lengths. The most expert of botanists also would sometimes find himself at fault. Yet so English in character and, in general, so English in execution is this woodwork that it is difficult to confine my remarks to a brief epitome. Few but those who have had lengthened opportunities of studying it on the spot could fully appreciate the charm arising from a close inspection of the infinite variety and extraordinary richness of these interminable lengths of chiselled surfaces, running in ribband-like bands placed one over the other across the top of the dividing screen of the mediæval sanctuary; the beauty of the window tracery beneath, the mouldings and canopy work, the elegance of ogee curves and crocketed arches, the vinework trailing its lengths along, with here and there bunches of its fruit, here and there birds with their symbolism; the gnarled and twisted stems curling in and out of the leaf-work, or strained as it were into the semblance of binding cords; the open-worked and often deeply undercut branches and tendrils; the creeping and climbing hedge plants interspersed with wild rose or eglantine, with poppy-pods or clusters of nuts, even with small bouquets of wild flowers, and the hand grasping them as at Bridford; the interlaced and Celtic knots, sometimes of unusual design and of excellent simplicity, such as we find in the fillets round the doorways; the crestings of strawberry leaf, or of a series of five-lobed flowers alternately upright or reversed; the excellent freedom of the sharply chiselled outlines and the sure hand of the carver working, as is evident, straight from the head and following no mechanical rule; the admirable effect of the play of light and shade; the evidence of the consummate understanding by the designer of his work as a whole—all this and more, for justice to be done to it, would require the systematic visitation of church after church, and, for the reader, ample space for description and the most generous amount of illustration.[1]

---

[1] A very large number of plates would be necessary to illustrate the remarks upon the foliage character of screens in their present condition. It is impracticable to fulfil this requirement, on account of so many calls for illustration in other divisions of the subject. It is to be understood, therefore, that the descriptions given above do not apply to the cornices alone, but to that which is to be found also in the groinings, spandrels and window-traceries, in the filleting of doorways, on the panellings, in the pulpit work, and incidentally in

Amongst this wealth of fruit and foliage work it is remarkable that animal and bird life holds so small a place. Except here and there a bird or two pecking at the grapes, there is nothing. The fauna of Devon was fairly profuse. Yet, though their use as imagery also was well known, we find no fox, no badger, wild cat, otter, marten, stoat or other smaller inhabitant of woods; no wild cattle or swine, no eagle, hawk or heron; not even the ordinary denizens of the poultry-yard. The *Physiologus*, the Book of Beasts, or Bestiary, is absent. Yet in these same churches we have only to go to the misericords and bench-ends to find it in conjunction with this same foliage work. We cannot tell the influences which contributed to form the style of decoration which is so fully exemplified in these screens. The investigation of its origin and evolution still remains to be done. The ornamentation has, of course, followed from stone sculpture, but in origin it is derived from the Far East and filtered through Byzantine adaptations. Bishop Bruere, of Exeter, in the thirteenth century, travelled and resided many years in Eastern countries, and the stall work of Exeter may be due to him. Many a traveller, too, brought home his recollections of such works as the throne of Maximian

the borderings of the bench-ends. A certain selection of members from the cornices has been arranged on Plates LVII., LVIII., LIX., but it has to be admitted that this is by no means representative of the great diversity of this kind of ornament which prevails in Devon and elsewhere. We have also to consider the screens not only as they are now, but as they were in Catholic times. Many difficulties presented themselves in deciding upon any one general view. Such fine examples as those of Atherington, Lapford, Kenton, Kenn, High Ham, Fitzhead, and several others had strong claims, of one sort or another, for consideration, but, on the other hand, would have demanded more lengthy notices, and some involve questions of foreign influence, of transitional and mixed styles, and of pure Renaissance. It was therefore thought better to fall back upon portions of the screens of Banwell, in Somersetshire, of Chawleigh, and of East Portlemouth, which illustrate, to some extent, the cornice mouldings, vaultings with their fillings and bosses, window-traceries, crestings, and mutilations which are the most usual features of West Country screens as they now appear.

PLATE LVI

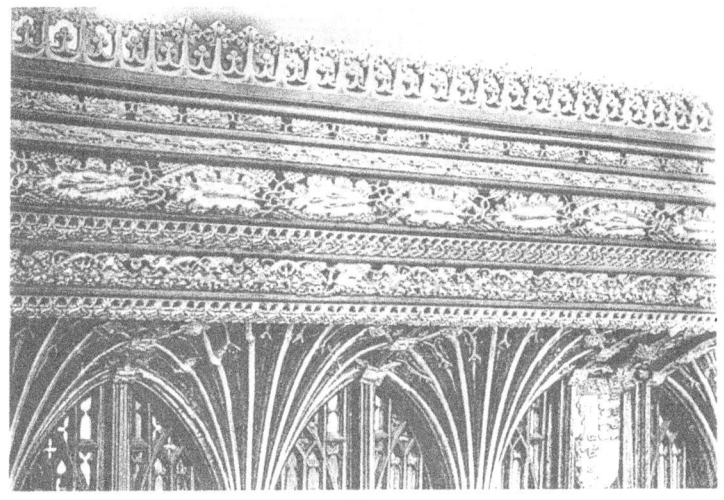

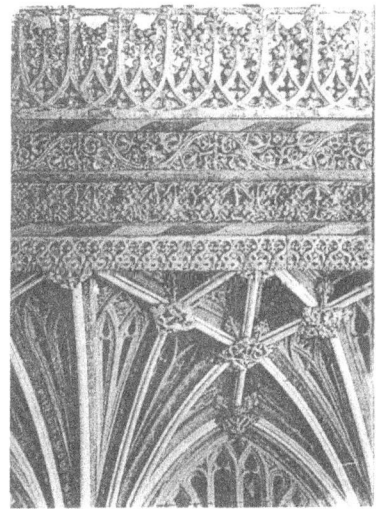

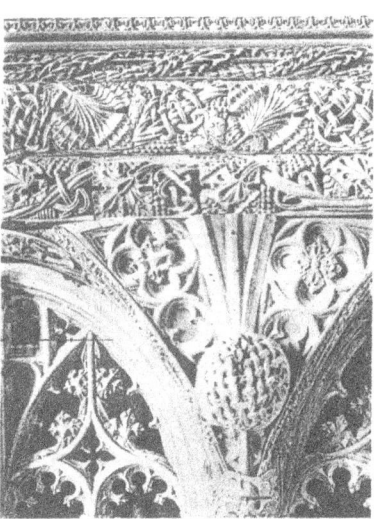

PARTS OF CHANCEL SCREENS
1. BANWELL. 2. CHAWLEIGH. 3. PORTLEMOUTH
PAGE 388

at Ravenna, the ornament of which is derived from Syria. Again, the crusader was always eager to take impressions of what he saw in the holy cities of Syria. Artists and artisans in their train no doubt returned home laden with models for sculptural ornament.

The prevailing system of the East could not have failed to make a deep impression, and there was ample material from which to elaborate any amount of fanciful imagery, adding their own national feeling. One does not forget, of course, that the earliest of our screens is some two hundred years later than Bruere's time, but the earliest existing is certainly not the first of its type. In these ages of Gothic art the root principle of decoration everywhere, upon capital and frieze, was this foliage interlacement, mingled with animal forms which Byzantine art had derived from Persia. The Celtic influence, which some see in these screens, is farther to seek. We find, it is true, the Celtic knot introduced occasionally, but the system and feeling are different. There is, however, no space here to follow out a question upon which but faint glimmerings of light are apparent. Yet a hint may be allowed at the strange relationship which in form and in decoration these cornices or bressummers present with such sculptures as those on the ruined edifices of Mschatta at Makam Ali on the Euphrates. The whole spirit is here the same: vast surfaces of convex and concave members covered with a similar treatment of vines and vegetation. These ruins of the fourth or fifth century lie in the land of Jordan, about 120 miles south of Damascus. For a full account the reader must be referred to the erudite article, amply illustrated, by Professor Strzygowski in the *Jahrbuch der Königlich Preuszischen Kunstsammlungen*, vol. xxv., 1904.

More puzzling than questions of style is that of

the sculptors by whom these works were executed. Within so limited a period as the hundred years or so embraced by these screens the similarity of style and design is so great that it must have been due to some systematic arrangement. In all probability the start was given from the monasteries. Possibly Torre and Tavistock and other abbeys sent out bands of monastic workmen. That would have been in accordance with their rule. Even to-day the monks of Buckfast are rebuilding with their own hands, on the old foundations, their abbey church on the banks of the Dart, and executing the whole of the carving in wood and stone. Some carved work, no doubt, would have been furnished by the guilds of the larger cities, and, as in the case of many bench-ends, may have been the work of local carvers in the parish itself. In those days the instinct for art had penetrated into the smallest villages. A certain type of figures, such as the angels common as corbel-heads and on the hammer-beams of roofs, was evidently turned out commercially in quantities; and there are many more of a ruder style which are village work copied from this commercial type, or from drawings or models, which, in one way or another, were at the disposal of the local carver.

Who, then, did this Western work? It is sometimes assumed that foreigners were called in, that the work was ordered from provincial centres such as Exeter—even from London—or executed by gangs of peripatetic craftsmen. All this may have been the case under varying circumstances of time and place. Then, again, no doubt such monasteries as Tavistock or Buckfast or Torre superintended or at least furnished plans and sketches. Nothing is more likely also than that monks were sent to work in the villages. At the present day there are extensive wood-carving establishments at Exeter which turn out screen and figure work of excellent quality in considerable quantities,

PLATE LVII

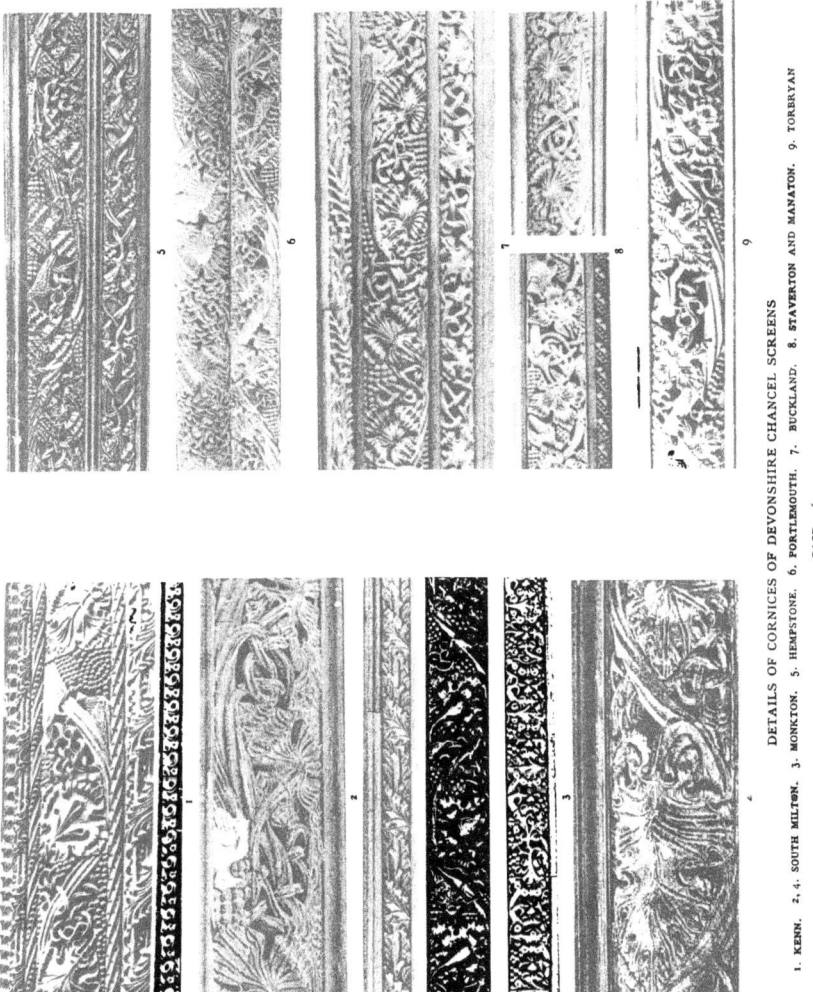

DETAILS OF CORNICES OF DEVONSHIRE CHANCEL SCREENS

1. KENN.   2, 4. SOUTH MILTON.   3. MONKTON.   5. HEMPSTONE.   6. PORTLEMOUTH.   7. BUCKLAND.   8. STAVERTON AND MANATON.   9. TORBRYAN

PAGE 396

sending it far and wide, even to the churches of the Australian colonies. Not a little also comes from Germany and from such places as Ober-Ammergau. What is not found now, but what was common in mediæval times, is the collaboration of the village craftsman. To him we doubtless owe many bench-ends, many angel figures in roofs, many misericords, perhaps even the beautiful canopies of honour over the roods, as at Lapford. Why not, also, much of such work as the foliaged cornices of the screens? A case in point is that of Crosse, the master carpenter of Yatton. If we may take it that he himself was the sculptor, probably such a one was to be found also in many villages. Intercommunication with larger towns was not such a simple matter in those days.

Although, then, we have little or no direct information, and the churchwardens' accounts—such of them as we have of the periods in question—are provokingly silent on the matter, nothing would have been more natural than that a parish priest and his parishioners should have done much of the carving. It is so even in our own day. The late Rev. J. L. Fulford of Exeter was a good amateur carver, as his son, the recently deceased vicar of Hennock, relates in a memoir of his father, and much work in Woodbury Church—bench-ends and poppy-heads—was done by him. So also in many other places, as at Ilfracombe, bosses of roofs and screen-work have been copied and restored from the ancient work by ladies and others of the parish.

The question of the employment of foreign workmen is one that in the absence of direct evidence presents many difficulties. Undoubtedly Flemish, German and Italian artists were at work in England. In the case of wood-carving we shall find the style of the last named especially abundant in the decoration of churches—such as King's College chapel —and in the staircases, ceilings and panellings of the great country-houses in the sixteenth and seventeenth centuries. On Devonshire screens and bench-ends much also is copied and adapted from Italian panels and doors in wood which are still existent. But when we come to particular cases of pre-Reformation screen-work opinions will differ. It is commonly held that that of Colebrook, Coleridge, Brushford, Kenton and other places is, in part at least, by foreign hands. But however much the style may point that way, however great may be the similarity to be found in the often adduced instance of the peculiar flamboyant style of the screen of Saint-Fiacre-le-Faouet in Brittany, the Flemish inspiration of Kenton or the Italian Renaissance character of the later screens, we need not be compelled to accept the inference. Even should it be suggestive, the great bulk of the design in general and the character of the tracery are English.

The glorious screen at Atherington—unique in the possession of its original gallery front—that at Lapford, and some others of mixed Gothic and Renaissance character, are usually attributed to Italian or other foreign workmen. Against this it may be said that the English carvers followed the universal taste and spirit of the time, and had no hesitation in copying to the best of their ability. At Atherington English mannerism is, to me, apparent. English are the large angels on the standards ; and, from the same chisel, English are the *putti* in the fillings of the vaultings. There is a lack of refinement and of Italian *cachet*, and creditable as they may be, I doubt that an Italian critic would accept them. The fine Renaissance bench-ends of Lapford have the solid character of English work. At the same time there are others— for example, the panelling at Warkleigh—which may call for a different judgment. So also in the case of bench-ends such as those in the church of Ashcombe, hidden away among the hills of the Teign valley.

However well supplied with models, these are too good for an untrained village worker. Reminding one of the spirit of the Japanese netsukes in their play of fancy, in the winged demons and symbolical imagery, and in the boldness and precision of the deep-cut carving, they are the work of a cultivated and learned man, as well as of an accomplished craftsman.

As a rule the village artist had little or no didactic intentions. When we find the appearance of these in late times they had probably lost their force, and were used, as we use such things to-day, without knowing precisely why we do so. Most likely a good deal of the earlier screen-work was not only directed from, but actually carried out by, carvers supplied by the monasteries, who during their stay in the villages would have instructed the local talent. Later on, when the number of schools and guilds increased, these would have been well supplied with French and Flemish and Italian pattern-books and models. And even the work of foreigners permanently settled in the country and assimilating their tastes to ours is rightly qualified as English, as in the cases of the silversmiths Lamerie, Kandler or Morel-Ladeuil, of the potter Solon, or of our naturalized English painters. Nor can we leave out of account the intimate relationships between our own and foreign monasteries of the same order and the interchange of their inmates.

It is often the case that a screen is reputed to have come from some local monastery at the dissolution. For example, the Brushford (Somerset) screen is said to have been carved by the monks of Barlinch for their priory church. The custom also was very general of ordering a new screen to be exactly copied from an already existing one, and this may account for a good deal of the family resemblance. In the highly interesting account-book of the High Cross

Wardens of the parish of Stratton we find an in-
denture of agreement in the year 1531 for the making
of a new rood-loft 'after the form and fashion in
everything as the rood-loft of St. Kew, with a crucifix,
with a Mary and John, and all other workmanship
after the fashion of Liskeard church'; and there are
other details, such as the provision of two images
and tabernacles, 'the one to be of Saint Armele, the
other of the Visitation of our blessed Lady.' And
there are sums of money paid to 'John Daw the
Kerver.' We note also the extreme care taken in the
choice of timber, which was all to be substantially
seasoned, and of one manner of drying. Seven years
was allowed for the completion of the work, and the
price to be xlvi^s· viii^d· the foot. In 1539 'the sold the
olde story of the old rood-loft. for vii^s· vi^d·' In 1549
there is an entry of the 'Taking down the rode and
the pagentes.' But on the 10th June the rebellion
broke out, so the churchwardens set them up again.
In 1572, alas, amongst other entries of destructions,
we have 'rec^d· of Master marrys for woden angells
iiii^d·,' and the next year the rode and loft are finally
got rid of. Extracts from other churchwardens'
accounts could be referred to, if space permitted, from
which the fortunes of the rood-screens in various parts
of the country, couched in quaint and, it must be said,
contemptuous language, might be gathered.

The striking character of English work is its
homeliness and sincerity. Throughout these mediæval
times the relationship was intimate between the artist
and the most humble of the public in whose interests
he worked. Art was the property of ordinary folk as
well as of the learned, and it was addressed in the
main to, or intended for the instruction of, those who
could read in no other way. The inhabitant of the
smallest village acquired the instinct of a refined
taste from his earliest years, and became in fact a

competent critic of the value of that of which he was called upon to bear his share of the organization and of the cost. The language which it spoke was not one appealing, as afterwards, to a privileged few, but to all. It was a necessity of existence, innate in every one, requiring for the public in general no teacher, no art schools, no museums, no pressure from a paternal government. In the case of the village artist himself, however naïve his ideas may have been, however crude his skill, there remains always the charm which the evidence of a loyal effort to overcome difficulties and the individuality of the worker cannot fail to produce. They are qualities which are rare, indeed, to find in our village life to-day. Mr. William Allingham, in his diary (published in 1908), forcibly asks, 'Where did the good taste and instinctive righteousness in former days come from, and whither has it fled?'

An examination of these screens opens up many questions of interest relating to the state of religious feeling in England immediately previous to and concurrent with the Reformation. Granted that much figure and painted work was destroyed, what remains shows a gradually increasing disuse of religious symbolism and devotional suggestion; a preference for the pagan sentiment of the Renaissance; a tendency to the personal glorification of individuals, such as the frequent use of shields of arms and royal emblems. There is but a last lingering trace of a desire to inspire devotion by figures of holy personages, such as the prophets (if such they be, and not divines of the new creed), in the Gothic but otherwise totally unreligious screen at Lustleigh. It is small wonder, indeed, that when art was divorced from the people in the sensuous and costly cult of the Renaissance, devotion went with it, and the people themselves lost their sense of refinement and any practice of art itself.

WOOD SCULPTURE

It would be a pleasant task to describe in detail the finer work of such noble specimens of wood-carving as the screens of Atherington, of Kenton, Lapford, Chulmleigh, Combe-in-Teignhead, Hartland, Holbeton, Kentisbeare, Plymtree and many more in Devon and Cornwall; to turn to Somerset with Banwell, High Ham or Fitzhead, or to go to Kent, to Norfolk and the East Coast, and to Wales especially, which presents so many points of interest, but a volume of the size of the present one would hardly suffice, and illustrations also would require to be plentiful. For much interesting information in detail, and for profuse illustration, the reader may be referred to the admirable works lately published by Mr. Francis Bond and Mr. Bligh Bond (see Bibliography).

In the condition in which we now find these screens, often shorn of their principal features, or disfigured by restorations, it is true that a certain amount of imagination is required to realize their appearance as they once existed. But if we should take any separate portion, a whole range of foliate cornice or a single specimen of fan-traceried vaulting, and inquire into the value of the carving and how far the carver fulfilled the best principles of his craft, we should find that he knew how to avoid the great fault of modern times and of some of the restorers of these screens. It is the fault to which Ruskin so forcibly alludes when he says: ' It is not coarse cutting, it is not blunt cutting which is bad: but it is *cold* cutting—the look of equal trouble everywhere, the smooth diffused tranquillity of heartless pains, the regularity of a plough in a level field. If completeness is thought to be vested in polish and to be attainable by help of sandpaper, we may as well give the work to the engine lathe at once. But right finish is simply the full rendering of a well-intended and vivid impression, and it is oftener got by rough than fine handling.' In these flowing masses of vegetable life, leaf and ten-

PLATE LVIII

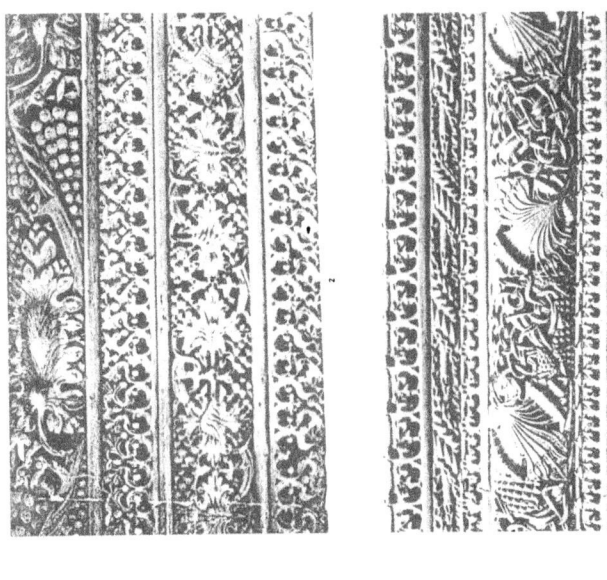

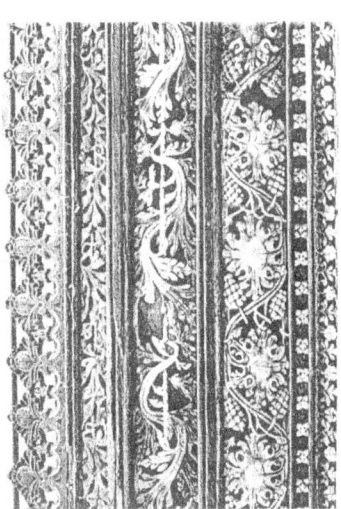

DETAILS OF CORNICES OF WEST COUNTRY CHANCEL SCREENS
1. ATHERINGTON. 2. PINHOE. 3. HIGH HAM. 4. DARTMOUTH
PAGE 398

dril contending for the mastery of growth, almost as the wild vine or clinging hopbine do amid the tangle of the lofty Devonshire hedge, the sculptor—to borrow once more from Ruskin—'paints with his chisel, puts power with his touches into the form. They are touches of light and shadow : they raise a ridge or sink a hollow to get a line of light or a spot of darkness.'

Characteristic, above all, in these masses of foliage which meet the eye in the cornices of every Devon screen are the grace and elegance of the vine work ; not symmetrical with leaves of identical form and bunches of fruit as we meet with elsewhere, but flourishing wild and free. Here, and in the rest of the tangled foliage, there is the spontaneous outcome of the carver's thoughts as he worked perhaps with no pattern before him. Here is originality, nothing stolen from great masters of engraving and etching. The impulse is from nature, but it is followed freely, every plant adapted to suit the purpose, almost regardless of absolute fidelity to truth of form, more careful to attract by the beauty of the long-rolling curves of the festoons of leafage contrasting with one another, curve competing with curve as they twine around the twisted ropes, or rough formed tendrils, which pass along from end to end ; careful too, that strength may not be sacrificed by undue undercutting or projections. And then, again, how true to the Gothic spirit are the lines of the traceried fenestrages ; that spirit itself derived, it has been said, from the suggestion of some leafy avenue, arches of branches and foliage meeting overhead, and what more appropriate material could we find to illustrate it !

Again carrying our thoughts back to the time when these screens were in the pride of their beauty, if we wish to realize the full intentions of their creators, we have to imagine them not with an aspect of the newly chiselled oak, not even with the mellow tone which age and use gives to wood, but brilliant with colour and gilding, not an inch of the surfaces left plain. In some cases the restorer has tried his hand at renewing this coloration also. But either because we are not in sympathy with mediæval feeling, or from want of skill, these attempts have in few cases been a success. The art is lost. In modern hands the results are glaring, tawdry, vulgar and shining with varnish. There is an entire absence of consideration for lights and shades, and for the atmosphere and conditions in which the work now finds itself. Doubtless those who made these screens were as well able as ourselves to appreciate the beauty and harmony of wood left in its original purity, toned down, perhaps, or waiting for the additional concord which time would supply. However this may be, there can be little question concerning the taste which will prefer Kenton, or Atherington, to the garishness of Bovey Tracey or Bradninch. Where the carver's work is missing, from destructions, we may be able to replace it by copying that which exists ; but the painter's is no longer before us : that is to say, in the spirit of the whole conception. On the other hand, the painting and gilding on the new screen at Littleham, near Bideford, has been executed in a manner which is probably much more in harmony with the mediæval system than we find in the restorations elsewhere.

Remains of colour and gilding are fairly frequent, and in some cases, as at Bridford, to a considerable extent. The general question of the polychromatic decoration of sculpture has already received attention here at considerable length and need not be repeated. The medium used for the screen - work is somewhat uncertain. Roughly speaking, it was a thin spirit, or the colour was ground in water with size, white of egg or other colloid : oil was seldom, if ever, used in the earlier mediæval times. Whatever the medium, it imparted a delicate bloom and did not conceal entirely the texture of the wood, even in the twists of red and white, black, or green and white, on the beads and columns. The great difference between the old colouring and the modern restoration shows that the one was done by an artist, the other in the spirit of the house-painter. In the earlier times we may remember that there were artists who could design and paint such admirable panels as those of Hennock. These are English work, the delicately drawn outlines having the sweep and decision of single stroke drawing. Doubtless the screen painters were equally able and refined. The artist kept in mind his subordination to, and dependence on, his surroundings in the general architectural scheme of the building, and the play of light and shade in his carved work. His foliage and fruit were not in one uniform stage of growth, and his colour of one uniform tone from one end to the other. His grapes are ripening or ripe, his leaves in summer bloom, or autumn decay, and, however wild and luxuriant the masses of foliage may be, the scheme is absolutely subordinate to the breadth of the masses of light and shade. The chisel and the brush worked together, and the wielder of both was careful not to overcharge the ornamentation. In this lies the true test of his work. In good work neither can be overdone. Remarks of this kind apply, of course, only to the best examples. It cannot be asserted that the merit is equal everywhere. Sometimes we find in the cornices—for example, at Bradninch—a monotonous regularity and repetition of the same motive: turned out by the yard, as it were, with the 'cold cutting' which has been quoted. And more than one contract stipulates, as in the Stratton accounts, the price per foot run. At Bovey Tracey the bunches of vine leaves and grapes on the cornices are too regularly repeated at intervals. We are not bound to admire everything because it is old.

The examination of these carvings could be pursued

to a length of which the plan of this book will not permit. In point of numbers alone the wood-screens since the unearthing process of the last twenty-five years or so, go far beyond what most people would imagine. In Devon, Messrs. Bond and Camms' work, the latest authority on the subject, includes no less than a hundred and forty in various states of original condition and restoration, and, besides fragments, a list of seventy-eight removed or destroyed during the last century. In Somersetshire upwards of seventy rood and parclose screens are noted, and throughout England and Wales the number is correspondingly large.

It is not without considerable reluctance that one like the present writer, whose acquaintance with the West Country and its churches has been lifelong, is compelled to treat the subject but superficially. There are few, indeed, familiar with Devonshire to whom the name alone does not recall pleasant memories of its vales and combes, its leafy high-hedged lanes, its ruddy soil and green-covered cliffs, contrasting with the peaceful blue of the calm estuaries, the valleys of Teign and Tamar and of Dart, the rich and flourishing farms and orchards, or the stretches of desolate moors so picturesquely broken by carn and crag and coloured heather. Apart from all this are the numberless shrines which hold the woodwork with which, however summarily, we have been occupied. In Devon and Cornwall, on whatever eminence we may chance to stand, we shall have in view hardly ever less than four or five typical churches with the long low roofs of the aisles and the stately pinnacled towers. Some, as at Kenton, are almost cathedral-like in dimensions and in remains of former magnificence. Some, again, of unaccountable spaciousness are to be found in the quietest of secluded villages, difficult of access, or, as at remote Morwenstow, where the builders could never have expected its solitudes to have tempted men to form a population equal

400

PLATE LIX

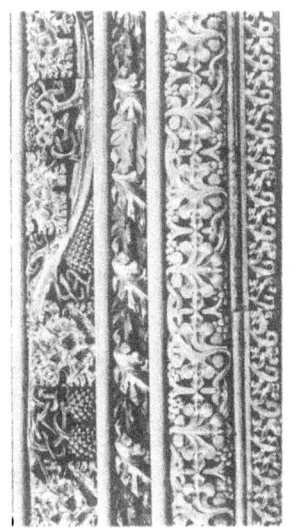

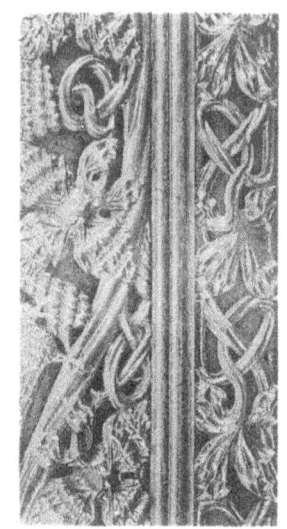

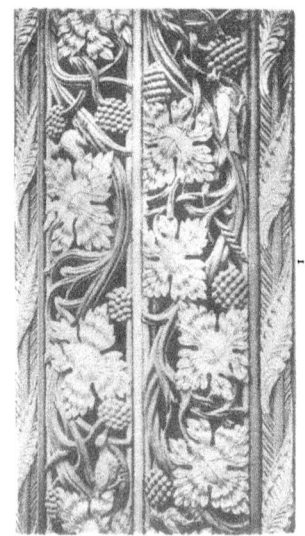

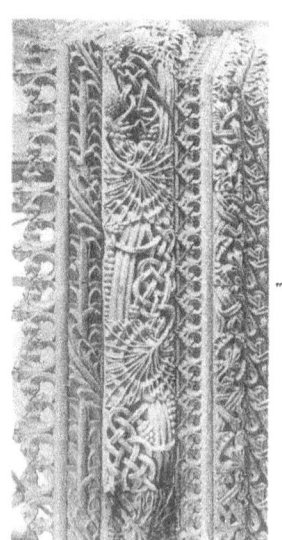

to the capacity of its church. Yet, as Hawker, the poet-vicar, loved to think, 'our forefathers purposely placed their churches far off in order that there might be a church path to be trodden as the journey of the worship day, a road of quiet thought.' Hardly one of these churches but is now adorned by specimens of English wood-carving. And if, when we look at the best examples we can imagine them as they were when doubtless a village festival celebrated their completion, I do not hesitate to say that we have as much reason to be proud of them as the Frenchman has of Amiens or the German of Ulm. Certainly, in no other land can such a profusion of wood-carving be found in village churches as in those of the two counties alone of Devon and Somerset.

CONCLUSION

IN the endeavour which has been made in the fore-going pages to follow a very comprehensive subject, our attention has been confined, for the most part, to the three centuries during which Gothic art may be said to have arisen, to have shaken off the torpor and subjection to hieratic prescriptions under which all forms of art had long suffered, to have attained its highest development, to have been influenced by and to have finally succumbed to the complete change of system that—speaking generally and without reference to its origins—we are accustomed to term the Renaissance. The spirit of Gothic, which although subordinate to religion had still worked in liberty with regard to details, died out and became replaced by a more regulated system based on forms and traditions derived from the classical antiquities of Greece and Rome. The superabundance of material is so great, that even while limiting our attention to the Western world it has been necessary to draw the line somewhere, and it is at this point—that is to say, at the period when the difference of styles was becoming definitely and universally marked—that a pause, at least, has been made. But much more remains to be noticed of the decorative and sculptural application of wood from this time to our own day.

From at least the middle of the fifteenth century the new system had imposed itself on sculpture in wood, on statuary and small figure work, and on the decoration of furniture no less than on great sculpture in marble or bronze, on goldsmiths' work, or on architecture.

402

CONCLUSION

Later on the arts became less and less the property of the people generally, who had until then shared them in common with the learned and wealthy. Religious changes caused a decline in the spirit of devotion, with the result that the lower orders lost their direct interest in the decoration of their churches, and, with it, their good taste and capability of expressing it. It was the beginning of an age of elegance, of refinement and of luxury. Courts and princes vied with each other in the patronage of the arts, led by Italy, which at the height of her prosperity under such princes as the Sforza, the d'Este, Lorenzo the Magnificent, or Leo x., sent out in all directions to discover the treasures of antiquity for the inspiration of the artists in their service.

Naturally there was a period of transition before Gothic feeling and ideas gave way completely to the new system. Nor must we forget also that the revival or Renaissance was no suddenly completed revolution, and that mediæval and classical art are logically and necessarily more nearly related than they may seem to be. It is not surprising that for a time the two went side by side. Instances could be multiplied in the figure and decorative sculpture in wood of every country, and it is not always easy to qualify the style which resulted from the mixture. Even so late as the first quarter of the sixteenth century the doors of the cathedral of Aix (of which excellent reproductions may be seen in the gallery of casts of the Kensington Museum) are evidences that the older feeling died hard. For however admirable, taken collectively, these sculptures may be, neither the canopies nor the ogee arches nor the floral borders can make them Gothic. In essentials, notwithstanding the motives borrowed from the earlier style, they are purely classical, even to the costumes of the prophets. So is it again with the charming furniture and other decorative carving in

403

walnut of the Château of Gaillon. This, entirely the work of French sculptors, despite the presence of, and possible direction by, Italian artists, is a mixture, or rather arrangement, of Renaissance and Gothic styles. The panellings are magnificent, with their semi-Gothic window - traceries, their semi - Renaissance pilasters covered with arabesques, their pointed arches enriched to overloading with cupids, vases and birds in full relief.

These two examples have been selected, because, although the same story of the invasion of the Italian Renaissance may everywhere be read, it was to be found exemplified in the highest degree in France, while, at the same time, there was no slavish following, but, on the contrary, a national independent movement.

In Italy the consideration of the choir and stall work which adorn innumerable religious edifices would open up so extended a subject, not only in Gothic, but also in Transition and in full Renaissance times, that sufficient space could not be devoted to it. Nor could it be entirely dissociated from the mass of marquetry work with which some of the greatest names are connected. We should find the latter not only in the veneered mosaic style of various coloured woods exhibiting landscapes, still-life, architecture, and figures to which the term *tarsia* is more properly applied, but also in the use of the symmetrically arranged geometrical inlays called *certosina*. This marquetry is intimately connected with the sculptured work, and it would be difficult to consider the one without the other. Had it been otherwise we should have noticed the entirely Gothic choir executed at Siena by Domenico di Niccolà in 1415, and many more either still purely Gothic or mixed with the newer style. For similar reasons of want of space it has been necessary to pass by such important examples of wood sculpture, and such prominent names, as the *cassoni*, candelabra, and the host

CONCLUSION

of other decorative furniture of a Baccio d'Agnolo or
of a Giovanni Barili, carver of the great doors of the
stanze of the Vatican. The marriage *cassoni* and other
carved chests alone furnish material for a very extended
notice. They were usually of walnut, of sarcophagus
form, the panels filled with mythological and historical
subjects deeply carved, relieved, or even completely
covered, with gilding, supported on claw feet, and often
bearing caryatid figures in the round at the angles.
Even the most ordinary furniture, such as chairs, was
richly carved with a similar character of figure work,
and amongst such things few are more striking than
the bellows, usually of walnut, of which, no less than
other great museums, our own at Kensington possesses
a rich collection.

In France, until well into the sixteenth century,
wood-carving continued faithful to Gothic traditions
and methods. Burgundy had been annexed to France
in the last quarter of the preceding century, and it is to
the influence of that school that we owe later on the
richest and most charming creations of the sculptors
of the monumental pieces of furniture. Mention has
already been made of Michel Colombe and the activity
with which wood sculpture was practised in Touraine
and all down the banks of the Loire. Here also
flourished later on Hugues Sambin, the great *menuisier*
of Dijon.

Although the art of the wood-carver of the sixteenth
century in France, and indeed in every other country,
has primarily to be considered as furniture, this does
not exclude ample material in the figure and other
decorative work which was so lavishly applied to it,
and would justify our regarding it from the same point
of view as in the earlier periods. When Gothic ideas
were dying or had died out, France, incited from Italy,
fell in with the idea of returning to the study of the
antique ; yet, though borrowing the Italian new methods,

405

she adapted them in her own way, impressing them with the unmistakable cachet of her own genius. The reign of François i. was characterized by immense luxury and display, not only in the architecture of the numerous palaces and châteaux, but in the furniture and sculptured woodwork which .adorned them. Till then the huchers and imagiers had kept in general to Gothic methods and traditions. Now, or at least in the reign of his son Henri ii., they are influenced by, and almost exclusively draw their models from, quite another class of artists. The inspiration is still architectural, but from civil instead of ecclesiastical precedents. They follow the designs prepared by architects, draughtsmen, and engravers of ornament, and we should find amongst the authors of these designs such illustrious names as the Burgundian Hugues Sambin, the Parisian Du Cerceau, Philibert de l'Orme, Bachelier of Toulouse, Pierre Lescot, Jean Bullant, Jean Goujon, and Germain Pilon.

In the sixteenth century the art of the wood-carver passes mainly into the domain of domestic furniture, applied to cabinets, tables, chairs, bedsteads, staircases, fireplaces, panellings, ceilings and a host of minor things, although at the same time much ecclesiastical ornament, such as rood-screens and choir-work, still calls for attention. It is the age of the great massive armoire or cabinet, the buffet and the huge imposing bedsteads decorated with the utmost profusion of carved figures and panels in high and low relief. The inspiration is still always from architecture, imitative of its general lines and classical entablatures, for decorative rather than for constructive reasons. Everywhere apparent are the designs of the great draughtsmen just mentioned: everywhere is the same prevailing taste for an astounding mixture of triumphs, pilasters, colonnettes, caryatid figures, festoons, scrolls, broken pediments, garlands, frets, and mouldings of all kinds, masks, strapwork, balusters, urns, arabesques, sirens, fauns, satyrs, griffins, nymphs and cupids, sphinxes, dolphins—a whole world of real and imaginary beings : overloaded perhaps, yet supremely elegant. How far the illustrious names of Sambin, to whom are attributed the great doors of the Palais de Justice at Dijon, or of Jean Goujon, for the doors of Saint Maclou, may be identified as the actual sculptors may be uncertain, but the influence of their designs is apparent. Casts of both works are in the Kensington Museum.

Although nothing would be more difficult—it might even be said hopeless—than an attempt to classify the schools of wood-carving in France of the fifteenth and sixteenth centuries, and to assign with certainty this or that piece to one or the other of them, yet we are able to connect them with certain names, and, in some cases, with certain styles. As a general rule oak is characteristic of the north, and hardly goes farther south than Burgundy, south of which region walnut prevails. Of the schools of Normandy, Brittany and the north generally we have the stalls of Amiens, the doors of the cathedrals of Beauvais and of Saint Maclou. The Ile de France, Touraine and the banks of the Loire are of the school of Philibert de l'Orme, of Pierre Lescot, of Jean Goujon, of Du Cerceau and of Germain Pilon. With Sambin we connect the Burgundian and Lyonese regions, and the neighbouring Dauphiny. At Toulouse Bachelier seems to have exercised the same influence as Sambin in Burgundy. Of this school is the choir of Auch. The wood sculpture of Auvergne is especially remarkable. If France has been able to keep for her own great museums the greater proportion of the splendid examples of wood sculpture which her genius produced in the sixteenth century, and if we possess comparatively little indeed at South Kensington or even in the Wallace Museum, we may be grateful that we have, in the Salting and Vaughan bequests, those splendid panels in walnut and pearwood which illustrate the school of Auvergne. Nothing could exceed the elegance and charm in treatment of these characteristic examples of the Renaissance art of the period of François I.: the busts of men and women issuing in three-quarter high relief from the circular medallions among delicate arabesques of leaf scroll work. Of the style of Philibert de l'Orme we happily possess also at Kensington a sufficiently characteristic example in such a cabinet as the one (No. 2573), completely covered with arabesques, sphinxes, caryatid figures, trophies of arms, Corinthian pilasters, masks and other ornament; and of the art, or influence, of Sambin, the walnut cabinet dated 1580 at one time in the Seillières collection. There is also, from the Soulages collection, a fine *dressoir* attributed to Bachelier, but this is somewhat later than his time.

We need not follow the effect of the Renaissance in other countries. The art of the sixteenth century was cosmopolitan, international. The models were the same everywhere. There was practically but one system, the subjection to the victorious Italian invasion, more or less refined in appreciation according to each nation's taste and genius.

In France from the seventeenth century there were no longer distinctive schools. The provinces were merged in that of Paris. Sculpturesque wood-carving declined: it was the age of marquetry and of dainty boudoir furniture enriched by the art of the bronze founder and chaser. Boulle, Gouthière, Riesener, David Roentgen and their contemporaries reign supreme. Without proposing the least in the world to enter into details which could have no place in such a summary as the present one, the reader may be reminded of a few names of other decorators who, with those just named, illustrate the history of sculpture in wood, as applied to furniture, from the beginning of the seventeenth to well on into the eighteenth century. Chief amongst them, and one of the earliest, was Charles le Brun, the director of a whole army of workers for the court of Louis XIV. under the protection of Cardinal Mazarin. In his employ, Jean Bérain, Jean le Pautre, Girardon, Jean Marot and his son Daniel are all names connected in one way or another with our subject. Daniel Marot is of especial interest to us. Exiled into Holland he was the means of disseminating the French style in our own country, where he died, and the indebtedness to him both of Grinling Gibbons and of Chippendale could not be overlooked. One more name amongst those who worked under le Brun must not be forgotten. This is the Italian Philippe Caffieri, who was especially distinguished as a wood sculptor. The fine doors of the great staircase at Versailles are his work.

Wood sculpture in England of the late fifteenth, of the sixteenth and of the seventeenth centuries possesses in its domestic character features of very strong national interest. Probably in no other country is there still existing, outside museums, such a wealth of carved woodwork as is to be found in the almost countless great country-houses throughout the land, where it serves the same purposes of ornament and usefulness, and is in many cases in the possession of the same historic families as in the days when it was erected or made. Not only is it to these great houses that we have to look for our treasures in wood in the shape of cabinets and decorative furniture of other countries, but it is in them that still exist, *in situ*, the massive carved staircases, doorways, chimney-pieces, panellings of rooms, mirror and picture frames, imposing bedsteads, tables, chairs and a host of other furniture of a period of at least two hundred years, during which the use of wood for decoration was so general. Nor should our interest be confined to these two hundred years only.

WOOD SCULPTURE

In mediæval times dense forests of oak abounded throughout the country, and afforded the most easily-worked material for the construction of whole cities. Houses were framed together, necessitating the use of vast posts or gigantic squared pillars—almost trees— such as we find in many a half-timbered church tower. The stories projected one over another, and this method of using large surfaces of exposed wood afforded considerable scope for carved work in the overhanging fronts, gable-ends, piers or corner posts, barge-boards, and hooded doorways. All this was enriched with delicate window tracery, niches filled with sculptured images, hammer-beams and brackets, corbels and pendentives carved, painted, and gilded. The later examples of the half-timbered style that are to be found most commonly perhaps in Yorkshire, Cheshire, Derbyshire, Worcestershire, Shropshire, and Suffolk are still evidence of every conceivable diversity of architectural ornament and small figure sculpture. In some cases they show the preservation to a late period of Gothic types and feeling. Others might be cited, but we may take, as one example, a seventeenth-century house in the Market Square, Shrewsbury, which is entirely Gothic, the barge-boards carved with vine-leaf and fruit, and scrolls of branch and leaf work. Or, for another the " Feathers " inn at Ludlow. Earlier ones still exist, even in London : for instance, the fifteenth-century building in Cloth-fair, Smithfield—now the " Old Dick Whittington " public-house—has some grotesque gargoyles still on the walls.

As in the case of mediæval screens, we have little knowledge of the actual carvers of this open-air decorative work, which is sometimes of the date of the screens, and of that for interior construction : so strong, so elegant, and yet so different in style and execution from the church work. That a certain amount is due to the foreigner—to the Italians brought over with

410

CONCLUSION

Torregiano, and, in the succeeding reigns, to the German and Flemish workmen and to imported goods, we know. We do not forget such examples as the Holbein chimney-piece of Reigate Priory, or Nonsuch House as it was, from which the Reigate chimney-piece came. Yet it is not to be too readily assumed that the uncouth is invariably of native, the refined and graceful of exotic origin. The stalls of Jesus College, Cambridge (1496-1506), of King's College chapel (1509-1528), or the panels of Queen's College (1531), all within the same university, are evidence of fine English work, even if the designs may have been inspired from Italy.

The field is scarcely less extensive in post-Reformation church wood sculpture of the sixteenth and seventeenth centuries. Such churches as Croscombe alone are mines for illustration, and without pretending even summarily to cover the whole subject, it will suffice to call attention to that which is involved in the numberless examples of screens, bench-ends, and pews. Some of the latter — known as squires' pews — are huge enclosures in themselves, covered with characteristic carved work. Amongst them there are, for instance, those at Stokesay (Salop), Whalley (Lancs.), Herriard (Hants), the Bluett pew at Holcombe Rogus, the Dropmore pew at Burnham, and—to take but one more—the superb work at Lavenham, Suffolk.

In the sixteenth and seventeenth centuries there must have been enormous activity in the use of carved wood for interior decoration. Whole forests of oak would have been required to supply even one great house, such as Aldermaston or Haddon Hall. A bare list of notable country-houses abounding in carved woodwork would fill, with their names alone, several pages. Many prominent examples occur at once to the mind. First of all there is Abington Hall, inexhaustible in interest, with its panels, often of the misericord style, the spoil, no doubt, of churches. Then there are Aldermaston

Court (Berks) and its noble stairway, with much evidence in its figure-work that English sculpture was not, at times, behind the rest of the world in delicacy of treatment, knowledge of anatomy, treatment of drapery, and power of execution. Or, as at Castle Ashby (Northants), again a remarkable staircase of the early seventeenth century, a most original treatment of tree-trunks intertwined with ivy, trailing vines, and other vegetation. Then, we have Burghley, built and ornamented by Germans (1577–1587) yet of English inspiration, for it would be difficult to find a prototype on the Continent, or anything like it. And, once more, Bradfield (Devon), where there is no end of quaint Elizabethan and Jacobean figure-work, in which the grotesque runs riot: barbaric, perhaps, but full of interest for costumes, and illustrative of the magnificence of a Tudor mansion. Again, we have Layer Marney and its linen pattern panels, Godinton, Burton Agnes, Longleat, Hardwicke Hall, Haddon Hall—the list is endless. All abound in panellings and majestic figure-work, especially in the characteristic giant terminal figures and other caryatid monsters so frequently used as jambs for the chimney-pieces. Uncouth though the latter may be—perhaps no better art sometimes than that of the sculptor of ships' figure-heads or of the Gog and Magog type—still, however open to criticism, they look well enough in the general scheme of decoration, and we cannot help but feel a national pride in it all. As an example of the houses of wealthy city merchants—numbers of which still exist in such towns as Exeter—the South Kensington Museum is able to show a complete room from the latter place.

An epitome of some of the most salient points in the history of English wood sculpture of the periods now in question could not, of course, avoid some mention of Grinling Gibbons, upon whom so much extravagant praise has been lavished, of Cibber, of Marot, of

412

CONCLUSION

Inigo Jones and of the influence of Sir Christopher Wren. But there is no place here to discuss the question of the position of Gibbons as a sculptor or of his art as a decorator. That the latter is highly decorative and pleasing from a certain point of view it would be impossible to deny, nor that amongst the profusion of work attributed to Gibbons there is to be found both the mediocre and the exceptionally fine. We may class among the very best such an example as the decoration over the dining-room mantelpiece at Keele Hall. Charming in their simplicity are the trails of foliage, the pendent drapery tasselled and looped, the floral frame of the portrait in the centre panel. We need not cavil at the imitative art. All is in harmony with the tone and details of the white marble mantelpiece, with the added ornaments which stand on it, and with the colouring of the adjacent panels. That is the whole secret of this style. Gibbons or some other may supply lengths of mechanically-cut work, more or less faithful, clever, admirable imitations of animal or vegetable life: not a little of the art lies in the man who selects and applies them, and who has studied the effects of light which their position and environments require. It is curious to observe that the art of Grinling Gibbons is altogether ignored by foreign critics. I know no reference to it whatever.

No more has been intended or could have been done within the limits of a short chapter than to give some general indication of the wealth of material which still awaits the student. Much more remains to be said in order even briefly to summarize the extensive range which the story of wood sculpture covers from the time of the triumph of the Renaissance to our own day. All with which we may connect it may not be art of the purest and highest kind perhaps, but all presents points of historical interest at least, and some may lay claim to distinction equal to any other sculpture.

Amongst the latter few things in decorative furniture stand out more prominently than the smaller work, such as the framings of mirrors, and other things of the kind, in which boxwood, pearwood, and similar soft woods were used. The small nude figure-work on such an example, for instance, as the mirror frame in the Kensington Museum (No. 1605 '55)—Flemish of the sixteenth century—is admirable. So, too, are such mirror frames as the Flemish ones, in the style of the northern French schools, with their rich decoration of strapwork, masks, and foliage, enclosing medallions with figures and scriptural subjects, of which there are fine examples in the Louvre and Munich Museums, and, formerly, in the Spitzer collection. So, again, musical instruments form a class apart, of which it would be no exaggeration to say specimens exist than which wood-carving of the best Renaissance times offers no more masterly work. We may take, amongst many, the lovely Pandurina, in beech or pearwood, at South Kensington, the back carved with a group of Juno, Diana and Venus, and with delicate tendril and strapwork. It is French of the second half of the sixteenth century. Or, again, for seventeenth-century German work, the finely carved head in boxwood of a viola di bardone. Nor could we neglect the many charming lutes—amongst them that known as Queen Elizabeth's at Helmingham—of which so many were exhibited in the historic Loan Collection of the Inventions Exhibition in 1885. Most interesting of all, to Englishmen, is the beautiful boxwood violin, completely covered with woodland scenes and figures, deeply carved, in the collection of the Earl of Warwick. This also is English work of about 1580, and said to have been Queen Elizabeth's.

Up to at least the end of the eighteenth century—that is to say, before the advent of utilitarian times, and when life proceeded more leisurely and there was more time to spare, people were fond of decorating the most ordinary things in common use. Without alluding even to such fine art as, for instance, an Italian knife-case at South Kensington, dated 1564, there are innumerable examples which would call for notice : not all great art, it may be, but interesting in the history of styles transmitted from generation to generation. There are toilet and table articles of all descriptions—combs, spindles, snuff-boxes, tobacco - graters, stick - handles, pastry moulds, fools' baubles, the curious Flemish ' Nativity' cribs known as *Repos de Jésus* of the fifteenth century (see NIFFLE-ANCIAUX in Bibliography), knife-handles, and a host of greater and lesser things. For knife-handles and the like it is probable that such artists as Fletner in Germany or Théodore de Bry in France made models for reproduction by the goldsmiths. Even the very tools the carpenter uses in his work—his planes, chisel-heads or mallets—were carved, sometimes with no mean' talent. And indeed we could not leave out of consideration the elaborate figure and other carved ornament of the state carriages, sedan-chairs, and sledges of the eighteenth century.

Until comparatively recent times woodwork generally appears to have suffered from unmerited neglect. But with the present rage for every description of fine art it is rapidly conquering its proper position. Any scrap of old panelling—even if quite undecorated—carved chests, and, above all, figures, are eagerly sought after and acquired at almost extravagant prices. Really fine examples of boxwoods will certainly become more and more rare and desirable, and perhaps realize as much as the rarest of mediæval ivories. Forgeries of wood-carving of the best styles and periods are not so common as is usually imagined. They are indeed beyond the capability, so far, of those who supply the Wardour Street type. On the other hand—from early neglect—we find but too often that pieces are put together and made up in the most incongruous fashion,

WOOD SCULPTURE

The object of this book has been to give some idea, to those hitherto uninstructed in the subject, of what is best worth study and appreciation in the remains of wood sculpture still existing, which is assuredly entitled to hold no mean position in the history of the arts.

INDEX

417

WOOD SCULPTURE

INDEX

INDEX

WOOD SCULPTURE

Printed by T. and A. CONSTABLE, Printers to His Majesty
at the Edinburgh University Press

Featured Titles from Westphalia Press

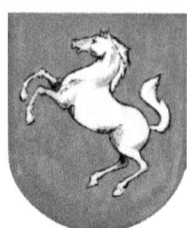

Peasant Art in Sweden, Lapland and Iceland
by Charles Holme

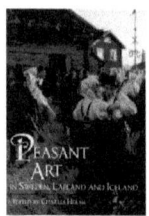

This particular work offers a carefully chosen selection of both the decorative and fine arts of Sweden, Iceland, and the northern most region of Finland. A comprehensive survey, it includes paintings, jewelry, textiles, metalwork, carving, furniture and pottery.

The Rise of the Book Plate: An Exemplative of the Art
by W. G. Bowdoin, Introduction by Henry Blackwel

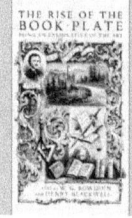

Bookplates were made to denote ownership and hopefully steer the volume back to the rightful shelf if borrowed. They often contained highly stylized writing, drawings, coat of arms, badges or other images of interest to the owner.

The Art of Table Setting, Ancient and Modern
by Claudia Quigley Murphy

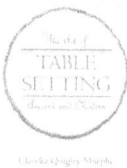

The arrangement of a table in terms of cutlery, arrangement, serving style, and timing of courses has changed a great deal over time and now is enjoying renewed interest. The History of the Art of Tablesetting was written by a true expert in the field, Claudia Quigley Murphy.

Understanding Art: Hendrik Willem Van Loon's
How To Look At Pictures by Hendrik Willem Van
Loon, Introduction by Daniel Gutierrez-Sandoval

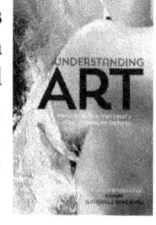

Hendrik Willem van Loon was a Dutch-American professor, journalist, prolific writer, and illustrator. His most famous work, "The Story of Mankind" earned him the prestigious John Newbery Medal.

The Etchings of Rembrandt: A Study and History
by P. G. Hamerton

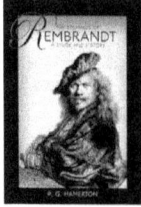

Philip Gilbert Hamerton (1834-1894) was an Englishman who was devoted to the arts in numerous forms. Due to the praise, Hamerton stuck with art criticism, and went on to write other works. He also wrote novels, biographies, and reflections on society.

Lankes, His Woodcut Bookplates by Wilbur Macey Stone

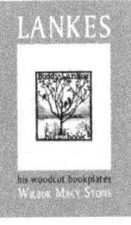

Julius John Lankes was born in Buffalo, New York in 1884, and became a prolific woodcut print artist, as well as an author and professor. As a child, he enjoyed working with the scraps of wood his father brought home from the lumber mill where he was employed. Lankes had a lifelong interest in art.

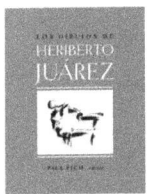

Los Dibujos de Heriberto Juarez / The Drawings of Heriberto Juarez, Edited by Paul Rich

That the drawings here are from life in México is not surprising because Juárez is constantly, and at times impishly, putting art into life and getting art from life. He doesn't think of art as something that is done just in a studio or for that matter kept in museums and looked at on Sundays.

The History of Photography: Carl W. Ackerman's George Eastman by Carl W. Ackerman, Introduction by Daniel Gutierrez-Sandoval

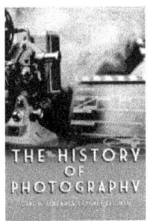

The life of George Eastman is very much a part of the history of contemporary photography. Founder of the Eastman Kodak Company, Eastman was an enthusiastic photographer himself who became instrumental in bringing photography to the mainstream.

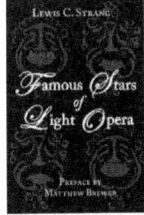

Famous Stars of Light Opera by Lewis C. Strang, Introduction by Matthew Brewer

Strang's attempts to quantify the humorous elements of each performer, as well as quotes from the performers themselves attempting to explain their own success, are an interesting exercise in attempting to explain the inexplicable.

The Historic Codfish
by George H. Proctor, Samuel D. Hildreth, William Frank Parsons

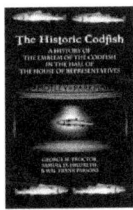

There may be 160 representatives in the Massachusetts legislature, but there is only one codfish. The nearly five-foot carving hanging from the ceiling is the third reminder of the importance of fishing to the state. The first was burnt in a 1747 fire and the second destroyed during the Revolution. The present fish was enshrined in 1784.

www.ingramcontent.com/pod-product-compliance
Lightning Source LLC
Chambersburg PA
CBHW072047190526
45165CB00019B/1956